Thorpe - Kevin

PATHWAYS TO EMPLOYMENT
FOR ADULTS WITH
DEVELOPMENTAL DISABILITIES

PATHWAYS TO EMPLOYMENT FOR ADULTS WITH DEVELOPMENTAL DISABILITIES

Edited by

WILLIAM E. KIERNAN, PH.D.
Director of Rehabilitation
Developmental Evaluation Clinic
Children's Hospital
Boston, Massachusetts
and

JACK A. STARK, PH.D.
Associate Professor of Medical Psychology
Departments of Pediatrics and Psychiatry
University of Nebraska Medical Center
Omaha, Nebraska

·P·A·U·L·H·
BROOKES
PUBLISHING C?

Baltimore • London

Paul H. Brookes Publishing Co.
Post Office Box 10624
Baltimore, Maryland 21285–0624

Typeset by Brushwood Graphics Studio, Baltimore, Maryland.
Manufactured in the United States of America by
The Maple Press Company, York, Pennsylvania.

Preparation of this text was supported in part by the University Affiliated Facilities
Networking Initiative for Services to Adults with Developmental Disabilities grant to
the Developmental Center for Handicapped Persons, Logan, Utah (Grant No. UT /59P
/40131/12) and the Developmental Evaluation Clinic, Children's Hospital, Boston,
Massachusetts (Grant No. 03DD0135/11) from the Administration on Developmental
Disabilities. The products reflect the efforts of the Pathways to Employment conference
held in Boston in October, 1984.

Library of Congress Cataloging-in-Publication Data
Main entry under title:
Pathways to employment for adults with developmental disabilities.

   Bibliography: p.
   Includes index.
   1. Developmentally disabled—Rehabilitation—United States—Addresses, es-
says, lectures.   2. Developmentally disabled—Employment—United States—
Addresses, essays, lectures.   3. Developmentally disabled—Services for—United
States—Addresses, essays, lectures.   I. Kiernan, William E.,
1945–   II. Stark, Jack A., 1946–
HV3005.P38   1986   362.1'968   85-19053
ISBN 0-933716-57-5

Contents

Contributors

Joyce M. Albin, M.Ed.
Research Assistant
Specialized Training Program
University of Oregon
135 College of Education
Eugene, OR 97403

Ansley Bacon-Prue, Ph.D.
Director
Mental Retardation Institute
Westchester County Medical Center
Valhalla, NY 10959

J. Michael Barcus, M.S.
Virginia Commonwealth University
1314 W. Main Street
Richmond, VA 23284

G. Thomas Bellamy, Ph.D.
Associate Professor and Director
Specialized Training Program
University of Oregon
135 College of Education
Eugene, OR 97403

Ted Bergeron, Jr., M.A.
Society to Advance the Retarded and
   Handicapped, Inc.
182 Wolfpit Avenue
Norwalk, CT 06851

Betty Jo Berland, M.A.
National Institute for Handicapped Research
Switzer Building, Room 3070
330 C St., S.W.
Washington, DC 20201

Robert H. Bruininks, Ph.D.
Professor
Department of Educational Psychology
University of Minnesota
178 Pillsbury Drive, S.E.
Minneapolis, MN 55455

Bruce A. Buehler, M.D.
Director
Meyer Children's Rehabilitation Institute and
Hattie B. Munroe Center for Human Genetics
University of Nebraska Medical Center

42nd & Dewey Avenue
Omaha, NE 68105

Carl F. Calkins, Ph.D.
Director
Institute for Human Development
University of Missouri at Kansas City
Kansas City, MO 64108

Ronald W. Conley, Ph.D.
Administration on Developmental Disabilities
Hubert Humphrey Building
200 Independence Avenue, S.W.
Washington, DC 20201

Jeffrey A. Ditty, Ph.D.
President
Ditty, Lynch & Associates, Inc.
301 West 4th Street, Suite 130
Royal Oak, MI 48067

Jean K. Elder, Ph.D.
Commissioner
Administration on Developmental Disabilities
Hubert Humphrey Building
200 Independence Avenue, S.W.
Washington, DC 20201

Beth Gibson, M.S.W.
Institute for Human Development
University of Missouri at Kansas City
2220 Holmes
Kansas City, MO 64108

Tammi L. Goldsbury, B.A.
Assistant Rehabilitation Psychologist
University of Nebraska Medical Center
Meyer Children's Rehabilitation Institute
42nd & Dewey Avenue
Omaha, NE 68105

Bradley K. Hill, M.A.
Associate Director
Center for Residential and Community Services
University of Minnesota
150 Pillsbury Drive, S.E.
Minneapolis, MN 55455

Mark L. Hill, M.S.Ed.
Rehabilitation Research and Training Center
Virginia Commonwealth University
1314 W. Main Street
Richmond, VA 23284

James Intagliata, Ph.D.
1160 S. Clinton Avenue
Oak Park, IL 60304

Orv C. Karan, Ph.D.
Director of Training and Clinical Services
Research and Training Center in Community
  Integration of the Mentally Retarded
Waisman Center on Mental Retardation and
  Human Development
University of Wisconsin-Madison
Madison, WI 53706

William E. Kiernan, Ph.D.
Director of Rehabilitation
Developmental Evaluation Clinic
Children's Hospital
300 Longwood Avenue
Boston, MA 02115

Catherine Berger Knight, A.B.D.
Doctoral Candidate
Department of Studies in Behavioral Disabilities
University of Wisconsin-Madison
Madison, WI 53706

John Kregel, Ed.D.
Virginia Commonwealth University
1314 W. Main Street
Richmond, VA 23284

K. Charlie Lakin, Ph.D.
Senior Scientist
Department of Educational Psychology
University of Minnesota
178 Pillsbury Drive, S.E.
Minneapolis, MN 55455

Kevin P. Lynch, Ph.D.
Vice-President
Ditty, Lynch & Associates, Inc.
301 West 4th Street, Suite 130
Royal Oak, MI 48067

David M. Mank, Ph.D.
Assistant Professor
Specialized Training Program
University of Oregon
135 College of Education
Eugene, OR 97403

Joseph Marrone, M.A.
Program Consultant
Massachusetts Rehabilitation Commission
20 Park Plaza, Room 1101
Boston, MA 02116

Marty Martinson, Ph.D.
Director
Human Development Program
University of Kentucky
114 Porter Building
730 South Limestone
Lexington, KY 40506-0105

John J. McGee, Ph.D.
Associate Professor of Medical Psychology
Department of Psychiatry
University of Nebraska Medical Center
42nd & Dewey Avenue
Omaha, NE 68105

Frank J. Menolascino, M.D.
Professor of Psychiatry and Pediatrics
University of Nebraska Medical Center
42nd & Dewey Avenue
Omaha, NE 68105

John H. Noble, Jr., Ph.D.
Professor
School of Social Work
Allen Hall
State University of New York at Buffalo
Buffalo, NY 14214

Mark B. Ostrowsky, M.A.
Director of Training and Employment Programs
Department of Mental Health/Division of Mental
  Retardation
160 N. Washington Street
Boston, MA 02114

Susan Perschbacher-Melia, Ph.D.
Associate Planner
Massachusetts Developmental Disabilities Council
1 Ashburton Place
Boston, MA 02108

Larry E. Rhodes, Ph.D.
Research Associate
Specialized Training Program
University of Oregon
135 College of Education
Eugene, OR 97403

Robert L. Schalock, Ph.D.
Consulting Psychologist
Mid-Nebraska Mental Retardation Services,
  Region III
P.O. Box 1146
Landmark Center
2727 West 2nd
Hastings, NE 68901

Sheila Scott, B.S.
Assistant Director
Goodwill Industries of Hagerstown, MD
223 N. Prospect Street
Hagerstown, MD 21740

Stephen Shestakofsky, J.D., LL.M.
Program Director
Supported Work for Mentally Retarded Persons
Bay State Skills Corporation
101 Summer Street
Boston, MA 02110

Bryan C. Smith, Ph.D.
The Developmental Center for Handicapped
    Persons
Utah State University
Logan, UT 84322

Vanessa C. Smith, B.S.
Director of Work Adjustment
Goodwill Industries of Indianapolis
1635 W. Michigan
Indianapolis, IN 46222

Jack A. Stark, Ph.D.
Associate Professor of Medical Psychology
Departments of Pediatrics and Psychiatry
University of Nebraska Medical Center
42nd & Dewey
Omaha, NE 68105

Margaret M. Van Gelder, M.A.
Coordinator
Work Experience Program
Developmental Evaluation Clinic
The Children's Hospital
300 Longwood Avenue
Boston, MA 02115

Hill M. Walker, Ph.D.
Director
Center on Human Development
Clinical Services Building
College of Education
University of Oregon
Eugene, OR 97403

Paul H. Wehman, Ph.D.
Director
Rehabilitation Research and Training Center
Virginia Commonwealth University
1314 W. Main Street
Richmond, VA 23284

Carolyn C. White, B.A.
Junior Scientist
Department of Educational Psychology
University of Minnesota
178 Pillsbury Drive, S.E.
Minneapolis, MN 55455

Claude W. Whitehead, M.A.
Director
Employment Initiative Program
National Association for Developmental
    Disabilities Council
1234 Massachusetts Avenue, N.W.
Washington, DC 20005

Foreword

THE AUTHORS AND PARTICULARLY THE EDITORS FEEL BOTH A SENSE OF ACCOMPLISHMENT AND A challenge as we present this book. Our feelings of accomplishment come from knowing that major authorities in the field have come together to write the most thorough book possible. It has been enjoyable and gratifying to work with persons who have chosen to spend their lives working on behalf of individuals with developmental disabilities. The authors, dedicated professionals with significant experience and expertise, have devoted a substantial amount of time examining the state-of-the-practice in an area where there is a paucity of data. Their resolve to advance the knowledge base in providing services to adults with developmental disabilities is apparent throughout this text.

Writing and editing this book were far more difficult than many of us anticipated. Although most of us have worked with citizens with developmental disabilities for many, many years, much of the information on this group of individuals was taken for granted. Not until the task of compiling the data by the editors and authors was undertaken was there a realization of how little data are available and how difficult it is to have access to the available data.

In addition, the task of developing a new model required a considerable amount of individual and group discussion and dialogue. All of us have come to realize the tremendous capabilities of such a collection of invested professionals and colleagues. We must also acknowledge that a developmental disability is more of a sociopolitical phenomenon with environmental limitations, barriers, and prejudices, than a human deficit.

We experience a sense of humility when we consider the work that lies ahead. We always seem to know more about what to do than we can presently deliver. However, we remain idealistic and optimistic, with a real sense of concern over the future. Our efforts are directed at ensuring that information, knowledge, and activity about current services and future trends will facilitate the development of an optimal person environment fit assisting adults with developmental disabilities in increasing their degree of economic self-sufficiency by maximizing their employment potential.

It will take an enormous effort on all our parts to gain the sense of acceptance so eloquently stated by Eleanor Roosevelt in *You Learn by Living:*

> There is another and perhaps greater danger involved in the matter of accepting the limitations of others. Sometimes we are apt to regard as limitations qualities that are actually the other person's strength. We may resent them because they are not the particular qualities which we may want the other person to have. The danger lies in the possibilities that we will not accept the person as he is but try to make him over according to our own ideas.

Jean K. Elder, Ph.D.
Commissioner
Administration on Developmental Disabilities

Acknowledgments

THIS BOOK IS THE RESULT OF TWO YEARS OF WORK BY MANY INDIVIDUALS IN ACADEMIC institutions, community programs, and state and federal agencies. The need for a comprehensive book on employment opportunities for the adult with developmental disabilities has become more essential in recent years. However, the funding for such a project was lacking until the Commissioner of the Administration on Developmental Disabilities, Dr. Jean Elder, made adult services a national priority. As a result of her and her staff's efforts, as well as Congressional support, funds were allocated to the University of Utah Exceptional Child Center (now Center for Exceptional Individuals) to coordinate a national project to evaluate the issues of employment, independent living, learning and adjustment, and health. Much of the extensive research and data collected by this project are reported in this book.

We would like to thank Marvin Fifield, Bryan Smith, and their staff in supporting this project. We also appreciate the efforts of each of the chapter contributors. They are very busy people who gave freely of their time because of their firm belief in the concepts reported in this book.

Of course, we would not have been able to complete such a project without excellent supportive staff. The staff at Boston Children's Hospital (UAF), including Allen Crocker, Margaret Van Gelder, Cindy Thomas, Sheila Lynch, Lisa Brinkman, and all those who assisted in the National Conference, deserve a great deal of credit for the success of the book. In addition, the preparation, typing, and design of the artwork for the book was superbly handled by Vicki Morrison and Tammi Goldsbury. To them, we owe a great deal of respect, appreciation, and our sincerest thanks for a difficult job that was well done. Last, we hope that this book will make a difference in the lives of the adults with developmental disabilities and their families who have supported us over the years.

∞ Section I ∞

OVERVIEW

WHY DO WE NEED A BOOK ON ASPECTS OF EMPLOYMENT FOR ADULTS WITH DEVELOPMENTAL DIS-abilities? To answer this question and set the tone for this book, the first section discusses its mission. Legislative efforts in the late 1960s and throughout the 1970s reaped enormous benefits for the school-age developmentally disabled child. School systems rapidly expanded—both qualitatively and quantitatively—their special education services. The result was a considerable elevation of the *expectations* for these young people. However, as the data began to come in on what happens to these individuals after ''graduation,'' it soon became clear that the majority of them (80%) were not making a smooth transition into the community because they were un-employed or underemployed after the first year. This national dilemma—some might call it a crisis—is what this book is all about. What do we do with these individuals, and how can we best accomplish this challenge?

Employment, as defined in its broadest context, is both an inherent right and essential component of one's well-being. As this first chapter points out, we have learned a great deal from our past experiences (and mistakes) on how to structure our current and future service delivery system. To be successful, however, we must be acutely aware of the ever-changing world of work and how these changes have an impact on the ability of the adult with developmental disabilities to realize increased levels of economic self-sufficiency through employment.

Let the needs of the developmentally disabled adult serve as your guide in reading this book. By reviewing those designs and strategies that are and will need to be developed to make the goal of employment a reality, the process described here can serve as a benchmark in providing a new conceptual model of service.

∞ Chapter 1 ∞

The Adult with Developmental Disabilities

William E. Kiernan and Jack A. Stark

The American ideal was stated by Emerson in his essay on politics. "A man has a right to be employed, to be trusted, to be loved, to be revered." It does many men little good to stay alive and free and propertied if they can not work. (William O. Douglass: dissent, *Barsky v. Regents*, April 26, 1954).

SINCE THE BEGINNING OF TIME, AN INDIVIDUAL's worth has been viewed by others according to his or her contribution to the good of the whole. In ancient times, status reflected the work an individual could accomplish to preserve the community. During the agricultural period when families remained stable over several generations, each member was expected to contribute both effort and skill to the maintenance and growth of the family. With the onset of the industrial age and the increased mobility of both people and products, the family unit became more decentralized. Work incentives, such as piece-rate pay and bonuses for production, replaced the sense of belonging to a cohesive environment. The separation of work from the residential and social elements of the total environment became more pronounced as the country moved into the age of automation and industrialization (Obermann, 1965).

The move from a frontier and agricultural society to an industrialized one resulted in greater specialization and separation of activities for the individual. Societal growth had a significant effect on the life-style of its members, resulting in less interaction between the individual's work, residential, and social spheres. The role of work became more and more significant, both financially and socially. Monies earned replaced the earlier, more direct barter systems. This change meant that, without a job and source of revenue, maintaining independence within the community became more difficult. Unemployed individuals were viewed as socially less acceptable, as work became the measure of both worth and social status.

For the disabled individual, these changes meant that social acceptance was even more difficult to achieve. Ironically, the entrance into the industrial age with its focus on productivity and technological advances, particularly in its early stage, meant reduced opportunities for disabled individuals to engage in meaningful and significant work. It was not until a time of high demand and a reduced labor force, as in World War II, that many disabled individuals were permitted to move into the employment market. The worth of disabled individuals became apparent as their productivity on the job increased. Yet, for certain disabled individuals, particularly developmentally disabled adults, employment opportunities were extremely rare even during limited labor resource periods because of inadequate training, misconceptions regarding capacity, and a lack of willingness of employers to re-structure jobs.

Sheltered work programs were believed to provide the answer to the employment problems of disabled individuals. Many professionals felt that these environments could give the amount of supervision, training, and special care required for the developmentally disabled adult to be productive. Industry could subcontract with these programs and utilize the productive capacity of this work force without having to deal with these persons in either a social or a work setting (Whitehead, 1981).

As with the nondisabled worker in industrial society, the life of the disabled worker was separated out so that there was limited interaction between work, social, and residential environments. This view of the person as a series of separate and discrete entities did not acknowledge the relationship of those entities to each other socially, emotionally, or physically. The need of the whole person was seen as secondary to the individual's work, social, or residential needs (Scheerenberger, 1983).

LESSONS TO BE LEARNED FROM PAST EXPERIENCES

The move to an industrial society has provided both opportunities and limitations for the developmentally disabled adult. In times of limited labor resources, disabled persons have shown that they can do the job (Horner & Bellamy, 1979). Yet, at times, increasing production demands and expanded production technologies have limited employment opportunities for disabled persons. Greater mobility—both in the employment and residential settings—has become the rule, rather than the exception. Flexibility and independence are assumed, with limited support given to those who may need either extended periods of adjustment or even continuous assistance to accommodate to change.

Institutions and sheltered work and living environments were intended to replace the extended family in providing supports to the developmentally disabled individual. However, experiences in the last few decades have shown that these types of isolated environments do not provide realistic and appropriate places of residence or work. The movement to a more decentralized service environment is now well underway. A variety of community residential alternatives with varying degrees of support is showing that the individual with developmental disabilities can reside in the community. Paralleling this *shift* in residential services, the movement from sheltered work settings to industry-based programs has demonstrated that even those who are most severely disabled can be productive in a normalized work setting. As is the case in residential programs, the degree of support in the work setting varies in both intensity and duration. This support allows the worker to remain in a productive and socially more appropriate setting (Schalock, 1983; Wilcox & Bellamy, 1983).

The lessons of the past have taught that it is necessary to be responsive to the whole person if gains in independence are to be realized. The experience of creating an artificial or isolated environment, one in which the needs of the developmentally disabled adult are attended to, may provide for basic needs but does little to establish a role in society for this individual as a full and respected member (Albin, Stark, & Keith, 1979). Members of subcultures generally have second-class citizenship. A coordinated approach to the vocational, residential, and social needs of the developmentally disabled adult in an integrated setting that provides opportunities for interaction with nondisabled persons will yield the greatest return for all.

CURRENT DIRECTIONS

Over the years, the nondisabled worker has learned to accommodate to separation of the work, social, and residential spheres by expanding his or her social networks, developing recreational activities, and utilizing neighborhood associations or other similar strategies that create small support and interest groups. These groups in turn provide assistance, enjoyment, and information for their members.

As services for developmentally disabled

adults continue to be developed in more normalized settings, their residential, social, and vocational needs must be dealt with in a comprehensive fashion.

As with nondisabled workers, social networks are important for the developmentally disabled adult. Because of their special individual circumstances, these adults may need assistance in the form of case management in order to gain access to community resources. This service could serve as a bridge into the groups, activities, and associations that are available to nondisabled persons. A measure of acceptance may be the frequency with which the developmentally disabled adult employs this bridging resource to gain access to community services. In many ways the establishment of the case manager is a method of re-creating communal experiences that existed before the emergence of the industrial society. The attributes of a supportive, structured, consistent, and integrated preindustrial society are being re-created as a means of facilitating the adjustment of the developmentally disabled adult to the decentralized environments of the 21st century.

The need to acknowledge the whole person does not obviate efforts to be more responsive to the individual aspects of the vocational, residential, or social spheres. Establishing new and unique methods of dealing with the individual spheres of need is as important as the coordination of all the elements of need for the developmentally disabled adult.

EMPLOYMENT OPPORTUNITIES: A CHANGING WORLD

Employment opportunities beyond those that are customarily viewed as appropriate and typical for the developmentally disabled adult must be explored. The move from an industrial society to a service and information society requires some adjustments in both training programs and placement efforts. For example, only 5% of almost 20 million new jobs created in the 1970s were in manufacturing. Information, knowledge, and service jobs represented 90% of the new jobs. By 1979 the largest job category in the United States was clerk, which succeeded laborer, which in turn succeeded farmer (Nessbitt, 1982).

These trends show the emergence of new employment opportunities for both nondisabled and developmentally disabled adults. High technology can provide both training strategies and employment opportunities. Future training and employment programs for the developmentally disabled adult must reflect the changes underway in society today—the movement from manufacturing toward information transfer and service—as well as the anticipated changes of tomorrow (see also Chapter 22 "Current and Future Directions").

Similarly, residential and social programs for the developmentally disabled adult must be dynamic. They must be able to react to the changes in society while being responsive to the needs of those they are to serve. Business as usual will lead to a system that is incompatible with the future shape of society.

The future of the developmentally disabled adult is a complex one. The needs of the whole person must be addressed, yet providing greater varieties of options within the vocational, residential, and social spheres is essential. Case management and a focus on stimulation of new initiatives will be the benchmark of success for those who seek to provide comprehensive, integrated services.

COORDINATION, ROLES, AND RESOURCES

The change in the role of the family as the central support resource and focus for its members has created an increased demand for coordination of services. Vocational, social, and residential needs must be dealt with consistently and often simultaneously Targeted services that focus on employment needs without acknowledging the residential and social needs of the individual frequently fall short of their goals. Work represents approximately one-fourth of the available hours per week, yet frequently there is an exclusive focus on this need while the residential and social needs of the individual are ignored. Unmet residential or social needs can often have a direct impact on performance in the work place (Schalock, 1983). Interfering events, occurrences, and factors external to the workplace more often lead to termination of an employment situation than the lack of capacity to perform on the job (Rosen, Clark, & Kivitz, 1977). Inadequate living space, lack of social opportunities, fears of loss of public financial or medical benefits, and numerous nonproduction-related issues are cited by the developmentally disabled individual as reasons for termination on a job (Hammerman & Maikowski, 1981).

There are similar problems in the residential sphere. Many states require an active day program for all disabled adults in a residential service system. Although the intent is laudable, in certain cases any day program is sought in order to comply with the regulations. This type of programming fits the individual into the available resources, rather than looks at his or her needs and matches or creates resources when appropriate.

Recreational and social activities frequently are less well developed than either residential or vocational programs. Recently, the assumption that recreational needs are less important than vocational or social ones has been challenged as issues of social isolation have been identified more accurately. Lack of social options can have significant impact on both the residential and vocational areas as the individual becomes more and more distressed and unhappy with his or her course in life (Kiernan, 1979).

Each of the areas—vocational, residential, and social—by itself must be given special consideration. Yet, it is essential to acknowledge the needs of the whole person and to integrate all life activities. The coordination of services is a total effort, involving key participants in the implementation of the plan dealing with the needs of the whole individual (Wolfensberger, Nirge, Olshansky, Perske, & Roos, 1972). There is a clear need for vertical linkages between education, vocational rehabilitation, and adult service agencies and for horizontal linkages between vocational, residential, and social spheres. Fiscal, administrative, and programmatic impediments to the establishment of these linkages will need to be addressed (Magrab & Elder, 1979).

THE NEED FOR CHOICE

Creating opportunities for the developmentally disabled adult is a necessary step in improving any service system. The range of choice within each sphere of life activity must be sufficiently broad so that all developmentally disabled adults can have access to a service that capitalizes on their strengths, rather than limitations. Opportunities for movement within the system must be available so that permanency in a program is a choice made by the individual and not a necessity imposed by the lack of opportunities (Smith, 1981).

Policies, programs, and services that do not allow the developmentally disabled adult to become involved in the decision-making process and to have an active role in the development of the plan will have minimal success. Personal investment will be less to those individual plans of service that have not cultivated the commitment of the individual for whom the plan is designed.

The goals of the service system of the next decade should be ones of involvement and development. A coordinated and integrated system that allows the developmentally disabled adult to become an active participant in the decision-making process will encourage investment on the part of all involved in constructing a viable service plan. It is the role of the provider to ensure that the developmentally disabled individual knows the options available, if in fact he or she is to participate meaningfully in the decision-making process. The developmentally disabled adult must also learn to accept the responsibilities associated with the decision once it is made. Along with the right to choose must also come the responsibility of choice.

NEEDS OF THE ADULT WITH DEVELOPMENTAL DISABILITIES

A focus on the needs of the developmentally disabled adult is a relatively new phenomenon.

The political, legislative, and service efforts of the 1960s and 1970s resulted in unprecedented educational programs for developmentally disabled children. These children have now grown up. The great majority have already or are in the process of graduating from school programs (Kiernan & Pyne, 1982). Although much still needs to be done with our educational system, we are even further behind in setting up a service system for the developmentally disabled adult (Will, 1984). Currently, developmentally disabled individuals are graduating from school with limited options and often no place to live, work, and/or socialize. The net result is that these individuals will, as some already have, remain in a dependent status indefinitely. Teachers are disappointed that their students graduate and lose the gains made in school; the developmentally disabled adult becomes disillusioned, and societal expectations are diminished. This downward expectational spiral only serves to reinforce the negative concepts of the developmentally disabled adult.

MISSION OF THE BOOK

The charge to the contributors to this book was to provide solutions to these above-mentioned problems. The contributors address the needs of the developmentally disabled adult by pro-viding a new conceptual model of service and strategies that will best meet those needs through economic policy and administrative redesigns.

Section 2 addresses the critical definitional issue of who is the developmentally disabled adult by looking at the prevalence of developmental disabilities in the population and reviewing past employment statistics for these persons. Section 3 focuses on the important economic, legislative, and policy implications for providing new services to this population. Programs have been less than satisfactory in the past, perhaps because of flaws in the basic concepts of service. Section 4 proposes a new model for habilitation, with an emphasis on transition, supported employment, and time-limited training strategies. A suggested review of outcome criteria is also presented. Evaluation and training practices are also addressed in Section 4, along with a discussion of those severely disabled adults who do not enter the system. Section 5 provides a comprehensive analysis of the residential, learning, and adjustment needs of the developmentally disabled adult. Section 6 addresses the future service, training, research, and program evaluation needs of the delivery system designed for this population. In closing, Section 7 reviews the major factors over the next two decades that will have a dramatic impact on the role of the developmentally disabled adult in the future.

REFERENCES

Albin, T., Stark, J., & Keith K. (1979). Vocational training and placement: Behavioral analysis in the natural environment. In G. T. Bellamy, G. O'Connor, & O. Karan (Eds.), Vocational rehabilitation of severely handicapped persons: Contemporary service strategies (pp. 161–180). Baltimore, MD: University Park Press.

Hammerman, S., & Maikowski, S. (Eds.). (1981). The economics of disability: International perspectives New York: Rehabilitation International.

Horner, R., & Bellamy, G. T. (1979). Structured employment: Productivity and productive capacity. In G. T. Bellamy, G. O'Connor, & O. Karan (Eds.), Vocational rehabilitation of severely handicapped persons: Contemporary service strategies (pp. 88–101). Baltimore, MD: University Park Press.

Kiernan, W. Rehabilitation planning. (1979). In P. Magrab & J. Elder (Eds.), Planning for services to handicapped persons: Community, education, health (pp. 137–171). Baltimore, MD: Paul H. Brookes Publishing Company.

Kiernan, W., & Pyne, M. (1982). Hard to train: A history of vocational training for special needs youth. In K. P. Lynch, W. E. Kiernan, & J. A. Stark (Eds.), Prevocational and vocational education for special needs youth: A blueprint for the 1980s (pp. 3–13). Baltimore, MD: Paul H. Brookes Publishing Company.

Magrab, P., & Elder, J. (1979). Planning for services to handicapped persons: Community, education, health. Baltimore, MD: Paul H. Brookes Publishing Company.

Nessbitt, J. (1982). Megatrends—Ten new directions transforming our lives. New York: Warner Books, Inc.

Obermann, C. F. (1965). A history of vocational rehabilitation in America. Minneapolis, MN: Denison & Co., Inc.

Rosen, M., Clark, G., & Kivitz, M. (1977). Habilitation of the handicapped: New dimensions in programs for the *developmentally disabled*. Baltimore, MD: University Park Press.

Schalock, R. (1983). *Services for developmentally disabled adults: Development, implementation, and evaluation*. Baltimore, MD: University Park Press.

Scheerenberger, R. (1983). *A history of mental retardation*. Baltimore, MD: Paul H. Brookes Publishing Company.

Smith, D. (1981). *Obstacles*. Special Committee on the Disabled and the Handicapped (3rd report). Toronto: Minister of Supply and Services.

Whitehead, D. W. (1981). *Final report: Training and employment of youth with disabilities: Bridges from school to work life*. Washington, DC: Position paper, Office of Special Education and Rehabilitation Services.

Wilcox, B., & Bellamy, G. T. (1983). *Design of high school programs for severely handicapped students*. Baltimore, MD: Paul H. Brookes Publishing Company.

Will, M. (1984). *OSERS programming for the transition of youth with disabilities: Bridges from school to work life*. Washington, DC: Position paper, Office of Special Education and Rehabilitation Services.

Wolfensberger, W., Nirge, B., Olshansky, S., Perske, R., & Roos, P. (1972). *Principles of normalization in human services*. Toronto: National Institute on Mental Retardation.

∞ Section II ∞

POPULATION CHARACTERISTICS

THIS BOOK ACCOMPLISHES THREE MAJOR OBJECTIVES: FIRST IT PROVIDES DEMOGRAPHIC DATA ON the developmentally disabled adult; second, it recommends a new model in serving this population; and third, it outlines future directions in service, training, and research, with an understanding of the barriers that must be overcome if the employment goals are to be achieved.

This section examines prevalence data and the characteristics of the developmentally disabled population. Surprising as it may seem, these two chapters were two of the most difficult to write. The actual writing of these chapters was relatively easy compared with the real chore—collecting the data. What the authors found is that people in the field of developmental disabilities are accustomed to operating in a data vacuum that perhaps contributes to the lack of a common language—definition of issues and terms—and confusion in characterizing this population.

Chapter 2 addresses the problems of defining this population; through legislative mandates, the definition has evolved from a categorical approach to an individual/functional approach. Applying this new approach to issues such as employment, work, and economic self-sufficiency required the authors to agree on the use of various terms found in this book.

With this basic foundation laid in Chapter 2, Chapter 3 expands this informational base through an analysis on the essential incidence and prevalence data. This was no small task. The authors of this chapter have made a major contribution to the literature by pulling together the essential data, which should serve as a standard in the developmental disabilities field. In addition, they provide a blueprint of the employment status of the developmentally disabled adult that allows for a more critical discussion of the development of the model of employment.

∞ Chapter 2 ∞

Developmental Disabilities
Definitional Issues

William E. Kiernan, Bryan C. Smith, and Mark B. Ostrowsky

ROLE AND FUNCTION OF DEFINITIONS

THE PRIMARY PURPOSE OF ANY DEFINITION IS to set forth criteria by which populations can be identified. The reasons for identification can vary and usually depend on the agency, organization, or individual utilizing the definition. Human services definitions have historically been used either for planning and policy development or to establish eligibility and/or declaration for entitlement purposes. Definitions used for planning and policy tend to focus more on populations and the needs of groups or clusters of people. Those used to establish eligibility look at individual needs and specific criteria to establish the right or authorization to receive services. In both cases a categorical approach is used to identify the group to which the policy or the individual will be assigned.

Use of a categorical approach to define groups of people leads to a policy, plan, or service that frequently does not acknowledge the individual differences of persons within the category. Policies in housing, employment, and health care can actually penalize the individual they are intended to help. Where eligibility for services is determined by a categorical approach and where there is not a clear match of the individual to the category, services may be and usually are denied (Bowe, 1983).

Definitions identifying those individuals who will be grouped into a specific category have become considerably more precise in the past 20 years. Before that, atypical features or behavioral manifestations were sufficient to make a diagnosis. This practice of diagnosis by intuition has been replaced by a more proscribed procedure. In certain medically based conditions, such as seizure disorders, more specific procedures have been utilized to refine the definition to diagnose more accurately persons having such a condition.

Before the definition of mental retardation was revised within the last two decades, diagnosis was often based on a poor performance on a standardized intelligence test. Currently, the definition of mental retardation is dependent not only on significant subaverage performance on an individually administered general intelligence test but *also* on the effectiveness with which the individual meets the standards of personal development and social responsibility expected for his or her age and cultural group. This definition incorporates intelligence test performance *and* the functional skill level of the individual.

This revised definition of mental retardation is an example of an effort to look at the functional skills of the individual in relation to an appropriate reference group. A move in response to some of the limitations of categorical groupings noted above, this new definition shifted the diagnostic process in the direction of a functional assessment of skill, utilizing a developmental criterion reference group.

Even with improved diagnostic procedures, the use of the categorical approach to defining terms has some limitations in fulfilling the main mandates of any definition, that of planning and policy development or eligibility and entitlement. The lack of sensitivity of the evaluation instruments, as well as the variability in both skills and needs for the persons within a categorical grouping, makes this type of grouping less sensitive to the needs of the individual person.

In addition to the direct services implications to an individual or group of individuals, definitions also serve a function in research. Fundamental to the study of any phenomenon is a clear identification of the members of the group to be investigated. Broad-based definitions without associated classification systems are of little value to research. Utilizing such imprecise definitions in research for purposes of studying specific hypotheses may lead to erroneous findings and, in general, cannot be considered sound. The broad categorical groupings do not allow for sufficient control to test hypotheses accurately or interpret findings. For the purposes of research, more detailed identification of subject groupings is essential (Grossman, 1983).

Incidence, prevalence, and other descriptive statistics, on the other hand, can more effectively be derived from categorical groupings, particularly for purposes of macroplanning and policy review. Although still somewhat risky, the development of policy can be responsive to a greater variation in individual groupings than can the testing of specific hypotheses. The difficulty in using categorical groupings in planning and policy development arises when there is an overly rigid adherence to an established policy (Freedman, 1977). In these instances, the use of policy is more often one of exclusion than guidance in the development of services for a targeted group of persons. Typically, this type of problem is associated with eligibility criteria and attempts to control expenses associated with a specific service or program; for example, policy changes in the Medicaid program.

Definitions and Labels

If definitions are viewed as planning and policy tools, rather than diagnostic tools, then the issue of labeling and its negative effects can be put into perspective. Definitions tend to be categorically based and impersonal, whereas labels frequently accentuate differences (Grossman, 1983). Labels in and of themselves need not be bad. The perceptions, beliefs, and attitudes that society assigns to labels are more significant than the labels themselves. A risk of defining large groups of labeled individuals into categories is to have them viewed as a single unit and thus "all the same." The individual stereotypical perception of the members is generalized to the whole category (Summers, 1981). The dilemma of labels and stereotypical perceptions of groups has led many researchers to try to move away from the use of categories and toward a functional approach in defining groups of people.

There is some question whether the problems associated with labels can be resolved by using a functional approach to the definition of developmental disabilities. Although a functional approach to defining groups of people may provide information about skills and abilities in a way that is intelligible to society in general and may also identify needs and acknowledge differences within groups of people, efforts to resolve labeling problems will more than likely require attitudinal and behavioral changes in society. The trend is clearly in the direction away from categorical groupings and toward the use of functional descriptions of persons in both program development and service delivery.

Review of Current Definitions

Although definitions are used for the purpose of planning and policy development or eligibility and entitlement, their basic nature is changing. Until the passage of the Rehabilitation, Comprehensive Services and Developmental Disabilities Act (PL 95-602) in 1978, most definitions employed a listing approach to the identification of individuals for inclusion within each specific grouping. Although many pieces of legislation in the 1970s attempted to look at the individual, these acts, when focusing on the provision of a service, reverted to the use of a categorical or listing approach to identify target audiences (see Table 1).

A LOOK AT A FUNCTIONAL APPROACH

Since its inception, the concept of developmental disabilities has been directed toward a functional approach, rather than a diagnostic one (Boggs & Henney, 1979; Summers, 1981). The original proponents of PL 91-517 wanted a law that would address the needs of persons with severe disabilities related to mental retardation. Although the first definition of developmental disabilities attempted to look at the needs of a variety of individuals, program personnel in the state service system and those at the local level charged with the implementation of the law tended to look to the definition along rigid categorical lines. The categories of mental retardation, cerebral palsy, and epilepsy received most attention, with autism being added as a categorical focus in 1975 (PL 94-103).

Dissatisfied that another categorical definition was added to the legislation, Congress mandated the Secretary of Health, Education, and Welfare to conduct a study on the definition. A special study group, The National Task Force on the Definition of Developmental Disabilities, was appointed, representing parents, professionals, and providers. In November, 1977 it recommended to the Committee on Interstate and Foreign Commerce of the House of Representatives and the Senate's Committee on Human Resources that a new definition be incorporated into the 1978 Developmental Disabilities Act. That definition became the developmental disabilities definition for PL 95-602 and was the first time that a purely functional approach was utilized in legislation. PL 95-602 was the first piece of legislation that attempted to identify its target service group by describing the needs of the individuals who were to be served, rather than recounting the

characteristics and/or diagnosis of the group (Gollay, 1979).

Since the passage of PL 95-602 in 1978, there has been much debate about the utility of a functional definition. Some feel that the definition's immediate advantages—that is, the reduction in labeling, and its diagnostic and prescriptive potential—have yet to be realized (Summers, 1981). Much discussion has centered around the complexity of its implementation and the lack of clarity that arises from its use. Little has been done to refine the key elements of the functional definition, thus leaving a great deal to subjective interpretation by planners and policy analysis.

The shift to a functional definition has not changed the basic intent of the initiative. In general, the Developmental Disabilities Act is directed at the needs of those who are disabled early in life with a disability viewed as substantial and chronic. Since the passage of the first Developmental Disabilities Act, the focus has been on serving those disabled individuals whose disability occurred during the maturing years, with the impact affecting the development of the total individual. Such a disability is felt to affect many other aspects of development, so that what might start as a single deficit is likely to bring about difficulties in other areas (Final Report of the National Task Force on the Definition of Developmental Disabilities, 1977).

The noncategorical definition of developmental disabilities places emphasis on the criteria of chronicity, early onset, multiple impairment, and the need for ongoing services involving an interdisciplinary focus. Key concepts in the definition include the elements of substantiality and severity. Severity reflects a presence of significant limitations related to different specific life functions. Substantiality of a disability is reflected by an impairment in at least three major life activities. It is thus clear that individuals who through the old categorical approach would be considered to be developmentally disabled are not classified as such under the functional definition. The mildly mentally retarded individual, the person with controlled epilepsy, and the mildly spastic

Table 1. Definitions of disability by legislation

Title and number	Date of passage	Targeted service population	Definition of service population	Role of definition in act
Developmental Disabilities Service and Facilities Construction Act (PL 91-517)	1970	Developmentally disabled person	– Mental retardation, cerebral palsy, epilepsy, and other neurological conditions occurring before the age of 18	– Policy and planning
Developmental Disabled Assistance and Bill of Rights Act (P.L 94-103)	1975	Developmentally disabled person	– Mental retardation, cerebral palsy, epilepsy, autism, and dyslexia when associated with mental retardation, cerebral palsy, epilepsy, and/or autism, occurring before the age of 18	– Policy and planning

Rehabilitation, Comprehensive Services, and Developmental Disabilities Act (PL 95-602)	1978	Developmentally disabled person	– Attributable to a mental or physical impairment or combination of mental or physical impairment
			–is manifest before 22 years of age
			–is likely to continue indefinitely
			–results in substantial functional limitations in three or more of the following areas of major life activity:
			  –self care
			  –receptive and expressive language
			  –learning
			  –mobility
			  –self-direction
			  –capacity for independent living
			  –economic self-sufficiency
			and reflects the person's need for a combination and sequence of special, interdisciplinary, or generic care, treatment or other services which are of lifelong or extended duration and individually planned and coordinated
				– Policy and planning

Education for All Handicapped Children Act (P L 94-142)	1975	Handicapped children	-Handicapped children means individuals who: -have mental retardation, are hard of hearing, deaf, speech impaired, visually handicapped, seriously emotionally disturbed, orthopedically impaired, or have other health impairment -have special learning disabilities who, by reason thereof, require special services -are between 3-21 years of age	-Eligibility and entitlement -Policy and planning
Rehabilitation Act (P L 93-112)	1973	Handicapped person	-Handicapped person means any individual: -who has a physical or mental disability -who has a substantial handicap to employment -who is expected to benefit in terms of employment from the provision of vocational rehabilitation services -for whom an extended evaluation of rehabilitation potential is necessary for the purpose of determining whether he might benefit in terms of employability from the provision of vocational rehabilitation services	-Eligibility and entitlement
Social Security Act Disability Insurance, 1975	1975	Disabled recipients	-The individual must be: -unable to engage in any substantial gainful activity because of medically determinable physical or mental impairment that has lasted, or is expected to last, at least 12 months or to result in death -A disabled worker and wife must be over 62 years of age. Children under 18, or between 18-22 and attending school full-time, or age 18 or over with a disability that began before age 22 are also eligible for disability insurance	-Eligibility and entitlement

cerebral palsy adult in most instances would not be viewed as developmentally disabled because the elements of substantiality and severity are not present.

Major Life Activities

Probably one of the most frequently discussed aspects of the definition is how to operationalize the element of major life activities. Several reports and papers have looked at this issue (Boggs & Henney, 1979; Gollay, 1981; Summers, 1981). In each work, examples were given of how these major life activities could be identified, quantified, and put into operation. However, there remains a great deal of variability in the interpretation of this element (Cawood, 1979).

One of the most detailed discussions of how to operationalize the various elements of major life activities was presented by Boggs and Henney (1979). They gave examples of how each activity would be reflected in day-to-day interactions for the individual (see Table 2). For each age group certain life activities are more significant than others. For the infant, no major life activities apply directly. The major life activities for children and youth ages 3 to 17 tend to evolve around school. For the child, learning is a central function, with language, self-direction, self-care, and mobility the major learning areas. For the adult the major life activities are incorporated in the work setting. Economic self-sufficiency is pivotal to the capacity of the individual to function in society.

In addition to the variability in the definition of life activities because of age, degrees of impairment also vary. A developmental disability is defined as a severe chronic disability that is likely to continue indefinitely. Thus, how the impairment is manifested in the seven life activities changes over time. However, what does remain consistent is the element of substantial disability. Efforts to quantify the term "substantial" have met with little success. General descriptions, such as "requires frequent assistance from others," "requires the use of highly specialized devices," and "is extremely costly to develop and/or maintain,"

have been utilized. More specific guidelines for measurement—for example, the amount of time required, the amount of money required in comparison to nondevelopmentally disabled persons—have been suggested as a means of verifying the existence of a substantial impairment in the individual (Boggs & Henney, 1979). However, caution must be exercised in defining further the life activities incorporated in the term "developmental disabilities." Too extensive a focus on individual elements may cause one to lose sight of the fact that the intent of the legislation was to acknowledge the interaction among the disabilities and the magnitude of the impact on the individual over protracted and, in many instances, lifelong periods. Thus, the need for a detailed classification or quantification system for the major life activities may be somewhat questionable. The intent and focus of the act are to provide services to the more severely impaired in a multitude of different functional areas.

Implications for the Functional Definition

The strength of the functional definition of developmental disabilities is that it encourages individualization of program planning on a person-by-person basis. Having a highly specific definition implies the ability to pinpoint individual clients within that definition (Freedman, 1977). It is thus the hope of some planners that the functional approach would form a basis for defining eligibility and entitlement to services for the developmentally disabled individual. However, due to the lack of consistency in interpreting the various elements of the definition, its use for planning and policy development has come under question. In light of the legislative intent of the Developmental Disabilities act to provide a mechanism for comprehensive planning, the use of a functional definition may be less than optimal.

Since the adoption of the new definition, the focus of the act has been on planning and gap-filling within the service structure. The impact on services has been either indirect, through specific developmental disability council activities, or direct, through the use of exemplary service monies to the University Affiliated

Table 2. Major life activity in developmental disabilities

Major life activity	Key factors for the DD adult	Examples occurring in life activity
Self-care	−Long-term condition −Need for significant assistance in personal care	−Eating −Personal hygiene/toileting −Appearance/grooming/dressing
Receptive and expressive language	−Long-term condition −Limitations in communicating with others without the use of devices −Inability to articulate thoughts/ideas/information	−Use of voice to communicate thoughts, feelings, needs −Use of sign language or other −Devise independence in communication −Ability to understand words or lip read −Comprehend words, signs, or gestures

Learning	−Long-term condition
	−Significant interference with
	   −cognition
	   −visual abilities
	   −oral communications
	−Special attention/programs
		−Ability to understand/process, or recognize information
		−Capacity to recall immediate and remote information
		−Ability to apply knowledge and skills in new situations
		−Able to engage in abstract thoughts and processes
		−Ability to perform routine age-appropriate academic activities; reading, writing, manipulation of numbers

Mobility	−Long-term condition −Impaired fine or gross motor skills −Requires frequent assistance from another person or device to move from place to place	−Movement of limbs/crawling, walking −Gross motor control/sitting, standing −Fine motor control/manual dexterity −Coordinated activities/eye-hand-foot −Travel/movement from location to location

(continued)

Table 2. (Continued)

Major life activity	Key factors for the DD adult	Examples occurring in life activity
Self-direction	–Long-term condition –Needs assistance in making decisions –Unable to make social, financial, or personal decisions for self	–Ability to choose among leisure, vocational, or residential options –Awareness and/or ability to consider options –Ability to make even basic financial decisions
Capacity for independent living	–Long-term condition –Unable to perform normal societal activities –Unable or unsafe to live alone –Requires regular and frequent supervision over a long period of time	–Ability to maintain own living environment with minimal assistance, if any –Able to direct self or others in daily living activities –Ability to maintain financial resources in an independent or semi-independent fashion –Able to relate to immediate community to satisfy personal, social, and health needs –Able to move about community by self or with directed assistance
Economic self-sufficiency	–Long-term condition –Unable to work in regular place of work –Limited production capacity –Limited financial resources after expenses –Unable to generalize learned skills to new tasks or environments	–Able to work and earn above the poverty index –Able to perform tasks consistently on the job –Has good work and personal adjustment behaviors; punctuality, appearance, attitude –Able to travel to and from work in an independent or self-directed fashion

Facilities (UAFs), protection and advocacy programs, or other agencies involved in special projects. The planning function has been difficult to implement because most mandated services utilize a categorical approach to eligibility, with an intent to focus services on a specific life activity. Indeed, the planning function in developmental disabilities programs must look at all the component pieces and assume that they will be able to be integrated in such a fashion that the needs of the person can be met.

Although in the past there have been difficulties with the use of a functional definition for developmental disabilities, one should not overlook the unique strengths of the concept of developmental disabilities. It is the only federally sponsored initiative that looks at the needs of the person over a protracted period of time at different stages in the life cycle. It is also an initiative that focuses its efforts on more impaired individuals.

Probably one of the most significant contributions made by the functional definition of developmental disabilities is to articulate clearly the range of services that the individual may need. Through the use of the life activities approach, one is able to acknowledge both the assets and limitations of the individual. The development of a highly individualized service plan for a developmentally disabled person may then be achieved. It is this emphasis on examining and planning around specific strengths and needs of an individual that potentially has the greatest yield in developing prescriptive service programs.

The definition may also serve as a means of attitude change by more clearly delineating the needs of individuals and thus more specifically describing the person to others. There is less opportunity to fall into the trap of stereotypical views when a functional description of the individual is utilized. Therefore, despite difficulties with the use of a functional approach, the gains of using it may also be considerable.

RELATIONSHIP OF DEVELOPMENTAL DISABILITIES DEFINITION TO EMPLOYMENT

For developmentally disabled adults, as for most adults, one of the critical life activities is employment. Much of an adult's time is spent in work or work-related activities, including social activities that may have their origin in the greater work environment. Work also provides the means through which the individual can engage in other activities through the use of earnings to purchase living and social options (Flexer, 1983).

Historically, the measure of success in vocational rehabilitation has been the number of individuals who are placed in jobs (Kiernan & Pyne, 1982). Within the past several years, with an increase in mobility in both jobs and residential environments, the concept of permanency in employment or "the job" has changed. Job mobility is now the rule, rather than the exception. Thus, to measure vocational rehabilitation success solely on job placement does not reflect the current times. Employment involving multiple jobs that contribute to an individual's work history may be a more realistic outcome measure. Such a measure allows for mobility within the job market and reflects the dynamic status of working today (Wehman, 1981).

To take this logic one step further, examine the role of employment. Employment can be defined as the level of economic self-sufficiency afforded to the worker through wages earned on the job. Ultimately, the measure of success is thus the degree of economic self-sufficiency gained through employment. As was seen in Table 2 the degree of economic self-sufficiency is one of the major areas of life activities noted within the definition of developmental disabilities (Hammerman & Maikowski, 1981) and has significant impact on the individual's ultimate level of independence. Economic self-sufficiency is a functional description of an outcome resulting from maintaining oneself in an employment status (Conley & Noble, 1979).

The measure of economic self-sufficiency can be more diverse, quantifiable, and recordable than are simple statistics on placement. Its use as an outcome index provides a more sensitive measure of adjustment for the developmentally disabled adult and moves the concept of employment into a more functional one. A more thorough review of functional design and how it may relate to the typical options and choices that exist for all persons is presented in Chapter 7, "Comprehensive Designs for the Future."

SUMMARY

Since its inception, the definition of developmental disabilities has taken a more functional view of the population that it addresses. Concerns about how to operationalize such a definition led organizations to view the developmental disabilities population from a categorical perspective. With the establishment of the current functional definition and the expressed intent of Congress, the administration, and the proponents of the developmental disabilities movement, there has been a move from a categorical approach to a more descriptive one. This move has created some difficulties in operationalizing both the planning and service elements for developmental disabilities on a state-by-state basis. Much of the difficulty relates to a lack of specific guidelines for interpreting the elements of the definition, particularly major life activities. On the other hand, the definition has forced planners and service providers to focus on the needs of the individual and thus has reduced some of the negative aspects of labeling and stereotypical perceptions and attitudes. The advantage of the definition is that it looks at strengths and limitations of an individual and thus has an increased potential for developing prescriptive program planning and service delivery (Gollay, 1981).

The discussion of the pros and cons of a functional definition will continue. The use of such a definition creates some constraints on strategic planning and requires more varied program planning. However, it allows for a look at the whole person over a series of different developmental stages. This process can facilitate the continuity of service delivery for substantially disabled individuals of all ages.

REFERENCES

Boggs, E., & Henney, L. (1979). *A numerical and functional description of the developmentally disabled population in the United States by major life activities as defined in the Developmental Disabilities Assistance and Bill of Rights Act as amended in P.L. 95-602.* Unpublished paper. Philadelphia: EMC Institute.

Bowe, F. (1983). *Demography and disability.* Fayetteville, AS: Arkansas Rehabilitation Research and Training Center, University of Arkansas.

Cawood, L. (Ed.). (1979). *Work-oriented rehabilitation dictionary and synonyms.* Seattle, WA: Northwest Association of Rehabilitation Industries.

Conley, R., & Noble, J. (1979). *Worker's compensation reform: Challenge for the 80's.* Washington, DC: U.S. Government Printing Office.

Final Report of the National Task Force on the Definition of Developmental Disabilities. (1977). Cambridge, MA: Abt Associates Inc.

Flexer, R. (1983). Habilitation services for developmentally disabled persons. *Journal of Applied Rehab Counseling, 14* (3), 6–19.

Freedman, R. (1977). An analysis of a functional approach to the definition of developmental disabilities. In *Final Report of the National Task Force on the Definition of Developmental Disabilities.* Cambridge, MA: Abt Associates Inc.

Gollay, E. (1979). *The modified definition of developmental disabilities: An initial exploration.* Columbia, MD: Murgah Management Systems, Inc.

Gollay, E. (1981). *Operational definition of developmental disabilities.* Santa Fe, NM: Gollay and Associates.

Grossman, H. (Ed.). (1983). *Classification in mental retardation.* Washington, DC: American Association on Mental Deficiency.

Hammerman, S., & Maikowski, S. (1981). *The economics of disability: International perspectives.* New York: Rehabilitation International.

Kiernan, W., & Pyne, M. (1982). Hard to train: A history of vocational training for special needs youth. In K. P. Lynch, W. E. Kiernan, & J. A. Stark (Eds.), *Prevocational and Vocational education for special needs youth: A blueprint for the 1980s* (pp. 3–13). Baltimore, MD: Paul H. Brookes Publishing Co.

Summers, J. (1981). The definition of developmental disabilities: A concept in transition. *Mental Retardation, 19* (6), 259–265.

Wehman, P. (1981). *Competitive employment: New horizons for severely disabled individuals.* Baltimore, MD: Paul H. Brookes Publishing Co.

∞ Chapter 3 ∞

Demographic Characteristics

William E. Kiernan and Robert H. Bruininks

THE IDENTIFICATION OF SPECIFIC DATA RE-
flecting the prevalence and characteristics of a
population is essential if goods and services are
to be delivered effectively and efficiently. Information needed for social and economic
planning depends to a great extent on the availability, quality, and precision of data, as well
as the intended purpose for which that data are
collected. For the politician the collection of
data could include how many people are registered as Republicans or Democrats, how many
are of voting age, or what the past voting habits
have been in a geographic area. An industry
marketing effort might include questions about
households and the number and/or ages of
people within those households. The number
of school-age children is a critical issue for the
education administrator, as well as the local
taxpayer, when looking at budgets and use of
school resources in districts where there is a
change in the distribution of the student body.

In human services, information on the number of persons in a specific group is an important aspect of research, planning, and service
delivery. Program managers of specific services—residential, employment, income maintenance, and health care—often need precise
information about the characteristics of those
served. Their need to know is derived not from
curiosity but from the desire to be able to be
responsive in a timely and effective fashion.

The authors of this chapter examine the
population of disabled individuals and, more
specifically, persons with developmental dis-

abilities in the world of work. Examining the
problems without considering the magnitude of
the need would be of little value. The authors
have looked at previous research on incidence
and prevalence of various disabling conditions
and at data reflecting rates of employment for
the developmentally disabled adult. This effort
provides a means of verifying a major concern;
that is, the lack of employment opportunities
for these people.

DEFINITIONS AND THEIR
IMPACT ON DATA COLLECTION

Essential to the development of reliable data
for planning service programs is a clear definition of the members of a target group. In the
past, a categorical approach to defining disabled individuals resulted in a somewhat proscribed system of determining which individuals would be members of the target group.
With the establishment of a functional definition of developmental disabilities, a new set
of criteria must be developed if a thoughtful
examination of population trends and data is to
be realized. Because most past efforts centered
around categorical groupings, the move to a
functional definition has presented many problems in assembling information pertaining to
the service needs of developmentally disabled
individuals.

With the adoption of a functional defintion
in the Developmental Disabilities Act, the
states encountered great difficulties in defin-

ing, enumerating, and projecting the number of developmentally disabled individuals needing services. A recent analysis of 46 state plans by one of the authors found little indication that states could project the numbers of developmentally disabled individuals with clearly defined functional limitations.

Existing data must be reexamined in light of this definitional change. The functional definition does not include individuals who would have been considered as developmentally disabled under the old, more categorically oriented definition. The bias in the new definition is clearly toward the more severely disabled individual; thus, the less impaired individual who was considered as developmentally disabled may not qualify for assistance under this new definition. Chapter 2 provided an overview of the impact of the shift from a categorical to a functional definition in developmental disabilities.

In addition to the impact of this definitional change it is important to consider how the data were used and the reason for which the data were originally collected. Inferences must be made if existing data are to be used for another purpose. Many assumptions must be made if the data from national data bases, such as the Bureau of the Census, Public Health Service, Vital and Health Statistics, and the Social Security Administration survey information, are to be useful in dealing with the developmentally disabled population (Boggs & Henney, 1979). Because there is no dedicated data base dealing specifically with the developmentally disabled population, the strength of the interpretations from those statistics is dependent on the soundness of the assumptions and methodologies utilized. Often, variations in the reported statistics of the characteristics or size of the developmentally disabled population nationally are more a reflection of different assumptions and procedures than true variations in population statistics. Much of the current information on developmental disabilities comes from the analysis of the 1976 Bureau of the Census' Study on Income and Education (SIE) (Boggs & Henney, 1979). As

is seen later, the SIE study serves as the primary source for many of the assumptions made about the developmentally disabled population in various studies.

PREVALENCE STATISTICS IN DEVELOPMENTAL DISABILITIES

In any attempt to look at populations it is important to establish certain basic statistics. Epidemiologists use incidence and prevalence statistics to describe the general or anticipated size of target populations. Incidence data reflect the rate at which new cases of an illness or condition appear in a population; it is expressed as the number of persons developing an impairment or condition per unit of population within a specified time period. Because there are many reasons why an individual might be considered as having a developmental disability at one time or another, and in light of the fact that age of onset is highly variable, this statistic is of limited value.

Prevalence data reflect the number of persons in a population who have an illness or condition during a specified time period. Prevalence data are much better suited to describing a chronic condition, such as developmental disabilities. Here, however, there is difficulty in identifying the population because of the ambiguity in the use of a functional definition and the methodology used to record population statistics in national studies. Much of the national census data and national statistics cannot be easily interpreted in relationship to criteria in the functional definition.

As is seen in the next section, numerous studies have been done on the prevalence of such conditions as mental retardation, cerebral palsy, epilepsy, and autism. However, as was noted earlier, not all of these individuals would be classified as having a developmental disability. A more specific discussion of employment and employment statistics for the developmentally disabled adult follows. This discussion deals with the diversity of definitions at many levels and the incompatibility of various sources of information.

Methodologies for Determining
Prevalence of Developmental Disabilities

Estimates of the developmentally disabled population in need of assistance can vary greatly in terms of questions to be answered, precision, information produced, and costs. Warheit, Bell, and Schwab (1974) have described five commonly used approaches to needs assessment in the field of mental health. These methods are the key informant approach, the community forum approach, the rates-under-treatment approach, the social indicators approach, and the direct survey approach. Each of these approaches, which may be applied to planning services for individuals with developmental disabilities, presents advantages and disadvantages, as can be seen by the information summarized in Table 1.

All the approaches summarized in Table 1 are viable methods of estimating the prevalence of developmental disabilities. The direct sample survey method is generally the preferred approach, but the costs involved make it impractical in many community studies. Such surveys are best conducted on a larger geographic scale.

Typically, the approach used to estimate prevalence of developmentally disabled individuals is the application of national prevalence estimates to the national population. Under this procedure, service needs are assessed through multiplying prevalence estimates for various handicapping conditions by the number of people residing in a specific geographic area. For example, if the prevalence of severely retarded children is approximately 0.3%, and if the number of school-aged children in an area is 10,000, the expected number of severely retarded children in need of service would be 30. Although this technique is widely used to estimate service need, it possesses a number of built-in deficiencies.

1. Prevalence estimates in many cases are not based on empirically derived findings. For example, many prevalence estimates of mental retardation are often based on projections, rather than actual documentation

derived from the normal, theoretical distribution of intelligence test scores.

2. These estimates are derived and reported at a single point in time and thereby ignore cyclical trends in the incidence of disabilities resulting from major changes in medical practice and social philosophy (e.g., epidemics, such as rubella).

3. Application of reported nationwide estimates to particular geographic areas is frequently inappropriate because it ignores local characteristics that could influence the prevalence of disabilities (e.g., per capita wealth, adequacy of health care).

Surveys of community agencies are another popular means of assessing demands for service. As with the previously discussed method, this voluntary reporting or key informant procedure also contains a number of limitations. Projections of service needs based on this method are limited by the peculiarities of agency intake policies, difficulties in developing consensus on definitions of disabilities and the extent to which they present significant needs for services, the problem of achieving comprehensive survey coverage among agencies with conflicting and overlapping jurisdictions in large geographical areas, and questions related to the confidentiality of agency records. Even with these limitations, Wishik (1956) reported a 63.4% agreement among case findings obtained through voluntary reports from agencies and a diagnostic sampling study in two different communities in Georgia. On the basis of these results, he concluded "that voluntary reporting, even lay reporting, is an important case finding device that should be given serious consideration" (p. 199). The reports of Wishik and others (Lemkau & Imre, 1969) indicate, however, that a major shortcoming of this approach is that it tends to yield conservative estimates of the actual number of disabled persons represented in the population.

Another approach that is often used to determine prevalence is the diagnostic survey method. This procedure entails the con-

Table 1. Needs assessment approaches

Approach	Source of information	Selected advantages	Selected disadvantages
Key informant	Secured from persons with knowledge of community's need and prevailing patterns of service	a. Low cost b. Broad participation c. Improvement of communication	a. Potential bias: personal and agency b. May inaccurately estimate needs
Community forum	Secured from individuals in a public meeting	a. Easy to arrange b. Low costs c. May increase community support and participation	Logistics
Rates-under-treatment	Description of persons using services in a community — location, SES characteristics, age, etc.	a. Low cost b. Increases awareness of service impact	Assuring confidentiality
Social indicators	Analysis of factors to be associated with persons in need through statistics in public records and reports. *Example:* Indices of poverty related to proportion of children in special classes by social status levels.	a. Useful predictors of need b. Useful in combination with other approaches c. Identify factors associated with service need and utilization	a. Provide an incomplete picture of needs b. Lead to incorrect and premature conclusions regarding causes of need c. Incomplete assessment of need
Direct survey	Persons in need of service are assessed directly, using standardized methods	a. Most accurate — possible to assess extent of error in survey b. Assessment is direct, not indirect c. Likely to produce more reliable and valid information than other methods	a. Costs can be very high b. Requires more sophisticated approaches than other methods c. Logistics

struction of random samples of the population and accurate assessments on each individual by an interdisciplinary team of specialists. It is the most rigorous and reliable case-finding approach of the various survey methods, but is also the most expensive. Few public agencies can afford the luxury of conducting comprehensive diagnostic surveys of populations.

This brief review of the issues involved emphasizes the importance of considering: 1) multiple factors—definitions, local considerations, methodological influences—in projecting the prevalence of the developmentally disabled population and 2) the relative limitations of single estimates as opposed to probable ranges derived from a variety of sources.

Prevalence Estimates

A number of studies and analyses have been conducted to estimate the prevalence of individuals with developmental disabilities. Most studies rely extensively on established diagnostic categories, which generally include mental retardation, cerebral palsy, epilepsy, autism, and associated disabilities. The tables found in the appendix at the end of this chapter present prevalence rates for these results of four categories of handicaps, which are often found in individuals who meet the criteria in the functional definition of developmental disabilities. Other serious mental or physical impairments also may result in substantial limitations in three or more areas of the major life activities and a need for extended assistance under the current definition. However, these estimates provide some basis both for identifying factors that influence the prevalence of developmental disabilities and for formulating a range of workable estimates for planning purposes.

Conclusions on Prevalence Estimates

The following conclusions seem warranted from a review of available evidence and projections of developmental disabilities.

1. The prevalence of categorical handicaps traditionally associated with the concept of developmental disabilities seems to range around approximately 1.0% for mental retardation (Bruininks, Rotegard, & Lakin, 1982), 0.35% for cerebral palsy (National Cerebral Palsy Medical Directory, 1983), 0.75% for epilepsy (Meighan, Queener, & Weitman, 1976), and 0.05% for autism (National Society for Autistic Children, 1983).

2. Under the new functional definition, a number of potential disability categories, with an anticipated relationship to the functional criteria, could be added to the population of developmentally disabled individuals (e.g., bilateral blindness, childhood psychosis, cystic fibrosis, bilateral deafness, deaf-blind, Huntington's disease, osteogenesis imperfecta, spina bifida, spinal cord injury, Tourette's syndrome, tuberous sclerosis, traumatic brain injury, etc.). In addition, more than one of these disabilities could be present in an individual. They are also infrequently represented in the United States population.

3. Due to medical advances and other factors, the prevalence of many disabilities is declining. For example, the Comprehensive Epilepsy Research Center at the University of Minnesota reports that 75% of the cases of epilepsy can be completely or partially controlled through drugs. The medical director for the National Association in Cerebral Palsy noted recently that the incidence of children born with cerebral palsy is decreasing.

4. Categorical definitions of disability and functional definitions of application criteria under Public Law 95-602 often overlap. A high correlation of these criteria often exists among developmentally disabled individuals. For example, in a recent New York state study, 80% of a large sample of individuals in programs for the developmentally disabled evidenced three or more of these functional criteria (Lubin, Jacobson, & Kiely, 1982).

5. Prevalence rates of developmental disabilities vary greatly by age, region, and circumstance. In a recent report to Congress on the implementation of Public Law 94-142 (and PL 89-313), approximately 8.8% of the school population received assistance through special education services. In specific examples such as the Turning 22 Survey in Massachusetts, 16.8% of the total school population is receiving special needs services. Using the existing functional or categorical definitions would likely produce a prevalence rate for developmental disabilities well in excess of 2.0%. Rates of developmental disability are considerably higher during the school years.

6. According to studies commissioned by the Administration on Developmental Disabilities (ADD), there is a wide diversity in estimates used by states to project the prevalence of developmental disabilities. The overall average across states was approximately 2.4% (Boggs & Henney, 1979). A recent report by Bruininks, Lakin, and Hill (1984) found wide variations in reported rates used by state councils.

7. A number of national surveys conducted by the Census Bureau have yielded estimates on the number of disabled individuals in the noninstitutionalized and institutionalized populations (Bureau of the Census, 1976). Many of these reports and other studies led ADD to project that 1.2% of the noninstitutionalized population is developmentally disabled (Administration on Developmental Disabilities, 1981). Adding those individuals in various residential arrangements—currently estimated conservatively at approximately 400,000 to 500,000 individuals—Lakin, Bruininks, Doth, Hill, and Hauber (1982) would increase this estimate by 0.2% or to a rate of 1.5% of the population. (The recent experience of the Center for Residential and Community Services at the University of Minnesota suggests that the Census Bureau survey,

based on the Master Facility Inventory, National Center on Health Statistics, seriously underestimates the number of developmentally disabled individuals in private, community-based residential facilities.)

8. The ADD's (1981) special report on the change in definition further estimated that individuals defined as developmentally disabled would comprise the following subcategories:

Mentally retarded	35%
Seriously emotionally disturbed	10%
Sensory impaired	17%
Physically impaired	38%
Total	100%

It should be noted that many developmentally disabled individuals in need of services would likely be represented in more than one category, and severity of disabilities may vary substantially within and across categories.

9. Based on a number of assumptions and a variety of statistical information, Boggs and Henney (1979) projected a prevalence rate of 1.65% for developmental disabilities. Henney (1980) later surveyed state reports and found a decreased prevalence estimate of 27% under the new functional definition. Given the lack of empirical basis for these state estimates, it is quite unlikely that this reported reduction can be defended with available information.

10. Using a variety of categorical statistics on school-aged and adult populations, plus assumptions on the possible overlap among categories (or duplicate counts), it is possible to estimate a defensible prevalence estimate of the developmentally disabled population. The estimate also makes the assumption that developmentally disabled individuals meet the substantial, severely handicapped criterion of the definition. (For example, if 75% of the cases of epilepsy can be at least partially controlled, the prevalence of epilepsy resulting in substantial limitations might be reduced to .19%.) Use

of available statistics, discounted by 25% for potential duplication and overlap, leads one to estimate a rate of 1.60% of the population as developmentally disabled. This projection is very close to the figure derived by Boggs and Henney (1979) using independent procedures and data.

Any population estimates regarding the prevalence of developmental disabilities should, however, be modified to reflect special circumstances. If the focus is on a specific age group, then consideration of increases or decreases in the population prevalence statistics reflecting the school-aged and the older developmentally disabled individual should be made. An increase in the proportion of the school-aged population defined as handicapped has been established (Report to the Congress, 1983; The After 22 Study, 1982). Not as well established is the potential increase due to age in the developmentally disabled population. As in all populations, there are certain events that may render an older person less able to perform daily activities: illness, reduction in strength, limitations in mobility, and so forth. Due to the aging process, certain individuals may, at some point in the future, experience substantial impairment in three or more of the major life activities. Although these individuals may require assistance similar to that needed by developmentally disabled individuals, they are generally not defined as developmentally disabled.

Other elements, such as poverty and economic indicators, have an impact on the developmentally disabled population. Data show a highly negative impact of poverty on the overall well-being of the entire population (Birch & Gussow, 1970). Poverty may have an even more significant impact on the developmentally disabled population. Such economic issues as unemployment rates and inflation can also inhibit the developmentally disabled adult from achieving a level of economic self-sufficiency that would enable him or her to move into a more independent status. In both of these instances, there needs to be an adjustment

in the local prevalence data to reflect their impact.

The next section covers data dealing with employment for the developmentally disabled population. These data have not been as well identified as the population data. Yet, with the key major life activities for adults focusing on employment and its relationship to economic self-sufficiency, there is a need to look at the prevalence of developmental disabilities in relationship to employment.

EMPLOYMENT AND THE DEVELOPMENTALLY DISABLED ADULT

As was noted earlier, in looking at population parameters, it is essential to have some consistency in identifying the target population and the definitions used. One persistent problem in research on adults is the inconsistency and difficulty in defining work disability and the nature and status of employment. Depending on the agency involved and the needs of that agency, the definition of employment, unemployment, not in the labor force, and work disability vary considerably.

Problems of ambiguity in defining terms related to work and employment are apparent in examining the information contained in Tables 2 through 5. In certain instances, where a question of eligibility is the determining factor, the measure of employment—as can be seen in Table 2—is very specific. Substantial gainful activity (SGA) has a specific dollar value attached to it. The Social Security Administration (SSA), for example, uses this dollar amount in part to determine ongoing eligibility for individuals who are disabled. The Bureau of the Census, on the other hand, groups individuals by the number of hours worked, rather than actual earnings. In that definition, an employed person is identified as an individual who has worked 15 hours or more in paid or unpaid work during a specific time period. For the Public Health Service, National Center on Health Statistics, an employed person is defined as an individual who is paid for work or is self-employed. Earnings or amount of time engaged in employment are not con-

Table 2. Employment

Term	Definition	Source
Employment	Person who: - as a civilian who, during the survey week, did any work at all as paid employee or in own business or own farm - has worked 15 hours or more of paid or unpaid work - is not working during the survey but has a job from which there is temporary absence - is age 17 or over during the interview period and has a job - is paid for work or self-employed in business - is unpaid for work in a family business or farm - is temporarily out of work due to illness, vacation, strike, or bad weather - is a freelance worker who has a definite arrangement with one or more employers to work for pay	Department of Commerce, Bureau of Census Department of Labor, Bureau of Labor Statistics Department of Health and Human Services, Public Health Service, National Center for Health Statistics
Substantial activity (employment)	Remunerative work: - is substantial as determined by the amount of money earned, the number of hours worked, and whether the work is in the general economy or sheltered - maximum monthly amount for 1980-1982 is $300 - minimum monthly amount for 1980-1982 is $190 - above maximum is viewed as substantial gainful activity - is between maximum and minimum with other factors considered	Department of Health and Human Services, Social Security Administration

sidered. In each case, the purpose of the data collection has determined the specificity with which employment and other related terms are defined.

Unemployment, on the other hand, presents fewer difficulties from a definitional perspective. For such agencies as the National Center for Health Statistics, an unemployed person is defined as an individual who has not worked for 2 weeks before the interview period, but who is actively seeking employment. The Bureau of Labor Statistics and the Bureau of the Census define an unemployed individual as one who is actively engaged in looking for work, but has not yet obtained employment. Thus, these definitions of unemployment all contain the element of an attempt on the part of the individual to seek out employment, which is his or her ultimate goal. Differences arise in the length of time that a person is unemployed and how they are counted by different federal agencies.

A terminology of a less popular nature reflects on those who are currently not within the labor force. According to the Bureau of the Census and the Department of Labor, an individual who is neither classified as employed nor seeking employment may not be con-

Table 3. Unemployment

Term	Definition	Source
Unemployed	Person who: - is 17 years or older who did not work or did not have a job during the 2–week period prior to the inteview - is looking for work - is on layoff but had a job	Department of Health and Human Services, Public Health Service, National Center for Health Statistics
Unemploy-ment	Person who: - was not working during census period but available to work - has engaged in any specific jobseek-ing activities within the past 4 weeks - is waiting to be recalled to a job from which there was a layoff - is waiting to report to a new job within 30 days	Department of Commerce, Bureau of Census Department of Labor, Bureau of Labor Statistics

sidered as part of the labor force. Generally, this classification is given to individuals who are unavailable for work due to a variety of reasons or are not interested in obtaining employment. No time limit to obtain employment is placed on those who are not in the labor force. For the National Center for Health Statistics, in order to be considered as not in the labor force, an individual must not be involved in looking for work nor engaged in any work activities for 2 weeks before the interview period. These definitions attempt to identify

Table 4. Not in the labor force

Term	Definition	Source
Not in labor force	Person who: - is 17 years or older - did not work during the 2–week period covered by the interview - is not looking for work - is not on layoff from a job - has a disability that excludes employ-ment	Department of Health and Human Services, Public Health Services, National Center for Health Statistics
Not in labor force	Person who is: - not classified as employed or unemployed - attending school - engaged in own home with housework - unable to work because of long-term physical or mental illness - retired - a seasonal worker not working at time of survey - voluntarily idle - a discouraged worker	Department of Commerce, Bureau of Conous Department of Labor, Bureau of Labor Statistics

Table 5. Work disability

Term	Definition	Source
Work disability	Work disability includes a person: - with a health problem or disability that prevents or limits kind or amount of work - with a service-connected disability, is retired, or has left job due to health reasons - who did not work in survey week due to long-term disability (physical or mental) - who did not work at all in 1981 due to illness or disability - who is under 65 years of age and is covered by Medicare - who is under 65 years of age and receiving SSI (Supplemental Security Income)	Department of Commerce, Bureau of Census
Disability	- Temporary or long-term reduction of a person's activity as a result of an acute or chronic condition Range of chronic activity limitation includes: - inability to work at a job - limitations in amount and kind of work (e.g., needs special aids/rest periods; not able to work full-time) - no limitations in regular work activity but limitation in other areas (e.g., sports, hobbies, civic projects) - no limitation in any activities	Department of Health and Human Services, Public Health Service, National Center for Health Statistics
Disability	A person who is: - unable to engage in substantial gainful activity due to medically determined physical or mental impairments that can be expected to result in death or to last for a continuous period of not less than 12 months.	Department of Health and Human Services, Social Security Administration

those individuals who have either not engaged in employment or have become discouraged and have withdrawn from the labor force.

By far, the most complex definitional issue involves defining a work disability. The Bureau of the Census defines a work disability as a series of problems or conditions that prevent or limit an individual from engaging in employment. For certain individuals, the limitations are a result of age, whereas in other instances, they are in response to a disability. The definition of disability of the National Center for Health Statistics is much more specific; it identifies temporary or long-term disability as the reduction of a person's activity as a result of an acute or chronic condition. It further defines the range of chronic activity limitations from a complete disability to no limitations in employment activities. Through this system, the National Center for Health Statistics is attempting to establish a range of disabilities as opposed to a specific time period of disability. Lastly, the SSA, being an entitlement service, defines disability as an impairment that limits an individual's ability to engage in SGA. Thus, it defines disability in light of the economic return or lack of economic return that the individual is able to achieve.

Problems of ambiguity in defining terms related to work and employment are apparent in examining the data presented. When a question of eligibility is the determining factor, as with Social Security data, the measure of employment is very specific. For purposes of grouping individuals, the Bureau of the Census uses the number of hours worked, paying little regard to actual earnings. For another data base, employment activities are defined by a series of descriptions with no reference to hours worked or amount earned. In each case the purpose of the data collection has determined the specificity with which employment and other related terms are defined. These definitions serve as the base on which many of the economic and employment indices are developed. The following section examines more closely some of these economic indices in relationship to the developmentally disabled adult population.

General Economic and Employment Indices

Frequently an overall index—entitled the Labor Force Participation Ratio—is reported by the Department of Health and Human Services. This figure represents the percent of the working-aged population employed or unemployed in comparison to the total working-aged population. This rate over the past few years has averaged about 63.9% (U.S. Government Printing Office, 1983b). Thus, about 36 of every 100 individuals 16 years of age or over are neither employed nor unemployed and there-

fore are not counted as part of the labor force. The labor force participation ratio varies for both age and sex. No specific analysis has been done on the number of disabled individuals included in this ratio. It could be assumed, however, that many of the developmentally disabled individuals who are of working age are not counted as part of the statistics and thus are not considered as part of the labor force (Bowe, 1983).

In addition to the labor force participation ratio, two terms have been used to reflect those who are not working: *unemployed* and *not in the working force*. The former is included in the labor force participation ratio, whereas the latter classification is not. The term "unemployment" reflects the state of not working during a specific time period (see Table 3). Not in the labor force, on the other hand, reflects those individuals who are not able to be classified as employed or unemployed for numerous reasons (see Table 4).

Much discussion has revolved around the use of employment and unemployment as measures of economic stability (Poindexter, 1981) for developmentally disabled adults. These measures frequently do not reflect the employment status of the disabled adult. The official unemployment rate for disabled persons in March 1982 was reported to be 16.8% (Bowe, 1983). This statistic, however, does not show what percentage are considered not in the labor force. Because many developmentally disabled individuals have not had jobs, the number considered not in the labor force could be substantial and is a very important statistic to consider in evaluating the need for training and other essential services.

When looking at the general issue of employment and unemployment for the developmentally disabled adult, there is also a need to look at those who are underemployed. For some developmentally disabled adults, a minimum-wage job without benefits may be the level of current employment. The present Bureau of Labor Statistics data tend to hide the magnitude of underemployment for all workers, particularly in times of a depressed economy (Poindexter, 1981). The concerns about underemployment are apparent when the reported earnings of the male and female disabled worker are compared with the nondisabled worker, as seen in Table 6. These data reflect all types of disabilities and do not focus specifically on the developmentally disabled worker. The table clearly shows that earnings for the disabled individual are less than those of the nondisabled worker. Underemployment continues to be a problem that must be monitored if, in fact, equal employment opportunities are to be a reality for developmentally disabled individuals.

Incompatibility in definitions and design of the current data bases makes an analysis of any data on employment status for the developmentally disabled adult difficult at best. Such terms as employment, unemployment, not in the labor force, and work disability are defined in many different ways. The lack of consistency in the definition makes the cross-referencing of statistics from the various sources less reliable. In order to keep data on employment status for the developmentally disabled adult in perspective, it is important to examine the prevalence of developmental disabilities in adults. These data give some idea of the number of persons who might potentially be in the labor pool and can serve as a base for comparison against some of the general placement and employment data that has been reported.

Employment Status of Developmentally Disabled Adults

Prevalence statistics for the total population of developmentally disabled individuals were discussed earlier. It is now appropriate to look more closely at developmentally disabled adults and their role in employment. The major life activity for adults is work. In looking at the data that deal with work and the disabled individual, the Study of Income and Education (SIE) done by the Bureau of the Census in 1975 is the most comprehensive survey to date. This survey examined those who are prevented from working or limited in their work done because of a disability. It provided the base from which Boggs and Henney (1979) developed their report on the numerical and functional descriptions of the developmentally disabled population.

Table 6. Underemployment and the disabled worker

		Employment income in 1980[a]	
		Part-time	Full-time
Male	Disabled worker	$12,579	$18,755
	Nondisabled worker	16,367	20,644
Female	Disabled worker	5,335	10,569
	Nondisabled worker	7,771	12,021

[a]Based upon Current Population Reports Series P-60, No. 138 (U.S. Government Printing Office, 1983a).

The SIE study's definition of work disability was consistent with that of the Bureau of the Census (see Table 5). Within the category of work disability, the SIE study established three groupings: prevented from working, not able to work regularly, and able to work regularly. Those prevented from working were defined as having a limiting health condition that has made or will make work at any job at all for a long period of time impossible. For those not able to work regularly, data on hours worked per week and total weeks worked in 1975 were collected. These data, however, reflected all disabled persons and not only those who were developmentally disabled.

In examining the data, adjustments are necessary to reflect information and needs of the developmentally disabled population. Age of onset and severity of disability are the key elements that identify a developmentally disabling condition. Boggs and Henney (1979) assumed that those prevented from working and those who work less than 16 weeks in a year were the most severely disabled. The SIE data showed that 44% of those who were not able to work regularly worked less than 16 weeks during the year. When applying these assumptions and adjusting for the age of onset of disability—that is, before age 22 years—1.49% of the adults between the ages of 18 and 64 were felt to be developmentally disabled and have a substantial limitation in economic self-sufficiency (Boggs & Henney, 1979).

These basic assumptions may be challenged. However, the Boggs and Henney (1979) study stands as the most detailed effort in identifying how many developmentally disabled adults have limitations in their degree of economic self-sufficiency. Although several other data bases report disabilities in the general population, only the SIE provides sufficient data to allow for the development of a realistic estimate of the prevalence of developmental disabilities among adults and the number of those adults who have a work disability. By definition, because there are limitations in the degree of economic self-sufficiency realized, it would be thus assumed that most, if not all,

individuals who are developmentally disabled are also unemployed or considered not in the labor force.

A second study, the 1978 Survey on Disability and Work, was published in May 1982 by the Office of Research Statistics, SSA (U.S. Government Printing Office, 1982a). As in the case of other studies, this examined all disabled persons and did not separate out disability in such a way as to make possible direct comparisons of the data with the population of developmentally disabled adults. The data do, however, note that 17.2% of all adults—21.5 of the 127 million adults—consider themselves as having a work disability (see Table 5). About 11 million of those adults reported that they were either unable to work at all or unable to work regularly. For those aged 18 to 65 years old with a work disability, 55.81% were not considered as in the labor force, as compared with 17.4% for those with no work disability. As would be expected for those who reported severe work disability, the percentage not in the labor force was even higher (86.4%). These statistics show that many persons with a disability are either not in the labor force or experience regular periods of unemployment. The 1978 study, as did the previous SIE study, did not allow for direct reporting of the employment status of the developmentally disabled worker. However, most of those who are developmentally disabled would be assumed to be placed in the severe work disability group.

A more specific study done by the Boston Center for Independent Living (BCIL) (January 1983) shows that, for severely physically disabled individuals between the ages of 18 and 59, 74% were either unemployed or not in the labor force. Of this group, 34% indicated a willingness to become employed if given the opportunity. Although the sample size (n = 105) in this study was somewhat small, it indicates that many disabled adults who might have been included in the 1978 Social Security study and labeled as not in employment might be interested in securing employment if given the opportunity. Although the 1978 Social Security study reports a somewhat lower rate of unemployment and not in the labor market for disabled persons, the rate was still significantly higher than that reported for nondisabled adults.

If the 1.49% prevalence rate is accurate, there would be 1,893,000 developmentally disabled adults in a total labor force of 127 million adults in 1978. Assuming that most developmentally disabled adults would be considered as having a severe work disability and in light of the findings of the Social Security study, 1.64 million of these developmentally disabled adults would either be unemployed or not in the labor force. If the findings of the BCIL study were utilized, about 1.4 million developmentally disabled adults would be unemployed or not in the labor force. What may, however, be a more significant fact is that, according to the BCIL study, 34% of those individuals who were unemployed or not in the labor force reported that they were interested in working. This finding would imply that about 475,000 developmentally disabled adults would like some assistance in seeking employment and would consider entering employment if given the opportunity.

The service system with a primary responsibility for providing employment training to disabled and handicapped persons is the vocational rehabilitation system. The statistics on employment closure reported by state vocational rehabilitation agencies represent the number of persons who are placed in competitive, sheltered, or homebound employment during a specific time period. Again due to data collection problems, the developmentally disabled population is not recorded separately; thus, inferences must be made about the number of developmentally disabled adults served by this system. For the period from 1978 to 1980, about 12% of those persons served by vocational rehabilitation agencies were mentally retarded. Although not all mentally retarded persons would be considered to be developmentally disabled, it can be assumed that the population of developmentally disabled persons served by the vocational rehabilitation system would not exceed this 12% figure. This assumption is based on the stipulation that a reasonable expectation for achieving employ-

ment be present if one is to be considered as eligible for vocational rehabilitation services. In many instances, adults with more severe disabilities would not be considered as eligible clients for vocational rehabilitation.

Of those persons with mental retardation served by vocational rehabilitation, 62% enter competitive, sheltered, or homebound employment at the completion of their rehabilitation program. This statistic would imply that a total of approximately 7.5% of the persons served by vocational rehabilitation who achieve an employment outcome have a diagnosis of mental retardation. However, as was noted, approximately 475,000 developmentally disabled persons each year would be interested in receiving assistance directed toward obtaining employment. It is clear that the need for employment training among developmentally disabled adults far exceeds the capacity of the rehabilitation system presently.

Several problems emerge when using data based on the rehabilitation service delivery system. Vocational rehabilitation agencies have strict eligibility criteria, and the possibility of the developmentally disabled adult not qualifying for service is high. In addition, the major disabling conditions reported are incompatible with the functional definition of developmental disabilities. Furthermore, rehabilitation data do not delineate those who go to competitive employment and those who go to sheltered employment. If the vocational rehabilitation data are to be utilized, many assumptions must be made, and such terms as "rehabilitated" need to be clarified. Because there are strict eligibility criteria, the data derived from this system reflect placement rates of eligible recipients and not the needs of the total developmentally disabled adult population. These stipulations make the vocational rehabilitation data extremely limited in its capacity to predict needs for the total population.

Other data bases, such as the Social Security statistics, have similar problems. The diagnostic groupings utilized by the SSA require that many assumptions be made if the functional definition of developmental disabilities is to be utilized. Records of earnings reported to the

SSA reflect revenues received from multiple sources and not just from employment. At times, eligibility for entitlement under Social Security may exclude certain developmentally disabled adults from participating. As in the case of the vocational rehabilitation system, the SSA records report data for highly specific purposes. Neither data base reflects the total picture for the developmentally disabled adult and employment.

It would seem that although some reasonable estimates of prevalence of the developmentally disabled adult are possible, employment and unemployment data are extremely limited. However, available information shows that developmentally disabled adults have an extremely high probability of not being in the labor force or of being underemployed.

SUMMARY

The development of precise estimates of the developmentally disabled population has been complicated by the adoption of the functional definition of developmental disabilities and the incompatibility of the existing data resources and collection methodologies. Reasonable estimates of prevalence and employment needs, however, are possible with certain adjustments made for age variation and economic factors. Given the inferences that must be made, a prevalence rate of 1.49% of the general adult population is realistic. Overall, the prevalence rate across all ages would be closer to 1.6%.

An analysis of the employment status of the developmentally disabled adult is further complicated by an inconsistency in definitions. Such data bases as the vocational rehabilitation system show rates of employment only for those who meet the eligibility criteria for service. No data reflecting those developmentally disabled adults who are deemed as ineligible exist within this system. For the vocational rehabilitation system, data reflecting placement in various types of employment settings are necessary. With the acknowledgement of the need for longer supports, as noted in Chapter 7, data reflecting hours worked and rates paid may be more significant than the number

placed or not placed, especially for the developmentally disabled adult.

Social Security data may provide some specific information about the economic self-sufficiency of disabled individuals. However, changes in revenue reported or degrees of economic self-sufficiency realized may not be exclusively related to employment activities. More precise measures of reasons for changes in earnings would be required if any inferences regarding enhanced achievements in employment for developmentally disabled adults are to be made.

The problems of identifying the magnitude and the effectiveness of placement in employment for developmentally disabled adults are significant. It is essential to establish a methodology that clearly identifies those individuals who are considered as developmentally disabled and to document the number of these individuals who have or could achieve economic self-sufficiency in an employment setting. With some modifications of the data collection procedures utilized by the Bureau of the Census, the current prevalence estimates of the developmentally disabled could be verified. From the employment perspective, a more accurate measure of earnings per hour and hours worked per week would give a more accurate estimate of the level of economic self-sufficiency achieved by the developmentally disabled worker. As noted above, the current system of measuring employment does not allow for measurement of smaller gains in earning capacity for more severely developmentally disabled individuals. A dedicated collection and tracking system for identification of developmentally disabled individuals and measures of economic self-sufficiency is essential if state and local agencies are to plan effectively. Strategies for evaluating employment outcomes for developmentally disabled adults are reviewed in more depth in other sections of this book.

Despite problems of definition and the absence of uniform means of maintaining information, available data do show serious levels of unemployment and underemployment among developmentally disabled adults. From

74% to 86% of the developmentally disabled adults are either unemployed or not considered to be in the labor market. This high level may reflect a lack of opportunity to enter employment, rather than a reluctance or inability on the part of the individual to move in this direction. The challenge is thus one that looks to not accepting the "state of the practice," which indicates that the developmentally disabled adult is not employable, but rather to establishing a "state of the art" that expands both training and the creation of employment opportunities for the developmentally disabled adult.

The need for expanded training and employment opportunities for developmentally disabled adults is obviously critical to increase economic self-sufficiency and social assimilation. Without that opportunity, the productive contributions of over a million of our citizens are needlessly limited.

REFERENCES

Abramowicz, H. K., & Richardson, S. A. (1975). Epidemiology of severe mental retardation in children: Community studies. *American Journal of Mental Deficiency, 80*(1), 18–39.

Administration on Developmental Disabilities. (1981). *Special report on the impact of the change in the definition of developmental disabilities*. Washington DC: Author.

Birch, H. G., & Gussow, J. D. (1970). *Disadvantaged children: Health, nutrition and school failure*. New York: Brace & World, Inc.

Bloom, B. (1982). *Current estimates from the national health interviews survey: United States, 1981*. (Series 10–Number 41). Washington, DC: U.S. Government Printing Office.

Boggs, E., & Henney, R. (1979). *A numerical and functional description of the developmental disabilities population*. Washington, DC: EMC Institute.

Bowe, F. (1983). *Demography and disability*. Fayetteville, AS: Arkansas Rehabilitation Research and Training Center, University of Arkansas.

Brask, B. H. (1970). A prevalence investigation of childhood psychosis. In *The 16th Scandinavian Congress of Psychiatry*.

Braunstein, W. (1977). Gainful employment: The myth and hope of rehabilitation consumers. *Journal of Applied Rehabilitation, 8*(1), 22–27.

Bruininks, R. H., Lakin, K. C., & Hill, B. K. (1984). *Client oriented statistical indicators*. Minneapolis, MN: University of Minnesota (unpublished report).

Bruininks, R. H., Rotegard, L., & Lakin, K. (1982, August). *Epidemiology of mental retardation and trends in residential services in the United States*. Paper presented at the NICHD Conference Concerning Research on the Impact of Residential Settings on Mentally Retarded Persons. Lake Wilderness, Washington.

Bureau of the Census. (1976). *Survey of institutionalized persons*. Washington, DC: Author.

Conley, R. (1973). *The economics of mental retardation*. Batimore: Johns Hopkins University Press.

Croxen, M. (1982). *Overview: Disability and employment*. Report for the Commission of the European Communities.

Cruickshank, W. M. (Ed.). (1976). *Cerebral palsy: A developmental disability* (3rd ed). Syracuse, NY: Syracuse University Press.

Davenport, C. (1923). The ecology of epilepsy. II. Racial and geographic distribution of epilepsy. *Archives of Neurological Psychiatry, 9*, 554–566.

EMC Institute. (1979). *Program review data: A compilation of rates of prevalence of the developmental disabilities*. Philadelphia: Author.

EMC Institute. (n.d.). *Program issue review: The prevalence of the developmental disabilities*. Philadelphia: Author.

Farber, B. (1968). *Mental retardation: Its social context and social consequences*. Boston: Houghton Mifflin Co.

Feller, B. (1981). *Prevalence of selected impairments: United States–1977*. (Vital and Health Statistics, Series 10–Number 134). Washington, DC: U.S. Government Printing Office.

Gentile, A. (1978). *Disabilities days: United States–1975*. (Vital and Health Statistics, Series 10–Number 118). Washington, DC: U.S. Government Printing Office.

Green, G., & Epstein, R. (1983). *Employment and earnings* (Vol. 30, No. 12). Washington, DC: U.S. Government Printing Office.

Grossman, H. (1973). *Manual on terminology and classification in mental retardation*. Washington, DC: American Association on Mental Deficiency.

Hauser, W. (1978). Epidemiology of epilepsy. *Advances in Neurology, 19*, 313–338.

Hauser, W., & Kurland, L. (1975). The epidemiology of epilepsy in Rochester, Minnesota, 1935 through 1967. *Epilepsia, 16*, 1–66.

Henney, R. L. (1980). *The impact of the amendment of the definition of "developmentally disabled" on the DD Program in FY 79 and FY 80*. Washington, DC: Institute for Comprehensive Planning.

Howie, L., & Drury, T. (1978). *Current estimates from the health interview survey: United States–1977*. (Series 10, No. 126). Washington, DC: U.S. Government Printing

Office.

Kirk, D. (1978). A community prevalence study of mental retardation in New York State. *Journal of Special Education, 12*(1), 83–93.

Jones, L. A. (1979). Census-based prevalence estimates for mental retardation. *Mental Retardation, 17,* 199–200.

Lakin, K. C., Bruininks, R. H., Doth, D., Hill, B. K., & Hauber, F. A. (1982). *Sourcebook on long-term care for developmentally disabled people.* Minneapolis, MN: Center for Residential and Community Services, University of Minnesota.

Lemkau, P., & Imre, P. (1969). Results of a field epidemiologic study. *American Journal of Mental Deficiency. 73,* 858–863.

Lindberg, D. (1976). *Prevalence of developmental disabilities in West Virginia.* Elkins, WV: Davis and Elkins College, Department of Sociology and Anthropology.

Lindberg, D., & Putnam, J. (1979). *The developmentally disabled of West Virginia: A profile of the substantially handicapped who are not in institutions.* Elkins, WV: Davis and Elkins Colege.

Loring, M. (1983). *Unemployment survey/study.* Boston: Boston Center for Independent Living, Inc.

Lotter, V. (1966). Epidemiology of autistic conditions in young children: I. Prevalence. *Social Psychiatry, 1,* 124–137.

Lotter, V. (1967). Epidemiology of autistic conditions in young children: II. Some characteristics of the parents and children. *Social Psychiatry, 1,* 163–173.

Lubin, R., Jacobson, J. W., & Kiely, M. (1982). Projected impact of the functional definition of developmental disabilities: The categorical disabled population and service eligibility. *American Journal of Mental Deficiency, 87*(1), 73–79.

Luckey, R. E., & Neman, R. (1976). Practices is estimating mental retardation prevalence. *Mental Retardation, 14*(1), 16–18.

Meighan, S., Queener, L., & Weitman, M. (1976). Prevalence of epilepsy in children of Murnomon County, Oregon. *Epilepsia, 17,* 245–256.

Metropolitan Council. (1977). *Developmental disabilities: Trends in the Twin Cities Metropolitan area.* St. Paul, MN: Metropolitan Council, Developmental Disabilities Task Force of the Metropolitan Health Board.

Miller, D. L., & Ross, E. M. (1978). National childhood encephalopathy study: An interim report. *British Medical Journal, 2,* 992–993.

National Center for Educational Statistics. (1982). *Conditions of education, 1981 edition.* Washington, DC: Government Printing Office.

One in eleven: Handicapped adults in America. (1975). Washington, DC: President's Committee on Employment of the Handicapped.

Poindexter, J. (1981). *Macroeconomics* (2nd ed.). New York: Dryden Press.

President's Committee on Mental Retardation. (1970). *The six-hour retarded child.* Washington, DC: U.S. Government Printing Office.

Renker, K. (1982). World Statistics on disabled persons. *International Journal of Rehabilitation Research, 5* (2), 167–177.

Report to the Congress. (1983). *Employment and training report of the President, 1982.* Washington, DC: U.S. Government Printing Office.

Richardson, W. P., & Higgins, A. C. (1965). *The handicapped children of Alamance County, North Carolina: A medical and sociological study.* Wilmington, DE: Nemours Foundation.

Ries, P. (1979). *Acute conditions: Incidence and associated disability: United States, July 1977–June 1978.* (Vital and Health Statistics, Series 10, No. 132). Washington, DC: U.S. Government Printing Office.

Rigby, D., & Ponce, E. (1982). *The supplemental security income program for the aged, blind and disabled: Selected characteristics of state supplementation programs as of January 1982.* Washington, DC: U.S. Government Printing Office.

Rose, S., Penry, J., Markush, R., Radloff, L., & Putnam, P. (1973). Prevalence of epilepsy in children. *Epilepsia, 14,* 133–152.

Rutter, M., Tizard, J., & Whitmore, K. (1970). *Education, health and behavior.* London: Longman.

Stein, L., Susser, M., & Saenger, G. (1976a). Mental retardation in a national population of young men in the Netherlands. I. Prevalence of severe mental retardation. *American Journal of Epidemiology, 103,* 477–485.

Stein, L., Susser, M., & Saenger, G. (1976b). Mental retardation in a national population of young men in the Netherlands. II. Prevalence of mild mental retardation. *American Journal of Epidemiology, 104,* 159–169.

Taylor, J. L. (1965). *Mental retardation prevalence in Oregon: A survey by the Oregon State Board of Health.* Portland: Oregon State Board of Health.

The after 22 survey. (1982). Boston: Division of Special Education, Massachusetts Department of Education.

Treffert, D. (1970). Epidemiology of infantile autism. *Archives of General Psychiatry, 22,* 431.

U.S. Department of Education. (1982). *Fourth annual report to Congress on the implementation of Public Law 94-142: The Education of All Handicapped Children Act.* Washington, DC: Author.

U.S. General Accounting Office. (1983). *Federal job training: A comparison of public and private sector performances.* Gaithersburg, MD: Document Handling and Information Services Facility.

U.S. Government Printing Office. (1975). *A summary of selected legislation relating to the handicapped–1974.* Washington, DC: Author.

U.S. Government Printing Office. (1977). *Key federal legislation affecting the handicapped, 1975–76.* Washington, DC: Author.

U.S. Government Printing Office. (1982a). *1978 survey on disability and work.* Washington, DC: Author.

U.S. Government Printing Office. (1982b). *Selected data on persons with disability: 1976 survey on income and education.* Washington, DC: Author.

U.S. Government Printing Office. (1983a). *Characteristics of the population below the poverty level: 1981.* (Current Population Reports Series P-60, No. 138). Washington, DC: Author.

U.S. Government Printing Office. (1983b). *Employment and training report of the president.* Washington, DC: Author.

Van den Berg, B. (1974). Studies on conclusive disorders in young children. III. Recurrence of febrile convulsions. *Epilepsia, 15,* 177–180.

Warheit, G., Bell, R., & Schwab, J. (1974). *Planning for change: Needs assessment approaches.* Bethesda, MD:

National Institute of Mental Health.

Wing, L., Yates, S., Brierley, L., & Gould, J. (1976). The prevalence of early childhood autism: Comparison of administrative and epidemiology studies. *Psychological Medicine, 6,* 89–100.

Wishik, S. (1956). Handicapped children in Georgia: The study of prevalence, disability, needs and resources. *American Journal of Public Health, 46,* 195–203.

APPENDIX

Tables A.1 through A.4 of this appendix present prevalence rates of mental retardation, cerebral palsy, epilepsy, and autism.

Table A.1. Illustrative prevalence rates for mental retardation

Study/source	Population	Method	Results	Comments
EMC Institute (1979)	Mental retardation	Nationally accepted standard	3%	
EMC Institute: *Program issue review: The prevalence of the developmental disabilities*. No date given.	Mental retardation	Based on reports from state DD offices Mean *prevalence* rate Nationwide $N = 44$ states *Range*—high prevalence rate $N = 1$ low prevalence rate $N = 1$ Standard rate	44 state plans were reviewed 2.47% 6.8% 0.1% 3.0%	Methods of obtaining prevalence data varied from state to state, e.g., direct survey, review of literature, estimates from national organizations
Grossman (1973) AAMD suggested rates	Mental retardation	Not specified	2.3%-3% of general population	
Bruininks, Rotegard, and Lakin (1982)	Mental retardation	Compilation from a large number of empirical studies	Actual prevalence of MR is close to 1%	Based upon a review of reported incidence and prevalence studies
President's Committee on Mental Retardation (1970)	Mental retardation	Nationally accepted standard	Reasonable and widely accepted prevalence estimate = 2.7%	
National Center for Educational Statistics (1982) — reported by Office of Special Education	Mental retardation 1980-81 school year	Rates-under-treatment 1980-81 school year	1.8% of general school population	
Luckey and Neman (1976)	Mental retardation	Key informant = questionnaire distributed to state offices of MR (40 offices responding)	Range of prevalence estimates = .35-5.0% mode = 3%	

Author (Study)	Problem	Method	Rate / Prevalence	Comments
Rutter, Tizard, and Whitmore (1970) (Isle of Wight Study in England)	Mental retardation	Direct survey Screened 3,519 children age 9–11 years.	Rate of severe retardation = 3.9/1,000 = .39% Rate of mild retardation = 11.1–21.1/1,000 = 1.1–2.1% overall	Very systematic attempt to identify all MR — not just those so labeled — but still focused on IQ as criterion
Miller and Ross (1978) (Riverside, CA)	Mental retardation	Direct survey + rates-under-treatment Screened sample of 7,000 households for MR + agency survey to identify residents classified as MR	Prevalence estimate for IQ scores below 70 = 2.14 per 1,000 = 2.14%	When adaptive behavior was included, the prevalency rate dropped to 9.7 per 1,000 = .91% (decline was among blacks and Mexican Americans, not whites)
Stein, Susser, and Saenger (1976a,b) (Netherlands)	Mental retardation	Direct survey 400,000 19-year-old men	Rate for severe retardation = 3.8/1,000 = .38% Rate for mild retardation based on: clinical diagnosis = 61 per 1,000 = 6.1% special schooling = 30 per 1,000 = 3.0%	Highly systematic and standardized examination carried out for the purposes of military induction
Abramowicz and Richardson (1975)	Mental retardation (severe only) IQ < 50	Review of literature Reviewed 27 community studies of severe retardation	4 per 1,000 = .4%	19 were considered to have reliable prevalence data
Taylor (1965) (Oregon)	Mental retardation	Rates-under-treatment Survey of agencies serving approximately 1/3 of population of Oregon (215,000 people identified)	1.9%	
Lemkau and Imre (1969) reported in Conley (1973) (Maryland)	Mental retardation	Direct survey Screened all children over age of 1, adults under 35 not completing high school, and adults over 35 who had not completed 8th grade	Rate with IQ<70 = 8.2%	Administered IQ tests to all subjects

(continued)

41

Table A.1. (Continued)

Study/source	Population	Method	Results	Comments
Kirk (1978)	Mental retardation	Direct survey Questionnaire regarding prevalence completed by school districts, state training schools, social service agencies, and the public	1,070 classified MR in a population of 220,000 = .55%	
Jones (1979)	Mental retardation	Direct survey 1976 survey of income and education — 150,000 representative U.S. households	.43% estimated national prevalence	Does not include persons in institutions, unrelated persons under 14 living in the households, or persons under 3 years of age
Farber (1968)	Mental retardation	Review of literature Review of approximately 10 studies conducted in U.S. between 1953 and 1962	General agreement among studies that 2–3% of population is mentally retarded	
Richardson and Higgins (1965) (North Carolina)	Mental retardation	Rates-under-treatment Review of agency records Direct survey Survey of 5% of households including clinical examinations	Prevalence rate for IQ below 70 = 77.0 per 1,000 = 7.7%	
Metropolitan Council (1977) (Minnesota)	Mental retardation (severe)	Rates-under-treatment Survey of **severely** mentally retarded receiving services in special education programs, vocational training programs, and so forth	0.330%	Metropolitan area only
Lindberg (1976) and Lindberg and Putnam (1979) (West Virginia)	Mental retardation (substantially handicapped)	Direct survey Surveyed 35,142 residents of 45 representative districts	0.81% of noninstitutionalized population	Noninstitutionalized developmentally disabled were not distributed randomly throughout the state

42

Table A.2. Illustrative prevalence rates for cerebral palsy

Study/source	Population	Method	Results	Comments
Minnesota United Cerebral Palsy (Personal communication, 1983)	Cerebral palsy	Not specified	3.5 persons per 1,000 = 0.35%	
National Cerebral Palsy Medical Directory (Personal communication, 1983)	Cerebral palsy	Not specified	3.5 persons per 1,000 may be too high since the incidence of CP at birth is decreasing	
EMC Institute: *Program review data: A compilation of rates of prevalence of the developmental disabilities.* No date given.	Cerebral palsy	Nationally accepted standard	.35%–.55%	

EMC Institute: *Program issue review: The prevalence of the developmental disabilities.* No date given.	Cerebral palsy	Based on reports from state DD offices
		
		Mean *prevalence* rate nationwide N=46 states
		Range–high prevalence
		    rate N=1
		    low prevalence
		    rate N=1
		    standard rate
			
			.42%
			
			1%
			
			.034%
			.35%–.55%
				Methods of obtaining prevalence data varied from state to state, and so forth, direct survey, review of literature, estimates from national organizations

(continued)

Table A.2. (Continued)

Study/source	Population	Method	Results	Comments
Cruickshank (1976) (reporting on Schenectady County Study conducted in 1949)	Cerebral palsy	Not specified	15%	64.1% required ambulatory services 8.3% required prolonged care 18.8% required institutional placement
Metropolitan Council (1977) (Minnesota)	Cerebral palsy	Rates-under-treatment Survey of number served in state hospitals, special education programs, and so forth	0.03%	Metropolitan area only
Lindberg (1976) and Lindberg & Putnam (1979) (West Virginia)	Cerebral palsy (substantially handicapped)	Direct survey Surveyed 35,142 residents of 45 representative districts	0.09% of noninstitutionalized population	Noninstitutionalized individuals with developmental disabilities were not distributed randomly throughout the states

Table A.3.　Illustrative prevalence rates for epilepsy

Study/source	Population	Method	Results	Comments
Davenport (1923)	Epilepsy	Direct survey (# rejections for draft for WWI — males only)	*Incidence* 5 per 1,000 = 0.5% (also said prevalence was 5/1,000) Geographic variation 1.6/1,000 in North Dakota 18/1,000 in Vermont	Reviewed in Hauser (1978)
Hauser (1978)	Epilepsy	Review of literature	*Incidence* Average annual incidence rates for recurrent seizures 30-50 per 100,000 = 0.3%-.05% Differences among geographic regions may be more likely due to study methods *Prevalence rates* cluster around 3-6 per 1,000 population .3%-.6%	Active cases at a given time — individuals taking anti-convulsants or experiencing seizures within given time period prior to the survey
Hauser and Kurland (1975) Rochester, MN, 1935-1967	Epilepsy (recurrent)	Rates-under-treatment (review of medical records from community)	*Incidence* 48 per 100,000 = 0.048% recurrent seizures, not febrile seizures (fever related) *Prevalence, Jan. 1, 1960* 5.5 per 1,000 = 0.55%	

(continued)

Table A.3. (Continued)

Study/source	Population	Method	Results	Comments
Hauser and Kurland (1975) (cont.)	Epilepsy		*Prevalence, Jan. 1, 1965* 5.4 per 1,000 = .54% *Prevalence, Jan. 1, 1977* 6.5 per 1,000 = 0.65%	
Rose, Penry, Markush, Radloff, and Putnam (1973)	Epilepsy Washington County, MD	Direct survey Questionnaire sent to all 3rd graders	Prevalence afebrile seizures, 14–18 per 1,000 = 1.4%–1.8%	Children are considered a high-risk group
Van den Berg (1974)	Epilepsy San Francisco	Direct survey Longitudinal – followed cohort of 18,500 births in San Francisco for 5-year period	1% had afebrile seizures by the time they were 5 years old	
Meighan, Queener, and Weitman (1976)	Epilepsy Multnomah County, OR	Direct survey	7.8–12.8 per 1,000 = 0.78%	
Minnesota Epilepsy League (Personal communication, 1983)	Epilepsy	Not specified	1%–2% of U.S. population = 2,293,070–4,586,140	(Seemingly a high estimate)
EMC Institute: *Program review data: A compilation of rates of prevalence of the developmental disabilities.* No date given.	Epilepsy	Nationally accepted standard	2%	

Source	Disability	Description	Rate	Comments
EMC Institute: *Program issue review: The prevalence of the developmental disabilities.* No date given.	Epilepsy	Based on reports from state DD offices Mean *prevalence* rate nationwide N = 46 states *Range*-high prevalence rates N = 18 low prevalence rate standard rate	0.97% 2% .0087% 1-2%	Methods of estimating data varied from state to state, i.e., direct survey, review of literature, estimates from national organizations
Metropolitan Council (1977) (Minnesota)	Epilepsy (severe)	Rates-under-treatment Survey of number served in state hospitals, special education programs, and so forth	0.025%	Metropolitan area only
Lindberg (1976) and Lindberg and Putnam (1979) (West Virginia)	Epilepsy (substantially handicapped)	Direct survey Surveyed 35,142 residents of 45 representative districts	0.35% of noninstitutionalized population	Does not include those controlled with medication

Table A.4. Illustrative prevalence rates for autism

Study/source	Population	Method	Results	Comments
Wing, Yates, Brierley, and Gould (1976)	Autism	Reviewed previous prevalence studies		
Lotter (1966, 1967) (England)	Autism	Direct survey Screened 78,000 8-, 9-, and 10-year-olds in Middlesex, England	$N = 4.5$ out of 10,000 = 0.045% (35 out of 78,000)	Methodological problems such as: initial screening consisted of questionnaires completed by teachers regarding child's "aloofness" and so forth
Brask (1970) (Denmark)	Autism	Rates-under-treatment Examined case notes of all children age 2–14 who were in psychiatric hospitals, MR services, and so forth—screened 1,500 out of 46,000 in chosen age range	$N = 4.3$ per 10,000 = 0.43% (20 out of 1,500 were classified as autistic by Brask)	Did not include anyone not receiving service
Treffert (1970) (Wisconsin)	Autism	Rates-under-treatment Reviewed computer printout of 280 children age 3–12 receiving services based on diagnosis of childhood schizophrenia; further subdivided that group excluding deaf and other organic causes	$N = 2.5$ per 10,000 = 0.025% (number autistic not given; N of 3 to 12-year-old population = 899,750)	Based solely on computer printout — much subjective judgment involved — questionable results
Wing, Yates, Brierley, and Gould (1976)	Autism	Direct survey and rates-under-treatment Surveyed 854 children: 107 receiving service, 747 screened by interviewing teachers with follow-ups, if appropriate	$N = 4.8$ per 10,000 = 0.048% (total population age 5–14 = 25,000)	Quite well-controlled study — thorough assessment of final cases

Source	Category	Method/Description	Prevalence/Rate	Comments
National Society for Autistic Children (Personal communication, 1983)	Autism		Approximately 340,000 people are autistic in U.S. (prevalence) 1.5% *Incidence* — 4-5 per 10,000 live births .04%-.05%	
Development Disabilities. (EMC Institute) No date given.	Autism	Nationally accepted standard	4 per 10,000 .04%	
EMC Institute: *Program issue review: The prevalence of the developmental disabilities.* No date given.	Autism	Based on reports from state DD offices Mean-*prevalence* rate nationwide $N=46$ states *Range*-high prevalence rate $N=1$ low prevalence rate $N=3$ standard prevalence rate	.03% .2% .005% .04%	Methods of estimating prevalence data varied from state to state (i.e., direct survey, review of literature, estimates from national organizations)
U.S. Department of Education (1982)	Seriously emotionally disturbed	Rates-under-treatment Reports by states of numbers served during school year 1980-1981 (94-142 and 89-313)	$N=348,954$ U.S., July 1, 1981 population 229,307,000 (school-age population unknown)	

(continued)

Table A.4. (Continued)

Study/source	Population	Method	Results	Comments
Metropolitan Council (1977) (Minnesota)	Autism	Rates-under-treatment Survey of number served in state hospitals, special education programs, and so forth	0.020%	Metropolitan area only
Lindberg (1976) and Lindberg and Putnam (1979) (West Virginia)	Autism	Direct survey Surveyed 35,142 residents of 45 representative districts	Three cases in 35,142 .0085% of noninstitutionalized population	

∞ Section III ∞

LEGISLATIVE AND ECONOMIC CHARACTERISTICS

READERS OF THIS BOOK MAY FIND THE COMPREHENSIVENESS—AND LENGTH—OF THIS BOOK QUITE demanding and therefore may review less critically the sections of the book that do not directly apply to them. Because a smaller number of agency staff is involved in legislative and economic decision making, many readers may decide to skim this section. Do not do so! These three chapters contain information that is not always easy to understand, but is essential for program success. We can talk about implementing a new model and analyzing future directions all we want, but if the legislative system and the funding mechanism that guides it are not changed, our efforts won't be successful.

Three experienced professionals teamed up to write this three-chapter section. Each brings with him or her a wealth of diverse experiences and knowledge in economics, administration, and policy. Together, they interweave their respective views on each major issue. For example, in Chapter 4, Elder, Conley, and Noble review the characteristics and employability issues for the severely disabled adult through macroanalysis of the service delivery system. They conclude by recommending a holistic approach to program development while devising policies that promote employment initiatives.

Chapter 5 provides a comprehensive analysis of the problems of our current service delivery system through a review of the *disincentives* to work, particularly those deriving from the major income support and health care programs. Conley, Noble, and Elder carefully walk us through the maze of federal payments, from SSI and SSDI to Medicaid and Medicare, and illustrate how such systems are sometimes disincentives to work for developmentally disabled adults.

The authors cogently present social goals in Chapter 6 that will help accomplish the task of placing developmentally disabled adults in substantial gainful employment. They present options that will shape and determine the success of these social goals, as well as the funding mechanism essential to the achievement of these social goals.

∞ Chapter 4 ∞

The Service System

Jean K. Elder, Ronald W. Conley, and John H. Noble, Jr.

FOR MANY YEARS PUBLIC POLICY HAS BEEN guided by the widespread belief that there are large numbers of individuals with disabilities who are incapable of substantial work. As a result, massive and well-intentioned public programs have evolved to provide income support and medical care to these people.

In recent years, this belief has been sharply challenged. Increasingly, it is argued that many people with severe disabilities are able to work in positions paying significant earnings, provided that suitable job opportunities are offered and appropriate services are provided.

If, however, many—and some would say most—people with severe disabilities are capable of substantial work, then the premises that underlie large public programs are incorrect. The structures of these programs need to be reexamined to determine whether socially beneficial changes can be made in them.

In this and the next two chapters, the authors examine existing public programs and their effects on the employment of persons who are mentally retarded and/or developmentally disabled. The first chapter reviews the characteristics and employability of such persons and describes the programs that provide services to them. The second chapter outlines the major ways in which the current service system impedes substantial employment. The third chap-

ter sets forth options for changing the service system in order to improve the employment prospects of these adults with handicaps.

WHOM ARE WE TALKING ABOUT

Although the focus of this chapter is on mental retardation, almost all the problems that are described apply with equal force to persons with other types of developmental disabilities, as well as to all persons with severe disabilities.

The term "mental retardation," as with most terms applied to people with disabilities, has a technical definition that is poorly understood by most people. Moreover, this technical definition has little value from an evaluative, analytic, or planning standpoint. To be useful for these purposes, a definition of mental retardation must encompass the full population of persons who may require specialized services because of their intellectual limitations, which, as this chapter shows, the technical definition does not.

The most commonly used definition requires that two conditions be met before a person is considered mentally retarded. First, he or she must show signs of significant intellectual limitation. This condition is usually satisfied if the person has an intelligence quotient (IQ) of 70 or less. Second, the person must be unable to

This paper was written by the authors in their private capacity. No official support or endorsement by the U.S. Department of Health and Human Services or the Virginia Department of Mental Health and Mental Retardation is intended or should be inferred.

participate in activities that are age appropriate. This condition is called the criterion of social competence (Grossman, 1977).

Although the primary characteristic of mental retardation is severe intellectual limitation, professionals usually insist on adding the criterion of social competence to this definition because they question the reliability and validity of existing intelligence tests. It is generally acknowledged that these tests, at best, measure only part of intelligence. Moreover, these tests produce varying results for the same individuals over time, and varying results for different individuals with identical intelligence, because of such factors as cultural differences, test conditions, attitudes of the testee, and physical handicaps. At a clinical level, professionals resist labeling a person as mentally retarded on the basis of such imprecise measures of intellect. The primary value of the criterion of social competence is that it serves to validate intelligence tests.

Unfortunately, the use of the criterion of social competence creates numerous problems:

It confuses cause and effect. Social incompetence, if it exists, may be caused by intellectual limitations, but it is of dubious value as a defining characteristic of mental retardation.

It implies that social incompetence must always exist among people with mental retardation, a conclusion that runs counter to the purposes of many programs that strive to promote independence and normalized living.

It obscures the fact that social incompetence may result from many factors other than limited intellect (e.g., negative attitudes, lack of developmental training), and thus may obscure the need for comprehensive planning to reduce or eliminate impediments to employment from these sources.

It creates a tendency to overlook the fact that large numbers of intellectually limited people exist—about two thirds of all persons with IQs below 70—who are employed and are generally socially competent. Most of these persons are mildly

mentally retarded (IQ 50 to 70). They are sometimes described as the ''invisible mentally retarded population.''

Why is it important to include socially competent persons with low IQs in the population of persons with mental retardation? One reason is that many persons who have low IQs become socially competent only as a result of the prior provision of educational, rehabilitative, and other services. Another reason is that some of these persons require services occasionally because of such episodic events as unemployment, illness or injury, personal problems, or other misfortunes. These services may be different in nature or more extensive than those required by the general population for the same type of problems. Unless the existence of the ''invisible mentally retarded population'' is explicitly taken into account when planning programs, their special needs will not be met.

Because of these problems in using the criterion of social competence, the term ''mental retardation'' is used to refer to all persons whose intelligence, if accurately measured, would correspond to an IQ level of approximately 70 or lower. The advantages of this approach are:

It defines mental retardation by its primary characteristic, which is a substantially limited intellect.

It specifies the full population who need or who may need special services because of limited intellect, including ''invisible mentally retarded'' persons.

It emphasizes the need to identify specifically those factors other than limited intellect that impede employment, and thus it greatly improves the basis for designing appropriate employment programs.

It should be stressed that this definition of mental retardation is meant to be used only for analytic, evaluative, and planning purposes. As a practical matter, we agree that no individual should be labeled as mentally retarded on the basis of I.Q. alone until greater agreement is reached about the validity of I.Q. tests. Even then, we believe labeling people with this diagnosis should be avoided whenever possible because of the negative effects that inevitably spring from its use.

MISCONCEPTIONS
ABOUT EMPLOYABILITY

There are three widely held misconceptions about the employability of persons with mental retardation. The first misconception is that they cannot work, except possibly in sheltered work environments. Until recently, this belief has prevailed among persons, including professionals, who are not directly engaged in working with persons with mental retardation. Even among professionals who work with persons with mental retardation, there has often been great skepticism about their capacity for substantial employment. As noted above, this bias is reflected even in the most common definition of mental retardation that requires that a person be socially incompetent before being considered mentally retarded.

Negative attitudes about the employability of adults with mental retardation may stem from existing follow-up studies, most of which have reported a substantial lack of employment among persons with mental retardation. Unfortunately, these studies are very misleading. Most of them were conducted shortly after the individuals with mental retardation had left school when most were teenagers. Although their employment rates and earnings levels were low, so are the employment rates and earnings records of most teenagers (Conley, 1973).

When the data from these studies are correctly analyzed according to different age and sex groupings, the employment rates and earnings levels of persons with mild mental retardation are found to rise rapidly when they reach their early 20s. In fact, one study estimated that 87% of the noninstitutionalized men identified as mildly mentally retarded while in school were gainfully employed as adults (Conley, 1973). Among women identified as mildly mentally retarded while in school, the comparable rate was 33%. Many women with mild mental retardation choose to marry and become full-time homemakers, rather than accept the menial jobs available to them. The study found surprisingly high earnings— slightly over 85% of the norm—for both men and women with mild mental retardation.

Until recently, it was generally assumed that people with IQs below 50 could not work. During the last 10 years, however, a number of organizations have sprung up that specialize in placing persons with severe handicaps in regular jobs. Although the evidence is still largely anecdotal, the increasing number of successful job placements, some of which are reported in this volume, is encouraging. A large number of persons with severe mental retardation who were formerly thought capable of working only in workshops, may, with suitable assistance, be able to engage in substantial employment (Bellamy, Rhodes, Bourbeau, & Mank, 1982; Bellamy, Sheehan, Horner, & Boles, 1980).

The second misconception about persons with mental retardation is that their productivity and earnings will necessarily be low or minimal. This misconception is based on the fallacious belief that productivity varies directly with intelligence; hence, the more severe the level of intellectual limitation, the lower the productivity and earnings.

The productivity of a worker can be defined as the value of what he or she adds to the value of output. In a private company, productivity can, in theory, be measured by the addition to total revenues that would accrue as a result of hiring a worker minus any increase in costs other than the wages paid to the worker. Clearly, a worker is not normally paid more than what he or she adds to the net value of output because otherwise the company would gain by discharging the worker.

What determines an individual worker's productivity? Productivity is dependent on the following three variables, as well as others not necessary to this discussion.

1. *The value of the items or services that are produced* Something must be produced, at least in the private sector, for which people are willing to pay (e.g., an automobile, a mown lawn, a clean room). The

more they are willing to pay, the greater the productivity associated with producing that item or service. Thus, technical improvements in a product will, in effect, increase the productivity of workers by making the products that they produce more attractive to consumers.

2. *The efficiency of the productive process* The greater the number of units of output produced, and the lower the value of inputs (costs) other than the wages paid to the workers, the greater the productivity of the workers. From this, it follows that the productivity of workers can be increased through the use of capital (e.g., power mowers, vacuum cleaners, robots to produce automobiles), better technology, increased specialization of work tasks, reduction of waste, improved management, and in numerous other ways.

3. *The appropriate placement of the worker* A worker's productivity depends on finding an appropriate niche in a production unit where he or she can make a significant contribution to output. It is important that workers locate employment that takes advantage of their physical attributes, aptitudes, training, and other characteristics. Place a learned professor on a job using a pick and shovel and he may be hard pressed to earn the minimum wage. The problem, of course, is that he would not be doing a job that makes the best use of his training and intellectual capabilities.

Most persons who are mentally retarded can find or be helped to find a job that makes use of their existing intellectual and physical capacities and that will enable them to make a substantial contribution to output. This premise is supported by the observation that most persons with mild mental retardation are employed, as are growing numbers of persons with severe mental retardation.

Will substantial productivity be reflected in substantial wages? Two facts must be recognized. First, workers with mental retardation who find jobs in which they can fill a regular niche become fully contributing employees of established and profitable economic enterprises with a demonstrated capacity to pay prevailing wages. Second, in most cases these workers are part of a production team. In these cases, productivity must be measured as the joint output of the entire group, rather than for individual workers. Workers do not produce cars by themselves; they produce a small component of a car. Dishwashers do not prepare meals, but are part of a team that includes managers, cooks, waiters, and bus persons, each of whom performs an essential function in the preparation of meals.

The earnings of individual members of the team are, in effect, a way of allocating the overall productivity. If workers with mental retardation are performing the work that non–mentally retarded workers would otherwise perform, there is no economic justification for paying them any less than non–mentally retarded workers would have earned on those jobs. The rate of earnings paid for different jobs is tied not as much to individual productivity as to bargaining power, scarcity of the supply of employees with particular skills, and tradition. Although some workers may be paid more than others, they are all essential to the productive process. If workers with mental retardation are paid less than more skilled workers, this may partly reflect their weaker bargaining position; if they are paid less than non–mentally retarded workers doing the same job, this represents exploitation.

What advantages do persons who are not mentally retarded have over workers with mental retardation? Obviously, non–mentally retarded persons can acquire skills that command a higher rate of pay than persons with mental retardation can earn. Another important advantage is their superior ability to perform a wider variety of existing jobs. They thus have less difficulty in locating work. A third and often critical advantage is their superior ability to shop around, try different jobs, and eventually find one that more nearly suits their capacities and interests. Persons with mental retardation, in contrast, usually have fewer types of jobs that they can perform and much less knowledge about how to locate and obtain them. Persons with severe mental retardation, in particular, are very dependent on assistance in locating suitable work. Of course, there are some persons with mental retardation whose job limitations are so severe that they have little prospect of obtaining a job that would otherwise be filled by a non–mentally retarded person. This topic is considered below.

The third misconception is that the intellectual limitation is the primary reason why suitable work is not found. However, the very large percentage of persons with mild mental retardation (roughly those with IQs of 50 to 70) who successfully obtain substantial work and the size and diversity of the job market should make it obvious that limited intellect is not a major barrier to employment for them. Probably, it is not a significant barrier to employment for many persons with even lower IQs. In the job market, there are thousands of types of jobs, each requiring a different combination of reasoning ability, strength, dexterity, experience, training, and other traits. There are many jobs that can utilize persons with limited intellectual capacities, and there will probably continue to be many such jobs in the foreseeable future. Most persons with mental retardation, if given the opportunity, can carry out these jobs as well as non–mentally retarded people.

What contributes to job failure? Failure to obtain and retain employment can result from many different and often interrelated causes.

Many persons with mental retardation, particularly severe mental retardation, have concomitant emotional and physical handicaps. As noted above, there are many jobs that can be performed by persons with limited intellectual capacity. But if because of a physical handicap, persons with severe mental retardation are also excluded from many of those unskilled jobs, then the number of jobs within their capability is greatly reduced. The difficulty of finding appropriate jobs becomes formidable. Similarly, few employers would care to employ persons with mental retardation who are also belligerent, recalcitrant, or withdrawn. Such behaviors disrupt production and employers avoid hiring people—mentally re-

tarded or not—who exhibit these characteristics. However, state-of-the-art behavior modificaton techniques applied by skilled practitioners can extinguish most types of adverse behavior.

There are other personal attributes of persons with mental retardation that affect their prospects for employment:

Are their attitudes favorable toward work? Do they want to work? Are they frightened at the prospect? Can they get along with their fellow workers? Do they even believe that they are capable of working?

Have they learned such fundamental prerequisites to job success as punctuality, proper attire, and use of public transportation?

Do they encounter job discrimination because of their handicap, age, sex, or race? Do employers fear, as has been reported by Berkowitz, Fenn, and Lindbrinos (1983) and Grossman (1972a, 1972b), that hiring workers with mental retardation causes the costs of production to rise, due to the sometimes higher use of sick leave and higher health care costs?

Many other factors influence whether people with mental retardation obtain work, including the availability of services, the strength of the economy, their acceptance by nonhandicapped workers, fear of loss of public benefits, and the luck (or lack of it) of being in the right place at the right time.

In summary, many factors determine whether a person with mental retardation obtains work. Limited intellect by itself does not preclude work, except in very severe cases. Usually, two or more work impediments must interact to cause failure in obtaining or maintaining employment, particularly in the case of persons with mild mental retardation.

WHERE SHOULD PEOPLE WITH MENTAL RETARDATION WORK?

Many adults with mental retardation are employed in workshops rather than in regular jobs. During 1976, slightly less than 90,000 persons with mental retardation were placed in workshops: 16% were in regular sheltered workshop programs, 12% were in training and/or evaluation programs, and 72% were in work activity centers (U.S. Department of Labor, 1979). With minor exceptions, all persons in regular sheltered workshop programs must be paid at least one-half of the federal minimum wage. The only stipulation for clients in work activity centers or in training and/or evaluation programs is that they must be paid according to their actual productivity. During 1976, earnings amounted to $1.21 per hour for clients with mental retardation who were in regular workshop programs, and $.39 per hour for clients with mental retardation who were in work activity centers (U.S. Department of Labor, 1979). Few clients worked a full week. During 1973, clients with mental retardation who were in regular workshop programs worked an average of 26 hours per week, and clients with mental retardation who were in work activity centers worked an average of 21 hours per week (U.S. Department of Labor, 1977). From this information, it appears that roughly half of the clients with mental retardation who were in sheltered workshops or work activity centers received $10 or less per week in 1976.

Sheltered workshops and work activity centers must be certified by the U.S. Department of Labor. However, even the minimal pay requirements for work activity centers can be avoided by placing adults with mental retardation in day activity programs that are called by various names in different states. In view of the low productivity of clients in work activity centers, the temptation must be great to move clients into non–vocationally oriented day programs. A survey by Bellamy and Buckley (1985) reported that during the 1983–1984 time period, about 136,000 clients were served in day activity programs or work activity centers that received funding from state agencies for persons with mental retardation or developmental disbilities. Because some of these programs were also certified as work activity centers by the U.S. Department of Labor, it cannot be determined how many persons with mental retardation were placed in day activity programs as compared to work activity centers. Needless to say, the earnings of the vast majority of the day activity program clients are inconsequential.

In his introduction to the comprehensive study of sheltered workshops conducted by the U.S. Department of Labor, Ray Marshall, former Secretary of Labor, defined the two purposes of workshops as: " . . . preparing the less severely handicapped worker for employment in the competitive labor market, and providing long-term sheltered employment and supportive services for the more severely handicapped person who is not likely to function independently in the community" U. S. Department of Labor, 1977, p. 10). Unfortunately, workshops, with some notable exceptions, have dismal records in attaining these two goals in the case of clients with mental retardation. Few clients with mental retardation who are in sheltered workshops, work activity centers, or day activity programs move onto competitive employment; in fact, Bellamy et al. (1982) reported that only about 3% of the clients with mental retardation who are in both work activity centers and in day activity programs move to a higher level of vocational activity each year. However, the U.S. Department of Labor study (1977) on sheltered workshops reported that 15% of the clients with mental retardation who are in sheltered workshops and 7% of the clients with mental retardation who are in work activity centers move on to competitive employment each year.

The low wages of persons with mental retardation who are in sheltered workshops are usually ascribed to their low productivity. One recent study, for example, reported that "[c]lients in the work activities centers represent a level of functioning from which only a minimal degree of work productivity can be expected . . . Therefore, the amount of their remuneration would be quite minimal" (Greenleigh Associates, Inc., 1975, p. 80). The comprehensive study on sheltered workshops conducted by the U.S. Department of Labor also indicated that the low earnings of work activity centers clients were due to their

" . . . generally low productivity level . . . "
(U.S. Department of Labor, 1977, p. 6).

As was indicated above, however, the productivity of workers, whether handicapped or not, is highly dependent on the efficiency of the productive process and the value that society places on what is produced. There are a number of reasons to believe that the low earnings of many workshop employees should be attributed to the inherent inefficiency of most workshops, rather than to the limitations of the workers. Among the reasons are the following:

During 1972, over 55% of the workshops in which persons with mental retardation were the primary group served had fewer than 50 clients in average daily attendance (U.S. Department of Labor, 1977). The small size of many workshops adversely affects productivity in several ways. It makes it difficult to accept large subcontracts, which, in turn, makes it difficult to take advantage of economies of scale, and presumably causes a number of promising subcontract opportunities to be lost. Small size also limits such important business activities as marketing products, recruiting business, and investing in capital stock and equipment.
Most workshops, particularly those that are small, are limited in the variety of jobs they offer, making it difficult to place clients in jobs that are suitable to their capabilities.
Most workshops are restricted in their ability to employ efficient methods of production because they usually must attempt to utilize large numbers of severely limited workers and too few skilled workers.
Most importantly, most workshops cannot match the productive efficiency of private firms. They lack the capital, experience, technical knowledge, employee skills, size, and marketing capacity, and are probably disadvantaged in other ways as well.

A study of sheltered workshops in Japan demonstrates the relationships between low productivity and workshop inefficiency; it also indicates that American workshops could have higher productivity (Cho, 1981). Japanese workshops seem to have much higher productivity than American workshops because of the more favorable mix of high technology machines and the use of nonhandicapped workers as well as workers with handicaps. The combination of machines and nonhandicapped workers compensates for the limitations of the workers with handicaps.

The obvious conclusion is that, whenever possible, persons with mental retardation should be placed in regular jobs in private or public employment. The great number and diversity of jobs in the economy make regular employment sites a much more likely source of suitable jobs than those available in workshops.

Yet, not all persons with mental retardation can, even after extensive preparation, perform jobs at the same level as would normally be performed by non–mentally retarded workers. This is not, however, an indication that these persons should be placed in workshops.

Employers can sometimes be encouraged to modify existing jobs in ways to accommodate workers with severe handicaps (e. g., by reducing the expected level of hourly output from the worksite, permitting part-time work, simplifying the job, or providing special tools.

Sometimes, workers with mental retardation, whether or not they require modified jobs, require a great deal of supervision and counseling in order to obtain and maintain employment. Many organizations, such as the Bay State Skills Corporation in Boston, where support, counseling, and other services are provided to clients with mental retardation for a period of time after job placement, have been established to serve workers with mental retardation. Then many employees with mental retardation are able to handle the job on their own.

However, these time-limited services are not always adequate. Some employees with mental retardation may still require much longer periods of support before they are able to work independently, and some never achieve this goal. Approaches to employing this low-functioning group are only now being developed and take many forms. Long-term periodic counseling and emergency support from a service organization are needed by some workers with mental retardation. Another method is the "enclave" method in which a unit of workers with mental retardation who are in an enterprise is placed under the supervision of an on-site staff person who oversees production and provides support, encouragement, and training. The "crew" model is still another approach, in which a group of workers with severe handicaps under the charge of a crew chief travels from site to site (e.g., cleaning hotel rooms, doing yard and maintenance work).

Even these approaches are sometimes insufficient for persons with very severe handicaps. A program called the "Specialized Training Program" (STP) has evolved at the University of Oregon to serve persons with severe retardation. Although STP is basically a workshop program, its goal is to provide remunerative long-term employment to persons with severe and profound mental retardation (IQ less than 40). To date, STP programs have specialized in electronic assembly and have emphasized high-quality production. In a recent report covering the first 9 months in 1983, the average monthly wage of 180 workers in 11 STP programs was $38, and the average hourly wage was $1.46 (University of Oregon, 1983). The STP programs have avoided some of the problems associated with workshops described above by employing talented managers who strongly emphasize maintainenance of a work-oriented environment and the use of efficient production methods. The continued success of STP programs as the number of such programs increases depends on their ability to attract dedicated and capable staff and to find other production opportunities in addition to those that have been found in electronic assembly.

It is possible to develop many varied approaches to helping persons with severe handicaps obtain and retain employment. These approaches must reflect the needs of the clients with mental retardation and the business conditions that prevail in the locales in which employment is sought. Success is dependent not only on developing the capabilities of clients with mental retardation but also on the business acumen of the program managers who must seek out contracts, raise capital, organize suitable production lines, and negotiate with industry.

SYSTEM OF SERVICES

Persons with mental retardation have the same basic needs, and are subject to the same problems as everyone else. Most of the public services utilized by persons who are mentally retarded or disabled are also used by persons without a handicap (e.g., food stamps, Aid to Families with Dependent Children, Supplemental Security Income, public housing, public transportation). To list and analyze all the programs that serve persons with mental retardation, directly or indirectly, would require a discussion of most public programs, an obviously unwieldy task. Therefore, the following discussion is confined to the larger programs.

Income Support Programs

The most imortant programs providing income support to persons with disabilities are the Social Security Disability Insurance Program, the Childhood Disability Program (these two programs are jointly designated as the SSDI/CDB program), and the Supplemental Security Income (SSI) Program. These federally funded and administered programs provide monthly benefits to workers unable to engage in substantial work as a result of a disabling condition. In addition, the SSDI program provides monthly benefits to qualifying spouses and dependent children.

The SSDI program was primarily established to provide income protection to workers who become disabled. Eligibility depends on the number of quarters of coverage that workers have accumulated. A quarter of coverage is earned when a worker pays social security taxes on earnings that reach a predetermined level. In 1984, this level was almost $400 of earnings per quarter. To qualify for SSDI benefits, workers must be fully and currently insured at the time of the onset of disability. A worker is fully insured if he or she has accumulated 40 quarters of coverage during his or her lifetime, has one quarter of coverage for each year after 1950, or has one quarter of coverage for each year after attaining the age of 21 (a minimum of six quarters is required). A worker is currently insured if he or she has 20 quarters of coverage during the 10-year period preceding the onset of disability, or if under age 31, was covered for half of the quarters after attaining age 21 (a minimum of six quarters is required). Blind persons need only be fully insured to qualify for benefits.

The Social Security Childhood Disability Program provides a monthly benefit to adults with disabilities (age 18 or over) whose disability began before age 22. To be eligible, the beneficiary must be a dependent son or daughter (or an eligible grandson or grandaughter) of a retired, deceased, or disabled worker who is eligible (or whose survivors are eligible) for Social Security benefits.

The Supplementary Security Income (SSI) program was established to provide a basic level of cash income to needy persons who are aging or disabled and who are not adequately covered by one of the Social Security retirement or disability programs. It pays benefits to qualified persons who do not qualify for Social Security or whose Social Security benefits are less than the basic level established for SSI beneficiaries. To qualify, claimants must be unable to work because of disability, but, in contrast to SSDI/CDB requirements, they must also have extremely limited assets. The SSI program was initiated in 1974 and partially replaced earlier state-operated categorical welfare programs for persons who are aging, blind, or disabled; 26 states supplement the federal SSI payment.

Health Care Programs

The Medicare and Medicaid programs are the two principal public programs that fund health care to persons with disabilities. The Medicare program is federally funded and administered and provides benefits to persons with disabilities who qualify for SSDI/CDB after a 2-year waiting period. (There is no waiting period for retired Social Security beneficiaries.) As with SSDI/CDB, eligibility for Medicare does not require that the applicant meet an asset test. As with private insurance, Medicare has co-insurance and deductible provisions that determine the reimbursement levels for specific health services.

Medicaid reimburses the cost of providing specific health services to needy persons. Unlike Medicare, it is state-administered, although subject to extensive federal regulation, and usually provides full reimbursement for medical expenses. Almost all people who are eligible for SSI are also eligible for Medicaid. In addition, some persons with disabilities receiving SSDI/CDB may receive Medicaid during the 2-year waiting period before becoming eligible for Medicare. They must qualify on the basis of limited income and assets. Some persons who are unable to pay for the co-insurance and deductible provisions under Medicare may receive Medicaid to cover the difference. The federal government reimburses states about half of the costs of the Medicaid program.

Employment Programs

The most important employment program for persons with disabilities is the state-federal vocational rehabilitation program. This state-administered program provides a wide range of services to people with disabilities (e.g., counseling, vocational training, medical restoration). These services are directed at assisting people to return to work.

The Department of Labor also operates several important programs. The Job Training Partnership Act (JTPA) provides federal funds for a wide range of state-administered services to economically disadvantaged persons and others who face serious barriers to employment. Among these services are work-study programs, work transition activities, job development, and literacy training. The Department of Labor also funds the operation of state employment services that can play an important role in assisting persons with developmental disabilities to locate suitable employment.

A different approach is utilized by the Targeted Jobs Tax Credit (TJTC) program, which gives employers a tax credit of 50% of earnings up to $3,000 for the first year for each person with disabilities that they hire, and a credit of up to $1,500 during the second year.

Other Programs

The Intermediate Care Facilities for Mentally Retarded (ICR/MR) Persons program (a component of the Medicaid program) pays for residential care and other needed services to persons with mental retardation and related conditions needing 24-hour care. To qualify for reimbursement, clients must need and be engaged in an active treatment program of health or habilitative services.

The federally funded Food Stamp program is administered by state public assistance offices. Food stamps are distributed to low-income persons who must satisfy a combined income and asset test.

The Department of Housing and Urban Development provides a rent subsidy to low-income persons who reside in public housing. Some persons with developmental disabilities have benefited from this program.

Of enormous importance to persons with mental retardation has been Public Law 94-142, the Education for All Handicapped Children Act. This Act requires that all children with handicaps be provided a free and appropriate public education, regardless of the severity or type of handicapping condition.

The Administration on Developmental Disabilities (ADD) in the U.S. Department of Health and Human Services (DHHS) funds a number of activities that are intended to improve the system of services to persons with developmental disabilities. Persons with mental retardation who have substantial functional limitations fall within the statutory definition of developmental disabilities. Every state receives a basic grant to establish a state developmental disabilities council to assist in planning and coordinating services to persons with developmental disabilities. In addition, the states are awarded grants to establish protection and advocacy (P&A) agencies to protect and secure the rights of persons with developmental disabilities. The Administration on Developmental Disabilities also funds University Affiliated Facilities (UAFS), the primary purpose of which is to train personnel to provide services to persons with developmental disabilities.

A full listing of the programs that can affect the lives and the employment of persons with mental retardation is extensive. It includes the Maternal and Child Health and Crippled Children programs, the Railroad Retirement and Disability programs, the federal and state Civil Service retirement and disability programs, workers' compensation, veterans' programs, and many others. In addition, there are a wide range of programs operated exclusively by state and local governments.

Although the discussion of work impediments (in Chapter 5) is based primarily on the SSDI, SSI, Medicare, and Medicaid programs, it must be emphasized that many of the problems that are identified in these large programs also exist to varying degrees in the other programs.

HOW MANY PERSONS WITH MENTAL RETARDATION DO NOT WORK?

One way to estimate the number of persons with mental retardation who do not engage in substantial work, that is, on jobs paying the substantial gainful activity (SGA) wage of $300 per month or more, is to consider the number of persons with mental retardation receiving SSDI/CDB or SSI. Almost all persons receiving benefits from these programs are earning below the SGA level. Unfortunately, these programs do not routinely collect and report data by type of disability. Special tabulations relating to persons awarded benefits during 1982 indicated that 2.4% of the workers with disabilities awarded SSDI benefits were diagnosed as mentally retarded (Social Security Administration, 1984). During 1976, 13.2% of the adults and 56.1% of the children with disabilities awarded SSI benefits were diagnosed as mentally retarded (Social Security Administration, 1980). Recent information is not available on the percentage of persons who are awarded Childhood Disability Benefits because of mental retardation. However, earlier data indicate that the percentage is large, roughly 65–70 percent (Conley, 1973).

If we assume: 1) that the percentage of persons with mental retardation initially awarded benefits is about the same as the percentage of persons with mental retardation among all beneficiaries, and 2) that these percentages as reported above for different years have been roughly constant over time, then a rough estimate can be made that the SSDI/CDB and SSI programs combined were making about 800,000 benefit payments monthly during 1984 because of mental retardation. Of this number, roughly 635,000 payments were made to persons between the ages of 18 and 65. About half of the benefit checks paid to persons in the 18 to 65 year age group were paid to persons receiving Childhood Disability Benefits, and a little less than half were paid to persons receiving SSI. The SSDI program accounts for only about 9.7% of the benefit checks. It should be observed that the number of workers with mental retardation who are receiving SSDI may be rising. Recent tabulations from the Social Security Administration (1985) indicate that the percentage of beneficiaries with mental retardation among persons awarded SSDI benefits during 1983 was 3.1%, up considerably from the 2.4% awarded SSDI benefits during 1982.

These estimates obviously involve double counting because some persons receive both SSDI/CDB and SSI benefits. This is particularly true for the Childhood Disability Beneficiary program, where, as of March, 1984, about 38% of all beneficiaries also receive SSI. The percentage of Social Security Disability Insurance beneficiaries who received both adult disability payments and SSI is much lower–8.1% (Social Security Administration, 1984). On the assumption that the same percentages apply to beneficiaries with mental retardation, the number of beneficiaries with mental retardation who receive SSDI benefits (both childhood and adult benefits) and SSI is about 125,000 persons. After subtracting this

estimated number of double-counted beneficiaries from the aforementioned estimate of 635,000 monthly benefit payments to persons 18 to 65 years of age, it is estimated that about 500,000 adult persons with mental retardation received income support from these programs during 1984. These figures are rough estimates of the number of adults with mental retardation or developmental disabilities who are earning less then $300 per month and, therefore, are not quite the same as the number who are not working.

Yet, the figure of 500,000 may be an underestimate of the number of adults with mental retardation who are not working or are working at less than the SGA level for the following reasons:

1. Some multiply handicapped, mentally retarded persons are given a primary diagnosis other than mental retardation as the basis for their Social Security or SSI disability award.

2. Similarly, it is possible that large numbers of "invisible" mildly mentally retarded persons who are gainfully employed or who function as homemakers for a number of years eventually suffer additional functional limitations that, in combination with mild mental retardation, qualify them for disability benefits. As just mentioned, mental retardation would not always be identified as the primary cause of disability.

3. This figure has not taken account of persons with mental retardation who are awarded disability benefits under income support programs other than SSI or SSDI/CDB, such as the federal Civil Service or the Railroad Retirement programs, both of which have childhood disability beneficiary programs.

4. Finally, it is highly probable that a large number of adults with mental retardation who lack substantial employment do not receive benefits from these programs. One reason is their failure to realize that they are eligible for benefits. In one study (Schultz, 1984), it was reported that only

12% of the persons with disabilities surveyed mentioned knowledge of SSI as a
source of financial assistance. Another
reason may be that they or their guardians
believe that there is a stigma attached to
accepting these benefits. Still another
reason is that some potential beneficiaries
may be ineligible for SSI benefits because
they have too many assets, perhaps as the
result of an inheritance.

Another way of estimating the number of
persons with mental retardation who are not
working is to examine follow-up studies of the
community adjustment of persons who have
been identified as mentally retarded. One such
estimate was derived about 15 years ago on the
basis of existing follow-up studies (Conley,
1973). In that study, it was estimated that 13%
of men with mild mental retardation were not
employed. At that time, about 9% of the males
in the general population were also not employed. In the usual approach to estimating
employment loss due to mental retardation, it is
assumed that the 4% difference between these
two figures (13%–9%) represents the pre-
centage of working age males who are not
working due to mental retardation. The authors
do not believe, however, that this figure is a
meaningful estimate of the number of persons
with mental retardation who would work if a
suitable job opportunity were offered, which is
a slightly different, but considerably more relevant question, cf. Chapter 3.

The crucial point is that most nonworking
adult males who are not mentally retarded
would work if they were given an opportunity
to do so. Some of these nonworking adults are
involuntarily unemployed, some have serious
physical or emotional impairments that prevent
them from working, some are temporarily ill,
and some are temporarily laid off. There are, of
course, some males who have taken advantage
of early retirement provisions of the Social
Security or corporate pension programs, and a
very few who could be classified as the "idle
rich." But, by and large, the great bulk of adult
males would prefer work to idleness. The authors believe that this is also true for adult
males who are mentally retarded.

There is, of course, a much higher percentage of adult women with mild mental retardation who do not work. Although some of
these women would undoubtedly choose to
work if given an opportunity, many others are
married and have no interest in working outside
the home.

Assuming that: 1) 13% of the nonworking
males with mild mental retardation would work
if they could, and 2) a comparable percentage
of nonworking women with mild mental retardation would work if they could, then there
are roughly half a million Americans with mild
mental retardation who are not employed but
who would accept employment if it were
offered. This estimate is probably low since the
prevailing level of unemployment in the United
States is higher than it was when most of the
follow-up studies were conducted, and unemployment among persons with mental retardation should be correspondingly higher.

This estimate of employment loss among
adults with mild mental retardation is about
three times higher than would be obtained by
making a strict comparison of employment
rates between persons with mild mental retardation and the general population. The authors
believe, however, that it is a more realistic
approach to estimating the target population for
employment programs.

This estimate does not include lack of employment among persons with IQs below 50.
Although a large number of these persons are
employed in work activity centers or sheltered
workshops, they appear, for the most part, to
be working at jobs paying inconsequential
wages. Estimates vary, but there are approximately 350,000 to 400,000 Americans with
IQs below 50 (Conley, 1973). If this total is
added to the estimated number of Americans
with mild mental retardation who are not working, then the estimated number of adult persons
who are not working or who are working on
jobs that do not pay substantial earnings because of mental retardation rises to 850,000 to
900,000. This estimate is quite consistent with
the earlier estimate that 500,000 adults with
mental retardation currently receive SSI or
SSDI/CDB benefits. It reflects the reality that
large numbers of adults with mental retardation

neither work (or have inconsequential earnings) nor receive SSI or SSDI/CDB benefits.

NEED FOR HOLISTIC APPROACH

Four important observations must be made. First, many people with mental retardation receive various types of support and services from public and private agencies. Second, many separate and distinct programs provide support and services to persons with mental retardation. Third, many persons with mental retardation receive services from more than one of these programs. For example, at the same time, a person could receive Social Security Childhood Disability Beneficiary payments supplemented by SSI benefits, Medicare benefits supplemented by Medicaid, food stamps, a rent subsidy, help from social services agencies, and possibly vocational rehabilitation services. Last, the types of support and services that are received and the conditions imposed on their receipt will have an important influence on whether persons with mental retardation seek work.

From these observations, the authors draw a critical conclusion. When examining the effects of these programs on the employment of persons with mental retardation, a holistic approach must be taken—evaluating, analyzing, and planning as though these separate programs represent a system of services. Each program has not only an independent effect, but also displays interactive effects with other programs. In consequence, devising efficient policies to promote employment for adults with mental retardation will require an examination of the combined and interacting effects of all programs that may affect employment; namely, income support, health care, vocational rehabilitation, and many others. This need for a holistic approach to assessing the effects of programs is true not only for employment, but also for housing, recreation, transportation, and most areas in which persons with mental retardation may need assistance.

As obvious as this conclusion may appear, the sad fact is that programs are usually evaluated and modified as though their effects are independent of other programs. This often leads to unintended and unfortunate consequences.

REFERENCES

Bellamy, G. T., & Buckley, J. (1985). *National survey of day and vocational programs, a 1984 profile.* In preparation.

Bellamy, G. T., Rhodes, L. E., Bourbeau, P. E., & Mank, D. M. (1982). *Mental retardation services in sheltered workshops and day activity programs: Consumer outcomes and policy alternatives.* Paper presented at the National Working Conference on Vocational Service and Employment Opportunities. Madison, WI.

Bellamy, G. T., Sheehan, M. R., Horner, R. H., & Boles, S. M. (1980). Community programs for severely handicapped adults: An analysis of vocational opportunities. *Journal of the Association for the Severely Handicapped, 5*(4), 307–324.

Berkowitz, M., Fenn, P., & Lindbrinos, J. (1983). The optimal stock of health with endogenous wages. *Journal of Health Economics, 2,* 139–147.

Cho, D. W. (1981). Japanese model factory employment of handicapped persons. *Evaluation Review, 5*(4), 427–450.

Conley, R. W. (1973). *The economics of mental retardation.* Baltimore: The Johns Hopkins University Press.

Greenleigh Associates, Inc. (1975). *The role of the sheltered workshops in the rehabilitation of the severely handicapped* (3 vol). Report to the Department of Health, Education, and Welfare, Rehabilitation Services Administration. New York: Author.

Grossman, H. (1977). *AAMD manual on terminology and classification in mental retardation.* Washington, DC: American Association on Mental Deficiency.

Grossman, M. (1972a). On the concept of health: Capital and the demand for health. *Journal of Political Economy, 80,* 223–255.

Grossman, M. (1972b). *The demand for health: A theoretical and empirical investigation.* New York: Columbia University Press.

Schultz, J. H. (1984). SSI: Origins, experience, and unresolved issues. In *The Supplemental Security Income Program: A 10-year overview.* An information paper prepared by the Special Committee on Aging, United States Senate. Washington, DC: U.S. Government Printing Office.

Social Security Administration. (1980). *Social Security bulletin: Annual statistical supplement.* Washington, DC: U.S. Department of Health and Human Services.

Social Security Administration. (1984, March). *Table Q-1. OASDI benefits in current payment status: Number and percent of OASDI beneficiaries in current receipt of federally administered SSI payments by type of beneficiary* (unpublished data). Washington, DC. U.S. Department of Health and Human Services.

Social Security Administration. (1985). Tabulations from Continuous Disability History Sample (unpublished data). Washington, DC. U.S. Department of Health and Human Services.

U.S. Department of Labor. (1977). *Sheltered workshop study, a nationwide report on sheltered workshops and their employment of handicapped individuals* (Vol. 1 and Appendix). Washington, DC: Author.

U.S. Department of Labor. (1979). *Sheltered Workshop study, a nationwide report on sheltered workshops and their employment of handicapped individuals* (Vol. 2). Washington, DC: Author.

University of Oregon. (1983, December). *Specialized training program newsletter*. Eugene: Specialized Training Program, University of Oregon.

∞ Chapter 5 ∞

Problems with the Service System

Ronald W. Conley, John H. Noble, Jr., and Jean K. Elder

THE LAST 25 YEARS HAVE SEEN AN ENORMOUS increase in the resources expended by federal, state, and private programs for support and services to persons with mental retardation and developmental disabilities. As a result, the social adjustment and quality of the life of many such persons have been greatly improved. Nonetheless, there are still many aspects of the existing system of services that stand in the way of their substantial employment.

WORK DISINCENTIVES

One of the most pervasive problems with today's public programs is the major work disincentives that they create, particularly by the income support and health care programs. These programs create work disincentives in at least three different ways: 1) by reducing the net gain from work, 2) by fostering dependency and negative attitudes toward work, and 3) by offering greater income security to persons who continue as beneficiaries of these programs than could be obtained in regular employment.

Basic Fallacy

These work disincentives are an unintended consequence of the restrictive legislative man-

date of these programs, which is to provide basic income support and health care financing to persons with disabilities only if they are unable to engage in substantial work because of disability. The Supplemental Security Income (SSI), the Social Security Disability Insurance and Childhood Disability (SSDI/CDB) programs, and, by extension, the Medicaid and Medicare programs, define disability as the

> . . . inability to do any substantial gainful activity by reason of a medically determinable physical or mental impairment which can be expected to result in death or which has lasted or can be expected to last for a continuous period of not less than 12 months . . . A person must not only be unable to do his or her previous work or work commensurate with the previous work . . . but cannot, considering age, education, and work experience, engage in any other kind of substantial work which exists in the national economy. (U.S. Department of Health and Human Services, 1982, p. 81)

Substantial gainful activity (SGA) is defined as earnings of $300 or more per month (U.S. Department of Health and Human Services, 1982). Thus, eligibility for the SSDI/CDB and the SSI programs requires that a person with disabilities be unable to earn approximately $1.75 or more per hour on a full-time basis at a job somewhere in the United States. The Social Security Handbook states that "[i]t is imma-

This paper was written by the authors in their private capacity. No official support or endorsement by the U.S. Department of Health and Human Services or the Virginia Department of Mental Health and Mental Retardation is intended or should be inferred.

terial whether such work exists in the immediate area, or whether a specific job vacancy exists, or whether the worker would be hired if he or she applied for work'' (p. 81). In effect, applicants for these programs can be denied benefits because they are deemed to have the capacity to earn slightly over 50% of the federal minimum wage, even though they may have almost no chance of obtaining such work. Economic conditions, discrimination, and cost of relocation are not viewed as being relevant in these considerations.

Persons who are blind may receive considerably more favorable treatment. For persons who are blind and are receiving SSDI/CDB, the SGA level is $610 per month in 1985. Persons who are blind and who apply for or receive SSI are not subject to an SGA determination. Eligibility is based solely on the existence of a medical condition (Code of Federal Regulations, Section 416.983).

How accurate is the process for distinguishing between those who can and cannot engage in substantial employment as a result of a disabling condition? The disability determination process is based on the implicit assumption by legislators that the knowledge and technology exist that enable bureaucrats to determine who, among all of the persons applying for disability benefits, is unable to earn about 50% of the federal minimum wage on some existing but not necessarily vacant job, which need not even be in the vicinity of the disabled person's residence.

Work capacity depends on a great many variables in addition to disability, age, education, and work experience. Inherent capacity and aptitudes, motivation and outlook, sex, race, and numerous other variables affect capacity to work. Neither the individual nor the interactive effects of these variables are well understood. This is well documented by the very high percentage of permanent partial disability cases in worker's compensation that are litigated over the extent of loss of ability to work (Conley & Noble, 1979). Determinations that applicants for SSDI/CDB or SSI are unable to engage in substantial work are extremely judgmental and, in the authors' opinion, sub-

ject to substantial error. The reliability of these decisions is further compromised because the initial determination of disability is made by the disability determination service, usually located in the state vocational rehabilitation agency solely on the basis of forms and medical reports transmitted by the Social Security Administration district office. The applicant is not even seen by the person making the initial determination. The Social Security Administration has developed a lengthy listing of impairments that, in the absence of other evidence (such as earnings above the SGA level) are considered severe enough to prevent a person from doing any gainful activity, which simplifies the process, but adds little to accuracy.

The premise that decisions can be made distinguishing between those who can and cannot engage in substantial employment is unrealistic. Furthermore, very few people are so severely disabled that they cannot possibly engage in substantial work. The authors believe that most people with severe disabilities can, with appropriate assistance, engage in substantial work (i.e., earn $70 per week or more). However, it must be emphasized that these persons are severely disadvantaged by their physical and mental limitations and perhaps by other problems as well. Many will require extensive assistance over long periods of time and, in some instances, indefinitely, in order to find and retain appropriate jobs. In some cases, the job may require modification.

Thus, a more realistic approach to the determination of disability would distinguish between: 1) persons who clearly can engage in substantial gainful activity; 2) persons who are very unlikely to be able to do so; and 3) persons for whom it will be difficult and will depend on a great many variables, including the availability of appropriate services. It is the authors' belief that many persons currently receiving income support and/or health care benefits fall into the last category.

For reasons to be described below, the requirement that persons with disabilities be unable to engage in SGA as a condition of eligibility and continued receipt of income support and health care benefits substantially reduces the chances that beneficiaries will seek, or even accept, substantial work if offered. This is particularly true when the jobs that are offered provide little security and low pay.

Net Gain from Work

The net gain (or loss) from taking a job varies widely from beneficiary to beneficiary. It depends on the level and types of benefits received, prospective earnings, and the availability of other sources of income. This discussion first focuses on the individual effects of each program.

The potential for reducing work incentives is particularly strong in the SSDI/CDB program. Under current law, persons qualify for SSDI/CDB if they are a childhood disability beneficiary or are an adult with sufficient quarters of coverage, and are unable to earn over $300 per month ($610 if blind), after deduction of extraordinary impairment-related work expenses (e. g., unusual transportation costs). Beneficiaries who return to substantial work are entitled to a 9-month trial work period to ensure that the work effort is successful. However, the intent of the trial work period is often nullified because any month in which beneficiaries earn $75 or more must be considered part of the trial work period, causing some beneficiaries to use up the trial work period in inconsequential activity. The trial work period need not be continuous, and only one trial work period is allowed per worker. At the end of the trial work period, the beneficiary is reevaluated, and if thought capable of earning $300 or more per month, then benefits are terminated. However, the beneficiary does not actually have to achieve this level of earnings. He or she must only be judged capable of it. Theoretically, this rule frustrates deliberate efforts to underpay workers or to restrict the number of hours they work in order to keep earnings below the SGA level. By the same token, however, earnings that are above the SGA level need not signify that the worker is capable of work at this level if it can be shown that part of the earnings represents a wage subsidy.

In order to determine the net income gain (or loss) for SSDI/CDB beneficiaries who return to work and consequently lose their benefits, the following deductions must be made from gross income:

The benefits formerly received from the SSDI/CDB program Theoretically, in the SSDI/CDB program, family benefits may exceed $2,000 per month, and individual benefits may run as high as $1,000 per month. Of course, the great majority of beneficiaries receive far less than these amounts.

Any income taxes that must be paid In almost all cases, these will include Social Security and Medicare taxes of approximately 7% (the rate is higher if self-employed) in addition to federal and possibly state and local taxes. Social Security and SSI benefits are not taxable.

Any normal work-related expenses, such as special clothing costs, lunches, child care, or bus fare.

Clearly, the disincentives to work can be substantial for many persons, particularly since the benefits under SSDI/CDB sometimes actually exceed the level of earnings at termination of benefits. Moreover, normal work expenses are sometimes very high (e.g., in the case of a woman with disabilities who must pay for child care in order to return to work).

Work disincentives are much less dramatic in the SSI program, partly because maximum benefits are much smaller and partly because of the effects of major legislation passed in 1980. In determining the monthly benefits to be paid to SSI beneficiaries, the following calculations are made. The first $20 of earned or unearned income and the next $65 of earnings are exempt from consideration. As much as $85 per month may be earned without penalty. Thereafter, benefits are reduced by $1 for every $2 of earnings over the exempted amount. Benefits are reduced by $1 for each $1 of unearned income over the exempted amount. It should be noted that there is no reduction of benefits for SSDI/CDB beneficiaries who earn less than $300 per month. In addition, extraordinary impairment-related work expenses are deducted from the earnings of SSI recipients before the reduction in benefits is calculated. SSI recipients who are blind are given even more favorable treatment because the extra-ordinary impairment-related work expenses are deducted from what would otherwise be the deduction in the SSI payment. It should be noted that, unlike the practice in the SSDI/CDB program, extraordinary impairment-related work expenses are not deducted from the earnings of SSI applicants for purposes of determining whether they are working at an SGA level when evaluating their eligibility for the program.

Beginning January 1, 1985, the basic SSI payment was $325 per month for an eligible individual, and $488 per month for an eligible couple. At these levels, all federal SSI payments cease when earnings reach about $735 per month for a single individual, and $1,061 per month for an eligible couple without any nonearnings income.

Prior to 1981, an SSI recipient would be placed on a nine-month trial work period after he or she began to work (unless he or she was blind). At the end of the trial work period, the beneficiary would be reevaluated and, if found capable of earning more than $300 per month, SSI payments would cease. As in the case of the SSDI/CDB program, any month in which the beneficiary earns $75 or more was considered as part of the trial work period. In the case of persons who are blind, benefits continue as long as earnings and other income are below the point at which all benefits are offset. If no benefits are payable, beneficiaries who are blind are not reevaluated to determine if they are still disabled. Instead, benefits are suspended and resumed if income declines to a point where benefits are again payable.

Consider two cases based on the 1985 benefit levels, but applying the rules governing benefits that existed before 1981. In the first case, an SSI recipient accepts a job paying $250 per month, and the second case is an SSI recipient who accepts a job paying $350 per month. At the end of the trial work period, the higher-paid worker would lose the entire $325 SSI payment and end up a net increase in gross income of only $25 (see Table 1, Columns A and B). The worker making $250, however, would still receive an SSI payment of about $242 per month, thereby having a gross income of $492 per month. The lower-earning recipient would actually end up with $136 more per month than the higher-earning recipient.

Clearly, any rational SSI recipient would choose the job paying the lesser wage, if possible. If only the higher-paying job were available, and its terms could not be altered, it is doubtful that the recipient would feel, that the job was worth accepting, particularly because taxes and normal work expenses would also have to be paid.

Recognizing these problems, Congress authorized a special 3-year demonstration program beginning on January 1, 1981—incorporated as Section 1619(a) of the Social Security Act—that permitted working SSI recipients to continue to be paid SSI benefits as long as their earnings were below the federal breakeven point, based on a $1 reduction in benefits fo each $2 in earnings. The recipient making $350, for example, would continue to receive an SSI payment of about $192, and his or her gross income would be about $542 per month (see Table 1, Columns C and D). This amount would seem to provide a reasonable incentive to work, unless taxes and work expenses consumed too large a portion of the increase ($218) in gross income over the benefit ($325).

The initial legislative authority for this special 3-year demonstration came to an end on December 31, 1983. At that time, it was believed that an extension was needed in order to collect additional, more conclusive data on the program's effects on the employment of SSI recipients. However, Congress did not approve an extension of this demonstration until September, 1984. In order to maintain the program in place during most of 1984, the U. S. Department of Health and Human Services approved a 1-year project that continued the demonstration for persons who were eligible for SSI benefits at the beginning of 1984.

It should be noted that slightly over half of the states supplement the federal SSI benefits. At the begining of 1984, the amount of the

Table 1. Calculation of SSI benefits after trial work period for individuals

	Pre-1981 rules		Under Section 1619(a)	
	(A)	(B)	(C)	(D)
1. Earnings (monthly)	$250	$350	$250	$350
2. Less $85 disregard equals	165	a	165	265
3. Deduction from benefits (Row 2 × 0.5)	82.50	a	82.50	132.50
4. Benefits (1985) equal	325	325	325	325
5. Benefits after deduction because of earnings (Row 4 − Row 3)	242.50	a	242.50	192.50
6. Total income after employment (Row 1 + Row 5)	492.50	350	492.50	542.50
7. Increase in income due to employment (Row 6 − Row 4)	$167.50	$25	$167.50	$217.50

aBenefits are terminated at the end of the trial work period.

supplement varied from $1.70 per month in Oregon to $252 per month in Alaska for individuals, and from $8.80 per month in Hawaii to $414 per month in California for a couple (Schultz, 1984). These supplements usually increase work disincentives, depending on the amount of the supplement and State practices (e.g., some states terminate the entire supplement when federal benefits end, whereas other states continue the $1 reduction in benefits for each $2 in earnings.) In addition, the mobility of SSI recipients may be reduced because of the conditions sometimes attached by states to the receipt of supplements (e.g., the person with disabilities may be required to be a resident of a licensed home for adults in order to qualify for state supplementary payments).

For persons with handicaps, continuation of health benefits is often as important, if not more important, than continuation of income payments. In some cases, the value of medical benefits exceeds the value of income support. Medical expenditures are frequently unpredictable, and sometimes are very large and ongoing. The problem is complicated by the fact that some SSI and SSDI/CDB beneficiaries with disabilities who return to work are unable to obtain health care coverage either as a fringe benefit where they work or as an individual because insurance companies often do not cover people with certain types of pre-existing conditions.

What happens if SSDI/CDB beneficiaries return to substantial work? Before 1981, a return to work paying the SGA wage led to termination of cash benefits and loss of eligibility for Medicare after a trial work period. In 1980, however, Congress changed the law so that SSDI/CDB beneficiaries could continue to receive Medicare coverage for 36 months after a determination that the beneficiary is capable of working at an SGA level. (Technically, the extended period of eligibility is 24 months after the last month in which a cash benefit is received, or 24 months after the 15-month extended period of eligibility following the trial work period and a determination that the beneficiary is capable of working at an SGA level, whichever is later.) In addition, Congress eliminated the 24-month waiting period for Medicare coverage in the case of former SSDI/CDB beneficiaries who become reentitled to SSDI/CDB benefits within the 5-year period after cessation of cash benefits.

What happens if SSI recipients who are eligible for Medicaid return to substantial work and lose eligibility for SSI? Before 1981, many beneficiaries who lost their eligibility for SSI also lost their Medicaid coverage. Some states, however, maintain a "medically needy" program paying the medical expenses of persons whose income is too high to qualify for SSI benefits. Consequently, some former SSI recipients continued to qualify for Medicaid coverage under this program.

In 1980, Congress authorized a 3-year demonstration program beginning January 1, 1981—Section 1619(b) of the Social Security Act—to provide continued Medicaid coverage to SSI recipients who return to substantial work, even if their income is too high to qualify for federal SSI payments. In order to qualify for continued Medicaid benefits, it was stipulated that the recipients must continue to have a disabling condition; have difficulty maintaining their employment without medical coverage; and lack earnings high enough to pay for benefits equivalent to the combined value of the federal SSI payments, state supplementary payments, and the Medicaid coverage that they would have continued to receive in the absence of employment.

Although these benefit provisions for Medicaid and Medicare should greatly reduce the work disincentives that existed before 1981, they do not eliminate all such disincentives. For example, consider the following.

1. Some SSDI/CDB beneficiaries may be concerned about the loss of Medicare benefits that will occur 3 years after they lose their entitlement to cash benefits.
2. Some SSI recipients may fear that Congress will not extend indefinitely the special Medicaid demonstration project. In fact, the initial 3-year authorization ended on December 31, 1983, and was not reauthorized until September, 1984. As in the case of Section 1619(a), the special cash benefits demonstration, Section 1619(b), was extended until June 30, 1987. Also as with Section 1619(a), the Department of Health and Human Services continued this Medicaid demonstration by means of a 1-year demonstration project during 1984.
3. SSI beneficiaries are eligible for extended

Medicaid benefits under 1619(b) if their income is below a threshold amount. This threshold amount differs from state to state and is equal to the federal breakeven to an individual living in his or her own household (calculated on an annual basis), plus 2 times the state supplement for 1 year, plus the average Medicaid expenditure for SSI beneficiaries who have disabilities and who live in the state. Because of differences in the supplements and expenditures on Medicaid beneficiaries who have disabilities by state, this threshold amount varies broadly. In 1984, the threshold amount varied from $8,500 to $21,500. If the individual's earnings exceed the threshold amount, the Social Security Administration checks to see if actual or anticipated Medicaid expenditures are greater than the state average. If they are greater, then these higher Medicaid expenditures rather than the state average expenditure are used to calculate the threshold amount for the individual. Despite this modification of the threshold amount, major and obvious inequities remain among states. Moreover, important work disincentives will continue for SSI beneficiaries whose income exceeds the threshold amount, but who cannot obtain medical insurance privately or as a fringe work benefit. Future medical expenditures are unpredictable, potentially large, and always a source of great concern for persons who have handicaps and their families.

4. Not everyone receiving SSI is automatically entitled to Medicaid or Section 1619(b) benefits. Twenty of the states in early 1985 used their own definition of who is entitled to Medicaid benefits (U.S. Department of Health and Human Services, Social Security Administration, 1985). In consequence, some SSI beneficiaries may not be eligible for Section 1619(b) benefits if they return to work.

In addition to the aforementioned effects on income support and health care coverage, beneficiaries who have disabilities and who accept substantial work may also lose their eligibility for social services. The rules governing the provision of social services are determined largely by state and local governments, and receipt of these services is often conditioned on meeting certain income and asset tests.

Security of Income

Decisions about when and where to work, or whether to work at all, are based not only on the amount that an individual can earn, but also on how secure the job is. Often, people may forego a higher paying but less secure job to remain in a position that is protected by union rules, seniority provisions, tenure, or civil service regulations, or has some other type of protection against the swings of the business cycle.

The desire for income security creates a strong work disincentive among beneficiaries of public income support and health care programs. It is not reasonable to expect these beneficiaries to give up easily what appears to be a secure monthly cash income and assured medical care in exchange for jobs that are often temporary or insecure and that may pay little more (or possibly less) than their monthly benefit.

In the 1980 Amendments to the Social Security Act, Congress attempted to reduce the fear that beneficiaries returning to work might have about the loss of their job. For both the SSDI/CDB and the SSI programs, the 1980 Amendments provide for a 15-month "reentitlement" period following the trial work period and a determination that the beneficiary is capable of working at a SGA level. The beneficiary with disabilities automatically becomes reentitled to disability benefits if the work attempt proves unsuccessful during this period. In the case of the SSDI/CDB program, the reentitlement period is equivalent to an extension of the trial work period, although SSDI/CDB benefits are not paid during the extension unless earnings drop below the SGA level. This would also be true for the SSI program, except that some beneficiaries may

still receive cash benefits from the Section 1619(a) demonstration program described above while the 15-month reentitlement period is running.

Other provisions of the 1980 Amendments that may reduce the fear of job insecurity are the extension of Medicare coverage for 36 months after cash benefits cease for SSDI/CDB beneficiaries, and the elimination of a second 24-month waiting period for Medicare coverage for persons who become reentitled to SSDI/CDB benefits within 5 years.

Obviously, these provisions do not reduce all fear of job loss. For one thing, some beneficiaries may feel that the 15-month "reentitlement" period is not sufficiently long. Even more importantly, they may fear that engaging in SGA for an extended period of time may lead to reevaluation of their case and the finding that they are no longer disabled and that they would then no longer be eligible for SSDI/CDB benefits, regular SSI benefits, or even Section 1619(a) benefits. Even the 15-month reentitlement period may be terminated if beneficiaries are reevaluated during this period and found not to be disabled. This fear is quite justified, because earnings above the SGA level are a specific indication to the SSA that the case should be reconsidered. Moreover, some cases are slated for periodic reevaluation because medical improvement is anticipated.

Even beneficiaries who lose their jobs may have their benefits terminated unless they can show that the job loss was due to their disability. If, however, their job loss is due to such factors as cyclic swings of the economy, use of new technology by the employer, loss of business by the employer, or any of a number of reasons that also cause nonhandicapped employees to lose their jobs, then the worker will probably lose his or her entitlement to benefits. Despite the fact that the beneficiary has shown a capacity to earn the SGA wage under certain circumstances, it may be a long time, if ever, before he or she can find another job. It is disconcerting that, despite the well-meaning intentions of the Congress in passing Sections 1619(a) and 1619(b), Americans with handicaps may still find themselves in jeopardy because of the way that these provisions of the law are now implemented.

Surprisingly, SSI beneficiaries who receive Section 1619(a) benefits lose their entitlement to regular SSI benefits after the 15-month reentitlement period. If, after this period, their earnings fall below the SGA level, their disability status must be reexamined to determine whether they still qualify for SSI benefits. If their income declined for reasons not connected to their disability (e.g., their employer goes out of business), it is conceivable that this would cause them to lose their entitlement to both regular SSI benefits as well as benefits under Section 1619(a).

Further, Medicare coverage of SSDI/CDB beneficiaries who return to work is not provided indefinitely, and after 5 years, beneficiaries who return to work face another 2-year waiting period before becoming eligible for Medicare if they become reentitled to SSDI/CDB benefits.

Attitudes toward Work

A third major work disincentive arises from the need for applicants to prove that they are unable to engage in SGA in order to establish eligibility for SSDI/CDB or SSI. The process of determining eligibility may last from 2 months to 1 year, and, during that entire period, applicants are impelled by the system to prove that they are unable to engage in substantial work.

Assistance in documenting work disability is solicited and usually obtained from vocational specialists, doctors, lawyers, social workers, family, friends, and others. In fact, these "supporters" sometimes coach applicants in methods to gain eligibility. In one state, a special project has been funded to train mental health professionals and legal aid providers to document work incapacity. Is it any wonder that the process of documenting work disability convinces applicants of their inability to work and the folly of attempting to work?

Negative attitudes toward work are further reinforced by the fact that benefits will continue to be paid to successful applicants only if they can demonstrate ongoing inability to work.

In this regard, it is noteworthy that one study of workers' compensation shows that claimants who do not need to prove the extent of their injuries generally fare better in employment than those with comparable injuries who become involved in litigation over the extent of their work disability (Ginnold, 1984). Clearly, the eligibility determination process and the conditions attached to continued receipt of benefits may destroy the will to work.

Multiple Benefits

Many people receive benefits from more than one program. In these cases, it is necessary to measure the combined value of all of the program benefits that must be given up as a consequence of engaging in substantial gainful employment in order to obtain a full asessment of the work disincentives facing these beneficiaries. Several different types of problems emerge as a consequence of persons receiving multiple benefits.

First, the number of programs that provide support and services is substantial. Obviously, most people who receive income support (SSDI/CDB, SSI) also receive health benefits (Medicare, Medicaid). Other benefits that people may receive because they are unable to work include Food Stamps, rent subsidies, public housing, state social services, school lunches, Aid to Families with Dependent Children, and private insurance.

During 1982, over 91% of SSI recipients also received Medicaid benefits, 45% received Food Stamps, 12% received school lunches, and 15% were in public housing (Congressional Research Service, 1984). Because about three-fourths of SSI recipients under 65 years of age are women (Noble, 1984), it is likely that a substantial percentage also receive Aid to Families with Dependent Children.

The total value of these multiple benefits can be substantial. The basic SSI payment for an individual is about $3,900 per year (1985). Depending on the state of residence, Food Stamps could add between $120 to $560 per year—in Hawaii, this aid amounts to $1,260 per year per person (Congressional Research Service, 1984). Medicaid may amount to $1,500 to $2,000 per year. The value of Medicaid benefits may, of course, be much higher to beneficiaries who are unable to obtain private insurance or who experience unusually high medical expenses. Thus, the basic level of benefits for most SSI recipients with disabilities receiving benefits as individuals is about $6,000 per year. For many individuals, this amount is much higher because other benefits are received (e.g., state supplements to SSI). In the case of couples receiving SSI and Medicaid benefits because of disability, the basic level of benefits is closer to $9,000.

Although many SSDI/CDB recipients receive benefits comparable to the SSI level or even lower (a large percentage of CDB beneficiaries must also apply for supplemental SSI benefits because their SSDI/CDB benefits are so low), some SSDI/CDB recipients receive benefits substantially higher than those paid by SSI. Consequently, in some cases, the value of benefits from all programs exceeds, sometimes by a considerable margin, $10,000 per year. The problem, of course, is that the full amount of these benefits may be placed in jeopardy by a return to work.

Additional problems associated with the receipt of multiple benefits are caused by the different eligibility conditions associated with the different programs. Consider the following two situations.

If SSI beneficiaries who reside in Medicaid approved and funded facilities, such as Intermediate Care Facilities for the Mentally Retarded (ICFs/MR) accept work while continuing to live in the facility, they will continue to be eligible for Medicaid provided that their earnings are sufficiently low to sustain federal SSI eligibility if they were not in a residential facility. Beneficiaries whose earnings are less than the SGA level will generally continue to be eligible for Medicaid under this standard.

In addition, states have the option of imposing a less stringent income standard for persons residing in Medicaid-funded institutions. Federal regulations permit states to receive Medicaid reimbursement for institutional services provided to residents whose total income does not exceed 300% of the SSI benefit amount payable to an individual living in his or her own home who has no other income. Under Section 1619(b), however, these earnings limits may be substantially increased since entitlement to Section 1619(b) may be continued as long as gross earnings are below the threshold amount (see above) that may include actual or anticipated Medicaid expenditures, an obviously vital consideration since institutional costs may exceed $30,000 per year, sometimes by a large margin. As noted above, however, about 20 states impose their own standards for Medicaid eligibility.

However, federal regulations governing reimbursement for care in Medicaid-approved facilities stipulate that the payment made to these facilities must be reduced by any amount of income in excess of a personal needs allowance, which may be as low as $25. Although this provision was designed to offset non-earnings income, it clearly may have a dramatic effect on work incentives because it may amount to virtually a 100% tax on earnings.

In the second situation, the Social Security Administration has interpreted Section 1619(a) to mean that, after the trial work period and 15-month reinstatement period, a person is eligible for a special SSI benefit only if he or she received an SSI cash benefit in the previous month—either a regular SSI benefit, a special Section 1619(a) benefit, or a state supplement. Similarly, a person is eligible for Section 1619(b) coverage only if he or she received an SSI benefit or a Section 1619(b) benefit during the previous month.

If a beneficiary does not receive an SSI benefit during the previous month, then he or she loses the program connection and must be recertified for regular SSI benefits, which means that he or she must be evaluated as too severely disabled to earn the SGA wage. Similarly, a person who becomes ineligible for a Section 1619(b) benefit also loses the program connection and must be recertified as eligible for the basic SSI program before further benefits can be provided. If earnings are above the SGA level, it is unlikely that the person will regain entitlement to SSI or Medicaid benefits.

These administrative provisions can result in capricious loss of benefits, substantial hardships, and inequities. Consider the following examples.

A beneficiary covered by Sections 1619(a) and 1619(b) who is earning $350 per month received a one-time gift or bequest that causes him or her to temporarily lose entitlement to both programs. It would require a relatively small amount of unearned income to eliminate the federal SSI payment—$265 to be exact. Depending on the state of residence, however, the one-time windfall would need to be considerably higher to terminate eligibility for Section 1619(b) coverage (i.e., generally in excess of $4,000).

Similarly, an individual may lose entitlement to these programs if assets other than a home, burial plot, insurance, automobile, and household goods and effects exceed $1,600 for a single individual and $2,400 for a couple (1985 limits).

Suppose a beneficiary receives both SSI and SSDI benefits, say $300 from SSDI and $45 from SSI. The total benefit is $20 higher than the maximum benefit for SSI alone because the first $20 of income from any source (here SSDI) is disregarded when calculating the SSI benefit. Assume as well that there is no state supplementary payment. Now suppose that the beneficiary accepts a job paying $250 per month. Obviously, the federal SSI payment is terminated since the breakeven amount is only $175. The SSDI payment is unaffected since the beneficiary is earning less than the SGA wage. However, the beneficiary is better off than if he or she was eligible for SSI alone since total income under SSDI is $550 ($300 + $250). Under SSI alone, total income would have been $495 per month ($242.50 + $250).

Suppose, however, that the beneficiary subsequently obtains a "merit" pay increase to $350 per month. After the trial work period, he or she is reevaluated and found not eligible for SSDI since earnings are above the SGA level. Now the beneficiary is markedly worse off than if he or she had received solely SSI since total income drops to $350, whereas, had SSI benefits been payable to the individual at the end of the trial work period, total income would be $542.50 per month ($350 plus $192.50). In other words, a beneficiary's monthly income varies substantially depending upon whether or not he or she was fortunate or unfortunate enough, depending on his or her other income, to have obtained sufficient quarters of coverage to be eligible for SSDI or was the dependent of a parent who is deceased, retired, or disabled.

Given these eligibility conditions, one would expect that some beneficiaries would seek to avoid such threatening events as yearend bonuses and holiday overtime if they would cause the breakeven point to be exceeded.

These situations, which arise partly from the complex rules governing the different programs, highlight the importance of considering these programs together as a system and developing a coordinated set of operating procedures. Although whether or not a given level of earnings will actually terminate eligibility for Section 1619(a) and/or Section 1619(b) benefits depends on a number of circumstances such as the level of state supplementary payments and the rules governing these supplementary payments as well as the level of a state's Medicaid expenditures on beneficiaries with disabilities, the capriciousness and inequity inherent in the Section 1619(a) and 1619(b) programs exist in all states. Only the cutoff points differ.

Work Decisions

Do these work disincentives actually have an impact on the decisions made by the beneficiaries of these programs? The response of SSI beneficiaries has been small to the special demonstration programs that provide special cash benefits—Section 1619(a)—and continued Medicaid benefits—Section 1619(b)—to SSI recipients who return to work. At the end of 1982, 2 full years after the extended benefits went into effect, fewer than 500 SSI benefici-aries were receiving special cash benefits. However, almost 5,600 former SSI recipients whose cash benefits were terminated, pre-sumably, in most cases, because their earnings exceeded the federal breakeven point, retained their eligibility for Medicaid benefits (Social Security Disability Benefits Reform Act, 1984).

The lack of a large-scale response to the provisions of the special demonstration pro-grams may reflect many factors other than unwillingness or inability to work. In par-ticular, knowledge of the special demon-stration programs has been quite limited. In approving the extension of Sections 1619(a) and (b), Congress required that SSA personnel be trained to implement these special pro-visions and that information on them be dis-seminated to the public.

In any event, one must ask why many people actually believe that the complicated rules governing eligibility for these programs do influence the job decisions made by persons with developmental disabilities. If the reader has found it difficult to follow the analysis of how the rules work, then consider the plight of persons with a developmental disability trying to figure out the risks and benefits of accepting a job paying "n" amount of dollars.

The authors believe, however, that these work disincentives do have a powerful indirect impact. Many persons influence the decisions made by persons with developmental disabili-ties. Will social workers who have struggled to place a person with severe handicaps in a community-based residence counsel him or her to risk a secure SSI or SSDI/CDB cash benefit or Medicaid or Medicare entitlement in order to accept work that provides little additional in-come? Will private operators of board and care homes, the financial solvency of which is de-pendent on a high bed occupancy and assured rental payments, actively encourage their tenant/client to seek employment with its at-tendant risks? Will relatives who are concerned about their legal or moral obligations and who themselves may be partially dependent on the income support payment be anxious to see a relative with developmental disabilities give up a secure benefit to accept a job?

OTHER EFFECTS OF PROGRAMS

Several other aspects of existing programs that discourage employment should be noted.

Intermediate Care Facilities for the Mentally Retarded (ICF/MR) Program

The ICF/MR program is a component of the Medicaid authority that funds residential care and needed services for persons with mental retardation or other related conditions re-quiring health-related or habilitative care. States have a strong incentive to place persons with severe mental retardation in ICFs/MR because the program pays all reasonable costs of providing care. There is little, if any, incen-tive for states to seek out less restrictive care alternatives.

One condition of eligibility for the program is that the resident be in need of 24-hour-a-day care. This strict requirement almost eliminates the prospect of substantial gainful employ-ment. The problem, of course, is that the de-termination of who requires 24-hour-a-day care is as unreliable as the determination of who is incapable of working at an SGA level. Thus, states may easily place residents with mental retardation in ICFs/MR who could be placed in less restrictive care that would en-courage care.

Asset Test

In order to qualify for SSI, applicants and recipients must meet a number of asset tests. In general, they can own a home without restric-tion as to value, and an automobile with a value up to $4,500. They may own a burial plot up to a value of $1,500, insurance up to $1,500, and household goods and personal effects with a value not to exceed $2,000. Other assets (e.g., cash, bank accounts, stocks) may not exceed $1,600 in the case of individuals, and $2,400 in the case of couples (as of 1985).

It is unlikely that the requirement of "near poverty" as a condition of eligibility for SSI and Medicaid discourages work. It does, however, create a strong incentive for SSI recipients to spend, rather than save. Of course, few SSI beneficiaries have an income sufficient to permit significant savings, but there are exceptions. In any event, thrift is one aspect of normalization and should be encouraged, rather than discouraged. It is particularly important because the accumulation of a small bank account may play an important role in stimulating a desire for independence among persons with developmental disabilities and perhaps in motivating them to work.

STRUCTURAL PROBLEMS

The authors have stressed the importance of examining the entire system of programs and services available to persons with mental retardation and other developmental disabilities. This section analyzes structural problems in the system of services that reduce the prospects of employment.

Coordination Problems

For years, analysts in this area have lamented the lack of coordination and integration of the available services. In effect, the system does not operate as an entity with clearly articulated parts that move cooperatively and efficiently in the achievement of social goals. Instead, it is a loose aggregate of independently functioning components that on occasion clash and interfere with each other's operations, and frequently fail to achieve desirable social goals, such as employment. There are a number of reasons for this lack of coordination.

First, these programs were created to deal with specific problems, and it was generally assumed that each program would, in and of itself, resolve its designated problem. For example, Medicaid and Medicare would meet health care needs, SSDI/CDB and SSI would meet income support needs, and vocational rehabilitation would meet employment needs. Rarely was consideration given to how these programs might interact, or, in some instances, clash, with one other.

Second, consistent with their independent origins, these programs are managed independently of each other for the most part, and each has its own set of goals, priorities, eligibility conditions, and operating procedures. Program managers often tend to be quite unconcerned whether these goals, priorities, eligibility conditions, and operating procedures support or interfere with those of other programs.

Third, the inherent difficulties of making these programs operate as a system are further complicated because some programs are managed at a federal level (e.g., SSDI/CDB, SSI, and Medicare), others at the state level (e.g., vocational rehabilitation, Medicaid), and yet others at the local level (e.g., some social service and housing programs).

Fourth and most important, the programs that comprise the system of services do not operate in a coordinated fashion because they do not have a set of consistent and uniform goals. Rather than providing services aimed at achieving a common set of social goals, they tend to have more limited programmatic goals that may interfere with the achievement of other goals, such as employment. It cannot be overemphasized that the center of the problem is this lack of a set of social goals for which each program accepts a share of responsibility. More than any other reason, the authors believe that this shortcoming explains why the system performs in a fragmented and counterproductive manner. As examples of clashing goals, consider the following:

The large federally funded income support and health care programs focus on identifying and providing support and services to persons unable to engage in SGA rather than on assisting them to return to work.

It is often alleged that lawyers, relatives, and even vocational rehabilitation counselors discourage workers' compensation claimants from accepting vocational rehabilitation services if they are litigating over the size of their award.

Some persons working with beneficiaries with mental retardation place a higher priority on ensuring the client a secure future income than on helping the client find and retain employment. Group home operators and some social workers, for example, often have strong incentives to counsel clients to avoid risking their secure benefits.

The requirement of 24-hour-a-day care in small community ICFs/MR is incompatible with promoting substantial employment of residents.

Many other examples of the perverse effects of the failure of the service system to act in a coordinated and integrated way can be cited. The above examples emphasize one intractable effect—the creation of major work disincentives. Other structural problems in the service system, some due to coordination problems, are worth noting.

Periodic Reviews

The Social Security Disability Amendments of 1980 required periodic review of SSDI and SSI beneficiaries at least once every 3 years in order to confirm their continuing eligibility, except where there was a finding of permanent disability.

On the surface, there would appear to be little reason to object to periodic reviews to confirm whether persons receiving these benefits were incapable of substantial work and therefore should be continued on the rolls. Yet, implementation of these reviews has resulted in major controversy and has led to tragic results in some cases. Although extreme in its consequences, the case of Gordon D. of Eugene, Oregon, a childhood polio victim diagnosed as paranoid schizophrenic, epitomizes the impact of these reviews. After the SSA dropped him from the disability rolls and denied his appeal, he wrote to his family, "I no longer have any income whatsoever and there is no way I can work . . . . I have no life any more . . . . I can't afford to eat . . . . I don't even feel like a man any more." In August, 1983, he committed suicide (Mental Health Law Project, November 29, 1983).

It should be noted that many of the decisions against beneficiaries are reversed, and benefits are often restored on appeal to the level of the administrative law judge (Noble, 1984).

What is wrong with these periodic disability reviews? The basic problem is that they fail to take account of the fact that the functional limitations of most persons with serious handicaps often make it difficult for them to locate work, may result in prolonged periods of joblessness, and may cause profound discouragement, regardless of whether or not they are believed to be capable of earning the SGA level of $300 per month or more. Although many SSI and SSDI/CDB beneficiaries are capable of working at an SGA level, they often need extensive assistance, assurance, and a considerable period of preparation before they are likely to find substantial work. During this time, these beneficiaries will continue to need income support from SSI or SSDI/CDB.

If the transition to work is to be effective, it must take place gradually, not abruptly. Unfortunately, the present periodic review procedures do not permit a gradual transition to work. Beneficiaries are notified that they are capable of substantial work and thus no longer eligible for income support. Little or no provision is made to help them find gainful employment or to refer them to agencies that will provide the needed services that will enable them to return to work. No transition period is permitted. No assurance is made of continued income support in the event that the assessment that they are capable of substantial work is incorrect. Unfortunately, the Social Security Disability Benefits Reform Act of 1984 does little to correct these problems. Although the 1984 Amendments require continuation of benefits during the appeals process, this provision will, if anything, further reduce work incentives because beneficiaries who appeal will strive to prove their utter incapacity for work.

Eligibility Problems

Another example of the perverse effects of an uncoordinated system of services occurs when persons with disabilities who are in need of assistance have difficulty establishing eligibility for services. Bradley (1978), after reviewing the operations of the SSI program in one state, reported that "[s]ome disabled persons have reportedly been denied SSI benefits on the grounds that their disability was not sufficiently severe and yet have been denied VR [Vocational rehabilitation] services because their prognosis for employment was too poor" (p. 53). It is difficult to think of a single reason why motivated persons with handicaps should not be assured of needed assistance in finding appropriate work if they do not qualify for income support (except possibly in the case of a person with a handicap that is sufficiently mild that it does not interfere with his or her ability to work).

Problems in Changing Programs

The transition of residents from institutions to the community is sometimes hindered because it usually takes 60 or more days before persons leaving an institution are declared eligible for SSI benefits, and consequently, needed funds may not be available at the time a resident is ready to be placed in a community-based living arrangement (Bradley et al., 1978). In addition, the problems encountered by graduating students with handicaps as they shift from services provided by the educational system to adult services (i.e., the "aging out" problem) have received a great deal of attention in recent years.

Staff Inadequacies

It is sometimes questioned whether the large generic programs, such as the income support and health care programs, have staff who are sufficiently knowledgeable about the specialized needs of persons with mental retardation and other developmental disabilities to provide services effectively (Bradley et al., 1978; Gettings, 1981).

Complexity of Service System

The very number and complexity of service programs make it difficult for persons with developmental disabilities to identify and gain access to them. Often, they or their guardians are not even aware of the programs or the criteria for judging eligibility for services. A primary role of a case manager is that of directing persons toward needed services and

expediting their acceptance into service programs. In effect, the case manager tries to make the programs operate as a system.

Resistance to Change

State and local governments tend to be resistent to major changes in the service system. Efforts to phase down large institutions, for example, have met with determined resistance from employees, whose jobs are threatened, and local communities, which may owe a large part of their existence to the institution payroll and business orders from the institutions. Conversely, efforts to place persons with severe handicaps in community residences may also meet with angry resistance. State legislators are obviously influenced by these considerations.

Widespread stereotyping of persons with severe handicaps also creates skepticism and resistance to change, particularly among legislators who are concerned about the political consequences of phasing down an institution. The resistance to phasing down these institutions may be further enhanced in the case of legislators who remember having voted for substantial funds to improve the institution so that it would qualify for ICF/MR funding.

Emphasis on Maximizing Revenues

A major goal of many legislators is to shift as large a part of the cost of operating the service system as possible to other levels of government. As far as state and local governments are concerned, the most efficient way to minimize their fiscal burden is to place clients with mental retardation in programs that are funded partly or totally by the federal government. Thus, clients with mental retardation are placed, if possible, in residential facilities that qualify for Medicaid funding through the ICF/MR program. An increasing number of states are funding small community-based residences through ICF/MR funding. When this is not possible, clients with mental retardation are assisted to apply for SSI benefits to pay for their care. In effect, these federal funds are sometimes perceived and used as if they were a free good rather than a scarce resource to be carefully husbanded. Even worse, clients may be placed in these programs even though it may not be in their best interests. As the authors have observed, both the SSI and the ICF/MR programs contain serious work disincentives. This phenomenon, more than anything else, explains why local governments, which often do not share in the cost of institutional care, are willing to see the state and federal governments pay institutional costs running to $60,000 or more per year.

Problems of Federal Oversight

In principle, federal oversight is intended to prevent problems such as inappropriate placement of persons with mental retardation in ICF/MR facilities. Unfortunately, this oversight is often inadequate. In part, this is because the technology for carrying out meaningful oversight is limited. There is, for example, no really good criteria for determining when placement of a client in an ICF/MR is inappropriate. In addition, federal oversight is often much more preoccupied with complying with the letter of the law, than with effective programming. Recent federal attempts to disallow some state expenditures for ICF/MR residents on the grounds that they were being improperly used for vocational purposes is a case in point. Moreover, federal oversight is sometimes confusing. The failure of the Health Care Financing Administration to clearly define when services will be considered as vocational in nature and not eligible for Medicaid funding is an example of this problem. Finally, federal oversight sometimes takes the form of asking the states to designate one agency to oversee the operations of other state agencies (e.g., the use of the state Medicaid agency to monitor the operations of other state agencies that receive Medicaid reimbursement for the services they provide) To expect one state agency to disallow reimbursements for substandard practice and thereby increase total program costs to the state is unrealistic.

Other Problems

Several interesting examples of the lack of a systems outlook in the programs that provide support and services to Americans who are elderly and have disabilities were reported at a recent Virginia legislative hearing (Richmond Times-Dispatch, September 15, 1984).

A grocery store must pay the state a 4% sales tax on the surplus food that it gives to the poor, but there is no tax if the food is thrown away.

An unemployed single mother living in a $100,000 condominium need not count the value of her home when applying for AFDC, but a poor mother living in a shack on 11 acres of land is ineligible if the land if worth $60 per acre.

Physicans keep elderly patients in hospitals longer than necessary, creating large Medicaid bills, because there is no room for them in the inexpensive Meals on Wheels program.

Lack of transportation prevents some poor people from getting to the welfare department to sign up for Food Stamps or to pick them up after being declared eligible.

ABSENCE OF SERVICES

Another reason why the service system does not always effectively assist persons with mental retardation to obtain and maintain employment is that appropriate services are often not available. Sometimes, the lack of services is due to low levels of funding, particularly social service programs. Of equal and perhaps greater importance is the fact that most state and local programs, other than education programs, exist largely because of federal legislation and funding. New services are not usually created without the federal stimulus because states constantly strive to minimize their costs by shifting the cost burden onto the federal government. To do do, states put most of their limited resources into programs for which federal financial participation can be obtained, rather than create more appropriate programs.

One of the most glaring examples of this problem is the lack of programs that provide long-term assistance to persons with developmental disabilities who seek to obtain and maintain themselves in employment on a regular job site. Despite its many successes, the state-federal vocational rehabilitation program is primarily oriented toward providing the short-term services needed by many clients to obtain a job, after which relatively little, if any, support is available. This model of service delivery is unsuitable for many persons with developmental disabilities.

The number of organizations that place persons with developmental disabilites in substantial employment in regular job sites and then provide follow-up with necessary support services for varying periods of time is increasing. However, most persons with severe mental retardation and other disabilities do not have access to these services. Moreover, few organizations provide indefinite support in regular job sites. Sheltered workshops and work activity centers are then the primary source of long-term employment support. However, as has been discussed, sheltered workshops and work activity centers should be a last resort for long-term employment, rather than the primary means of such employment.

Not only does the federal government not support programs to fund long-term employment services, but, because of the rules governing Medicaid funding, states face major disincentives to placing persons with disabilities in vocational programs in sheltered workshops, work activity centers, or in programs on regular job sites if they reside in Medicaid-approved residences.

Several states have attempted to utilize Medicaid to fund employment services to persons living in either ICFs/MR or in community residences receiving funds under the Medicaid Home and Community-Based Services Waiver program. There is, however, great controversy around this issue. Medicaid regulations specifically prohibit the use of Medicaid funds for vocational training (CFR 441.13[b]). However, Medicaid regulations also specifically require that "active treatment," which must include social services directed toward the goal of "maximizing the social functioning of each resident," be provided to all residents of ICFs/MR (CFR 442.494). These ICF/MR require-

ments appear contradictory because work, in the view of most people, is one of the highest social functions that people perform.

In the case of the Home and Community-Based Services Waivers program, an explicit goal, and condition of participation, is that the cost be less than would be incurred by Medicaid if residents were placed in institutional care. Ironically, the restriction on the provision of vocational services sometimes impedes the attainment of this goal because, often, vocational services are less costly and more beneficial than the alternative day care programs that are often provided.

In other words, sometimes compliance with Medicaid goals and regulations for the ICF/MR and Home and Community-Based Waivers programs seems to depend on the provision of a prohibited service. The dilemma faced by the states is even more evident when it is noted that vocational training is sometimes barely distinguishable from other habilitation services and that considerable uncertainty exists as to what is allowable and what is not allowable under Medicaid for federal financial participation in this area. In sum, states have a strong financial incentive to place persons with developmental disabilities in facilities for which they can receive Medicaid funding. But, if they do so, they are prohibited from spending Medicaid funds to provide the services that are often needed to achieve both social and programmatic goals.

Finally, lack of family support is another serius deficiency. Families with a member with mental retardation who is at home may face such extraordinary burdens as social isolation and/or rejection by kin or neighbors; the need to provide direct care, sometimes on a continuous basis; and the need to locate and transport the family member with mental retardation to needed services. These burdens may create major financial losses due to reduced opportunities for gainful work, and eventually wear down the most dedicated of parents. Families often need training in developing the adaptive behavior skills of persons with mental retardation, and sometimes need counseling to help them cope with the almost inevitable family stresses. These problems increase as the primary family members grow older. Lack of support to cope with these burdens has led some families to institutionalize their dependent child rather than maintain a place for him or her in the community.

State funding support is extremely limited, ranging from $3.6 million annually in Penn-

sylvania for supportive services to 11,548 persons, and $23,000 in Connecticut for cash subsidies to 15 families. Federal support for family support services is extremely limited and thus places the fiscal burden for such services on state or local revenues (Human Services Research Institute, September 15, 1984).

REFERENCES

Amendments to the Social Security Act. (1980). Legislative history and summary of provisions. *Social Security Bulletin, 44*(4), 1–17.

Bradley, V., Allard, M., Annikis, M., Billingsley, K., Liegey, A., & Cravedi. (1978). *Developmentally disabled persons in the federal income maintenance programs: A critique of issues in SSI and SSDI*. Washington, DC: National Association of State Mental Retardation Program Directors.

Code of Federal Regulations, Title 20, Chapter 3, Section 416.983.

Congressional Research Service, Library of Congress. (1984). Legislative history, trends, and adequacy of the supplemental security income (SSI) program. In *The Supplemental Security Income Program: A 10-year overview*. An information paper prepared by the Special Committee on Aging, United States Senate. Washington, DC: U.S. Government Printing Office.

Conley, R. W., & Noble, J. H. (1979). Workers' compensation reform: Challenge for the 80's. In R. W. Conley (Ed.), *Research reports of the Interdepartmental Workers' Compensation Task Force* (Vol. 1). Washington, DC: U.S. Government Printing Office.

Gettings, R. (1981). Generic vs. specialized services: The ying and yang of programming for developmentally disabled clients. In T. C. Muzzio, J. J. Koshel, & V. Bradley (Eds.), *Alternative community living arrangements and non-vocational social services for developmentally disabled people* (pp. 19–37). Report to the Administration for Developmental Disabilities, U.S. Department of Health and Human Services. Washington, DC: The Urban Institute.

Ginnold, R. (1984). A follow-up study of permanent disability cases under Wisconsin worker's compensation. In R. W. Conley (Ed.), *Research reports of the interdepartmental worker's compensation task force*

(Vol. 6). Washington, DC: U.S. Government Printing Office.

Human Services Research Institute. (1984, September). *Supporting families with developmentally disabled members: Review of the literature and results of a national survey*. Draft report to the Office of Human Development Services, U.S. Department of Health and Human Services, Boston.

Mental Health Law Project. (1983, November). *Letter from Norman S. Rosenbery, Director*. Washington, DC: Author.

Noble, J. H. (1984). Rehabilitating the SSI recipient—Overcoming disincentives to employment of severely disabled persons. In *The supplemental security income program: A 10-year overview*. An information paper prepared by the Special committee on Aging, United States Senate. Washington, DC: U.S. Government Printing Office.

Richmond Time-Dispatch. September 15, 1984, pp. 3–5.

Schultz, J. H. (1984). Origins, experience, and unresolved issues. In *The supplemental security income program: A 10-year overview*. An information paper prepared by the Special Committee on Aging, United States Senate. Washington, DC: U.S. Government Printing Office.

Social Security Disability Benefits Reform Act of 1984. (1984). *Report from the Committee on Ways and Means, March 14, 1984*. Washington, DC: U.S. House of Representatives.

U.S. Department of Health and Human Services. (1982). *Social Security handbook*. Washington, DC: U.S. Government Printing Office.

U.S. Department of Health and Human Services, Social Security Administration. (1985). Program operating manual system—Part 05, Chapter 023, Subchapter 02. Washington, DC: Author.

∞ Chapter 6 ∞

Where Do We Go from Here?

John H. Noble, Jr., Ronald W. Conley, and Jean K. Elder

DURING RECENT YEARS IT HAS BEEN INCREAS-ingly recognized that persons with mental retardation and other developmental disabilities have much greater capabilities than had previously been believed. For example, all children with mental retardation are capable of learning. Now all children, no matter how severely handicapped, must be given a free, appropriate education. Likewise, almost all persons with severe mental retardation are capable of some degree of independence. The earlier practice of "warehousing" persons with handicaps in large segregated institutions is now generally discredited as being both unnecessarily expensive and destructive to human growth and development. More and more persons with developmental disabilities are residing in community-based housing. Children usually remain with their natural families. As adults, they may continue to live with their families, may move into small group homes, or may move into independent housing. Wherever they live, emphasis is placed on assisting these citizens to increase their ability to live independently and to integrate themselves into the community as much as possible.

It is also being discovered that most persons with developmental disabilities can be employed in meaningful, remunerative work. The authors believe that the nation is moving rapidly toward adopting a goal of placing most persons with mental retardation and other developmental disabilities in substantial gainful employment. Among the forces shaping this emphasis on substantial gainful employment are the following:

It is consistent with the almost universal acceptance of the goal of assisting people with developmental disabilities to live under conditions as nearly normal as possible.

It not only enriches the lives of such persons, both spiritually and financially, but also reduces the taxes that must be paid for income support, medical care, and the supervision and services that would have to be provided if they were not employed.

Because of Public Law 94-142, more students with severe handicaps are completing their education. Neither they nor their families are willing to accept institutionalization or sterile day care upon graduation. Employment is the next natural step for persons who complete their education.

Unfortunately, achievement of the goal of employment is sometimes thwarted because most public funds expended on persons with developmental disabilities support programs

This paper was written by the authors in their private capacity. No official support or endorsement by the U.S. Department of Health and Human Services or the Virginia Department of Mental Health and Mental Retardation is intended or should be inferred.

that promote dependency and discourage employment. How can this be changed?

NATIONAL GOALS

The authors believe that there must be a major reappraisal and restructuring of existing programs so that they support rather than hinder the provision of the most beneficial and cost-effective services to persons with developmental disabilities. Two factors that have contributed to the inadequacies of existing programs should be emphasized. One is the revolutionary changes that have occurred in the goals being set for persons with developmental disabilities. As a result, existing program objectives and policies often lag behind what is technologically possible, particularly with respect to employment and community-based residences for people with severe handicaps.

The second factor is the lack of generally accepted and comprehensive goals for persons with mental retardation, on the basis of which individual programs can operate as part of a coherent and consistent system of services. Programs have usually focused on a single goal, such as providing basic income support for persons unable to work (the SSI and SSDI/CDB programs), or improving conditions in institutions (the ICF/MR program). Little consideration has been given to how achievement of these individual program goals affects the attainment of other equally important goals, such as employment and community-based living. As a result, there are sizable gaps in services, inconsistencies among programs, substantial incentives to provide inappropriate rather than appropriate services, and major work disincentives. The fact that individual programs were created at different points in time probably contributes to these problems. These problems are so pervasive that they almost defy the coordination efforts of well-intentioned practitioners and would-be program reformers.

There is a clear and compelling need to establish a set of generally accepted social or national (the terms are interchangeable) goals for the entire system of services for Americans

with developmental disabilities. Each program should then be evaluated according to its contribution to the achievement of this set of social goals. There will, of course, be inevitable conflicts among the goals, as increasing the level of achievement of one may decrease another goal's level of achievement. For example, the higher the level of income support under the SSI and SSDI/CDB programs, the greater the potential work disincentives. Compromises will have to be made. Yet, a clear set of social goals at least makes it possible to compare explicitly advantages and disadvantages of alternative ways of organizing and operating the service system with respect to all social goals, not just a single or limited subset of these goals.

Although this discussion focuses on persons with developmental disabilities, a set of national goals is equally applicable to all Americans with handicaps.

Establishing a set of consistent, generally accepted goals is one of the most effective ways of improving the coordination and integration of the various programs that compromise the system of services for persons with developmental disabilities. It also is an essential step in identifying the most advantageous ways of improving this system of services.

Creating a set of consistent, generally accepted goals will require prolonged discussions among program administrators, scholars, professionals, legislators, persons with developmental disabilities, and their relatives. Toward that end, the following tentative list of social goals is offered. It is not meant to be comprehensive; nor is the wording intended to be precise. It is simply a list of some of the areas in which more precisely stated social goals should be delineated.

1. Promoting and maintaining the employment of working-age persons with developmental disabilities, even for persons whose earnings will be low, who will hold less secure jobs, or who will be employed in jobs that will not be continuous, should be of high priority in every program.

Probably the goal of employment should even be extended to those persons with developmental disabilities who are past the customary retirement age who wish to work and are able to do so. The possibility of substantial gainful work should rarely be rejected, even for persons with very severe functional limitations.

2. Adequate income support should be provided to persons who are temporarily or permanently unable to work because of a disability. To what extent this income support should be subject to an asset test (as in SSI) or not subject to an asset test (as in SSDI/CDB) is an issue that the authors defer to subsequent discussion.

3. When protective oversight is needed, placement should be made in community-based residences. Moreover, these facilities should provide supervision and care only to the extent needed for personal development and rehabilitation. This practice is consistent with the principles of "normalization" and "least restrictive care."

4. Persons with developmental disabilities should be encouraged to participate in community activities appropriate to their age, sex, and education (e.g., use of public transportation, community recreational facilities, restaurants, and senior centers).

5. Persons with developmental disabilities should be provided with reasonable protection against the dangers of fire, criminal assault, and highway, home, and other accidents.

6. All children with disabilities should be provided with a free, appropriate public education and, as adults, should have access to appropriate habilitation services.

7. All services should be coordinated and provided in the most cost-effective manner.

These goals have the following characteristics. First, they are output oriented. If the national goal is employment, the goal statement should not include additional process goals, such as whether employment is achieved through the federal-state vocational rehabilitation program, the employment service, or some other program. This is an issue to be determined by assessment of the best way of achieving the goal of employment. Social goals should not be used to set procedural standards, such as the conditions of eligibility for program services.

Second, these social goals are described in terms of broad, long-term policy directions, rather than specific numerical objectives, such as the employment of "x" thousands of adults with mental retardation. Setting specific quantitative objectives/goals is more appropriate when planning annual program operations; it is a function of resource limitations and existing knowledge of the best ways to achieve social goals.

Third, most people agree in principle with these broadly stated social goals. Substantial disagreement will undoubtedly arise, however, over the extent to which certain goals, such as employment, are attainable, the speed with which specific numerical objectives can be achieved, the priority that should be placed on the achievement of different social goals when resources are limited, and the best way to achieve these goals. Nevertheless, establishing broad social goals will have the positive effect of focusing subsequent debate on issues of the speed and methods of implementation, and not on the desirability of the goals themselves.

Finally, establishing a set of social goals for persons who have developmental disabilities does not mean that each level of government should assume responsibility for full achievement of the complete set of goals. A national reappraisal of the appropriate roles and responsibilities of federal, state, and local governments in the funding and management of public services is currently taking place. A national consensus seems unlikely to emerge for several years. Nevertheless, the existence of a set of national goals might induce each level of government to plan, legislate, or operate programs that follow these two guidelines:

1. The effects of proposed or existing programs on all national goals should be carefully assessed, not only the effects on the immediate problem that the individual

program is designed to solve or mitigate. For example, the federal government must consider the effects of the Social Security programs not only on averting poverty but also on the employment of people with disabilities and the structural barriers that they contain that hinder effective coordination with other programs. Although goals often conflict we can attempt to maximize the beneficial effects of programs and to minimize their negative effects only by taking into account all consequences of programs.

2. Every effort should be made to ensure that the individual programs in the system of services do not interfere with the attainment of the national goals. Even though a given government does not accept full responsibility for all progams in the service system or for achieving the complete set of national goals, the interdependence of programs must be recognized. For example, the federally funded Medicaid program deserves careful review to determine if current policies encourage the states to place some persons with disabilities in unnecessarily restrictive residential facilities (institutions and nursing homes) in order to obtain federal reimbursement for their care.

OPTIONS FOR CHANGE

In this section, options are presented that the authors believe will greatly enhance the likelihood of persons with developmental disabilities obtaining and maintaining employment. The possible effects of these options on social goals other than employment are analyzed. These options are discussed in the context of the entire system of services that has been described, and not solely in the context of a single program. The options are presented according to the policy objectives that they are designed to achieve.

Objective 1 *Improve the integration and coordination of programs so that the system of services operates in a unified and consistent way.* As previously observed, some persons need several services simultaneously (e.g., vocational training, income support, and health care benefits). In addition, some workers with handicaps have intermittent periods of eligibility and need for benefits or services. A system for effectively coordinating services in these varying circumstances does not exist. Improving program coordination will require major changes in the way that most administrators perceive their programs. In particular, a strong vocational orientation and a holistic approach to achieving this goal will need to be adopted.

The authors believe that not only will the system of services become more effective and less costly if it operates in a more unified fashion, but that this will reduce resistance to change within the system, reduce the likelihood of the provision of inappropriate services, and improve the oversight over programs. One crucial option that the authors believe will greatly improve the coordination of programs within the system, namely, the adoption of a generally accepted set of national goals for people who have developmental disabilities, has already been discussed at some length.

A second option for improving the coordination of the system of services would be to develop a unified system for determining eligibility across programs. There are several advantages for doing so. First, it should reduce cost as multiple determinations of eligibility for different programs are consolidated into a single determination. Second, it would help ensure that clients are given the benefit of all available services to which they are entitled and that they need. Third, it would avoid the problem of persons falling between the cracks of programs. For example, it sometimes happens that a person is declared unfeasible for vocational rehabilitation on the grounds that he or she is too severely disabled, and is then refused SSDI or SSI on the grounds that he or she is not sufficiently disabled to qualify. There is no rationale for not declaring applicants eligible for one or the other of these programs (and possibly both).

A third option for improving the coordination of the system of services is to require unified, comprehensive service plans for each client. This plan would include programs for education, vocational rehabilitation, adult social services, health care, income support, and other services. The plan would include services to be provided under both public and private programs. More importantly, it would include joint planning by representatives at all government levels, federal as well as state and local. In many states, joint planning among state and local agencies already exists, and a plan is not valid until approved by the representatives of the different agencies. The authors are proposing that the process become mandatory and include the federally administered programs, such as Social Security and Medicare. A comprehensive service plan would not require that each agency give up its individual service plan, which is often required by federal law. Instead, the authors are proposing an amendment to existing procedures that would require: (a) assurance that the various individual plans are consistent with each other, and (b) extension of responsibility for implementing the plan to all agencies associated with the services that are defined as needed under the comprehensive plan.

Along with other options that are discussed below, a unified plan would prevent the problems that occur when beneficiaries are declared ineligible for SSDI or SSI, but are not provided with services and support needed to achieve the independence of which they are believed capable.

Objective 2 *Eliminate the emphasis on demonstrating inability to work as the condition of eligibility for program benefits.* The requirement that applicants for income support and health care benefits—SSI, SSDI/CDB, Medicare, and Medicaid—must demonstrate that they are incapable of working in order to be eligible for benefits inevitably creates severe work disincentives and negative work attitudes among program applicants and beneficiaries. Moreover, this requirement forces bureaucrats to reach critical decisions about the work capacity of program applicants that are impossible to make. The U.S. Congress is showing its lack of faith in these decisions by amending federal income support and health care programs to increase the incentives for program beneficiaries to return to work.

Eligibility for federal income support and health care programs should be changed to require only that program applicants prove that they have great difficulty in obtaining work because of their handicapping condition. In this approach, eligibility for benefits would be granted without the pejorative judgment about the applicant's incapacity for substantial work and the futility of providing employment services. In fact, under this new policy, it makes sense to grant eligibility for benefits quickly, and simultaneously to condition their receipt on the beneficiary's willingness to accept services designed to help him or her to return to work.

Under this approach to determining program eligibility, one important measure of success for the entire service system should be the number of persons who are accepted as eligible for income support and health care benefits and then enabled to return to work, with corresponding termination or reduction of these benefits. At present, the return of a person with handicaps to work without medical improvement implies a failure in judgment by the person who evaluated the case in the first place. Rather than find fault with the evaluation, it would be far better to claim success for the restored worker.

Objective 3 *Ensure that beneficiaries who return to work are always significantly better off than if they remain on the program rolls.* Most people work because they expect to be significantly better off than if they do not work. As was pointed out in Chapter 5, however, not only is it likely that a significant number of program beneficiaries would gain very little by returning to work, but also, some program beneficiaries even face a net reduction of income if they do so. It can be expected that many of these beneficiaries will resist returning to work, even if they would normally prefer work to leisure. There are a number of options to reduce this problem that must be considered.

Income Support Programs The special cash benefits paid to SSI beneficiaries who return to work under the Section 1619(a) demonstration program should be made a permanent part of the SSI program. Reducing the benefits by $1 for every $2 of earnings, and continuing benefits until earnings exceed the breakeven point rather than only until they exceed the level set for substantial gainful activity, ensure that no one will receive less cash income as a result of accepting employment than by not working. Of course, the incentive to work could be strengthened by decreasing benefits by a lesser amount, say $1 for every $3 of earnings. Yet, this approach has two disadvantages: it clearly would increase the cost to the U.S. Treasury, and it would substantially raise the current breakeven points. Under Section 1619(a), these breakeven points set the earnings level beyond which all SSI benefits would cease. Higher breakeven points may not be socially acceptable because current breakeven points are in excess of the earnings of a full-time worker receiving the minimum wage. The current reduction of $1 for $2 of earnings seems to be a reasonable compromise between the goals of maximizing work incentives and controlling the costs to the federal government.

Currently, there is no corresponding method of reducing SSDI/CDB benefits as the earnings of beneficiaries rise. Establishing a system for doing so in the SSDI/CDB program could be difficult and controversial because of the high benefit levels of some SSDI/CDB beneficiaries. For example, with an income disregard of $85 and a $1 reduction in benefits for every $2 in earnings (the procedure followed in the SSI program), an SSDI/CDB beneficiary who receives a benefit of $1,000 per month would not have benefits totally offset until earnings were over $2,000 per month—a level of subsidized income that might be unacceptable to many taxpayers. Nevertheless, there are ways in which work disincentives can be substantially reduced in the SSDI/CDB program without incurring excessive costs.

Even if SSDI/CDB benefits were offset dollar for dollar as earnings rise, this approach would still be a great improvement over the present system. It would at least reduce the

likelihood that the worker would receive less cash income as the reward for returning to work.

A more reasonable alternative would be to set up a two-phase system for reducing benefits as earnings rise. In the first phase, all SSDI/CDB benefits up to the level of SSI benefits would be reduced at the same rate as in the SSI program. Beyond that point, benefits would be reduced at a higher rate, say $3 of benefits for each $4 of earnings. In the case of an individual SSDI beneficiary receiving $1,000 per month, the breakeven point would be about $1,635 per month, when benefits above the SSI level of $325 are reduced by $3 for every $4 of earnings and there is no unearned income. The calculation is a breakeven point of $735 for the first $325 in benefits plus a breakeven point of $900 for the next $675 in benefits ($675 × 4/3). Suppose this beneficiary accepted a job paying $400 per month. Instead of losing $600 per month of net income after the trial work period as would occur under current policy, the beneficiary would continue to receive an SSDI benefit of $843 per month (see Table 1, case 1). This amount, plus $400 in earnings, is $243 greater per month than the $1,000 monthly SSDI benefit alone. If a beneficiary accepted a job paying $1,000 per month, he or she would continue to receive an SSDI benefit of about $476 per month; the $1,476 gross income would be $476 higher than the $1,000 monthly SSDI benefit alone (see Table 1, case 2).

Under a two-phase system for reducing SSDI/CDB benefits, SSDI/CDB beneficiaries whose earnings were less than the SGA level of $300 per month would fare less well than under the current system; they currently can earn up to $300 per month without any loss of benefits, whereas under the system described above, benefits would begin to be reduced after earnings exceed $85. This situation could be avoided by establishing a higher level of initially disregarded earnings under SSDI/CDB than under SSI. For example, disregarding the first $300 of earnings of SSDI/CDB beneficiaries would have the effect of making the SSDI/CDB breakeven point $215 ($300 − $85) higher than the breakeven point for SSI for identical levels of benefits. It would, however, ensure that no current SSDI/CDB beneficiaries would be made worse off by returning to work.

Many variations are made possible by a two-phase approach to reducing work disincentives in the SSDI/CDB program. They could be created mainly by varying the rate at which benefits are reduced for earnings above the SSI breakeven level, and by varying the amount of the initial income disregard. At this time, it is impossible to determine which of these many variations would best balance the competing goals of minimizing work disincentives and controlling program costs. However, any of these variations would be a vast improvement over the present system. In any event, any revision of the current system should be carefully evaluated once in effect.

For persons receiving benefits from both the SSI and SSDI/CDB programs, all benefits should be combined for purposes of calculating the benefit reductions that occur as a result of accepting substantial work. What happens if the income disregard established for the SSDI/CDB program is greater than the income disregard established for the SSI program? If this occurs, the least difficult and least controversial approach would probably be to use the higher income disregard in the calculation of benefit reductions. (Obviously, the higher the income disregard, the smaller the reduction in benefits.)

Taxes The preceding discussion did not account for the fact that Social Security and income taxes must be paid on earnings, but not on SSI, Medicaid, or Medicare benefits, and only on a limited basis on SSDI/CDB benefits. Taxes cause a reduction in net income for SSDI/CDB and SSI beneficiaries who return to work beyond the reduction in the benefit payment itself. Sales and excise taxes and most property taxes, on the other hand, must usually be paid whether income is derived from disability benefits or from earnings and thus, in principle, have no effect on the incentive to work.

Social Security taxes complicate matters because almost all earnings are subject to a Social Security tax of about 7% (the rate is higher if the worker is self-employed). A person earning $350 per month nets only $325 after deducting Social Security taxes (and before paying any other taxes), although the $1 for $2 reduction in SSI benefits is calculated on the basis of earnings of $350. Thus, the worker's net increase in income (under Section 1619(a)) is not $217 (see Table 1, Chapter 5) but $192 per month, a difference that could considerably reduce the eagerness to work.

Table 1. Calculation of SSDI/CDB benefits assuming an $85 disregard, a $2 reduction in benefits for every $1 of earnings up to the federal breakeven amount, and a $3 reduction in benefits for every $4 in earnings above the federal breakeven amount for a single individual

		Case 1	Case 2
1.	Earnings	$ 400	$1,000
2.	Less $85 disregard equals	315	915
3.	If amount in Row 2 is less than the SSI breakeven amount, then deduction from benefits equals Row 2 X 0.5.	157.50	N/A
4.	If amount in Row 2 is over SSI breakeven amount, then subtract SSI breakeven amount ($735) from Row 1.	N/A	265
5.	Row 4 x .75 equals benefit reduction for SSDI/CDB benefits above the SSI benefit level		198.75
6.	SSDI/CDB benefit	1,000	1,000
7.	Benefit is reduced by amount in Row 3 if earnings are less than SSI breakeven amount. If greater, reduction equals amount in Row 5 + SSI benefit	157.50	523.75
8.	Equals benefits after employment (Row 6 − Row 7)	842.50	476.25
9.	Total income (Row 8 + Row 1)	1,242.50	1,476.25
10.	Increase in income after employment (Row 9 − Row 6)	242.50	476.25

One can argue that the present treatment is appropriate on the grounds that Social Security taxes directly benefit the wage earner because they provide the basis for the worker's retirement benefits and disability benefits if needed. Unfortunately, most beneficiaries will probably perceive these taxes as a work disincentive. One option for substantially reducing this work disincentive would be to calculate the reduction in benefits on the basis of income after payment of Social Security taxes. If benefits were reduced by $1 for every $2 of earnings, then persons whose earnings are below the breakeven points would have their net income reduced by only about one-half of the Social Security taxes they pay. Under present rules, an SSI beneficiary earning $350 per month and paying 7% in Social Security taxes (actually, the current Social Security tax is 7.05% and is scheduled to rise) would have his or her SSI benefits reduced by $132.50. If earnings after Social Security taxes were used as a basis for calculating benefits, the reduction would be $120.25. The work disincentives resulting from Social Security taxes are obviously higher for persons who are self-employed and will increase as Social Security taxes rise in the future.

It is more complicated to reduce the work disincentives caused by payment of federal, state, and local income taxes. The best solution would be to subject all SSI and SSDI/CDB benefits, and any other income support payments, to income taxation so that people could not avoid tax liability by choosing to receive public income support instead of employment earnings. This approach is not as draconian as it sounds. Many people receiving SSI or SSDI/CDB do not have income sufficient to incur federal income tax liability. In the case of beneficiaries whose total income is sufficient to incur federal income tax liability, there is little justification for exempting income from public support programs from taxation. It is not equitable to permit people with income from public support programs to incur lower tax liability than people with the same gross income who receive their income from employment (or interest or dividends).

A basic argument against taxing Social Security benefits is that, under the existing system, workers incur income tax liability on the earnings that are used to pay Social Security taxes. Thus, taxing Social Security benefits would cause double taxation: once when the tax is paid, and once when retirement or disability benefits are received. The easiest solution to this problem would be to forego taxation of income paid as Social Security taxes. This would be consistent with the treatment of many forms of deferred income retirement plans (e.g., I.R.A. and Keogh accounts). A second possibility, and one that is now used by the Internal Revenue Service for many types of retirement and disability benefits, is to subject Social Security benefits to taxation only after the total benefits paid exceed the amount of the initial taxes paid in. Federal civil service retirement benefits are taxed on this basis. Another reasonable solution is to tax only half of the SSDI/CDB benefits on the grounds that half of the premiums were derived from the matching contributions of employers who paid no income taxes on these matching contributions. The federal income tax has recently adopted a variant of this approach. Currently, Social Security beneficiaries are taxed on one-half of their benefits if their income exceeds $25,000 per year.

One can also argue that SSDI/CDB benefits received for disability are fundamentally different from those received for retirement. Social Security taxes to support retirement are paid into a trust fund, and it is anticipated that there will be a rough correspondence between the amount people pay in and the benefits that they eventually receive. Thus, taxes for retirement are similar to savings. In contrast, taxes to support disability benefits are separately levied and are more similar to insurance premiums (i.e., a payment for protection from a disastrous event) rather than savings. Given these considerations, one can argue that disability benefits should be subject to full taxation regardless of how retirement benefits are treated. Note that the potential problem of double taxation applies only to Social Security benefits, not SSI benefits. The authors believe the optimal solution to be full taxation of all income support benefits. However, given current practices regarding IRA and Keogh accounts, and treatment of other forms of employer fringe benefits, the authors also believe that taxes paid into the Social Security program should be exempt from income taxation.

Child Care Beneficiaries who must pay for child care if they return to work have a major work disincentive. One option to deal with this would be to disregard payments for child care, that is, subtract these payments from earnings when calculating benefits under both the SSI and SSDI/CDB programs as earnings rise. Of course, this approach assumes that the SSDI/CDB program adopts a system of reducing benefits as earnings rise. As the SSDI/CDB program is currently operated, child care expenditures could only be disregarded in the determination of whether the beneficiary is engaged in substantial gainful activity. A limit of $50 to $100 per month in child care payments could be established for the child care disregard. Of course, it must also be stipulated that any amount disregarded could not be used as a tax deduction.

Normal Work Expenses One reasonable option for reducing work disincentives would be to disregard normal work-related expenses (i.e., consider only earnings net of these expenses) when calculating benefits, up to some reasonable limit (perhaps 10% of earnings). At present, only extraordinary impairment-related work expenses are disregarded. Because this is likely to be administratively troublesome, another option would be to increase the amount of earnings that are disregarded when determining benefits (currently $65) to serve as a rough approximation of the costs of normal work-related expenses.

Health Care Many persons with severe handicaps are unable to obtain health insurance if they lose their Medicaid or Medicare entitlement. Two options for consideration follow.

1. The special extended Medicaid benefits paid to SSI beneficiaries under Section 1619(b) of the Social Security Act could be made a permanent part of the Medicaid program.

2. Lifetime eligibility for Medicaid or Medicare could be provided to beneficiaries with disabilities who qualify for benefits under these programs, even if they return to work and cash benefits are terminated (unless there is medical recovery or an error in the original disability determination). At present, Medicare benefits are provided only for 3 years after cash benefits cease.

To be most effective, these eligibility rights should have the following features. First, they should be available only if the beneficiary is unable to obtain comparable private health insurance. Second, they should not be subject to any income limitations. In Chapter 5, it was noted that the special Medicaid benefits under Section 1619(b) are subject to some income limitations. Third, beneficiaries who obtain private coverage and give up their Medicaid or Medicare coverage, but who subsequently lose their private health benefits, should be entitled to renewed Medicaid or Medicare benefits. This unpredictable loss of health care benefits must be a common occurrence among former beneficiaries who lose or change jobs. At present, beneficiaries who return to work and give up their entitlement to Medicaid because their earnings are too high to qualify them for Section 1619(b) coverage have no guarantee that they can reestablish eligibility for Medicaid benefits if their earnings decline. In fact, because they must generally show that they are incapable of working at an SGA level, it is likely that most of these beneficiaries will not be able to reestablish entitlement to health care benefits.

It is important to note that there is no reason to pay Medicaid or Medicare health care benefits for employed persons solely out of tax dollars. Employers who deny medical benefits to employees with disabilities could reasonably be required to pay an amount into the Medicare Trust Fund, or into a special Medicaid Trust Fund, equal to the average amount that they spend on the employees for whom they provide health insurance. In addition, persons receiving benefits from these programs could be reasonably required to make a contribution to the costs of running these programs over and above their regular Medicare tax. In effect, these contributions would be in lieu of the insurance premium that they would otherwise pay, and could vary depending on their income. Any health insurance contributions above the normal Medicare tax paid by the employer on behalf of these beneficiaries with disabilities could be used to reduce the beneficiary's liability to contribute to these programs.

Objective 4   Ensure that beneficiaries with disabilities who accept gainful employment and have earnings that terminate their income support or medical benefits will be reentitled to SSDI/CDB, SSI, Medicare, or Medicaid benefits if they lose their jobs for reasons other than voluntarily quitting, even if the subsequent job loss does not take place for many years. Many persons with severe disabilities require extensive assistance and sometimes a substantial period of time in order to locate a suitable job. Given the possibilities of firms having to cut back or go out of business due to variations in the demand for their products, or of jobs becoming obsolete because of technical progress, some persons with disabilities will inevitably lose their jobs at a later date.

Because the difficulties that persons with severe disabilities have in obtaining suitable work usually continue to exist in case of subsequent job loss, the only way to eliminate the work disincentives stemming from the ensured payment of public benefits would be to grant SSI, SSDI, Medicaid, and Medicare beneficiaries with disabilities who return to work lifelong reentitlement rights to these programs in case of job loss. In effect, having once made the determination that these beneficiaries face lifelong impediments to locating and retaining work, these public programs would guarantee that beneficiaries will quickly become reentitled to benefits without undergoing repeated formal determinations of their disability status. Such a reentitlement provision should encourage beneficiaries to accept jobs that are known to be insecure or temporary because

benefits would automatically resume when the work ceased. In the case of persons receiving Medicare or Medicaid, lifelong entitlement is necessary not only to ensure beneficiaries of continued medical protection, but also to ensure that they are not made financially worse off by accepting employment (Objective 2).

Circumstances under which these lifelong reentitlement rights might be withdrawn include medical recovery in the sense of a demonstrable improvement in mental or physical capabilities, an error in the initial disability determination, entitlement by a beneficiary to retirement benefits (which should trigger a change in the benefit package), job termination without good cause, or the failure of the beneficiary to make a good faith effort to become employed. This option would eliminate the current inequity where a temporary rise in income could cause a person subject to Section 1619(a) or 1619(b) to permanently lose his or her entitlement to these benefits.

If lifetime eligibility appears excessive, one might adopt a less comprehensive measure, such as providing for reentitlement for 5 years instead of the current 15 months after the trial work period. There are, of course, other ways of reducing the drastic and capricious effects of a temporary increase in income (e.g., specifying that a cash benefit must be lacking for 6 months before entitlement to benefits is terminated instead of the current 1 month.)

Objective 5   Prevent persons with serious handicaps from sinking into dependency. The objective should be to reach persons with handicaps early (i.e., before they fall into the habits and attitudes of dependency). There are a number of options that might be considered.

Persons with handicaps should not be required to give up work entirely before becoming eligible for benefits. If: (a) they are severely handicapped, (b) their income is such that they would be eligible for income support benefits if they were program beneficiaries (e.g., if their earnings were below the break-even point under Section 1619a), and (c) they are otherwise eligible (i.e., have sufficient quarters of coverage or meet the asset test), then they should be provided with the same

Social Security or SSI benefits that they would receive if they had become beneficiaries of these programs before returning to work. Similarly, if employed persons with handicaps are unable to obtain health care coverage, then Medicaid or Medicare coverage should be granted regardless of the level of earnings if they meet the asset test for Medicaid, or the quarters of coverage test for Medicare. This approach assumes that provisions are made to reduce SSDI/CDB benefits as earnings rise, and to require some payment for medical benefits by the employers of these beneficiaries and the beneficiaries themselves if their earnings are sufficiently high.

Another option that merits consideration is to disregard extraordinary impairment-related work expenses for applicants to SSI, as is done for SSDI/CDB applicants. At present, these expenses are disregarded when calculating the benefits for SSI beneficiaries and for both applicants and beneficiaries under SSDI/CDB.

Applicants for SSDI/CDB and SSI benefits might also be allowed to disregard some part of normal work expense from their earnings in order to be consistent with the option given under Objective 2.

Objective 6 Set more realistic monetary values for substantial gainful activity (SGA) and redefine the trial work period. If the preceding options were adopted, the breakeven points for the SSI and SSDI/CDB programs would effectively become the SGA levels, and a trial work period would no longer be used. Until that time, however, it is unrealistic to define SGA by a wage that is only slightly more than half of what would be earned by a full-time worker at the federal minimum wage. Raising the SGA earnings level to at least the amount that would be earned at the minimum wage (i.e., about $580 per month) would be a more realistic approach. Another, and probably preferable, approach would be to use the same SGA level for all beneficiaries with disabilities that is used for recipients of SSDI/CDB who are blind. This SGA level for persons who are blind in 1985 is $610, and it is adjusted annually for changes in the cost of living. If the SGA amount were raised, it

should be accompanied by some provision to reduce benefits for persons on SSDI/CDB if earnings exceed a given amount. At present, they are allowed to keep all earnings below the SGA level.

Counting any month in which a beneficiary earns $75 or more as part of the trial work period is hardly realisitic because this amount represents less than $.50 an hour for a full-time worker. Many sheltered workshop employees and even some work activity center employees exceed this level of earnings, despite the fact that they are far from ready for a regular job. There is, in fact, little reason to count a month as part of the trial work period unless the beneficiary has earnings at the SGA level, or could have made this amount.

Objective 7 Expand the service system so that long-term vocational services are available to persons with severe handicaps who require these services. The authors predict the emergence of a wide range of diversified employment programs in each state that will reflect each state's industrial and agricultural base. There are already models in which crews of workers with developmental disabilities are transported to jobs under the supervision of non-handicapped workers, or where workers with severe handicaps are placed on jobs in private firms under a supervisor who is trained to work with handicapped persons (the enclave model). Although many other models could be described, and are described elsewhere in this text, the essential point is that a flexible source of financing is needed to support these various employment activities. In the short run, these work programs may receive some support from federal research and demonstration funds. However, a more stable long-term source of funding is needed. At least part of the assistance for long term supported employment should come from the federal government. This would stimulate state and local governments to undertake the hard task of establishing these services.

In states that fear the loss of other federal funds (e.g., funding for day care under Medicaid), it would also offset the disincentives to place persons with severe disabilities in supported work. There are several ways of providing the needed federal support. First, Congress could permit Medicaid funds under the Medicaid ICF/MR and Home and Community-Based Waivers Program to be used to provide long-term vocational services, including supported employment in workshops or in regular worksites. Doing so would remove a major disincentive for states to provide these services. However, there are three disadvantages to this option. First, it takes the Medicaid program further away from its primary mission of financing medical care. Second, Medicaid is a program designed to serve people in poverty, whereas a major objective of funding services to assist people with disabilities to become employed is to move them out of poverty. Under present Medicaid rules, needed services could be terminated if beneficiaries began to earn wages sufficient to enable them to escape poverty. However, adopting the options described earlier regarding Medicaid would largely resolve this problem by ensuring continuing Medicaid coverage. Third, the Medicaid program only funds services for persons in ICFs/MR, or those who are at risk for institutionalization if it were not for services funded by the Home and Community- Based Waivers program. Long-term vocational services, however, are needed by a much broader spectrum of persons with severe handicaps.

Another way to fund these services would be through the federal-state vocational rehabilitation (VR) program. Not only is the VR program established for the express purpose of assisting people with disabilities to work, but Congress has also mandated that priority be given to serving individuals with the most severe handicaps. One problem with using the VR program is that its counselors and administrators would probably be inclined to provide services to the traditional VR clientele before serving the more severely handicapped clients who require long-term support. Another problem is that VR resources are already inadequate to serve all the traditional VR clientele.

If the VR program is chosen as a mechanism for funding long-term vocational support, then in order to ensure that these services are made available to persons with severe handicaps, it would probably be desirable to designate a given amount of funds to be used for long-term supported work. One approach would be to expend these funds only on clients for whom the traditional rehabilitation closure after 60 days in employment is not feasible. Obviously, there should be separate reporting and a rigorous evaluation of such a program. Such a program should probably be instituted as an add-on to the existing VR program and should not divert funds from the traditional clientele.

A third approach would be to utilize generic programs, such as those supported by the Administration for Developmental Disabilities and the National Institute of Mental Health. This approach's advantages are that it would target populations most in need of this type of support and would place responsibility for these services in agencies that have specialized understanding of the needs of persons with severe disabilities. One disadvantage of this approach is that these programs would not serve all persons with severe handicaps who need long-term vocational support.

A fourth approach would be to modify the program by which the Social Security Administration (SSA) reimburses vocational rehabilitation agencies or, in some cases, contractual agencies or individuals, for rehabilitating SSI and SSDI/CDB beneficiaries. Under the provisions of the Omnibus Budget Reconciliation Act of 1981, reimbursement is made only if the beneficiary is sustained in employment paying SGA level–wages for a continuous period of 9 months. Unfortunately, these reimbursement criteria do not fully correspond to the work capacities and service needs of some beneficiaries in these programs. Not all beneficiaries will be able to earn at an SGA level after rehabilitation, and some will require ongoing long-term services. Consideration should be given to two changes in the program: (a) permit a waiver of the requirement that beneficiaries must earn at the SGA level before reimbursement for vocational rehabilitation services will be made by Social Security in cases where beneficiaries are determined to be working at the highest vocational capacity of which they are capable; and (b) provide ongoing long-term reimbursement in cases where long-term vocational services are needed to assist SSI and SSDI/CDB beneficiaries to continue working (i.e., cases for which the traditional vocational rehabilitation closure is not feasible). In these cases, vocational services should be reimbursed not only if they enable beneficiaries to return to work, but also if they assist beneficiaries to maintain and even enhance their earning capacity over time.

A fifth approach would be to make use of two or more of the preceding options. Such a broad-based approach would not be duplicative because clients would not receive the same services from more than one agency at any point in time. A case could be made that a pluralistic approach would, in the aggregate, be less costly and more effective than placing all of the support for long-term services in a single agency or program. Such an approach would add an element of competition among the agencies, perhaps stimulating them to be more innovative, and would encourage different approaches to developing employment opportunities.

A final possibility for funding long term vocational services would be to develop a long-term care block grant for persons with mental retardation and developmental disabilities that would permit states to use the funds to purchase vocational services. Presumably, such a block grant would be primarily constructed from funds currently being used to support the ICF/MR and the Home and Community-Based Waiver programs. Many state governments would favor this approach because of the flexibility it would afford them, particularly if there were assurances that a reasonable inflation allowance would be built into the block grant.

One problem with this option is that long-term vocational services are needed by many disabled persons who are not developmentally disabled. One possibility would be to establish several different block grants to support long-term care services, each one serving a different group. Another possibility would be to establish a single block grant that extended eligibility to all persons with severe disabilities, not just those who are developmentally disabled.

Objective 8 *Develop methods of subsidizing employers who employ people with severe disabilities.* The reasons for providing a subsidy to employers who employ individuals with very severe disabilities or multiple handicaps are to pay for the additional costs incurred by the employer, and/or to subsidize the wages of the workers unable to achieve normal productivity. One approach would be to specify conditions under which employers could continue to earn a tax credit under the Targeted Jobs Tax Credit program for employees with severe handicaps beyond the current 2-year limitation. In effect, doing so would lower the cost of hiring these employees. It may not involve a major net cost to the government because, under the current program, some workers with disabilities may change employers after a period of time, and so may already be causing tax credits to be paid for a period longer than 2 years. In addition, persons with disabilities who are employed as a result of this program will pay taxes and receive less public income support.

Another approach to subsidizing employers would be to utilize whatever program(s) is established not only to provide long-term vocational support to persons with severe handicaps (Objective 7) but also to pay a subsidy to employers when appropriate. This latter approach is more target-efficient than the Targeted Jobs Tax Credit program because it would limit this type of support to those workers with severe disabilities who, in the judgment of vocational counselors, require it in order to be employed. It is worth noting that such a program might be almost self-financing if the subsidy paid to the employer (say about one-half of wages) is roughly equal to the reduction in SSI benefits, which are reduced by $1 for each $2 of earnings after the $85 disregard. An advantage of this second approach is that it could provide assistance to employers who do not benefit from the Targeted Jobs Tax

Credit program (i.e., nonprofit firms and public agencies).

It would be desirable, but difficult, to devise a system that would calibrate the level of tax credit or wage subsidy and the severity of the functional limitations of the employees that benefit from these provisions.

IMPLEMENTATION

Adoption of the foregoing or similar options will not be as difficult as may initially appear. Many programs already exist to serve persons with disabilities. Primarily, what is needed is reorientation of the system toward work, and better coordination among existing programs. The major current gap is in the lack of funds to support long-term vocational services.

Nor are these options a major departure from current policy. Many of the options that the authors have offered for consideration are basically logical extensions of the 1980 Social Security Disability Amendments. For example, the authors suggest making Sections 1619(a) and 1619(b) permanent and creating a similar program for SSDI/CDB. Granting lifetime eligibility for the income transfer and health financing programs is basically an extension of the 15-month reentitlement period after the trial work period. Of equal importance is the fact that all of the authors' proposals to reduce work disincentives already exist in the SSI program for persons who are blind. Basically, the authors are suggesting that the SSI policies already adopted for persons who are blind be extended to all persons with severe handicaps. Persons who are blind are not subject to the SGA test of income adequacy at application for SSI benefits, only to an asset test (Code of Federal Regulations, 416.983). They are not subject to a 9-month trial work period or to a reentitlement period of 15 months because they are not subject to redetermination of their work capacity even though their earnings exceed the SGA level for an indefinite period of time. They are only subject to the reduction of their benefits up to the federal breakeven point on a $1 for $2 of earnings basis. Whenever earnings fall below the break-even point, SSI benefits are automatically restored.

Three further points should be made. First, although rigorous benefit-cost studies have not been conducted, it seems that, in some instances, the costs of providing oversight and other services needed to maintain people with severe disabilities in gainful employment will exceed the wages they earn. This obviously raises the question of whether the provision of services is worthwhile in these cases. One can always argue, of course, that there are non-monetary benefits to employment that make it worthwhile. However, it must be emphasized that the relevant benefit-cost comparison is not between the earnings and costs of a single employment program, but rather between the earnings and costs of an employment program and the alternative benefits and costs that would be incurred if the employment program did not exist. The alternative is likely to include either institutionalization or day care, either of which usually involves higher costs than the employment program, as well as minimal benefits. In conducting benefit-cost studies, it is essential to compare the costs of the employment program and all of its benefits, where benefits include not only client earnings but also the savings in the costs of the alternative forms of care (e.g., benefits might equal earnings plus the costs saved by averting institutionalization).

Second, in principle, implementation of the foregoing options should reduce the costs that society incurs as a result of disability. Unfortunately, the data are not available to prove this assertion. And there are at least two reasons why legislators and program administrators may be concerned by these new approaches. First, these options represent a major reorientation in program philosophies and activities, with uncertain effects on the number of people served or the services received. In addition, some persons with disabilities not now eligible for income support or health care benefits may become eligible under these options, with resulting increases in program costs.

However, these options would assist people who are currently totally dependent on income support and health care programs to become paritally or totally independent, thus reducing costs. Moreover, even though some persons will become eligible for Medicaid or Medicare who would not otherwise have done so, this effect should not be construed as a net social cost because someone—the government, insurance companies, private employers, or the person with disabilities—must bear the cost of illness, either by paying for medical care, or suffering unnecessary morbidity or mortality. In the long run, assisting persons with handicaps to achieve partial or total independence is a more humane and cost-effective way of containing the costs of the income support and health care programs than by placing restrictions on eligibility.

Third, creating a system a services that is fully effective takes time. Professionals must gain expertise in techniques that help persons with severe disabilities to obtain and maintain work. An adequate supply of suitably staffed work programs will need to be developed. There will be a substantial period of trial-and-error before the most effective combination of work programs and community support is discovered, particularly because there is still a great deal to learn about the most effective ways of providing work opportunities. And most important, changing public and professional attitudes about the employability of persons with severe mental retardation and developmental disabilities will be a lengthy process.

ROLE OF THE FEDERAL GOVERNMENT

Although the role of the federal government in relation to state and local governments in the system of services has not been fully agreed on, it is clear that the federal government will have a major influence on the way the system of services evolves.

Funding

Although there is great resistance to federal funding of new programs, a large percentage of the funds used to support the service system comes from the federal government, particu-larly for the income support and health care programs. Because of this factor and the inevitable interaction among programs, the rules and regulations imposed by the federal government have a dominating and often disturbing effect on the way states expend their resources. As examples, consider the following:

> Medicaid regulations have caused states to allocate a large proportion of their funds to upgrade the physical plants of large institutions, rather than developing small community-based residences.
>
> Because SSI is often used to pay the rent of persons with disabilities in board and care homes, states place little emphasis on providing vocational services to residents of these homes (Dittmar, Smith, Bell, Jones, & Manzanares, 1983); employment would jeopardize their eligibility for SSI.
>
> When VR agencies do not accept persons with severe disabilities, these persons are often placed in an ICF/MR with a day program, rather than a supported work program, in order to capture federal matching funds.

There are three ways to avoid these distorting effects of federal funding: (a) eliminate federal funding, (b) enact new programs to fill the gaps in federal programs, or (c) ease the restrictions on the use of federal funds. The last of these options is likely to be the most viable one at present. Some of the foregoing alterations proposed for the network of services for persons with handicaps would remove many of the principal distorting effects of federal funding. Other solutions might take the form of more extensive use of block grants.

Research and Demonstrations

The federal government is generally in a better position than state or local governments to fund high quality and systematic research and demonstration projects for the employment of people with severe mental retardation and developmental disabilities. It is usually more efficient to fund a few large and well-crafted research and demonstration projects than to fund numerous small and possibly duplicative state or local government projects. Moreover, federal funding of demonstration projects spreads out the initial risks of trying out new methods of providing employment services. Finally, the federal government is in a strong position to compare and contrast different approaches to employing people with disabilities throughout the country.

The authors believe that this is an opportune time to increase federal research efforts in the area of employment of Americans with the most severe disabilities.

Data

The federal government is also the logical locus for developing and maintaining a consolidated national data base that indicates how many people with severe disabilities are being helped to obtain jobs, the characteristics of these individuals, the types of jobs they obtain, their wages, and other relevant information. This information is needed to chart progress toward achieving national goals and to help identify which states, agencies, and types of services are most effective.

Such a data base does not currently exist, but consideration should be given to its creation. If created, the focus should clearly be on a broad range of disabilities and not be limited to persons with developmental disabilities.

Information Dissemination

Research and evaluation studies, statistics, or demonstration projects serve little purpose unless their results are carefully evaluated and widely disseminated. In general, the federal government is the logical point at which to undertake this information exchange. An effective information exchange would have the following characteristics.

1. It would make available at reasonable price copies of reports on research and demonstration projects and on collected data.
2. It would provide information promptly. Reports on data collection or research and demonstration projects should be available within a few months after the data are collected or the projects are completed, not 1 or 2 years later, or even longer as is often the case. In the fast-changing field of employment, the failure to exchange information promptly causes much of its value to be lost.
3. Short summaries of completed research and demonstration projects and of collected data should be prepared and disseminated though newsletters and other means. Comprehensive summaries of research should be prepared at least annually and possibly semiannually. These activities would assist users of this information to ascertain significant developments without being inundated by thick reports.
4. Information from data systems would be carefully evaluated, and significant trends and findings clearly communicated. One of the most effective ways to assist a state to upgrade its employment programs is to indicate the effectiveness of the methods used by other states in employing persons with severe mental retardation and other developmental disabilities.

REFERENCES

Code of Federal Regulations, Title 20, Chapter 3, Section 416.983.

Dittmar, N. D., Smith, G. P., Bell, J. C., Jones, C. B. C., & Manzanares, D. L. (1983). *Board and care for elderly and mentally disabled populations: A survey of seven states*. Denver, University of Denver, Denver Research Institute.

∞ Section IV ∞

NEW CONCEPTS AND DESIGNS IN HABILITATION

THE PATHWAYS MODEL INTRODUCED IN CHAPTER 7 OF SECTION IV IS THE CORNERSTONE OF THIS book. Its focus is on outcome, the degree of economic self-sufficiency realized through employment, and through its principle of simultaneous choice, the model represents the decision process and opportunities available to the adult with developmental disabilities.

This model serves as a guiding concept to the options presented in the chapters of Section IV. The educational transition is a key element in the movement of the student into the adult world. In Chapter 8, the transition process and a three-stage model are presented by Wehman, Kregel, Barcus, and Schalock. This model presents a conceptual framework for viewing the complicated process of leaving school and entering the world of work. For many developmentally disabled individuals, this is a time of exit from a highly structured environment to one that is much less structured. To facilitate this transition, the authors suggest the development of a functional curriculum and an integrated educational setting with community-based training opportunities. They present strategies to meet these goals.

A somewhat newer concept—supported employment—is presented in Chapter 9 by Bellamy, Rhodes, and Albin. Supported employment, designed for more severely disabled individuals who require ongoing supports in order to maintain employment, attempts to provide a role for them in the employment world. Four supported employment alternatives, each with a somewhat different approach to supported employment, are presented by Mank, Rhodes, and Bellamy in Chapter 10. The authors note that there is no one single design of supported employment, but that all programs that provide ongoing support in a normalized industrialized setting clearly fit the definition of supported employment as presented. These programs are designed to meet the needs of severely developmentally disabled adults by providing vocational options that combine employment outcomes with community integration and ongoing employment support.

A second approach to supported employment is presented by Bergeron, Perschbacher-Melia, and Kiernan in Chapter 11. The approach presented has two variants, one where the supports are provided externally to the workplace and the other where extensive crew designs are used as severely developmentally disabled individuals move into industrial settings. Both Chapters 10 and 11 acknowledge that the nature of the supports offered in any supported employment design varies both quantitatively and structurally. However, the environment within which supported employment occurs should be based in the normal work setting.

Movement into independent employment reflects the more traditional time-limited programs offered through vocational rehabilitation. In Chapter 12, Whitehead and Marrone review many of the time-limited strategies offered by vocational rehabilitation and explore the opportunities for expanding time-limited training into the normal work setting. In contrast to the previous chapters, Chapter 12 presents a design in which ultimately all support services are eliminated and the individual is expected to maintain employment in an independent fashion. As is noted by Lynch, Ditty, Scott, and Smith in Chapter 13, the use of time-limited training procedures must accommodate to the needs of industry. This chapter reviews some of the changes that have occurred in industry over the past 10 years. These changes imply the need to modify the approaches used to help developmentally disabled individuals gain access to positions in the normal work setting. Their discussion notes the need for change within the rehabilitation world if the partnership between rehabilitation and industry is to be viable. In Chapter 14, Shestakofsky, Van Gelder, and Kiernan review two specific time-limited training strategies: a statewide model and one offered within a nonprofit health care setting. Both designs have the potential for replication and present strategies for training where developmentally disabled adults will eventually be placed in employment with minimal supports offered.

There are some severely developmentally disabled adults who will not enter employment. Chapter 15 presents a brief discussion of the characteristics of those individuals for whom employment is not a viable goal. Stark, Kiernan, Goldsbury, and McGee caution that there is a need to reevaluate the employment potential of such persons, particularly in view of future advances in training technologies and expanded employment opportunities.

∞ Chapter 7 ∞

Comprehensive Design for the Future

William E. Kiernan and Jack A. Stark

WORK IS VIEWED AS THE MEASURE OF ONE'S worth to society. Many people view those who choose not to work or are unable to work as less desirable socially. From a psychological perspective, being able to contribute to the good of others, and thus to be valued by them, is a significant factor in the stable development of one's perception of self-worth. Conversely, to be viewed as a failure, a noncontributor, or a liability to the community leads to a reduced sense of self-worth (Braunstein, 1977; Obermann, 1965). As a result of societal perceptions and each individual's need to belong, the concept of work has taken on a greater meaning in our culture. To be denied the opportunity to work is to be denied the chance to belong and develop a sense of self in a positive and constructive fashion.

There are limited opportunities for the adult with developmental disabilities to enter employment. Many developmentally disabled adults are not considered as part of the labor force, whereas others are frequently underemployed (see Chapter 3). In part, this employment status reflects the perceptions of employers, parents, and the disabled individuals themselves of their role in the world of work.

Frequently, because employers lack knowledge about the capacities of the adult with developmental disabilities, they have only limited expectations about the abilities of the disabled individuals in the workplace. Because of these low expectations, developmentally disabled adults have little, if any, access to jobs, and there is a tendency for them to be underemployed. Therefore it is essential that the employer learn about the abilities and capacities of the developmentally disabled individual as a worker.

Parents of developmentally disabled young adults are concerned about their children's security and stability and the lack of acceptance of their son or daughter in the workplace. Anxiety about the lack of security in the workplace as compared to the relative security of Social Security income and health care programs or the protective environment of the sheltered workshop limits the enthusiasm and support of parents as their child moves toward competitive employment. For parents, the desire to choose what would appear to be long-term security in lieu of a more normalizing setting is strong.

Having experienced limited success in the educational process, increased social isolation as their peers have matured and a move from the highly structured environment of the school, young adults with developmental disabilites are left with a sense of apprehension and bewilderment about their role in the adult world. The lack of knowledge about future options and the transition into the incompletely

The authors would like to thank G. Thomas Bellamy for his assistance in developing this conceptual model.

103

defined world of adult services contributes to their concerns about the future.

For employers, parents, and disabled adults, there is a need to increase awareness of options that should, could, and ought to be available as the special needs student makes the transition into the world of work. For the employer and the parent, this increased awareness may invoke both an educational process and a change in attitudes. Employers need to be willing to open up employment opportunities and to give greater access to jobs while encouraging mobility within the workplace to those developmentally disabled workers who are able to advance. Parents need to encourage the independence of their children and their movement toward competitive employment, thereby foregoing the secure but restrictive environments of the sheltered workshop. Critical to success of the transition process is the support of the family.

Likewise, the adult with developmental disabilities needs information about the future and should play a defined, active role in the decision-making process. In the school years, critical life course decisions are frequently made with little or no input from the individual for whom the decision is most important, the student with developmental disabilities. The decision process regarding major life courses starts early and requires a great deal of involvement by many persons, including the disabled individual, in exploring options, discussing risks, and making choices. The process does not begin at the time of graduation nor at the time of transition, but continues throughout the educational process and beyond.

The acknowledgement that individuals have a right to choose for themselves is an integral component of any decision-making process. However, along with this right comes the responsibility of choice. Critical to the success of any decision-making process is an understanding of the options available. Information about such options must be presented in a fashion compatible with the social and cognitive capacities of the individual. Once the options are understood, the individual must be willing to accept the responsibilities associated with any decision that is made.

It is the experience of participating in the decision-making process, understanding the options, and accepting the responsibility of the choice that helps the adult with developmental disabilities move from a dependent to an independent adult status. The opportunity to take risks and learn through experience is frequently denied as the transition into adult services occurs. However, it is just this process of learning through experience that will assist the student in moving from life at school to the school of life in a positive and constructive fashion.

A CONCEPTUAL VIEW

From an economic and psychological perspective, the world of work is significant for both the individual and society. The work role is central to personal identity and the achievement of economic self-sufficiency. In our society, work is viewed as the primary means of creating growth, as well as ensuring stability for all. There is a complex preparatory process directed at providing the individual with the skills and maturity to enter the employment system. Formal preparation in school must be directed at helping the student achieve viable outcomes as an adult, whereas society must provide a means through which the individual can enter as a worker.

A series of steps occur as individuals move from school to employment. These steps are not always predictable, but they seem to occur in some sequence. It is thus necessary and appropriate to develop a conceptual design what reflects that process.

A number of factors must be considered in the development of a conceptual design or model. Regardless of the process a model portrays, it must contain the following attributes. The model must be:

Sufficiently broad so that the outcomes presented within the model reflect those outcomes sought by the majority of persons for whom the model was designed

Sufficiently flexible so that individual variations in response may be accommodated through the range of outcomes offered by the model

Sufficiently specific so that the model is able to reflect what is, what could be, or what has happened as the individual moves toward an outcome

Able to accommodate a variability in skills, capacity, and degree of motivation brought into the process by each individual who enters it

A true and accurate representation of the process that it is designed to reflect

The Pathways to Employment for Adults with Developmental Disabilities Model (see Figure 1) presents a conceptual framework of the role that adults with developmental disabilities play in the decision-making process and the outcomes that may be achieved as a result of that process. It deviates substantially from the flow-through design of the more traditional vocational rehabilitation model, as it places less emphasis on sequential training or service activities and more on simultaneous options, choices, or paths for the individual. However, it does incorporate some elements of the more traditional view of vocational training activities while presenting other options for those developmentally disabled adults who may not be able to benefit from a sequential rehabilitation process.

The Pathways Model presents a framework within which the individual may make choices. It does not focus solely on specific service options, but rather it looks at process and outcome. It is a person-driven design where the individual is faced with a number of choices, all of which lead to an outcome of enhancing the degree of economic self-sufficiency realized through employment. Such an outcome is measured not by individual job placements but rather by the effects of moving the individual into an employment status. Employment status is viewed as a series of jobs, acknowledging job turnover not always as failure but in many cases as a sign of occupational growth and

development. Thus, employment is made up of multiple jobs, each leading successively to a more desirable outcome or environment for that individual. The measure of effectiveness or success in such a design is not job placement or "26," as in the vocational rehabilitation system, but rather is a measure of earnings in relationship to the level of financial independence realized by the individual.

A key concept of the design is its focus on expansion of environments in which outcomes should and may occur. The model is concerned with more than the creation of specific jobs; it attempts to look at work environments and to see what potential exists for the developmentally disabled worker in the widest variety of industrial and community settings. The design encourages exploration and the establishment of new environments and new methods in which the developmentally disabled adult may attain and maintain or be maintained in employment; thus, to be an asset to society, rather than an economic liability.

ELEMENTS OF THE PATHWAYS MODEL

The Pathways Model's focus on the range of choices that should be available to adults as they move toward employment points out the need to expand the environments within which employment can occur. Although the model does not stipulate the type of employment sought, past research has shown that the industrial or real work setting is most conducive to increasing the productivity and thus expanding the degree of economic self-sufficiency realized by the individual with developmental disabilities (Horner & Bellamy, 1979; Lynch, Kiernan, & Stark, 1982; Wehman, 1981).

As in any model, there needs to be sufficient flexibility to accommodate variations in ability, age, maturity, and motivation of those individuals who enter the decision-making process. The Pathways Model is consistent with and continues the transition activity as the student moves from school to work (Will, 1984). In certain instances where the individual has sufficient skills, the move from a

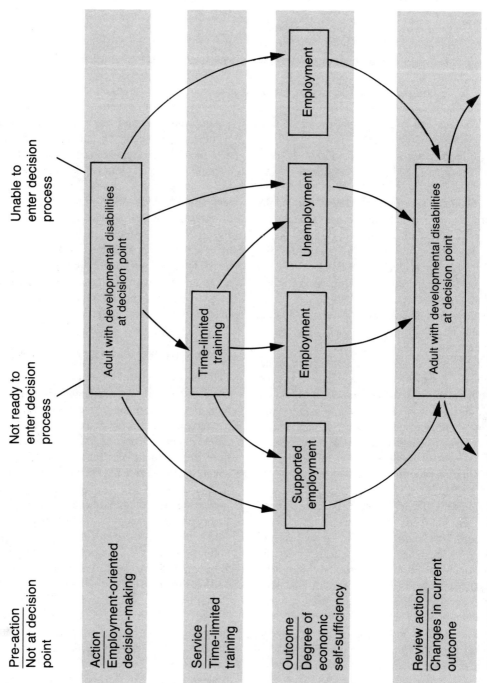

Figure 1. Pathways to employment for the adult with developmental disabilities. A habilitation model.

school-based program directly to an industrial-based employment setting is possible. Optimally, as schools expand training activities, fewer and fewer students will need additional vocational training services before entering employment. Currently, many students do not enter employment, but rather become unemployed or underemployed in sheltered employment. This employment status is due both to the training environment that the individual is in and the limited employment opportunities that are made available in the community.

The Pathways Model acknowledges that there are some students in academic settings who are not yet ready to enter the action or decision stage of the model. Because these individuals are too young or have not yet completed a training program, they have not yet reached the stage of making specific employment-related decisions (see Chapter 8).

In addition, some individuals are viewed as unable to enter the decision process because of the complexity or severity of their disability. However, past experiences have shown that, for many severely disabled individuals, the perception of their role or lack of role in employment may not be completely accurate. Programs now serving severely/profoundly mentally retarded individuals have demonstrated productivity and employment are in fact realistic goals for many developmentally disabled adults (Horner & Bellamy, 1979). Specific modifications and/or supports, however, may have to be provided at times to this group of workers. These supports, as is noted later, may be of an extended or even permanent nature for some developmentally disabled-adults (see Chapters 9, 10, and 11).

There remain those adults with developmental disabilities for whom entry into an employment-making decision process, in truth, is not a realistic or desired choice. Individuals with ongoing medical needs who are often considered as "medically fragile" are not able to move toward either employment or supportive employment. In addition, certain adults with developmental disabilities may not view employment as a desirable goal. Such factors as age, financial status, and individual expec-

tations may contribute to some people's reluctance to seek employment. Some cautions, however, must be exercised when looking at the choice made by these individuals because it may not be a fully informed or free one, but rather a forced choice. For instance, the economic and health disincentives to employment can drive a developmentally disabled adult to a nonemployment choice out of necessity, rather than desire. A further discussion of those developmentally disabled adults not entering the decision-making process can be found in Chapter 15 of this text.

Stages in the Model

In the Pathways Model, there are four stages in the process of making an employment-related decision: the action, service, outcome, and review stages.

In the action stage, the individual is about to make a decision. It is at this stage when attention must be paid to providing the individual with information about available options and the specific parameters of each option. As was noted earlier, it is imperative that these options be presented in a clear and detailed fashion so that they may be understood by the adult with developmental disabilities. The action stage leads either to a service stage or directly to the outcome stage.

When the individual makes a decision to obtain additional skill development before moving into the outcome stage, specific services may be sought and used. In this stage the individual usually has a general awareness of what he or she would like to do and an understanding that additional skills are necessary to attain this goal. The training or services offered should assist in the development of those skills that will lead to the outcome sought by the individual. Thus, to enter a training program focusing on knowledge of tools when, in fact, the individual is interested in working in a service area is inappropriate. Equally inappropriate would be entry into a program of work adjustment where the role models in the training environment have yet to establish acceptable work behaviors. Thus, a training environment in a sheltered work setting may have little value in assisting this individual in developing appropriate work skills and moving toward his or her desired outcome. Once the service or training is completed, movement into the outcome stage occurs.

Rather than present employment as the outcome, the Pathways Model defines outcome as the degree of economic self-sufficiency realized through employment. The outcome can be positive, as in the case of employment or supported employment, or negative, as in the case of unemployment. Whatever the outcome achieved, it must reflect the individual's informed consent and not what others think or feel he or she should do or what job happens to be available at the time. The pathways to the desired outcome are varied and diverse, reflecting the range of abilities, interests, and degree of motivation brought by the individual into the employment-related decision-making process. As is discussed later in this chapter, each activity leading to the outcome has different characteristics and qualities.

As in any dynamic model, there must be mechanisms to ensure that an individual can modify his or her current status—in this case, employment, supported employment, or unemployment—to achieve a more desirable outcome. In the review action stage, the individual has the opportunity to reexamine his or her decision and, when necessary, to modify that decision. Change need not be viewed as failure, but rather as a maturing process. Once this stage is completed, the individual returns to the employment-related decision or action stage. At this point, the entire process is repeated, and the individual again has access to services leading to outcomes or goes directly to an outcome.

The stages of the Pathway Model are intended to represent those stages through which all individuals go as they progress toward increased levels of economic self-sufficiency. For some persons, the level of complexity in the decision stage may be greater than for others; however, the process and stages are the same. Thus, the Pathways Model reflects the normal growth and development model used by all developmentally disabled adults as vocational decisions are made.

Components within the Model

Having looked at the stages of the Pathways Model, a closer look at its components may elucidate some of its underlying concepts. Individual choice and simultaneous options at the employment-related decision point make the model a person-driven design.

Time-Limited Training The more traditional vocational rehabilitation design is incorporated into the Pathways Model. The service stage reflects the movement of the individual through a time-limited training program that will lead to either employment or supported employment or to unemployment for those not completing the process. Time-limited training may take many forms, ranging from specific skill training, to work or personal adjustment training, to on-the-job training. More recently, supportive work programs utilizing the natural work environment, peer supports, and graduated expectations have been used to provide training in the natural work setting (see Chapter 14). The trend is to provide the service in the natural work setting as often as possible. The emphasis of time-limited training services is on specific and discrete supports that are discontinued as the individual moves toward the goal of increased economic self-sufficiency.

On completion of the time-limited training stage, the adult with developmental disabilities moves toward one of three outcome options: employment, supported employment, or unemployment. However, as can be seen in the design, some individuals bypass the service stage and go directly from their academic courses into employment or supported employment. For those making a job change, direct entry into either employment option may also be appropriate. Thus, one of the premises of the Pathways design is that there are many paths to an outcome, reflecting a range of choices any of which can be used, depending on the needs, skills, or interests of the individual making the choices.

Employment in the Natural Work Set-

ting Employment is viewed as the entry of the individual into a normal work setting. The pay received should be at least minimum wage or at the prevailing wage rate for that specific job. Although initially there may be a need for some accommodation, once the task has been learned, the expectations and wage rates for the worker who is developmentally disabled should be no different than for the nondisabled worker.

As was noted earlier, employment must be viewed not as synonymous with holding a single job, but rather with holding many jobs successively. An individual's employment history thus reflects the various jobs held and is a presentation of job activities over time. The Pathways Model presents a design where the individual may change jobs, yet maintain his or her degree of economic self-sufficiency by having minimal periods of time between jobs. Therefore, job placement thus should be viewed as a beginning step in ensuring that the adult with developmental disabilities can maintain an adequate level of economic self-sufficiency over time.

Supported Employment Supported employment is an employment option that recognizes the capacity of the adult with developmental disabilities while acknowledging his or her need for ongoing support. The nature of the supports required varies depending on the individual and the environment within which the individual works, resides, and socializes. The supported employment option looks at the supports that will enhance degrees of economic self-sufficiency, thereby making the developmentally disabled individual less dependent on others for economic support. For many persons entering supported employment, the level of reimbursement is less than that in employment because it is expected that their productivity will be less than that of the average worker in industry.

In the case of both employment and supported employment, the jobs held can be diverse. However, the environment within which the job is performed should reflect the natural or real work setting. From a planning and development perspective, there is a need to look at expansion of the types of jobs available, as well as the environments in which either form of employment can occur. In certain instances, the environment can be an integrated one, whereas in others the amount of stimulation in such an environment may be too great for the developmentally disabled worker to tolerate. Supervision and support can be the responsibility of the agency or organization involved, the industry, or a combination of both. With a reasonable degree of flexibility and creativity, the number and type of environments within which the developmentally disabled adult can work may be expanded.

Unemployment A word needs to be said about those who choose not to go into employment, the unemployed. Many economists view full employment as the condition when there is a job available for everyone who wants to work at the prevailing real wage. However, full employment does not imply that everyone is employed, but rather that there is a group who chooses not to work, is in transition between jobs, or is unemployed due to economic issues (Poindexter, 1981). Most economists accept an unemployment rate in the 4.5% to 5.5% range as full employment, acknowledging that about 5% of the total labor force population may choose not to enter employment. This level of unemployment should also be applied to the population of adults with developmental disabilities.

When considering those developmentally disabled adults not in employment, care must be exercised not to automatically assume that these individuals are fully aware of the benefits of employment. Some adults may feel that the risks and financial disincentives of working are too great. This group frequently chooses unemployment not because of a lack of skill, motivation, or desire but out of fear of losing current financial, medical, and/or social supports. As was noted in Chapters 4, 5, and 6, current public fiscal and health support systems create major disincentives for certain adults with developmental disabilities who are considering employment as an option. For other developmentally disabled adults, employment may not be a realistic option.

Monitoring and Assurance Needed

The various components of the Pathways Model lead to a common outcome: increasing the degree of economic self-sufficiency realized by the adult with developmental disabilities. The establishment of a single outcome allows for evaluation of the various paths an individual takes when making an employment-related decision. Less emphasis is put on the concept of case closure or placement because the model recognizes the factor of job mobility. Some developmentally disabled workers will need continuous intervention to maintain employment, others will require intermittent support, and still others will progress to full independence. The Pathways Model, in accommodating to this wide range of abilities, requires a coordinated approach to the delivery of services to adults with developmental disabilities. This section presents some of the monitoring and evaluation aspects that are necessary at various stages in the employment-related decision-making process.

Within any system, there must be check-points and mechanisms to guarantee that the system is in fact working and to monitor the progress of an individual through the process. The system must be designed so every individual who is served has had or will have the necessary supports to achieve the expected outcomes.

Because the focus of the Pathways Model is on the progress of the adult with developmental disabilities toward increased economic self-sufficiency, it must be able to ensure those who enter that an employment outcome is possible. According to the model, employment is viewed differently than job placement. In the latter case, the individual is placed in a specific job in which a specific set of activities or duties is performed. In employment, the individual may hold several jobs that are generally related to each other, but have varying activities and duties. Such changes require that there be a mechanism to monitor the change process and

to intervene when appropriate to minimize the time between jobs.

Critical points, such as at the time of decision making and job change, may require specific supports for the individual. Case management systems that ensure that the adult with developmental disabilities is informed of the options, able to understand the choices, and provided assistance with the choices when necessary will aid in reducing the risk of the person becoming "lost" to the system.

The nature of support required varies according to which stage the individual is at in the process. At one point, support may focus on facilitating decision making, at another on monitoring service, and then still another on stimulating change. This third role—stimulating change—is less clearly defined and is one that has seldom been emphasized in the past. Its focus is on encouraging mobility for the developmentally disabled adult in employment and other areas of his or her life.

Education/advocacy and information/referral for the adult with developmental disabilities are essential support services, as we move to the concept of providing supports over longer periods of time to certain individuals. Monitoring progress and ensuring that the adult with developmental disabilities plays an active role in determining his or her future are key elements, if the Pathways Model is to be effective. More specific discussion of strategies of monitoring, evaluating, and managing employment services is found in Chapter 21.

In any system or model of service delivery, there must be a mechanism of ensuring that the individuals who are to be served are indeed served. There is also need to evaluate the economic, social, and individual costs of such a system to see if the system is as efficient as it could be. Although not a focus of this chapter, the development of a monitoring capacity is essential to the design of any system or model. The criteria for measuring goal attainment for the individual in the system and for the system as a whole need to be clear and unambiguous. The Pathways Model puts forth alternative outcome criteria to the standard vocational rehabilitation system. It is a model that is able to respond to a wider range of individuals who are more severely disabled, yet are able to engage in employment when specific support services are offered.

SUMMARY

The Pathways Model focuses on the role of the adult with developmental disabilities in the decision-making process and looks at outcome not as job placement but as employment that leads to increased degrees of economic self-sufficiency for the individual worker. Involvement in the decision-making process ultimately increased the individual's investment in the implementation of the decision. Both the adult with developmental disabilities and his or her family, friends, and program personnel receive the message that adult status must be granted if adult behaviors are to be expected.

The use of a simultaneous set of choices, rather than a sequential course of action, allows for a more diversified response to the developmentally disabled population. One of the more significant elements of the model, however, is the use of employment not as an end in and of itself but as a means to an end. An increased degree of economic self-sufficiency through employment is in fact the desired outcome. Thus, those who enter employment but need support services over a protracted period of time or even permanently, may be considered as having achieved an acceptable and measurable outcome. Implicit within the Pathways Model is the need to have a wide range of environments through which an outcome can be achieved.

The Pathways Model is a conceptual model that makes the adult with developmental disabilities an active participant and stresses the development of alternative environments in which the adult may decrease his or her dependence. Both the individual's self-worth and society's perception of the contribution that the individual has made are thereby increased. It closely approximates the experiences of nondisabled individuals as they move from school to work and through the work cycle process. The Pathways Model looks at the adult with developmental disabilities not as different but as a person with strengths and needs similar to those of a nonhandicapped individual.

REFERENCES

Bellamy, G. T., O'Connor, G., & Karan, O. (1979). *Vocational rehabilitation of severely handicapped persons.* Baltimore, MD: University Park Press.

Braunstein, W. (1977). Gainful employment: The myth and hope of rehabilitation consumers. *Journal of Applied Rehabilitation, 8*(1), 22–27.

Horner, R., & Bellamy, G. T. (1979). Structured employment: Productivity and productive capacity. In G. T. Bellamy, G. O'Connor, & O. Karen (Eds.), *Vocational rehabilitation of severely handicapped persons.* Baltimore, MD: University Park Press.

Lynch, K., Kiernan, W. E., & Stark, J. (1983). *Prevocational and vocational education for special needs youth: A blueprint for the 1980s.* Baltimore, MD: Paul II. Brookes Publishing Company.

Obermann, C. F. (1965). *A history of vocational rehabilitation in America.* Minneapolis, MN: Denison & Company, Inc.

Poindexter, J. (1981). *Macroeconomics (2nd Edition).* New York: Dryden Press.

Wehman, P. (1981). *Competitive employment: New horizons for severely disabled individuals.* Baltimore, MD: Paul H. Brookes Publishing Company.

Will, M. (1984). *OSERS programing for the transition of youth with disabilities: Bridges from school to work life.* Position paper. Washington, DC: Office of Special Education and Rehabilitation Services.

∞ Chapter 8 ∞

Vocational Transition for Students with Developmental Disabilities

Paul H. Wehman, John Kregel,
J. Michael Barcus, and Robert L. Schalock

TODAY, DEVELOPMENTALLY DISABLED STU-
dents in most U.S. school systems are not
guided into employment opportunities compatible with their abilities. Although there are
varying degrees of vocational training and educational experiences made available to disabled students, usually there is no systematic
transition to positions in industry and business.
Similarly, communication between school personnel and adult service providers is typically
limited. Hence, those students in need of further intensive vocational training are not directed to the necessary services.

This vacuum of systematic vocational transition contributes significantly to the continued
high unemployment rate of disabled individuals. In 1983, the U.S. Commission on Civil
Rights reported that between 50% and 75% of
all disabled individuals were unemployed. An
excellent follow-up study of disabled students
in Vermont (Hasazi, Gordon, & Roe, 1985)
reflects similar figures of unemployment, as do
the preliminary results of a follow-up study
underway in Virginia (Wehman, Kregel, &
Seyfarth, in press). In Colorado, another
follow-up study indicates that, although over
60% of the recent special education graduates
were working, there was a high level of underemployment and very poor wages (Mithaug,
Horiuchi, & Fanning, 1985). Schalock (1984)

reports that almost 40% of mildly disabled
students in Southeast Nebraska were unemployed after graduation.

This problem has not escaped federal attention. New program initiatives are underway
through Public Law 98-199, the Education for
Handicapped Children amendments. These
amendments provide funds and support for
secondary education and transitional services.
In a rationale for the inclusion of transitional
services in the Act it was noted

> The Subcommittee (on the Handicapped) recog-
> nizes the overwhelming paucity of effective pro-
> gramming for these handicapped youth, which
> eventually accounts for unnecessarily large num-
> bers of handicapped adults who become un-
> employed and therefore dependent on society.
> These youth historically have not been ade-
> quately prepared for the changes and demands of
> life after high school. In addition, few, if any, are
> able to access or appropriately use traditional
> transitional services. Few services have been
> designed to assist handicapped young people in
> their efforts to enter the labor force or attain their
> goals of becoming self-sufficient adults, and con-
> tributing members to our society. (Section 626,
> PL 98-199)

Transition is a term that has been used in
professional circles frequently (Brown, Pumpian, Baumgart, Van Deventer, Ford, Nisbet,
Schroeder, & Grunewald, 1981). Only re-

cently however has strong emphasis been placed on providing quality services for all handicapped youth as they leave school. What specifically is vocational transition? For purposes of this chapter the authors have defined vocational transition as

> a carefully planned process, which may be initiated either by school personnel or adult service providers, to establish and implement a plan for either employment or additional vocational training of a handicapped student who will graduate or leave school in 3–5 years; such a process must involve special educators, vocational educators, parents and/or the student, an adult service system representative, and possibly an employer.

The key aspects of this definition are that: 1) members of multiple disciplines and service delivery systems must participate, 2) parental involvement is essential, 3) vocational transition planning must occur well before 21 years of age, 4) the process must be planned and systematic, and 5) the vocational service provided must be of a quality nature. Placing a severely handicapped 20-year-old student, who is learning letters of the alphabet, days of the week, coloring, and other minimally functional skills into an activity center with the same training objectives accomplishes little for either the individual or society and, in fact, distorts the purpose of the transition initiative.

This chapter presents a three-stage vocational transition model that encompasses the important components of facilitating the movement of developmentally disabled youth from school to the workplace. This model applies to all developmentally disabled students. The authors also analyze important aspects of appropriate secondary programs that facilitate meaningful transition. Lastly, there is a review of selected employment outcomes that need to be available for developmentally disabled graduates in the community.

A MODEL FOR VOCATIONAL TRANSITION OF DEVELOPMENTALLY DISABLED YOUTH

Facilitating transition from school to the workplace is not a one-step process, but rather requires movement through three stages: *school instruction, planning for the transition process,* and *placement into meaningful employment.* With the federal government's increased emphasis on transition, it is essential that service providers and agencies not focus exclusively on the transition process while ignoring the quality of the foundation services offered by public schools and the range of vocational alternatives offered by community agencies. In too many cases, previous efforts at interagency agreements that attempted to ameliorate transition problems actually resulted in movement of a student from an inadequate *school* program to an inadequate *adult* program.

Figure 1 presents a model that the authors feel overcomes the shortcomings of earlier attempts at transition and builds on earlier successful efforts. As illustrated, an appropriate special education program is characterized by a functional curriculum (Wehman, Bates, & Renzaglia, 1985) in a school setting that reflects integration with nonhandicapped peers (Certo, Haring, & York, 1983) and that provides for a community-based instructional model of school services (Wehman & Hill, 1982). These program characteristics are fundamental to vocational transition. The actual transition process includes a formal individualized transition plan with significant parental input and cooperation from key agencies, such as rehabilitation. Finally, neither the school program nor the planning process is sufficient without a range of varied work or employment outcomes available to students after graduation.

Public School: The Foundation of Effective Transition

Preparing students to have independent living skills and to be employable in the marketplace should be the major goals of the educational system. Without careful planning and preparation for postschool placement, however, these goals are seldom achieved by handicapped youth. Over the past few years, critical program characteristics that contribute to effective programming have been identified

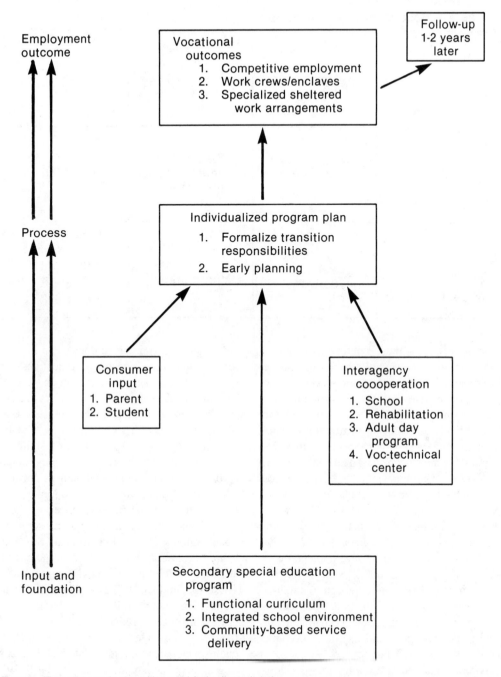

Figure 1.   Three-stage vocational transition model for handicapped youth.

(Bates, Renzaglia, & Wehman, 1981). These characteristics provide the foundation for meaningful transition from school to the workplace; therefore, it is of little value to discuss transition without analyzing them. The critical components of an appropriate secondary program include those characteristics illustrated in Figure 1 and in Table 1.

Functional Curriculum Training activities must be designed to prepare persons for vocational opportunities that are available in their community. To ensure this outcome,

Table 1. Secondary program components

Most effective ↑	Integrated service delivery	Classroom/ Community-based instruction	Functional curriculum
	Segregated service delivery	Classroom/ Community-based instruction	Functional curriculum
↓ Least effective	Segregated service delivery	Classroom-based instruction	Developmental curriculum

school personnel must continuously assess available community employment and analyze the specific skills required for successful job performance. The vocational curriculum for specific students can then be developed on the basis of this assessment. In designing functional secondary programs, selection of vocational skills must not be based on convenience, availability of equipment that has been donated to the school, nor on sterotypical views of what people believe disabled youth should do when they grow up. Instead, a functional curriculum reflects skills required in actual local employment situations. Usually, developmental curriculum materials and guides do not provide the most direct and efficient approach to employment preparation. The functional curriculum ensures that the training content can be generalized to potential jobs and facilitates eventual movement into the labor force.

Often, vocational training for developmentally disabled youth does not begin until they are 15–16 years of age. Because many disabled youth learn very slowly, common sense dictates that vocational experiences should begin early and should continue through the school years. Early vocational emphasis does not mean that preadolescents are placed

on job sites for training. It does mean that we select appropriate vocational objectives for training at each age level (Wehman, 1983). The objectives should reflect behaviors that are important to community functioning and employment, be useful for the student, and be consistent with the expectations of similarly aged, nonhandicapped peers. We must begin early to instill in children and their parents the feasibility of employment and the importance of work for a normalized existence.

Therefore, the functional approach to vocational training is also longitudinal. Students begin developing skills early, with increasing attention to this area as they become older. These longitudinal activities should result in gains in vocational skills (e.g., attending to a task, competitive production rate, broadened range of jobs a student can perform, production quality, etc.) and in job-related skill areas (e.g., independent mobility, appropriate selection of clothing, ability to interact socially with co-workers, etc.). As a result, students will graduate with an increased chance either of being employed already or being in an excellent position to become employed. The implementation of a functional curriculum is described below.

The curriculum focuses on three habilitation environments: work, living, and community integration. Students are assessed on core generalization skills involving communication, sensorimotor, cognitive/academic, and social competence. In addition, potential jobs are assessed in reference to *required* core generalizations skills and the tasks involved. This process is integrated into the student's Individualized Education Program (IEP) through the following three steps:

1. *Initial IEP meeting*
   a. Select with parents the functional activities from the student's potential work, living, and community integration environments.
   b. Classify those skills/activities into short-term and long-term goals and objectives.
2. *Assessment*
   a. Conduct an inventory with a non-handicapped person of the required skills for each functional activity. This is referred to as *an environmental/activity analysis.*
   b. Complete a student's profile on those required skills through descriptive analysis and assessing the "core generalization skills."
   c. Conduct a *discrepancy analysis* and recommend augmentative habilitation techniques directed at skill training prosthetics, and environmental modification.
3. *Develop, implement, and monitor the student's IEP.*

The Individual Transition Plan (ITP), as shown in Table 2, is developed jointly by the school and staff of the setting where the student is then placed and is attached to the student's IEP. The ITP is generally developed when the student is 16 years of age and is implemented as specified by the yearly ITP goal statements. As can be seen in Table 3, responsible persons, evaluation criteria, and completion dates are specified for each annual goal. Projected units of service are also associated with each goal to facilitate resource allocation and ITP monitoring.

The monitoring process employs a technique referred to as systems review (Schalock, 1984) that is conducted yearly during the regularly scheduled IEP/ITP review and update. This review process evaluates objectively whether the ITP objectives have been met as per the evaluation criteria and completion dates specified in the ITP (see Table 2). The number of actual units of service received during the year are also summarized for evaluating staff utilization patterns and costing/reimbursement purposes.

Integrated School Services It is generally accepted that in order to prepare persons for life and work in integrated settings, it is necessary to provide these individuals with exposure to and experience in dealing with the demands and expectations of these environments. Therefore, it is imperative that training occur in integrated settings. Emphasis needs to be placed on training that occurs as much as possible in integrated, as opposed to exclusively handicapped, facilities.

Just as integrated school programs serve disabled and nondisabled students of the same chronological age level, so the effective vocational training program also includes regular exposure to natural work settings. Natural work settings are defined as real job situations in the community. Students should train and work in the community whenever possible not only to expose them to the community and work expectations but also to expose future employers and co-workers to their potential as reliable employees. Fortunately, there is a slow but perceptible move toward integrated school environments in the country (Certo et al., 1983), and it appears that this form of service delivery will be a truly vital aspect of meaningful transition into natural work environments.

Community-Based Instruction Students over the age of 12 need to be exposed to vocational training programs for progressively extended periods of time. Job training sites should be established in vocations where there is a potential market for employment. Staff must be provided to conduct training and sys-

Table 2. Critical activities involved in transitioning students from school to work

Systems level activities

1. Survey community employers concerning desired skills and behaviors for entry-level employees.

2. Develop a **Student Competency Checklist** that incorporates the desired employee skills and behaviors.

3. Develop **Vocational Curriculum Teaching Modules** based on skill and behavior priorities identified by local employers.

4. Implement a **Resource-Teacher Training Plan** that develops teacher competencies in job analysis, job development, and on-the-job support activities.

5. Develop a **Program Handbook** of vocational services and activities that provides specific procedures to:

    a. Facilitate a cooperative working relationship between community employers, schools, and teachers.

    b. Encourage program ownership at the school district level through solicitation of school administrator and teacher participation and input in program-related decision-making processes and activities.

    c. Maintain a data base related to student and school characteristics, vocational education/training services, and specific outcome measures.

Student level activities

1. Start the ITP process at 16 years of age in cooperation with the parents.

2. Evaluate the student's interests, aptitudes, and temperament in reference to the entry-level skills outlined by the employer and obtained from a job analysis.

3. Provide job exploration and short-term on-the-job-training before final commitment. Assist the student considerably at first, but fade assistance as soon as possible.

tematic instruction at these community sites. Behaviors that should be targeted include acquisition of specific job skills, production rates, mobility, and interpersonal skills.

The need for community-based instruction is related to the two previously mentioned components of functional curriculum and integrated services. It should be clear that even the best curriculum in the most integrated school will still not enhance employment-focused transition without ongoing exposure to and experience in community work situations. In

Table 3. Individual transition plan[a]

Year	Goal(s)[b]	General procedure	Projected needed resources	Responsible persons	Completion date
1983	Arrange orientation meeting with parent regarding ITP goal for job placement in 5 years	ITP team contacts parents	Community job-training site and supervision	Vocational consultant Resource teacher	
1984	Locate job-training site for Chris (1-2 days per week during last part of school year)	Advise superintendent of need Contact community employers	Job site Transportation	Home school superintendent Vocational consultant	
1985	Have Chris in half-day job training	Orient employer Place and do work adjustment Conduct on-the-job assistance	Job site Transportation	Facilitator-enabler Employer	
1986	Coordinate job placement/training and transportation with community-based mental retardation program	Develop interagency agreement	Job site Transportation	Vocational consultant CBMR job supervisor and case manager	
1987	Have Chris participate in high school graduation program	Place name on office list Inform home district superintendent		Parent Resource teacher School principal	
1988	Have Chris maintain full-time employment with occasional follow-along assistance	Provide assistance units by CBMR staff	10 assistance units per month	CBMR job facilitator/assistance	

[a] Attached to the student's regular Individualized Education Plan.
[b] Begin at age 16.

119

the authors' experience, a principal reason for vocational failure on the part of significantly disabled individuals is their lack of exposure to natural job environments, such as hospitals, fast food restaurants, and offices.

In sum, functional curriculum objectives prepare students to learn appropriate skills, an integrated training environment enhances interpersonal skills with disabled workers and other peers, and community training improves each of these components by allowing students an opportunity to practice in real situations. Educational programming that reflects these tenets will help students prepare for the next phase in the model.

Planning for
Vocational Transition: The Process

As has already been observed, unless specific and formalized planning for vocational transition occurs, students will not receive a quality postsecondary program or enter the labor force. Therefore, even an excellent secondary program with good adult service alternatives available cannot benefit handicapped youth without planning and coordination of services. The three stage transitional model described earlier (see Figure 1) indicates the necessity of having a formal transition plan and delineating responsibilities of staff and participating agencies. Consumer input from parents and students and interagency coordination are essential. This process is briefly described below.

Formal Individualized Student Plans The focal point of the vocational transition process is the development of a formal, individualized transition plan for every disabled student. Without a written plan specifying the objectives to be acquired by the student and the transition services to be received prior to and following graduation, the other major elements of the transition model will have little impact. The plan should include annual goals and short-term objectives that reflect skills required to function on the job, at home, and in the community. Transition services should also be specified, including referral to appropriate agencies, job placement, and on-the-job follow-up.

Transition plans should be comprehensive in scope. Working in the community requires many different skills. In addition to specific job skill training, students must also be prepared to use community services effectively, manage their money, travel to and from work independently, and interact socially with other individuals. Plans must address all these skill areas to meet the comprehensive needs of handicapped students and, at the same time, should be individualized. Not every individual can be prepared for the same postschool environments. Similarly, each individual will require a different set of postschool services. In addition, transition plans should identify who is responsible for initiating and following through on each specified activity. This plan therefore dovetails nicely with the model recommended in Chapter 7.

Finally, transition plans must be longitudinal in nature. This requires the participation of all individuals and agencies involved in the transition process during the initial development of the plan. The plan should first be developed 4 years before an individual's graduation and should then be modified at least once a year until the individual has successfuly adjusted to a postschool vocational placement. While in school, the transition plan should be considered a section of the student's IEP. After leaving school, the plan can be a component of a client's Individual Written Rehabilitation Plan, if he or she is served by vocational rehabilitation, or part of the individualized service plan of a community service agency. Although the agency assuming major responsibility for services changes over time, the participants involved in developing and modifying the plan should remain the same during the course of vocational transition, thereby ensuring continuity of goals and services.

Consumer Input The informed participation of parents and guardians is a critical component of the vocational transition process. Parents should be made aware of the employment alternatives available to their son or daughter on graduation. They must be provided an opportunity to acquire the knowledge and skills needed to participate effectively in transition planning. Public schools should initiate parent education activities to provide consumers with background information. Systematically planned parent education programs will improve the effectiveness and duration of parent involvement in the vocational transition process.

Parent education activities should begin at least by the time the student reaches the age of 16. Content should be based on problems and concerns identified through needs assessment activities. Horton, Maddox, & Edgar (1983) have developed a parent questionnaire needs assessment that can be used to specify the needs of students and parents. The major areas of concern identified by the assessment process can then be addressed through parent meetings and program visitations.

Parent education meetings, sponsored by public schools or advocacy groups, are an effective method of training parents to represent their child's vocational interests. Meetings should: 1) orient parents to the community agencies providing postschool services to handicapped individuals; 2) familiarize parents with the specific responsibilities of special education, vocational education, vocational rehabilitation, and adult service programs in the vocational transition process; and 3) prepare parents to work with various agencies to develop transition plans and to apply for future services. Parental visits to local adult service facilities are also useful. School systems may be able to assist in arranging these visitations. They may also provide information to parents about what to look for during a visitation and ways to compare different service programs. This first-hand information should help alleviate parental concerns and fears about their child's future and should enable them to knowledgeably participate in transition planning.

When assisting students in making the transition from school to work, the resource teacher temporarily leaves the classroom to enter the community as a job trainer and advocate. The critical student level and systems level activities required in this process are outlined in Table 3. To ensure that the ITP works in harmony with the IEP, which is required by both state and federal agencies, the IEP should focus on short-term (yearly) objectives, and the ITP should target long-range (4–5 years) transitional plans (see Table 4 for a sample).

As illustrated in Table 2, the ITP process normally begins when the student is 16 years old and involves parents' acceptance of the long-range goal of employment. Procedures are based on the student and systems-level activities outlined in Table 3. The ITP frequently involves interagency coordination from its early phases, because the eventual follow-along assistance typically involves an agency other than the school system, such as vocational rehabilitation services or community-based mental retardation programs.

Interagency Cooperation   Interagency cooperation refers to coordinated efforts across such agencies as public schools, rehabilitation services, adult day programs, and vocational-technical training centers to ensure the delivery of appropriate, nonduplicated services to each handicapped student (Horton et al., 1983). The concept has been widely advocated (Greenan, 1980; Lacour, 1982) as an effective management tool that facilitates the development of fiscally accountable human service systems. Federal legislative mandates actively promote cooperative activities as a means of conserving resources and reducing inefficiency. The varied service needs of handicapped individuals demand the development of an array of available programs to meet the full service provisions of PL 98–199 and Section 504 of the Rehabilitation Act.

Unfortunately, efforts to encourage interagency cooperation have had little impact on the design and delivery of services. Although approximately 35 states have developed formal interagency agreements, and many communities have implemented local agreements, numerous problems persist. Agencies differ widely in their diagnostic terminology and eligibility criteria. Services continue to be duplicated while communities fail to initiate programs—for example, supported work placement—that are needed to complete a local continuum of services. Political and attitudinal barriers also inhibit interagency cooperation. Administrators often enter collaborative efforts suspicious of the intentions of other agencies, defensive of their own "turf," and fearful that interagency cooperation may lead to budget cuts and termination of programs.

A number of specific steps can be taken to overcome the obstacles cited above and increase the likelihood of cooperation. Information exchange must occur to identify the legislative mandates, types of services provided, eligibility requirements, and individualized planning procedures of each participating agency. Intensive staff development activities must then occur to enable administrators and direct service personnel to understand the regulations and potential contributions of other agencies. This information exchange should result in a restructuring of services to eliminate duplication and to guarantee that options are available to meet the service needs of all handicapped individuals. Finally, the process must result in the involvement of appropriate agencies in joint planning activities.

Multiple Employment Outcomes

The outgrowth of appropriate secondary special education and a meaningful transition plan should be employment. However, as was noted earlier, in many communities there are few or no employment opportunities. Obviously, it is essential that communities provide many different vocational alternatives, or successful transition cannot occur. The prospect of having an adult activity center that only focuses on activities of daily living or a workshop that provides only benchwork-contracted services is too limiting for the broad range of learning abilities of young developmentally disabled adults. In this section several types of alternatives for persons with all types of disabilities are presented not as a developmental continuum, but rather as a series of selected options or opportunities. Probably many other creative options or combinations of alternatives may be considered. Figure 2 presents a brief schematic of several of the outcomes described below.

Competitive Employment Many mildly handicapped individuals have the ability to work competitively if given the opportunity (Brolin, 1982). These individuals, who may have physical, sensory, or learning disabilities, require help from a work experience coordinator or rehabilitation counselor in job seeking and initial adjustment skills. If their school program experiences have been rich in quality and diversity, many disabled individuals will be able to work in a variety of fields, often beyond the stereotypical vocations of food service and custodial areas. Critical attention must be given to developing social interpersonal skills and providing more challenging types of jobs than have been performed in the past.

Competitive Employment with Support Competitive employment should also be made available to handicapped individuals who need more help in getting a job, learning and adjusting to a job, and holding a job (Revell, Wehman, & Arnold, 1984; Wehman, 1981; Wehman & Kregel, 1985). It is obvious from previous placement experiences that many persons with mild, moderate, and severe mental handicaps, autism, behavior disorders, or multiple handicaps do not fare well in competitive employment. Generally, there are difficulties in learning and performing the job, greater parental concerns, transportation problems, and also fear of losing Social Security payments. Yet, fortunately, there are programs and efforts underway that are now demonstrating how supported work through the ongoing services of a job coordinator can help this historically unemployed population gain entry into the labor force (Brickey & Campbell, 1981; Rusch & Mithaug, 1980; State of Washington Developmental Disabilities, 1984; Wehman et al., 1982).

An approach to competitive employment with support emphasizes structured assistance in job placement and job site training (Wehman, 1981). A job coordinator is available extensively for individualized one-to-one training and follow-up. Strong emphasis is

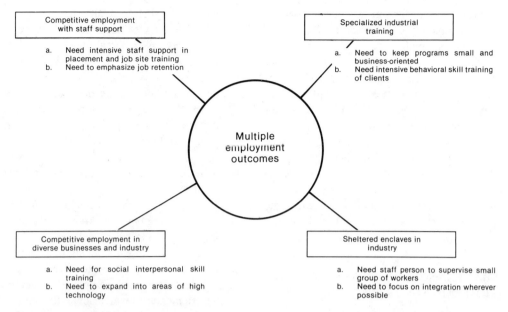

Figure 2.   Selected employment outcomes for youth with handicaps.

placed on helping individuals *maintain* their jobs. Although at first glance this approach may appear too expensive, in fact, there is a significant cost savings in comparison to long-term rehabilitation costs. The savings in reduced transfer payments also occur once employment is achieved (Hill & Wehman, 1983).

Enclaves in Industry   Another possible vocational outcome for more substantially disabled individuals is the sheltered enclave. In this approach, small groups of disabled individuals—typically less than six—are employed in business and industry under the daily supervision of a trained human service staff person. This approach is attractive because it offers disabled clients, who generally have been excluded from employment services, the opportunity to work in a natural work environment earning a decent wage. However, the hours and working conditions may be more limited compared to either of the previously mentioned alternatives. Fringe benefits are not usually an option. In addition, although breaks and lunch provide for integration with non-handicapped coworkers, in most enclaves disabled workers are placed together on a special set of tasks. The sheltered enclave may be a

good opportunity for some severely disabled workers to move into part- or even full-time competitive employment at a later time.

Specialized Industrial Training   Specialized industrial training is another employment option that usually takes place in a small industrial-oriented workshop setting. Contract revenue from business and industry provides wages for clients. This alternative has been available to severely and profoundly mentally retarded individuals, particularly in several states in the Pacific Northwest (Bellamy, Horner, & Inman, 1979; Paine, Bellamy, & Wilcox, 1984). This employment alternative is small, usually with less than 20 workers. Typically, programs are based in the community and provide employment through performance of complex assembly and production contracts. Successful training for electronic parts assembly, chain saw assembly, and varied high technology tasks has been accomplished, with these workers subsequently earning wages that they would never have realized in a traditional work activity center. In addition, nonhandicapped workers may be employed in the same program. The specialized industrial approach requires: 1) a staff trained in behavior modification and business and 2) a commitment to small, community-based vocational programs that focus on employment and earnings.

Other alternatives, such as mobile work crews, work stations-in-industry, resource sharing, and cooperative agreements with industry should also be considered. In planning for transition, options need to be evaluated carefully so that the best service delivery approach can be selected and the student, parent, and adult service providers can be prepared for the transition. There needs to be an ongoing exchange of information about the student between the school personnel and adult service providers.

WHAT CAN SCHOOL PERSONNEL DO TO ENHANCE TRANSITION?

Elementary Level

The teacher of a primary-age developmentally disabled child has a responsibility to focus part of the educational program on career and vocationally related activities. The teacher should not only work with students but also with parents and vocational experts within the school. The following four guidelines relate to the elementary educator's role in facilitating the transition process.

1. Let students sample different types of jobs in which they express an interest. Cleaning tables, emptying trash, washing blackboards, or taking messages to the office are good ways of improving career awareness. A major value of this exercise is that students, their parents, and educational personnel can evaluate strengths, weaknesses, and interests in relation to different jobs and assist in identifying areas for intensive work in a more concentrated career cluster as the student grows older.
2. Introduce such concepts as work, money, and employer relationships into the classroom. Students can run errands, empty trash, clean blackboards, and do other jobs not for the purpose of specific skill development but for acquiring the general

work skills that are central to all types of jobs. The lack of such broad work skills and behaviors frequently leads to the termination of employed disabled workers.
3. Explore the concept of work and its importance with the child's parents. Material can be shared with parents that emphasizes the employment potential of disabled youth and adults. Interested parents should be encouraged to visit successful work programs both at school and at local adult day programs.
4. Visiting senior-level and adult programs to observe the types of skills that are most important to the vocational success of severely handicapped students is essential. Communication among teachers at these different levels must take place in order for the elementary-level teacher to become sensitive to the curriculum changes that must be implemented in the earlier years. A list of sample vocational behaviors is provided by Lynch (1982, p. 2) for the elementary through secondary years.

Middle-School Level

Once a developmentally disabled child reaches 10 or 11 years of age, three additional areas of vocational education should be emphasized, along with continued communication with parents and senior-level programs. Teachers at the middle-school level must be aware that the student is a "product" whose later progress in vocational placements is highly dependent on the quality of the program provided at the middle-school level.

First, more attention and time must be given to developing general work habits, such as appearance, on-task behavior at the work station, and appropriate response to supervisor criticism. These skills were introduced at the primary-age level, but need to be expanded and practiced more often. General work habits are best taught in the context of specific vocational skills and with systematic instructional techniques. Related vocational behaviors can also be taught and reinforced in a variety of other curriculum areas and by staff other than teachers. Rusch and Schutz (1982) developed an excellent assessment tool to evaluate this progress.

A focus on learning specific vocational skills that will lead to increased employability in a marketable trade—for example, housekeeping—should be emphasized as well. The essential point is that teachers must teach students how to become proficient in a variety of jobs that, depending on the local job market, might include entry-level skills in farming, clerical, food service, housekeeping/custodial, or assembly/inspection work. Instructional techniques, such as task analysis, forward or backward chaining, shaping, and reinforcement, are commonly used to facilitate the development of specific skills (Bellamy et al., 1979). The purpose is to provide students with a repertoire of skills on which senior-level teachers may then build.

Toward the end of the intermediate-level period, teachers should assist students in identifying a vocational track(s) that can be emphasized in the senior level. For example, a profoundly retarded 13-year-old might be advised to spend a significant portion of time learning sheltered work skills that correspond to the requirements of local sheltered facilities. In contrast, a severely retarded youth might focus more time on janitorial skills, assuming that the local job market experiences regular turnover in maintenance-related positions.

Secondary Level

It is at this level that one can truly assess the success or failure of the vocational experiences provided in the earlier years. More time should be spent on vocational education at the secondary level. At least five additional areas need to be emphasized, as well as continued reinforcement of the activities and suggestions already mentioned.

1. *Focus on increasing or improving production rates.* The speed at which students work in an employment situation directly affects their employability and attractiveness to potential employers. Bellamy et al. (1979) have described in detail strategies for accelerating production rates.

2. *Focus on improving the quality of job performance.* The accuracy and care with which the job is completed influence the likelihood of being retained on a job, assuming of course that work proficiency, work speed, and general work skills are acceptable. The quality objectives are partially affected by the employer's or industry's standards of acceptance. Improving quality of work performance is best accomplished by providing reinforcement to students for committing progressively fewer errors and helping arrange a work environment that reduces the likelihood of failure.

2. *Focus on building up the student's endurance and stamina.* Increasing the number of work hours for the secondary-level student over a period of weeks substantially improves employability in adulthood. During the performance of workshop tasks, the student should be encouraged to stand, rather than sit all the time. Non-sheltered employment training should require the student to complete a series of tasks within a job without stopping for more than a brief period.

4. *Focus on providing vocational experiences in natural or real-life environments.* All too often, secondary-level students receive vocational (and other educational) services in highly protected classrooms and activity center environments. Although it may be understanding from the standpoint of efficient administration, this service delivery pattern leads to the student's inability to generalize vocational skills learned at the school or to relate to and interact with nonhandicapped individuals in the natural workplace. These critical deficits are usually best overcome by providing some training in natural work environments outside the classroom (Wehman & Hill, 1982) and/or by actually placing the student into a part-time or full-time job and then providing job-site training in a supported work model (Kraus & MacEachron, 1982; Wehman, 1981).

5. *When placement is not possible, do not let*

students graduate without a transition plan into an adult vocational services program that will provide necessary follow-through. A transition plan should list options available for the student in the community, identifying an advocate—a rehabilitation counselor or case manager—and describing strategies for ensuring a smooth change from school to adult-based programs (Wilcox & Bellamy, 1982).

NECESSITY OF STUDENT FOLLOW-UP

It is necessary for school systems to follow up their special education graduates. It will be very difficult for the field to assess the effectiveness of school instruction and adult service employment efforts until school systems begin to monitor more frequently the success or failure of their recent students' activities as adults. Regular follow-up of special education graduates on a minimum of every 2 to 3 years is essential if schools are to be able to monitor the transition process effectively. This evaluative data should be presented to the local school board and state agency to substantiate program effectiveness and facilitate strategic planning for those students yet to enter the transition process.

The follow-up process should uncover information concerning each individual's employment status, student and parent satisfaction with the individual's present status, employer evaluation of work performance, and consumer satisfaction with the transition program. Information regarding an individual's employment status, type of job, specific job duties, and current wages will aid in identifying the specific vocational training programs to include within the secondary curriculum. Discovering why some students are currently unemployed may reveal areas in which existing programs can be improved. Attention should also be paid to the individual's own perception of his or her present job status. Is the individual satisfied with the

current job? Is there interest in obtaining a different job or receiving additional vocational training? Are the individual's parents satisfied with the work their child is performing? This information will not only aid in program development but will also identify the support services most needed by program graduates. Employer evaluation of work performance will enable service providers to determine whether vocational training programs are equipping clients with all the skills necessary for success in employment. Finally, follow-up procedures should provide opportunities for former students, parents, and employers to express their opinions concerning the effectiveness of the transition process.

SUMMARY

In this chapter a rationale and definition for meaningful transition and a three-stage model for how to implement transition programs for handicapped youth have been presented. The importance of functional curriculum and integrated educational settings with community-based training opportunities has been emphasized. In addition, it was strongly suggested that written individualized transition plans be established with significant parental input. Finally, a series of employment opportunities were presented as community service vocational outlets for special education graduates.

Monitoring the transition process serves both a program evaluation and a planning purpose. The intensity of the focus on the transition from school to work is new, although the need is not. The new thrust is in response to the poor outcomes realized by those who have graduated and moved into a partially or fully independent status as an adult. The realization that the transition process is an evolving process has given the impetus for the educator and the adult service provider to work together in responding to the needs of the developmentally disabled student, the family, and the employment community.

REFERENCES

Bates, P., Renzaglia, A., & Wehman, P. (1981). Characteristics of an appropriate education for the severely and profoundly handicapped. *Education and Training of the Mentally Retarded,* April, 140–148.

Bellamy, G. T., Horner, R., & Inman, D. (1979). *Vocational training of severely retarded adults.* Baltimore, MD: University Park Press.

Brickey, M., & Campbell, K. (1981). Fast food employment for moderately and mildly retarded adults. The McDonald's Project. *Mental Retardation, 19,* 113–116.

Brolin, D. (1982). *Vocational preparation of persons with handicaps.* Columbus, OH: Charles Merrill.

Brown, L., Pumpian, I., Baumgart, D., Van Deventer, L., Ford, A., Nisbet, J., Schroeder, J., & Grunewald, L. (1981). Longitudinal transition plans in programs for severely handicapped students. *Exceptional Children, 47*(8), 624–630.

Certo N., Haring, N., & York, R. (1983). *Public school integration of severely handicapped students.* Baltimore, MD: Paul H. Brookes Publishing Company.

Greenan, J.P. (Ed.). (1980). *Interagency cooperation and agreements: Policy paper series: Document 4.* Champaign IL: College of Education, University of Illinois.

Hasazi, S., Gordon, L., & Roe, C. (1985). Factors associated with the employment status of handicapped youth exiting high school from 1979 to 1983. *Exceptional Children, 51,* 455–469.

Hill, M., & Wehman, P. (1983). Cost-benefit analysis of placing moderately and severely handicapped individuals into competitive employment. *Journal of The Association for Severely Handicapped, 8*(1), 30–38.

Horton, B., Maddox, M., & Edgar, E. (1983). *The adult transition model: Planning for postschool services.* Seattle, WA: Child Development and Mental Retardation Center, College of Education, University of Washington.

Kraus, M., & MacEachron, A. (1982). Competitive employment training for mentally retarded adults: The supported work model. *American Journal on Mental Deficiency, 86*(6), 650–651.

Lacour, J. A. (1982). Interagency agreement: A rational response to an irrational system. *Exceptional Children, 49*(3).

Lynch, K. (1982). Analysis of mentally retarded subjects' acquisition and production behavior in synthetic prevocational training environments. In K. Lynch, W. Kiernan, & J. Stark (Eds.), *Prevocational and vocational education for special needs youth: A blueprint for the 1980s* (pp. 81–106). Baltimore, MD: Paul H. Brookes Publishing Company.

Mithaug, D., Horiuchi, C., & Fanning, P. (1985). A report on the Colorado statewide follow-up survey of special education students. *Exceptional Children, 51,* 397–404.

Paine, S., Bellamy, G. T., & Wilcox, B. (1984). *Human services that work.* Baltimore, MD: Paul H. Brookes Publishing Company.

Revell, G., Wehman, P., & Arnold, S. (1984). Supported work model of employment for mentally retarded persons: Implications for rehabilitative services. *Journal of Rehabilitation, 50,* 33–39.

Rusch, F., & Mithaug, D. (1980). *Vocational training for mentally retarded adults.* Champaing, IL: Research Press.

Rusch, R., & Schutz, R. (1982). *Vocational assessment and curriculum guide.* Seattle, WA: Exceptional Education.

Schalock, R.L. (1984). *Services for developmentally disabled adults.* Baltimore, MD: University Park Press.

State of Washington Developmental Disabilities. (1984). Competitive employment summary update of placements made from adult day programs. Seattle, WA: Author.

Wehman, P. (1981). *Competitive employment: New horizons for the severely disabled.* Baltimore, MD: Paul H. Brookes Publishing Company.

Wehman, P. (1983). Toward the employability of severely handicapped children and youth. *Teaching Exceptional Children,* Summer, 219–225.

Wehman, P., Bates, P., & Renzaglia, A. (1985). *Functional living skills for moderately and severely handicapped individuals.* Baltimore, MD: University Park Press.

Wehman, P., & Hill, J. (1982). Preparing severely and profoundly handicapped students to enter less restrictive environments. *Journal of The Association for Severely Handicapped, 7* (1), 33–39.

Wehman, P., Hill, M., goodall, P., Cleveland, P., Brooke, V., Pentecost, J. (1982). Job placement and follow-up of moderately and severely handicapped individuals after three years. *Journal of Association for Severely Handicapped, 7,* 5–16.

Wehman, P., & Kregel, J. (1985). A supported work approach to competitive employment of persons with moderate and severe handicaps. *Journal of The Association for the Severely Handicapped, 10*(1), 3–11.

Wehman, P., Kregel, J., & Seyfarth, J. (1985). A follow-up of mentally retarded graduates' vocational and independent living skills in Virginia. *Rehabilitation Counseling Bulletin.*

Wilcox, B., & Bellamy, G. T. (Eds.). (1982). *Design of high school programs for severely handicapped students.* Baltimore: Paul H. Brookes Publishing Company.

∞ Chapter 9 ∞

Supported Employment

G. Thomas Bellamy, Larry E. Rhodes, and Joyce M. Albin

CONVENTIONAL MODELS OF THE WORK PREP-
aration process have either ignored persons
with moderate, severe, and profound mental
retardation and/or related disabilities or have
relegated them to nonvocational and prevocational services (U.S. Department of
Labor, 1977). As a result, the majority of these
developmentally disabled individuals have had
little work opportunity, receiving instead leisure, social, and prevocational skill training
with the expectation that this instruction will
develop readiness for later employment (Bellamy, Sowers, Horner, & Boles, 1980).

As research and demonstration projects
documented the employment potential of individuals with these severe disabilities, service
models that excluded them from employment
came under increasing criticism (Crosson,
1966; Gold, 1972; Horner & Bellamy, 1979;
Pomerantz & Marholin, 1977). Not surprisingly, efforts to reform vocational services
have attempted to provide alternatives for individuals previously considered unable to benefit
from vocational services. The Pathways Model
described in Chapter 7 of this book, an example
of such an alternative, is significant in its
complete absence of prevocational service
components.

This chapter provides a brief review of the
problems with the conventional service model
that have led to such widespread reconceptualization of new approaches. Supported
employment is described as the alternative to

prevocational programming as reflected in
recent federal legislation and regulations, as
well as in the Pathways Model presented in this
book.

PROBLEMS WITH CURRENT
SERVICE APPROACHES

Today's prevocational and nonvocational services are a natural outgrowth of the development of community services during the past
three decades. Sheltered workshops, which
were originally designed as places for protected, long-term employment, were encouraged by federal legislation to develop techniques for vocational rehabilitation (Dubrow,
1957, 1959; U.S. Department of Labor, 1977).
New services were developed to prepare individuals for competitive employment; these services emphasized work evaluation, work adjustment training, and counseling, whereas
sheltered work began to be viewed as a therapeutic modality for building tolerance for
future employment (Ruegg, 1981).

Vocational rehabilitation's federal mandate
in the 1950s and 1960s required services only
for those individuals for whom employment
was a feasible goal. Thus, there was a reduction in services for individuals with more severe disabilities. Day activity, day habilitation,
and work activities programs were developed
to respond to the needs of this unserved population. In both governmental policy and com-

munity practice, the purpose of these programs has been to provide educational opportunities and therapeutic programming that would prepare individuals to enter more advanced, work-oriented services (Katz, 1968). Together with the sheltered workshops, these programs made up a continuum of services through which individuals were expected to move as they developed prevocational skills, work habits, and tolerance for employment demands. At first, the logic of preparing individuals for higher levels of services and eventually employment was attractive, resembling the manner in which children advance in school from one grade to the next. However, neither the results nor the underlying logic of the flow-through continuum in adult services supports the application of this vocational preparation approach to adults with severe disabilities.

Lack of Accomplishments

The most important data—and thereby reason—for developing an alternative to day activity, work activity, and day habilitation services come from the outcome findings of these services. Movement to higher-level services—the central measure of success in the continuum concept—remains an illusion for most service participants. State studies of movement to higher-level vocational services consistently show that fewer than 5% of the participants advance each year (California Department of Finance, 1979; Minnesota Developmental Disabilities Program, 1982; New Jersey Bureau of Adult Training Services, 1981). Annual movement from the more advanced work activities centers is similarly low, estimated by the U.S. Department of Labor (1979) at 10%. Given the current rates of progress, individuals in day activity and work activity programs can therefore expect to spend much of their adult lives in these programs.

The failure of the current system of prevocational services is also evident in the wages earned by participants. A minimum of 40,000 adults are served in day programs in which state regulations specifically disallow work (Bellamy, Horner, Sheehan, & Boles, 1981). Another 60,000 persons with mental retarda-

tion are served in work activities centers, where the average wage in 1979 was $288 per year, or about $1 per working day (U.S. Department of Labor, 1979). These national estimates are supported by a study of programs in Minnesota. Forty-nine percent of a random sample of adult clients of that state's Developmental Achievement Centers had no earnings at all during 1980, whereas the average yearly earnings for the 51% who did report wages was $155 (Minnesota Developmental Disabilities Program, 1982). Clearly, current services do not offer participants the financial benefits associated with employment. Combined with the typical size and structure of current services, these results point to a life that is financially impoverished and segregated from the mainstream, with little hope of advancing to greater employment opportunities.

Conceptual Problems

The lack of successful outcomes in current day and work activity services should not be surprising. The flow-through continuum model of services is fraught with conceptual problems that would make it difficult, if not impossible, for local programs to accomplish placement goals.

Inefficient Technology Implicit in the design of prevocational and nonvocational programs is the belief that skills and behaviors acquired in those settings will transfer to later employment preparation and work settings (Brolin, 1976). Although such an assumption may well be defensible in relation to other consumers of vocational services, it is increasingly untenable for those with severe disabilities (Brown, Nietupski, & Hamre-Nietupski, 1976). In fact, more recent data support the interpretation that, for individuals with severe disabilities more than other consumers, it is critical that they receive training and other interventions in the settings and under the circumstances where performance is ultimately required. The absence of non-disabled co-workers and peers, the lack of pressure for work performance and quality, and the typically continuous presence of supervisors or teachers all represent radical differences from most vocational services and work settings. Even if prevocational skills were acquired in these programs, it is unlikely that they would then be generalized and performed in more advanced services or employment situations.

Distorted Service Objectives Day and work activity centers abound with tasks to increase hand-eye coordination, to enhance the ability to follow instructions, to remain on-task for extended periods of time, and to develop a capacity to fill out job applications. These are but a few of the typical objectives found in prevocational services that are often cited as entry requirements for sheltered workshops (Mithaug, Hagmeier, & Haring, 1977). A focus on these tasks in prevocational services reflects two faulty assumptions: their necessity for work performance and the need to master those tasks before work preparation can begin.

The skills typically considered prevocational are not necessary for work performance, as illustrated by the many reports of work competence by individuals who have mastered few, if any, of these skills (Boles, Bellamy, Horner, & Mank, 1984; Cook, Dahl, & Gale, 1977; Gold, 1972; Karan, 1978; Rusch & Mithaug, 1980; Wehman & Hill, 1982). The assumption that skills typically considered prevocational must come *before* employment preparation implies that there is a set hierarchy or sequence in which skills must be acquired. Data cited in the previous section suggest that it would be more efficient from a teaching standpoint to teach these skills in the actual work setting at the same time that the work skills themselves are being developed. Instead of providing the wages, benefits, and job satisfaction of employment, day and work activities centers typically focus their interventions on development of prevocational skills that have little relationship to success in employment. The primary barrier to paid employment for persons in these environments may not be lack of any personal or prevocational skill, but simply lack of an opportunity to perform paid work.

Funding Coordination Problems A third devastating assumption underlying the flow-through continuum of vocational services is that funding for individuals will remain available only as long as they move to higher levels of service. Instead, the cumulative effect of developing a continuum of program steps has been a maze of conflicting funding contingencies and regulations. Funding for day and vocational programs is available from many different state and federal agencies, and movement from one program level to another usually requires that one agency stop paying for services and another start doing so. Consequently, there are often powerful disincentives to movement for both services purchasers and providers. Medicaid, as was noted in Chapter 4, provides an example of the existing disincentives. In its Home and Community-Based Waiver Program, states are allowed to shift the costs of community services to Medicaid for which a relatively high share of program costs are paid by federal funds. However, regulations prevent the funding of vocational and prevocational programs, making federal financial participation available only for day activity services of a nonwork nature. States have no incentive to move individuals out of this level of service. Most states have applied for the waiver, with many promising that adult services will have no vocational or prevocational components, despite prevailing employment philosophies and supporting documentation that employment for adults with severe disabilities is a possibility.

The Transition Problem

The problem of day activity, day habilitation, and work activity programs are exacerbated by the growing number of unserved adults with severe disabilities. Severely handicapped children who entered public school programs rather than institutions after the passage of PL 94-142 are now adolescents, creating a national expansion in secondary-level classrooms. Research findings from the Department of Education in Oregon provide an example of the dramatically increased numbers of school-leavers who were faced with entering the adult service system. Five years ago, fewer than 15 students in Oregon reached the mandatory age of 22 when they could no longer be served and would enter the adult services system. Now, more than 100 students are projected to graduate each year for at least the next 10 years (Brodsky, 1983; McDonnell & Wilcox, 1983). Twenty-three percent of the students who graduated from 1976 to 1981 and required a day program on graduation were still waiting for such services up to 5 years later. Only 20% of the graduates had received any vocational rehabilitation services, and most of these were single disability determinations or vocational evaluations (Brodsky, 1983). These unserved graduates of public school programs may necessitate the expansion of an ineffective service system before alternatives that create real employment benefits can be installed.

SUPPORTED EMPLOYMENT

Joe normally would be considered a perfect candidate for the day habilitation and day activities programs described in the previous section. He is 51 years of age and had spent the first 35 years of his life in a large state institution (Washington state) for persons with mental retardation. Joe's diagnosis included cerebral palsy, quadraplegic spasticity, severe retardation, and diminished adaptive skills (i.e., difficulty telling time and handling money). When the state of Washington began deinstitutionalization efforts several years ago, he was placed in the "community" in a large congregate care facility. He also became a participant in a supported employment business where he has had the opportunity to learn electronics assembly work. In the ensuing 8 years, Joe has worked regularly doing circuit board assembly and volume control device assembly tasks. His earnings have gradually increased from less than $15 a month to $105 a month. In part because of his wages, he now has moved to an apartment that he shares with one other person with similar skills under general supervision from a social service agency. He works slowly and often engages in unusual behaviors while working. These behaviors continue to call for staff intervention. Joe is not cured. He still has severe disabilities and skill deficits that would place him in day habilitation programs in most areas of the country. Yet, as a participant in a supported employment business, he enjoys a quality of life in the community that day programs hold out only as a distant goal of their readiness and therapy activities.

Supported employment addressed the same service problem as that targeted by day activity programs: There are important discrepancies between the skills of many individuals with severe disabilities and the demands of the workplace that the limited services—both in time and resources—offered by the state vocational rehabilitation agency are unlikely to overcome. A daily occupation for these individuals is needed, however, as a part of the community support system. In the day service model, this descrepancy is treated as a problem of readiness: a need for the individual to develop skills and overcome disabilities so that he or she can enter vocational rehabilitation and employment at some future time. Supported employment takes a different interpretation of this discrepancy between the skills of individuals and job demands. Rather than seeing a need for readiness preparation, this approach sees instead a need for support while the individual is working.

This simple difference in interpretation has profound programmatic consequences. If the individual's readiness is emphasized, government services will focus on treatment and training services that attempt to prepare the person for employment. If the support interpretation is taken, adequate provision involves both a paid work opportunity and support services. Both approaches strive for the ultimate objective of a decent life in the community that includes productive work, independence, and social integration. The readiness approach of most current services addresses this goal by attempting to "fix" the individual by providing therapy, training, and related services in anticipation of a productive future. Supported employment provides immediate opportunities for work and community participation while offering a level of support reflective of an individual's needs.

Definition

Supported employment is defined similarly in the Developmental Disabilities Act of 1984 and the regulations under the 1984 Amendments to the Education of the Handicapped Act and the Rehabilitation Act (Federal Register, 1984). The term supported employment means paid employment that: 1) is for persons with developmental disabilities for whom competitive employment at or above the minimum wage is unlikely and who, because of their disabilities, need intensive ongoing support to perform in a work setting; 2) is conducted in a variety of settings, particularly worksites in which persons without disabilities are employed; and 3) is supported by any activity needed to sustain paid work by persons with disabilities, including supervision, training, and transportation (Developmental Disabilities Act of 1984). Several critical features of this definition are briefly described in the following sections. The presentation relies both on experiences from existing supported employment programs and planning documents from the U.S. Department of Education that clarify its supported employment initiative.

Target Population to be Served

By definition, supported employment is for individuals with disabilities who need ongoing support to work. This work may not meet productivity requirements for payment above the minimum wage. This definition excludes individuals who can work on their own after a period of vocational rehabilitation, but structures no minimum ability levels. Consequently, supported employment is unique as an employment initiative: It has no entry requirement analogous to the minimal feasibility criterion in vocational rehabilitation. This approach does not mean, of course, that all persons with disabilities should be forced into work roles. As is discussed in Chapter 15, persons of retirement age, those of independent means, individuals who are medically fragile, and others may choose not to be candidates for supported employment or employment of any type, regardless of the nature or degree of their disability.

Practically speaking, supported employment is designed to serve persons who participate in day habilitation and day or work activity programs who have not been accepted for vocational rehabilitation services. Of course, the exact group of persons needing ongoing support in any community reflects in part the quality of services and the employment opportunities in that locale. The more skilled the providers of time-limited services leading to independent competitive employment and the better the overall labor market, the smaller is the group who should need ongoing support.

Employment Opportunities

Supported employment is, first of all, employment. Employment exists when an individual's activities create goods or services that have economic value and when he or she receives payment for work from an employer or customer. Within the definition, supported employment may be part- or full-time, and although payment below the minimum wage is emphasized—implying a relationship between productivity level and need for support—wages can also be above this level. By establishing a simultaneous provision of employment opportunity and public support, supported employment is unique among vocational services. In order to provide employment, a job is required at the outset of service, not simply at its completion. That is, supported employment begins when the labor of an individual with a disability is successfully marketed to an employer. Most other employment programs are successfully terminated when employment begins.

Large-scale implementation of the supported employment approach to serve individuals with disabilities will be greatly assisted by putting into practice implementation of three emerging ideas. First, it is important for service developers to search out employment opportunities in every possible aspect of the labor market, not only the traditional areas. If we limit efforts to work that only has training value or that carries high social status, a large percentage of persons with severe disabilities would probably remain in day activity programs due to a lack of work opportunity. Second, incentives for employers to participate in supported employment programs are needed. Existing employer incentive programs address the excess costs that may be experienced in offering independent competitive employment, but comparable incentives for employers to participate in supported employment efforts are not yet available. Third, it is time to look carefully at the link between public policies for human services and economic development. The same communities that are developing services for persons with severe disabilities are often actively engaged in extensive economic development efforts designed to attract industry. Treating these as separate problems may well result in greater costs for the economic development efforts and inferior services for persons with developmental disabilities.

Ongoing Support

All of us receive some support at work from supervisors, friends, mentors, and others. The critical features of the "support" in supported employment are that it is necessary for the individual to maintain employment and that it is funded on an ongoing basis by public agencies. By implication, the individual would lose his or her job without access to this suport and, consequently, is not a candidate for less expensive and less intrusive programs for preparation of independent, competitive employment. Ongoing support involves the continuous expenditure of public monies and may involve constant or episodic intervention at the worksite. Obviously, worksite support involves more than the collection of follow-up data. It is intervention-oriented, designed to improve the work behavior of the individual or the related performance of co-workers and supervisors.

The support required to maintain employment may involve any of a variety of strategies. For example, as jobs change, extra supervision, ongoing training and counseling, transportation assistance, a personal care aide, or design of equipment that assists performance all constitute ongoing support needed by some developmentally disabled individuals. Such

support can be provided through several administrative arrangements. For instance, public funding for ongoing support may be used to create a not-for-profit community organization that offers employment opportunities through its own business programs. Or it may be allocated to a non-profit organization that supports people who work in other businesses or supports a co-worker who provides needed assistance at the workplace.

Objective of Supported Employment

Supported employment is designed to provide the benefits of working to persons with severe disabilities. This is a major shift from current service objectives, where skill development or service procedures are normally used as indices of service quality.

Persons with severe disabilities have the same goals from employment as the nondisabled. As most adults evaluate whether their current work is satisfactory or whether a new job opportunity represents a desirable change, they ask three general kinds of questions: 1) What income level will the job provide, and what kind of life-style can be purchased?; 2) How attractive is the work life? Will one be able to work with interesting people, do challenging work, be in a safe, high-status environment?; and 3) What security and/or benefits—job mobility, advancement, tenure, insurance—does the job provide? Naturally, individuals attach different values to income, quality of work life, and security. Most of us use some informal weighting system to evaluate our employment. Instead of measures of developmental growth, these three normal benefits of employment provide the yardstick by which program quality and success can be measured (see Chapter 21).

IMPLEMENTATION ISSUES

Although supported employment is a reconceptualization of services for severely developmentally disabled individuals, it does not negate all existing services. In fact, many of the service innovations of the last decade fit comfortably within its definition. The concept of supported employment provides a basis from which different kinds of employment services can emerge and to which current services can be compared in terms of consumer benefits and outcomes.

Many would argue that supported employment is no different from sheltered workshops since their inception. Indeed, some sheltered workshops do provide supported employment service, whereas others are designed as transitional programs leading to independent, competitive employment (Office of Special Education and Rehabilitation Services, 1984). Sheltered workshops, however, have seldom provided services to the full range of persons for whom supported employment is designed. Consequently, these workshops typically serve only those individuals who are the more capable and for whom supported employment may be inappropriate. Others (Rusch, 1986; Wehman, 1981) have repeatedly pointed out that many persons who can succeed in independent competitive employment with appropriate preparation are instead enrolled needlessly in segregated workshops.

Incorporating the supported employment concept into existing sheltered workshops would require a change in the target population served. The majority of persons for whom the supported employment program is designed are denied entrance to existing workshops on the basis of criteria that often have little to do with ability to work productively (Mithaug et al., 1977). Equally dramatic changes would be required in existing day habilitation and day activity programs. Although these services do typically include more of the adults for whom the supported employment initiative is intended, they seldom provide the opportunities of work-related benefits that are offered by supported employment. Exceptions do exist, however. Some programs originally established as sheltered workshops have accepted the challenge of serving persons with much more severe disabilities, and many programs funded as day activity centers have become effective businesses, marketing the labor of their participants.

The supported employment concept presents yet a further challenge to these innovative programs. By describing a support process that can rely on not-for-profit service organizations or on individuals or businesses, supported employment provides a new set of criteria against which existing services must be compared. Although many existing services may well meet the definition of supported employment, their value in the end must be determined in comparison to other programs that may be more integrated, more remunerative, and more able to accommodate persons with all levels of disability. The supported employment concept is an open invitation to the private sector to develop more effective and efficient methods of employing individuals who need ongoing support.

Funding and Administration

As with earlier day programs for this population, supported employment has no clear home in the federal government. Without this mandate, it is vulnerable to the conflicting priorities of different agencies with overlapping responsibilities. The federal agencies that provide support for most day programs for persons with severe disabilities—the Medicaid Home and Community-Based Waiver, the ICF/MR program, and the Social Services Block Grant—either explicitly prohibit employment-related activities or provide no guidance about the kind of services that are appropriate. On the other hand, the agencies that encourage employment services—the Rehabilitation Services Administration and various Department of Labor programs—typically discourage services to persons who need ongoing support, either by rigid service qualification, budget restrictions, or outcome requirements.

Funding under the Medicaid program now provides enormous incentives for states to establish nonvocational day habilitation programs that are in direct opposition to the supported employment emphasis on the developmental disabilities legislation. To provide a coherent funding and management structure within the federal government and to avoid the waste associated with directly contradictory program objectives, one of three changes seems necessary: 1) change the Medicaid regulations so that funds for day programs can be used for supported employment and give Medicaid primary responsibility for implementation of the initiative; 2) give responsibility for supported employment to vocational rehabilitation, change that agency's feasibility criterion for service eligibility, provide funding for supported employment, and eliminate contradictory incentives from Medicaid for states to offer nonvocational services; or 3) transfer the responsibility and funding for day programs for persons with disabilities from the Health Care Financing Administration (HCFA) to the Administration on Developmental Disabilities so that they can administer a program of supported employment outside the Medicaid program without competing incentives for states to establish nonvocational services under Medicaid.

Innovative Approaches

One of the most important aspects of the supported employment program is that it challenges the private sector—both profit-making businesses and not-for-profit service providers—to develop alternative service and employment models that fit different disability groups, different industries, and different communities. Most existing supported employment programs are minor variations on traditional service organizations, whereas the concept of supported employment invites creative program design within a much broader framework. No doubt, implementation of the supported employment program will result in organizational structures and relationships that have not yet been proposed.

Combining employment opportunities and ongoing supports represents an important new direction followed by most community service organizations. Without responsibility for the preparation of and placement in some "next environment," supported employment programs can be much more efficiently organized to accomplish the task at hand: to provide paid employment that provides the full range of employment benefits. One can well imagine

that this reorganization could result in much smaller and more specialized organizations, because much of the expensive overhead requirements of current community organizations comes from the effort to combine sheltered work and competitive job preparation functions. Smaller organizations can also maintain a clear business specialization, more like other successful small businesses, rather than the diversification that is now common in community programs.

Qualifications for personnel in supported employment programs are also quite different from those of earlier day activity or sheltered employment services, and new training programs may well be required that develop new combinations of skills in prospective service providers. For supported employment, staff need a combination of technical business skills associated with the work specialization and skills required for providing ongoing support, including training or rehabilitation engineering and service program management.

Measuring Outcomes of Supported Employment

The very broad definition of supported employment encompasses several program alternatives to ensure flexibility in providing supported employment in a full range of job possibilities to a very diverse group of persons with disabilities. Excluding some forms of supported employment from the definition would exclude some individuals from supported employment altogether. However, the inclusive definition also creates the risk that some persons may be served in employment situations with unnecessarily restrictive service methods and earnings opportunities. Consequently, there is a critical need to develop measures of supported employment outcomes that can be applied across program types and locations.

Wages are, of course, relatively easy to measure, and they provide a basic index of employment success. It should be noted, however, that most systematic efforts at statewide evaluation of wage levels have focused on hourly wages, which provide an index of individual progress in habilitation efforts, rather than a measure of weekly or monthly wages, which provide a better index of individual benefits of working. An exemplary effort to monitor wage levels in supported employment is underway in the state of Washington, where all day programs funded by the state's Division on Developmental Disabilities provide monthly information on the average monthly worker wage of service consumers, the cost of service, and other related measures of commercial activity. The state summarizes this information in regular reports to service providers, county purchasers of service, and case managers responsible for service referrals. It is consistent with the documented effects of similar feedback in other organizations (Prue & Fairbank, 1981) that, in the first year in which this information was regularly available, average earnings in the state's programs increased from $35 in July 1983 to $51 in July 1984.[1]

Although earnings provide the foundation for assessing the success of supported employment, they do not provide a complete picture. Other measures are needed to assess the quality of working life, including integration of the workplace and the security that work affords the individual. Both quality of working life and security encompass a number of interrelated characteristics of a job and are easily distorted by single-variable measures. Significant measurement problems need to be resolved in order to develop indices that are useful across the full range of circumstances in which supported employment can occur.

SUMMARY

The supported employment movement offers an alternative to the current service structure based on the flow-through model. The concept of individuals flowing from one service level to another has failed, both in moving individuals with severe handicaps to higher service levels and in achieving the wage and integration benefits normally associated with employment.

This failure of the current system stems from the original development of the service structure and from the patchwork of government agencies that define, fund, and regulate the continuum of services. Overlapping and conflicting regulations create a maze of confusion for service providers and disincentives to states for developing employment services for the most severely handicapped portion of the population. Federal regulations from at least one agency administering day and residential services for people with severe handicaps specifically prevent the funding of employment services.

For meaningful outcomes to be achieved for individuals with severe handicaps, the focus in adult day services must shift from perpetual *preparation* for the future to *employment* with ongoing publicly funded support. Overlapping or conflicting federal agency responsibility and regulations must be eliminated, and innovative approaches utilizing the full range of employment possibilities and potential support structures must be designed.

REFERENCES

Bellamy, G. T., Horner, R. H., Sheehan, M. R., & Boles, S. M. (1981). Structured employment and workshop reform: Equal rights for severely handicapped individuals. In J. Ansley & J. Lapadakis (Eds.), *Proceedings from the National Institute on Rehabilitation Facilities* (pp. 59–75). Menomonie, WI: University of Wisconsin-Stout.

Bellamy, G. T., Sowers, M. R., Horner, R. H., & Boles, S. M. (1980). Community programs for severely handicapped adults: An analysis of vocational opportunities.

Journal of the Association for the Severely Handicapped, 5 (4), 307–324.

Boles, S. M., Bellamy, G. T., Horner, R. H., & Mank, D. M. (1984). Specialized Training Program: The structured employment model. In S. C. Pain, G. T. Bellamy, & B. Wilcox (Eds.), *Human services that work: From innovation to standard practice* (pp. 181–208). Baltimore, MD: Paul H. Brookes Publishing Company.

Brolin, D. (1976). *Vocational preparation of retarded citizens.* Columbus, OH: Charles E. Merrill.

----

[1]Program output for "Chris System" developed under grant # 90DD0044/01, A Decision Support System for Managing Work Programs Serving Developmentally Disabled Adults.

Brodsky, M. (1983). *Post high school experiences of graduates with severe handicaps.* Unpublished doctoral dissertation, University of Oregon, Eugene.

Brown, L., Nietupski, J., & Hamre-Nietupski, S. (1976). The criterion of ultimate functioning. In M. Thomas (Ed.), *Hey, don't forget about me!* (pp. 2–15). Reston, VA: CEC Information Center.

California Department of Finance. (1979). *A review of sheltered workshops and related programs (Phase II): To Assembly Concurrent Resolution No. 2067, Volume II, Final Report.* Sacramento, CA: State of California.

Cook, D. F., Dahl, P. R., & Gale, M. A. (1977). *Vocational opportunities.* Palo Alto, CA: American Institute for Research in Behavioral Science.

Crosson, J. (1966). *The experimental analysis of vocational behavior in severely retarded males.* Eugene, OR: University of Oregon (Doctoral dissertation, Dissert. Abst. Int. 27:3304).

Dubrow, M. (1957). *Report of the institute held for the creative use of sheltered workshops in rehabilitation.* New York: Altro Health and Rehabilitation Services, Inc.

Dubrow, M. (1959). Sheltered workshops for the mentally retarded as an educational and vocational experience. In *New trends in rehabilitation.* Washington, DC: Department of Health, Education, and Welfare, Office of Vocational Rehabilitation.

Federal Register. (1984, September 25). Developmental Disabilities Act of 1984. Report 98–1074, Section 102 (11)(F).

Gold, M. (1972). Stimulus factors in skill training of the retarded on a complex assembly task: Acquisition, transfer and retention. *American Journal of Mental Deficiency, 76,* 517–526.

Horner, R. H., & Bellamy, G. T. (1979). Structured employment: Productivity and productive capacity. In G. T. Bellamy, G. O'Connor, & O. Karan (Eds.), *Vocational rehabilitation of severely handicapped adults: Contemporary service strategies* (pp. 85–102). Baltimore, MD: University Park Press.

Karan, O. (1978). *Habilitation practices with the severely developmentally disabled, Volume 2.* Madison, WI: University of Wisconsin, Research and Training Center in Mental Retardation.

Katz, E. (1968). *The retarded adult in the community.* Springfield, IL: Charles C Thomas.

McDonnell, J., & Wilcox, B. (1983). *Issues in the transition from school to adult services: A survey of parents of secondary students with severe handicaps.* Eugene, OR: University of Oregon (unpublished manuscript).

Minnesota Developmental Disabilities Program. (1982).

Annual Report—Minnesota Council on Developmental Disabilities. Minneapolis, MN.

Mithaug, D. E., Hagmeier, L. D., & Haring, N. G. (1977). The relationship between training activities and job placement in vocational education of the severely and profoundly handicapped. *AAESPH Review, 2,* 89–109.

New Jersey Bureau of Adult Training Services. (1981, June). *Movement of adult activities clients to vocational programs.* Paper presented at New Jersey Bureau of Adult Training Services Regional Supervisors meeting, Trenton, NJ.

Office of Special Education and Rehabilitation Services. (1984). *Supported employment for adults with severe disabilities: An OSERS program initiative* (unpublished manuscript).

Pomerantz, D. J., & Marholin, D. (1977). Vocational habilitation: A time for change. In E. Sontag (Ed.), *Educational programming for the severely and profoundly handicapped* (pp. 129–141). Reston, VA: The Council for Exceptional Children.

Prue, D. M., & Fairbank, J. A. (1981). Performance feedback in organizational behavior management: A review. *Journal of Organizational Behavior Management, 3,* 1–16.

Ruegg, P. (1981). The meaning and use of work as a modality in habilitation and rehabilitation of disabled persons in facilities providing vocational programs. In J. Lapadakis, J. Ansley, & J. Lowitt (Eds.), *Work, services and change: Proceedings from the National Institute on Rehabilitation Facilities.* Menomonie, WI: University of Wisconsin-Stout.

Rusch, F. (Ed.). (1986). *Competitive employment issues and strategies.* Baltimore, MD: Paul H. Brookes Publishing Company.

Rusch, F., & Mithaug, D. (1980). *Vocational training for mentally retarded adults: A behavior analytic approach.* Champaign, IL: Research Press.

U.S. Department of Labor. (1977). *Sheltered workshop study, workshop survey,* Volume 1. Washington, DC: Department of Labor.

U.S. Department of Labor. (1979). *Study of handicapped clients in sheltered workshops,* Volume 2. Washington, DC: Department of Labor.

Wehman, P. (1981). *Competitive employment: New horizons for severely disabled individuals.* Baltimore, MD: Paul H. Brookes Publishing Company.

Wehman, P., & Hill, M. (1982). *Vocational training and placement of severely disabled persons: Volume 3. Project employability.* Richmond, VA: Virginia Commonwealth University.

∞ Chapter 10 ∞

Four Supported Employment Alternatives

David M. Mank, Larry E. Rhodes, and G. Thomas Bellamy

As a combination of paid work opportunity and ongoing service, supported employment offers challenging flexibility to those responsible for planning and managing community day services for persons with severe disabilities. Differences in service needs, public resources, and labor markets combine to form an unprecedented array of possible program approaches. The purpose of this chapter is to illustrate the variety of supported employment possibilities by describing alternative service models with different organizational features, working conditions, and business specializations.

Development of supported employment opportunities for adults with severe disabilities has been limited by several factors. First, available work opportunities have traditionally been used by community services as a means of preparation for competitive employment and, consequently, have been given to persons with less severe disabilities (Ruegg, 1981). Second, funding mechanisms and regulations of many states specifically prohibit paid employment in programs for persons with severe disabilities. Third, because the technology for teaching vocational skills to this population is relatively

new, many program structures and staffing models were already in place before needed program features were developed.

Despite these constraints, the opportunity now exists to make rapid progress in developing employment options for persons with severe disabilities. As the first generation of persons with severe handicaps to be served in the public schools is making the transition to adult life, state service planners are confronting a rapidly expanding adult population requiring ongoing services. Two separate federal programs offer leadership and direction in the design of supported employment options for these individuals. The Office of Special Education and Rehabilitation Services has announced plans for a discretionary grant program that will assist states in shifting from day activity and day habilitation programs to supported employment (U.S. Department of Education, 1984). A complementary effort is promoted by the Developmental Disabilities Act of 1984, which places a new priority on employment-related services that must be addressed by state planning councils no later than 1987. Supported employment is one of the employment-related activities specifically de-

Preparation of this chapter was supported in part by grants to the University of Oregon from the Rehabilitative Services Administration (Grant No. 84.128A), the Administration on Developmental Disabilities (Grant No. 13.631), and the Office of Special Education Programs (Grant No. 84.158a).

fined in that act. Although no entitlement to employment or employment services exists, the present combination of federal initiatives and local service expansion creates important opportunities to develop supported employment services in local communities.

Creating the needed supported employment programs on the local level involves two distinct tasks. First, real employment opportunities must be developed and structured so that program participants experience the full range of work outcomes, including income, integration with people without disabilities, good working conditions, and other work benefits. Supported employment is successful only to the extent that these normal benefits of working are achieved by persons with severe disabilities. Accomplishing this task requires an important shift from earlier service models, where work opportunities and benefits were expected to emerge as the long-term result of prevocational preparation. In effect, supported employment reverses the traditional sequence of services, followed by employment, requiring that employment opportunities exist first as the context within which services are provided. Of course, the work opportunities that can be included in supported employment programs are extremely diverse, limited only by the economy of a community and the entrepreneurial skills of those responsible for program development.

Second, a successful supported employment program must offer ongoing support that allows persons with severe disabilities to perform the available work. Supported employment programs are successful to the extent that they can accommodate persons with the most severe disabilities. Because these individuals may bring to the workplace barriers associated with learning difficulties, physical limitations, behavior problems, health requirements, and transportation needs, the nature of the required ongoing support naturally varies from one individual and community to another.

There is a nearly infinite array of supported employment strategies and structures, each of which combines a particular kind of work opportunity with a particular method of ongoing support. Each, no doubt, has advantages and drawbacks in terms of generating real employment outcomes while overcoming barriers to employment experienced by the individuals with disabilities. No single alternative is ideal, and none fits all situations. Community development of supported employment programs requires adaptation to local employment opportunities and individual service requirements.

Employment models are needed that result in valued work outcomes for individuals with severe handicaps, yet vary enough to provide employment solutions in varied local communities. At the individual level, each supported employment alternative should be assessed as to whether or not it is the least restrictive alternative.

This chapter illustrates some of the variety in supported employment programs by describing four supported employment models. Each of these programs was developed by the University of Oregon's Specialized Training Program for replication in many communities. Each is supported by operations manuals, staff training guides, implementation procedures, and program evaluation protocols. The four models share many features with innovative programs that have existed for some time in rehabilitation services. They are unique, however, in their focus on persons with severe and profound mental retardation and related developmental disabilities. The chapter provides brief descriptions of each model's operations, service focus, outcomes and an overview of the issues involved in its implementation.

SUPPORTED JOBS MODEL

Perhaps the most direct way to offer supported employment is to place individual adults in regular community jobs and to provide support at the worksite as needed for the person to learn and perform the work. The Supported Jobs Model adopts this approach, building on methods used in earlier competitive employment training programs by adding procedures for ongoing support. In the Supported Jobs Model, a not-for-profit community agency is funded on the same basis as a day or work activity program. However, it has no building and provides no prevocational training. All the individuals served by it work in regular community jobs, and its program staff are responsible for job development, training on the job, and ongoing support at the worksite to maintain employment.

The work opportunities that form the basis for the Supported Jobs Model come principally from service businesses—restaurants, offices, hotels, and so on—although the model could theoretically provide support in many other kinds of jobs. Because of the interest in serving people with severe disabilities, program staff typically negotiate for positions of 3–6 standard hours of daily work, with the expectation that workers need not function at average productivity levels of nonhandicapped employees to perform the job successfully. Therefore, positions are sought that neither have time constraints nor require employees to work at high speed.

The employment strategy used in the Supported Jobs Model opens employment in integrated settings to many individuals previously denied such opportunity because of low productivity. By acquiring certification that allows payment below the minimum wage and ensuring that wages paid are based on productivity, the employer is not penalized for hiring an individual who performs at less than full productivity.

Consumers and Available Support

In the limited experience of a single demonstration project using the Supported Jobs Model, it is clear that individuals with severe disabilities can be successful employees. Individuals employed during the program's first year (1985) include those with little expressive language and with histories of many inappropriate behaviors. Support for individuals begins as continuous one-to-one training on the job site and is reduced to about 1 hour of support daily within a few months. Although this fading of on-the-job supervision is required if the program is to survive within typical adult service funding levels, it does create

some limits on the nature and severity of the handicapping conditions of those employed.

Three features of the model make it difficult to serve some individuals with more severe disabilities. First, the jobs themselves may create some training difficulties. Even though procedures for skill training have developed rapidly, entry-level jobs in service occupations often require day-to-day changes in tasks, performance criteria, and distractors that test the limits of current technology. Second, the work setting often imposes constraints on who can be served. Because the standards for acceptable social behavior are typically established by the host business, rather than by the service provider, individuals with more extreme behavior problems are difficult to serve. Finally, constraints on who can be included are created by the level of supervision available. Although our field has demonstrated that practically anyone can learn and perform under constant supervision and training, no such data are available when only periodic monitoring is possible. Even when a supported jobs program continues to receive funding equal to that available to alternate day programs, supervision can occur only during a fraction of the time at work.

The problem is not whether potential employees can learn to perform the job, but whether resources are available to support the employment of every potential employee. Individuals who require continuous supervision and support over long periods of time cannot be served successfully with limited resources. This model provides for support that can vary in type, as well as amount, yet it has a limit on the resources that can be expended in maintaining any single placement. Data from other supported employment programs in competitive job sites provide corroborating evidence: Although success with people labeled mildly and moderately mentally retarded is widely demonstrated, there are only isolated instances of successful employment of people with severe and profound mental retardation in individual worksites where supervision and training are only episodic (Hill, Hill, Wehman, Banks, Pendleton, & Britt, 1984; Rusch &

Mithaug, 1980; Vogelsburg & Williams, 1980; Wehman, 1981). Improvements in training and supervision technology should be expected to allow such programs to serve people with more severe disabilities. Until that time, the Supported Jobs Model and similar programs must be seen as extremely effective strategies for serving one part of the population needing supported employment services, but not as a panacea for all persons with severe disabilities.

Outcomes

Outcomes of the Supported Job Model can be presented only from the brief experience of the first demonstration site. However, preliminary data are encouraging. Five individuals have been placed on jobs during the first 7 months of operation. Average wages are approximately $210 per person per month, with each person working 4–6 hours daily. Before beginning their present jobs, two persons were unemployed, and three were in work activity centers earning less than $50 a month.

The cost for set-up and operation of this type of employment option is not yet known, given the brief experience of the demonstration site. It is anticipated however, that after an initial start-up year, the costs of ongoing operation will be similar to those of more traditional day programs.

Employees served in this model are integrated in both their jobs and communities. Each person performs his or her job duties in the same areas as other employees doing similar work. Breaks and lunches occur with other employees in the work setting, ensuring physical and social integration. Each person is trained to use public transportation to travel to and from work.

Implementation Issues

Important issues related to planning and implementation of the Supported Jobs Model include funding, coordination with families and advocates, and needed safeguards.

Funding The present demonstration program receives fees for service from the local developmental disabilities agency. This is the traditional source of funding for work activity centers, which are usually tied to facility-based and largely nonvocational programs. Individuals traditionally served in activity centers are the focus of the model, but the use of such funding to place and support people in jobs is a significant departure from the ways it has been used in the past. Typically, job placement programs have been funded through short-term and transitional monies from the vocational rehabilitation agency. The Supported Jobs Model focuses on employment outcomes, yet uses a source of long-term funding usually not associated with work outcomes.

This model also requires significant start-up funding. Initially, no more persons can be placed on jobs than there are trainers to teach job duties. As a result, high start-up costs are incurred in extra personnel over the first year of operation in order to secure jobs and train all persons placed.

Coordination with Families and Advocates Another area of need has been to secure the support of the families and residential service providers of individuals placed on jobs. Because most individuals referred to the model demonstration have been served in work activity centers, family members and others involved with these individuals have limited expectations regarding their employment prospects. Thus, it is important to hold discussions with family members and residential service providers to establish a commitment to work out such details as transportation and the handling of wages earned. Without the support and commitment of these significant others in the life of an individual placed in a job, there is a decreased likelihood of long-term success. As a result, the model has built-in procedures for working with families and significant others and includes an agreement with the individual and the family or residential service provider specifying each person's roles and responsibilities in supporting a job placement.

Needed Safeguards Any employment for less than a full hourly wage has the potential for exploitation of individuals. In order to avoid inequities and perceptions of inappropriate public subsidy of private enterprise, systems and documentation are needed to ensure fair and commensurate wages for work performed. Within this model, the support organization provides the documentation on a continuing basis of each person's productivity. These safeguards are important in order to make integrated employment a reality for more individuals with severe disabilities.

ENCLAVE MODEL

Another option for providing supported employment is referred to as an enclave. In its broadest application, an enclave is a group of individuals with disabilities who are trained and supervised among nonhandicapped workers in an industry or business. As a supported employment model, the Enclave Model is being developed by the authors in a small number of electronics companies. A supported employment enclave provides a useful alternative to both competitive employment and traditional sheltered employment. It maintains many of the benefits of integrated employment while providing the continuous, ongoing support required by some individuals for long-term job success.

In one enclave model, persons with severe disabilities perform work tasks within a host electronics company; a nonprofit organization funded by state service agencies provides support to the individuals and the host company. Up to eight persons with severe to moderate retardation are employed, working on a manufacturing line managed by a specially trained supervisor.

Within the enclave, payment for work performed is commensurate with pay to other employees within the host company doing the same type and amount of work. Access to work is guaranteed in the same manner as for other employees within the company. Persons with disabilities work alongside others doing the same work, although limited work abilities and behavioral needs may require that workers be situated in proximity to each other to enhance training and supervision. Employees with handicaps are subject to the same conditions— working hours, lunch and break times, and performance evaluations—as others in the company.

There are a number of incentives that enclave developers can offer to a host company. These include guaranteed productivity on a fixed cost basis, effective training and supervision techniques, detailed production information, affirmative action assistance, tax credits, possible reduction in employee turnover, and improved public relations.

A biomedical electronics device manufacturing company in the Pacific Northwest illustrates the use of the Enclave Model as a supported employment option (Rhodes & Valenta, 1985). The company employs approximately 900 people, including 250 electronics assemblers. Six individuals labeled severely handicapped are employed in a production line within the final assembly area of the plant. Ongoing supervision and training are provided by a lead supervisor and a model worker provided by the company with the goal of increasing productivity and wages. The supervisor is responsible for the production of the employees with handicaps. As with other lead supervisors within the industry, this person must also meet production schedules and ensure the high quality of production. The company provides a model worker in the same assembly area who has production responsibilities and assists the lead supervisor with the training and supervision of the individuals with handicaps. The lead supervisor and model worker within the company both assume responsibility to ensure that enclave employees learn to use the company cafeteria appropriately and to support day-to-day integration.

Consumers and Available Support

Individuals are employed in the initial program site who experience severe and moderate retardation and have histories of inappropriate behavior and difficulty attending and learning The enclave has two important advantages over the Supported Jobs Model that make it possible to accommodate persons with more severe disabilities. First, because it is often possible within larger corporations to select work that is relatively stable over time, it may be possible to train individuals who experience greater difficulty in learning the more varied tasks in service occupations. Second, the enclave of-fers the possibility of continuous supervision, with the result that the program should be able to accommodate persons who experience addi-tional learning and behavioral problems. There are, however, the following limiting factors: the ability of the lead supervisor to manage successfully the behavioral needs of up to eight individuals and the tolerance of particular be-haviors on the part of the host industry. With today's technology, these two factors may make it impossible to employ some individuals in an enclave who could be employed success-fully in other supported employment models.

Outcomes

The present demonstration has been in oper-ation for 2 years. Preliminary data on the suc-cess of this strategy as a supported employment option are positive. Before working in the enclave, two individuals were unemployed, and others attended work activity centers where their individual productivity was less than 25% and their average wage was $40 per month. After 8 months, all employees with disabilities were producing at or above 50% of the standard set by the company and earning an average wage of $295 per month. Wages of these individuals before beginning work in the enclave averaged less than $40 per worker per month.

Valued outcomes also occur in integration with co-workers. Enclave employees use pub-lic transportation to travel to work. They use the same lunchroom facilities and go to breaks and lunch at the same time and place as other electronic assemblers in the company. Physical and social integration occurs as a natural part of daily operation.

As individuals reach 65% productivity, they are hired by the company and receive a monthly salary of $639 and fringe benefits, such as medical insurance, vacations, and holiday pay. The company calculates that, if a person is producing at or more than 65% pro-ductivity, then an adequate contribution above costs is made and the worker is eligible to be paid as other employees, instead of based on productivity. Two enclave employees have

been hired by the host company (Rhodes & Valenta, 1985).

Initially, the lead supervisor in the demon-stration site was paid by the not-for-profit cor-poration. However, the company determined that the lead supervisor produced and managed a volume of work sufficient for the company to assume that cost. As a result, costs to the public sector in the form of fees for service have decreased dramatically. During the first 6 months of planning and operating, the total monthly cost to taxpayers was $3766 for all employees with disabilities. Now, the total monthly taxpayer cost is $650 and is dropping rapidly.

Implementation Issues

The most important implementation issues are the process of locating a host industry and the need for flexibility.

Locating a Host Industry   Significant re-sources are required to plan an enclave and locate a host industry. Our initial experience suggests that 3 to 9 months of planning and negotiation with a company may be required before employment of individuals with handi-caps actually begins. Because these costs occur before service starts, responsible state agencies must be willing to support program develop-ment for several months before realizing em-ployment outcomes.

Need for Flexibility   Many of the features that contributed to the success of the initial program may be due to the idiosyncracies of the host company. In all cases, the needs of the industry must be met, in addition to producing the outcomes of integrated employment. The Enclave Model is designed to be flexible enough to be successful in companies in other industries and within companies with different operating practices. This implies a need for greater flexibility and sharing of decision-making than is typical for a not-for-profit provider.

A final caution relates to the mechanisms for using public dollars within a for-profit com-pany. Safeguards are necessary to show that public dollars used to support a private cor-poration are used only for the extra costs of

MOBILE CREW MODEL

In both the Enclave and Supported Jobs Models, work opportunities are provided by existing community employers while a not-for-profit service agency provides needed support and training. This arrangement seems to be very successful in providing both income and integration opportunities, but it is now available to only a tiny fraction of those with developmental disabilities needing service. Although efforts to expand these arrangements should continue, there remains a significant need for models in which service providers establish commercial enterprises, providing work opportunities as well as services.

The Mobile Crew Model is just such a combination of service and business. Working from a van rather than a building, a crew of five individuals with disabilities spends its working day performing service jobs in community settings. Groundskeeping and janitorial work are the mainstay of income-producing contracts. This model has been designed to support employment in communities where there is a small service need, such as in rural settings or in small towns, and where a single large industrial base is unlikely. In addition, such areas are less likely to support the presence of more typical vocational programs for adults with severe disabilities because there are fewer persons needing service. The Mobile Crew Model also may be appropriate in urban areas where there are opportunities to acquire grounds maintenance and building maintenance contracts.

A Mobile Crew is set up as a small, single-purpose business, rather than as an extension of a large organization with many missions. A general manager is responsible for small crews, each with one supervisor and approximately five employees. Companies using the Mobile Crew Model are organized as not-for-profit corporations. Extra costs are incurred because employees produce at less than full productivity and require greater supervision than do workers without disabilities. (For a discussion of the extra costs resulting from reduced productivity, see Cho, 1983.) Such costs are covered by public funds. As with other supported employment options, the major outcomes of Mobile Crews are wages and community integration.

Consumers and Available Support

The experience of the two companies using the Mobile Crew Model demonstrates that individuals with significant and severe handicaps can be successfully employed. Employees include persons having moderate, severe, and profound levels of mental retardation, sensory and physical limitations, and behavior problems. Although continuous supervision available to the crew allows the program to include people who are difficult to serve, the constantly changing work tasks and public standards of acceptable behavior create some constraints. In addition, because funding for the crews approximates that available to other day services, supervision resources are not unlimited.

Typically, participation in the crew is inappropriate for individuals with significant physical or behavioral problems with training, supervision, and support needs that cannot be met by a single supervisor responsible for work performance and behavior change in community settings. However, persons with severe intellectual disabilities who have mild sensory impairments and some behavioral problems are successfully employed by these companies. Individuals are selected with attention to the resources available within the organization to meet individual needs. Often in rural settings and small towns there is a small group of individuals with severe handicaps whose needs differ greatly. Existing mobile crews have demonstrated that it is possible to have one member of the crew with more significant behavioral needs than the others and still provide training and habilitation services to meet the needs of all crew members.

The manager of such a crew distributes time across direct service and management functions to ensure that each worker learns and performs work tasks to customer specifications, to complete all jobs scheduled for that day, and to ensure that each worker has access to meaningful community integration.

Outcomes

Data from the two companies using the Mobile Crew Model show wages for individuals of $130 to $185 per month. The data also show that the Mobile Crew Model provides a broad range of social contacts with nondisabled citizens. Because workers move about their community in the performance of their jobs, there is constant physical integration. Training employees to use stores and restaurants individually as well as in a group helps create meaningful social integration.

Companies using the Mobile Crew Model can operate within the same funding levels as more traditional organizations serving individuals with similar needs. Such crews have start-up costs of approximately $5,000 to $8,000 for planning and initial acquisition of equipment to perform service contracts.

Implementation Issues

Two issues in employing individuals with severe disabilities using the Mobile Crew Model are of particular concern: commercial opportunities and operational problems.

Commercial Opportunities   As with any supported employment program, access to work contracts is of tremendous importance. Without work, there can be no wages. The experience of two companies employing this model demonstrates that suitable contract work can be available even in rural settings and small towns. Even though the two communities in which these companies are located have been plagued by economic difficulties and high unemployment, these companies have been able to acquire service contracts that result in work and wages.

The type of service contracts procured is also important. Clearly preferred are contracts where maintenance services are needed at regular intervals. To date, crews have been unable to fill all available standard hours with such repeating contracts. Instead, some crew

resources are spent performing such jobs as raking leaves and a one-time cleanup of lawns or buildings. These one-time jobs consume a disproportionately high amount of supervisor time and are difficult to teach because tasks are not available for repeated training. The more stable the contracts, the greater the outcomes of related productivity and wages achieved by workers with severe disabilities.

Operation   The small size of the mobile crew requires a small staff. The general manager is responsible for all aspects of the operation from training workers, maintaining the financial records, to writing and implementing individual habilitation plans. Although such multiple roles may make the position of general manager more interesting, they also require that he or she function in relative isolation from others. In the event of illness or a lengthy absence, the company's operation is severely hampered. One strategy to address this need is for an organization to operate several crews, increasing the number of staff to three or four. Such a strategy provides a critical mass of people and allows direct service and management functions to be shared among staff members within a small single-purpose organization.

BENCHWORK MODEL

The fourth supported employment model—the Benchwork Model—is designed to provide employment in electronics assembly work in a service agency that also functions as a business enterprise. It was developed in the early 1970s as an alternative to traditional day activity programs to provide long-term employment to individuals previously denied access to any vocational services. Contract work is procured from electronics firms and related industries. Individuals receive intensive training and supervision on contract tasks.

Operated as small, single-purpose, not-for-profit corporations, companies using the Benchwork Model provide employment and related services to approximately 15 individuals with severe and profound mental retardation and related disabilities. A small number of highly qualified staff are employed, maintaining at least a 1:5 staff-to-worker ratio.

Although designed for persons with more severe disabilities, the Benchwork Model shares many features and constraints with traditional sheltered workshops. Work is performed in the program's own workspace, reducing the opportunities for social integration during the workday. Further, successful employment depends entirely on the program's ability to secure an adequate supply of contract work, a result that has eluded most community vocational programs to date.

The Benchwork Model was designed in response to these constraints. Specializing in electronics work has enabled benchwork sites to invest in technical staff skills and equipment, build exemplary records for quality assurance and on-time delivery, and develop competitive pricing procedures. Several advantages follow from the electronics specialization. First, large capital investments are not required to begin operations. This is particularly important because most companies using this model begin without significant capital resources. Second, there are small initial requirements for space and equipment. Companies lease commercial space of up to 4000 square feet, minimizing both initial costs and ongoing overhead expenses. Third, the manufacture of small assemblies having little weight and requiring little space allows companies to contract work from customers several hundred miles away without incurring excessive shipping expenses.

Several procedures in the Benchwork Model are designed to overcome the barriers to integration inherent in a separate worksite. First, integration into the larger community surrounding work is addressed both in program design and individual services. Maintaining small, independent programs serving fewer than 20 people and locating work places in close proximity to stores, restaurants, and other community resources provide the capacity for integration into the workplace vicinity during work breaks, lunches, and immediately before and after work. A catalogue of these opportunities for vicinity integration ser-

ves as the "curriculum" for the program's nonvocational training, with related procedures for individual planning and intervention. Second, some possibilities for integration during the workday are available, as commercially successful programs hire workers without disabilities as production employees.

Consumers and Available Support

The structure of the Benchwork Model allows intensive training and support to employees with severe handicaps. Individuals receiving service in companies using this model are generally severely or profoundly mentally retarded. Some have significant behavioral problems, such as aggression, excessive self-stimulation, and pica behaviors. Individuals with moderate mental retardation have been employed when significant additional behavioral or physical disabilities prevented participation in less restrictive options.

With at least three staff, it is possible to devise and implement intensive training and continuous behavior management strategies to develop and maintain appropriate work behaviors. Ongoing support provided to individuals in settings that use the Benchwork Model includes individual training on contract tasks, available retraining when tasks or contracts change, individual training on community integration activities near the workplace, continuous supervision and behavior management intervention to maintain and increase work rates, and supervision and behavior management intervention to develop and maintain appropriate behaviors. The presence of these intensive supports implies that the model is inappropriate for individuals with less severe disabilities.

Outcomes

The Benchwork Model is being used by companies in 17 communities in five states and Australia. Recent data indicate that wages average twice the national averages for people in work activity centers (Boles, Bellamy, Horner, & Mank, 1984). For those companies that have employed this model for 5 years or more, wages average more than $110 per worker per month or more than four times the national average. In addition to work and wage outcomes, employees with severe handicaps receive training and support to enable them to participate in community access activities surrounding the workplace that any working adult might choose during a work day, such as using public transit to travel to and from work, going to lunch, or buying a few items at lunch time. Data in exemplary companies indicate an average of more than seven integrated community activities per person per week. It is important to note that these activities are almost exclusively performed individually and not with other persons with disabilities.

The long-term cost of operation of a setting employing the Benchwork Model is in line with the annual cost of operating a day or work activity center serving individuals with similar disabilities. The planning and initiation of a company using this model require minimally $15,000 to $25,000 capital to hire and train staff, acquire the most basic equipment, and begin operation.

Implementation Issues

The Benchwork Model provides job opportunities for individuals most often denied access to vocational services. The major issues for operation include its appropriate use and integration.

Appropriate Use of the Model The Benchwork Model is designed to employ individuals with severe disabilities who require intensive long-term support in order to achieve work outcomes. Its use for individuals with lesser needs is inappropriate. It has the advantage of being able to deliver intensive training and support, but this model does not represent the least restrictive vocational service alternative for individuals who require less support.

Work Opportunities Although the Benchwork Model provides supports that should be able to accommodate persons with the most severe learning and performance problems, it is successful only when the program also experiences enough commercial success to provide work opportunities for all participants. Many programs using the Model have provided suffi-

cient work opportunities, but others have been able to provide only periodic access to work. Without work, the Benchwork Model is little different from existing day programs that are justly criticized for unnecessary segregation and indefinite prevocational preparation.

Program Size Although initial Benchwork Model sites were designed to accommodate 15 persons with severe disabilities, it now appears that the programs may operate as equally effective businesses and more integrated services by employing only 6–8 persons with disabilities. Commercial success in existing Benchwork model sites provides the needed financial stability to explore this smaller program alternative.

State and local agencies considering the Benchwork Model as a strategy for providing supported employment should be certain: 1) that the community requires supported employment services for individuals who cannot be served in less restrictive programs, and 2) that sufficient work will be available for full employment of participants. If both these conditions are met, the authors believe the Benchwork Model is an important strategy for providing supported employment. However, the need for a model this restrictive should diminish over time as our technology for employment support improves, as public schools become more involved in vocational preparation of youth with severe disabilities, and as more effective incentives are developed for employers to offer on-site opportunities for supported employment.

IMPLICATIONS

The models discussed in this chapter are but four of an extremely large variety of options for the supported employment of persons who have severe disabilities. The four options differ in their business base and strategy for providing long-term support, but have several common characteristics. Table 1 provides a summary of the similarities and differences among the models on important operational dimensions. Each model has a clear focus on the consumer outcomes of access to work and meaningful wages. Each provides for long-

Table 1. Comparison of organization and procedures in four supported employment models

	Supported jobs	Enclave	Mobile crew	Benchwork
Organizational strategy and business base	-Nonprofit support to individuals and employers -Varied types of jobs	-Nonprofit support to host company -Target manufacturing companies	-Nonprofit -Crews operate from a van -Rural -Service contracts	-Nonprofit -Small electronics assembly businesses
Number of workers per job site	1 per job	6–8	5 per crew	8–15
Cost	Not yet known, expected to be similar to day programs	Less than ½ the cost of other day programs	Same as traditional day programs	Same as traditional day programs
Intensity of support	Low. Continuous initially, scaling to no more than 1 hour a day after several months	Medium. Continuous and long term	Medium. Continuous and long term	High. Continuous and long term
Training	Individual training for up to 4 months on: -job tasks -nonwork behaviors in and around job setting	Individual training on: -production tasks -nonwork behaviors in job setting	Individual training on: -service tasks -community integration activities	Individual training on: -contract tasks -community integration activities -nonwork behaviors in job settings
Supervisor	-Two - three supervisors for 12 employees in separate businesses	-One supervisor for 6–8 employees in host company -Host company assigns model employee as backup to supervisor	-One supervisor for five employees -Continuous presence of one supervisor on service jobs for all five employees	-Three supervisors for 15 employees -Continuous presence of more than one skilled supervisor in production area
Implementation issues	-Availability of local jobs -Matching employee needs to available support	-Availability of host company	-Availability of profitable, repeating service contracts	-Availability of contract work -Integration

term support to ensure working success. Each model is designed to employ people immediately, rather than to prepare them for some future role in the work force. The models also have common features related to organizational structure. All are small, specialized, single-purpose organizations that have the sole mission of employment of people with severe disabilities.

Although emphasizing employment, each option also includes procedures and strategies for teaching nonvocational behaviors and providing opportunities for physical and social integration. Nonvocational behaviors and community integration activities are focused, however, on those activities common to any working adult in a similar employment setting.

All these supported employment strategies rely on the presence of skilled personnel who are competent in management, business, and direct service. The organizational structures of each model rely on a small number of staff who share management, planning, and direct service functions. These are nontraditional staff roles and call for personnel with a wide range of competencies. A national move toward such supported employment options has important implications for the preparation of personnel to manage such companies.

Program Comparisons

Because the many types of supported programs share the objectives of providing normal employment benefits and involving persons with severe disabilities, comparisons among alternatives can address not only procedural differences and similarities but also the relative effectiveness of different models. Programs are more effective when they result in greater employment benefits and when they can include individuals with the most severe disabilities. Consequently, comparisons of quality should combine measures of employment outcomes and severity of disability. Such an evaluation strategy recognizes that it is more difficult to

serve persons with the most severe disabilities in a way that produces high wages and frequent integration. Table 2 compares the four programs on these indices, and Figure 1 presents a conceptual model for combining this information for quality assessment—by adding a program's success in achieving employment outcomes (wages, integration, other benefits) to its success in overcoming barriers to employment (degree of disability experienced by the individual and environmental constraints on employment). Although specific measures are not being proposed in this chapter, these measures can be developed and combined into useful indices of program quality. Of course, doing so requires that minimum criteria be established for each measure. Supported employment cannot be seen as successful when its participants do not have severe disabilities, regardless of the level of employment outcomes received. A program that involves persons with the most severe disabilities but fails to achieve employment outcomes is similarly ineffective.

SUMMARY

No single supported employment alternative is a "silver bullet." Every program must fit into a community's service need and business opportunity. To date, ongoing support in employment has been provided mostly in large, segregated work settings. Conversely, integrated employment typically has meant a lack of employment support after initial and temporary training. In order for citizens with severe disabilities to realize meaningful and integrated employment, it is incumbent on service professionals to design and make available vocational options that combine employment outcomes with community integration and ongoing employment support. What is needed is not more discussion of the ability of individuals with disabilities but widespread development of alternatives to support employment.

Table 2. Comparison of quality features in four supported employment models

	Supported jobs	Enclave	Mobile crew	Benchwork
Wages (exemplar)	Medium. $210/mo.	High. $295/mo.	Medium. $185/mo.	Medium. $118/mo.
Integration	High. Daily and continuous integration in individual job sites	High. Daily and nearly continuous integration with nonhandicapped peers in work area, break and lunch times	Medium. Breaks and lunch occur in community settings; work performed in community settings but interaction with nonhandicapped persons is low	Low. Community access activities scheduled during breaks, lunch, and beginning and end of day; integration on workfloor with nonhandicapped auxiliary employees
Other employment benefits	Medium. Benefits vary across jobs	High. Full insurance benefits for workers after hiring by company	Low. Job security and benefits depend on organization's commercial success	Low. Job security and benefits depend on organization's commercial success
Success in serving persons with the most severe disabilities	Medium. Participants must be able to work with very limited contact with service program	Medium. Participants' behaviors must meet standards of host company	Medium. Model can accommodate only one person with extreme service needs per crew	High. Model has accommodated people with extreme learning and behavioral difficulties
Success in overcoming environmental constraints to employment	Low. Few environmental constraints affect existing sites if transportation issues can be solved	Low. Few environmental constraints affect existing sites if transportation issues can be solved	High. Successful implementation in high-unemployment areas with little indigenous work	Medium. Successful development of businesses in some economically depressed areas

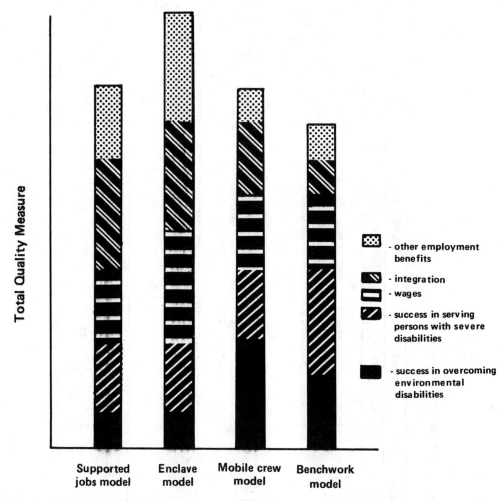

Figure 1. Quality comparisons among four supported employment programs (based on the high, medium, and low ratings from Table 2).

REFERENCES

Boles, S. M., Bellamy, G. T., Horner, R. H., & Mank, D. M. (1984). Specialized Training Program: The structured employment model. In S. Paine, G. T. Bellamy, & B. Wilcox (Eds.), *Human services that work: From innovation to standard practice* (pp. 181–208). Baltimore: Paul H. Brookes Publishing Co.

Cho, D. W. (1983). An alternate employment model for handicapped persons. *Journal of Rehabilitation Administration, 8,* 55–63.

Hill, J., Hill, M., Wehman, P., Banks, P. D., Pendleton, P., & Britt, C. (1984). Demographic analysis related to job retention of competitively employed persons with mental retardation. In P. Wehman & J. W. Hill (Eds.), *Competitive employment for persons with mental re-* *tardation: From research to practice, 1* (pp. 46–64). Richmond, VA: Rehabilitation Research and Training Center, Virginia Commonwealth University.

Rhodes, L., & Valenta, L. (1985). Industry-based supported employment: An enclave approach. *Journal of The Association for Persons with Severe Handicaps, 10,* 12–20.

Ruegg, P. (1981). The meaning and use of work as a modality to habilitation and rehabilitation of disabled persons in facilities providing vocational programs. In J. Lapadakis, J. Ansley, & J. Lowitt (Eds.), *Work, services and change: Proceedings from the National Institute on Rehabilitation Facilities* (pp. 5–22). Menomonie, WI: University of Wisconsin-Stout.

Rusch, F., & Mithaug, D. (1980). *Vocational training for mentally retarded adults: A behavior analytic approach.* Champaign, IL: Research Press.

U. S. Department of Education. (1984). 34 CFR Part 373.

Vogelsberg, R. T., & Williams, W. W. (1980). *Towards comprehensive services for developmentally disabled individuals: Independent living and competitive employment.* Burlington, VT: Center for Developmental Disabilities.

Wehman, P. (1981). *Competitive employment: New horizons for severely disabled individuals.* Baltimore, MD: Paul H. Brookes Publishing Co.

∞ Chapter 11 ∞

Supporting the Employment Initiative

Ted Bergeron, Susan Perschbacher-Melia,
and William E. Kiernan

ROBERT FROST AND HIS CELEBRATED POEM "Two Tramps in Mudtime," developed the separate themes of the need to work and the love of work. Although he agreed that "need was the better right," he concluded:

> My objective in living is to unite
> My avocation and my vocation
> As my two eyes make one in sight.
> Only where love and need are one,
> And work is play for mortal stakes,
> Is the deed ever really done,
> For heaven and future's sake.

By having the two themes converge, Frost illustrates the virtue of combining purposes to achieve a nobler perspective. Uniting the love and need motivations toward work is particularly meaningful and useful when carried into human services and applied to the employment future of individuals with developmental disabilities. It is meaningful because there is human growth in the motivation toward work and a sense of fulfillment in contributing to the experience of living. It is useful because there is a bonding relationship created in the service of a task or a product. Work becomes an event of human unity.

PREMISES

Ever since the words "dignity of risk" appeared in the literature, the challenge to enter the unknown with enthusiasm became clear not only to individuals with developmental disabilities but also to the receptive community around us (National Association for Retarded Citizens, 1973). The art of implementing that challenge, however, still calls for new ideas and more imagination in the development of community integrated employment (Rusch, 1979). In any design for creative alternatives to traditional models, it is important to note their worthy underlying premises before adding new ideas. Among these premises are the belief that work is a desirable, if not a necessary, life activity; the agreement that everyone involved will suspend the decision as to who should and who should not enter the marketplace for employment; the confidence that the working community will deal honestly with the needs of all individuals to be equally employed; and, ultimately, the recognition that everyone has potential and has the right to realize it.

MISSION OF HUMAN SERVICE PROVIDERS

The goal of ensuring successful access and retention in an integrated employment environment for individuals with developmental disabilities could be stated in a number of ways. For the purposes of this chapter, the goal

155

is seen as the removal of the attitudinal and physical barriers that inhibit any adult with a developmental disability from the benefit of integrated employment. Thus stated, the primary effort and reward rest with the individual employed; that is as it should be, and thus our role becomes one of "facilitator."

As facilitators we will have the opportunity to organize information in new ways for targeted audiences, to structure time as if it were in our control, to introduce the employable to the employing and the employed, and to modify enormous systems and biases.

In order to reach our goal in the working community, there are several steps that help identify the direction of our efforts.

1. Gain a commitment from human service and business leaders through their belief that all adults, without regard to the complexity of their handicaps, deserve the opportunity to enter the realm of employment.
2. Assess the immediate and future needs of the potential work force for those with disabilities.
3. Survey and prepare the employing community.
4. Design and implement a methodology that establishes integrated employment as a primary focus.
5. Develop a coordinated evaluation, placement, and follow-up system with community agencies providing similar services.
6. Provide ongoing advocacy and social services to the developmentally disabled individual in the work place.
7. Evaluate the concept and structural design.

Implementing the above steps invites as many possibilities as there are communities and employees with disabilities; even the sequence and the emphasis may vary from one location to another. In some models, for instance, an entire year is reserved to prepare the community employment environment before placing individuals. Strategies to educate industry were carefully prepared in advance to

appeal directly to the needs of the marketplace. In other programs, the emphasis is placed on building self-image and confidence before developing technical skills. Communication and interpersonal relationships are strengthened by allowing candidates for employment the opportunity of a visitor tour, without staff participation, through the facility. However, many pathways may be taken to an employment goal; the constant remains that the mainstream, even with all its imperfections, is still the better place to be.

TEC—A TRANSITIONAL CENTER AND MORE

It is not sufficient to develop the concept of supported employment without considering the parallel services that need to be in place to ensure the ongoing success of individuals with developmental disabilities. We are often reminded by parents and individuals with developmental disabilities of the disincentives that exist in our service system that pit the advantages of medical benefits, residential options, and integrated employment one against the other. Never before has more serious attention been paid to removing these disincentives than at the present time. This increased attention is almost entirely due to the proven success of individuals with developmental disabilities who have entered the world of work through job placement or supported employment. Their success in vocational pursuits not only points out the need for congruent regulations but also highlights all the other missing elements in the service system for adults with developmental disabilities as they move into the community (see Chapters 16 and 17).

The establishment of a model concept called Transitional Centers, designed to facilitate the move to employment, is a recent undertaking of the Society to Advance the Retarded and Handicapped, Inc. (STAR) in Norwalk, Connecticut. The actual design and implementation of such a center will vary from location to location, depending on the resources that unite to meet consumer needs. However, the following review is presented as a means of stimulating an interest in the development of similar resources.

A consortium of three agencies—two public and one private nonprofit—joined forces and resources to meet the advocacy, evaluation, transitional placement, and employment retention needs of individuals with disabilities from high-school age on. This joint venture, called The Training and Employment Co-op (TEC), is designed to supplement and, in many instances, supersede the functions of a traditional sheltered workshop or work activity center.

The three agencies represented are the Division of Vocational Rehabilitation (DVR), Cooperative Education and Services (CES), and STAR. Combining the advocacy and community services component of STAR with the intake and funding mechanisms of DVR has the obvious advantage of providing one-stop referral and entry for individuals seeking any combination of evaluation, training, placement, counseling, and social services. The same holds true in the relationship between DVR and CES for those within the mandated age who are preparing to make the transition from school to work.

Only a short distance from DVR and the evaluation areas of CES and STAR are the placement and marketing offices. Both offices, which are staffed by STAR, have the primary responsibility of linking the employment needs of individuals with disabilities to the working community. Two full-time placement coordinators engage in a wide range of duties, which include the usual scouting of the marketplace for job opportunities, determining with the individual and other involved parties the most realistic approach to employment, providing on-site training and follow-up, and ultimately phasing out that portion of the direct support that is no longer required.

The marketing representative in this design has a multifaceted role of negotiating subcontracts; developing satellite programs, enclaves, and small work crew ventures; and referring job opportunities to the placement coordinators. The many details involved in the coordination of each contract—time studies,

hourly and piece rates, volume, capacity, storage, shipping, attendance, and location in relationship to public transportation—require a thorough knowledge of the activities of the training facility, the viability of the marketplace, and most important, the interest and potential of those to be employed. Given the thrust of integrated employment without regard to level of function, the marketing position is not only significant in bridging the gap between the world of employment and human services but it is also critical in assisting individuals who need to leave sheltered employment through transitional sites in the community.

The strength of TEC is the proximity of the service agencies. The arrangement allows quick access to otherwise separate systems, avoids duplication of services and expensive testing equipment, economizes in administrative areas—for example, shared receptionist, computer, supplies, and office equipment—and provides an environment for professionals to pool their collective experiences to reach more solutions to human service challenges. Moreover, this triagency mall is located on the ground level in the middle of a major revitalization project.

To ensure philosophical continuity across agencies, the commitment of all staff to the values and principles that best foster entry and retention in the workplace needs to grow. To effect this common education, a large training and conference room is available for shared presentations and seminars.

Clearly, there are many ways to have a positive impact on the lives of those who seek employment in the community. TEC is only one of many ways to approach a systems design. It is hoped that it will stimulate other concepts and strategies for developing a coordinated and a long-term approach to the provision of services to the adult with developmental disabilities.

Principles of No Deposit, No Return

Among the most significant barriers to placement in the community is the fear shared by family members and individuals that, once they are placed out of the system, there is no return. Feeding that fear has been a history of cumbersome paperwork, delayed and incorrect support payment checks, inappropriate placement, and repeated layoffs. Separation anxiety between individuals with disabilities and the familiar setting of staff and friends can cause hesitation, if not reluctance, to pursue placement from the known to the unknown.

To address these fears and anxieties, TEC, which is located 4 miles from the vocational training center, handles the case management of all those who are already placed and no longer need to be monitored on a continuous basis. This function rests with the advocacy and community services branch of the agency. It is an ongoing service that ensures legal assistance, social services, counseling, and guardianship for as long as the individual with disabilities needs such service. One of the primary objectives of TEC is to develop strong self-advocacy qualities among adults with developmental disabilities by providing assertiveness training and forums on making choices and decisions. The importance of locating the stepping-stone component between sheltered and integrated employment is realized when participants in satellite programs, enclaves, or work crew ventures return to the training center only to feel out of place.

A response to this barrier is a "no deposit, no return" system design that expects everyone to graduate from training and become an integrated employee, even if it requires a long-term support system in the mainstream. In this context no deposit means that no one is placed in a sheltered workshop or work activities center forever. No return means that once an individual has completed training, there is no need to return to a training location if there is a change in employment status. The most convincing argument for this design comes directly from those who are placed. They remind us in their own words that their "future is out there."

Supporting Supporters

Civilization survives on the interdependency of its citizens. Success in the human service experience is based on the same relationship. Those who learn from teachers, teach teachers to learn more. So it is in vocational services. Once the commitment is made to enter the marketplace for employment, one of the most dramatic changes that occur is in the focus on who it is that needs the education. In a typical sheltered workshop or work activity center, it is the staff and sometimes the family who are trained first. In turn, they train the trainees. In the marketplace, the number of individuals needing training increases and the time for training decreases. Yet the results have been extraordinary, as the majority of supervisors and co-workers have risen to the occasion.

One way to provide supervisors and co-workers with the support they need is to include them when appropriate in the individual's planning process. To be part of the team fosters understanding, increases knowledge about specific goals and time frames, and offers an opportunity for input from the operational perspective of the working world. For the individual, the advantages of clarifying expectations, giving feedback in a setting other than the work environment, and enhancing social acceptance are the likely outcomes of this joint effort. Working relationships become as important a focus as task competency.

In the TEC Center, the potential for long-term supports outside the workplace is realized. The focus is on the environment within which the individual relates, with the realization that ongoing support over time may be necessary if the developmentally disabled worker is to remain productive on the job.

The approach of support on the worksite (as is seen in the later portion of this chapter and is discussed in other chapters in this book) fits more directly into the concepts of supported employment. The TEC design is a variation in the concept, with the focus for support on the extended work environment as well as the immediate workplace.

A SUPPORTED EMPLOYMENT DESIGN ON-SITE

When the move into an employment setting occurs, the adult with developmental disabilities may require specific supports.

Whereas the TEC model emphasizes support to the individual and the extended working environment, the Community Rehabilitative Employment Work Sites (CREWS) emphasizes support to the individual on-site. This model, an example of a supported employment design, assists the individual in adjusting to the job and the tasks of the job while utilizing a normal working environment.

The CREWS program is sponsored by the South Shore Rehabilitation Center (SSRC) in Quincy, Massachusetts. In the 15-year history of this program, it has been found to be a viable and practical means for individuals with developmental disabilities to leave workshops for community job sites and, in some cases, to move to competitive employment. Its emphasis is on individuals living and working in the community. It has been found that clients are more motivated and more productive with less behavioral problems if they work in a more naturalized setting (Rusch & Schutz, 1979; Wehman, 1981). As was noted in Chapter 10, the CREWS system of job development is better adapted to the economic needs of the community. The basic elements of the model include: 1) workers in groups, 2) supervision provided by staff through the rehabilitation agency, 3) employer payment to the rehabilitation center for work done, and 4) rehabilitation center payment to the workers according to productivity and the level of skills demonstrated on the job.

These elements make it highly adaptable for certain types of jobs in private industry and in government. Industry pays a set price for work completed, and individuals usually receive pay based on the rate of productivity achieved. Labor certificates are maintained by the rehabilitation agency.

Often, the work in private industry is similar to the subcontract work done in the workshop. The advantages to industry are that there is no shipping time, the company does not have to hire and fire, there is no requirement to carry workers' compensation, and the work is done on jobs with a traditionally high employee turnover rate. The job supervisors are trained primarily in the industrial job, rather than in the professional rehabilitation career tracks.

Current CREWS Activities

In 1985, there were 17 sites with over 200 workers. Eight sites are located in private companies. Private sites are identified by the rehabilitation center in industries that engage in such activities as assembly and packaging. The center negotiates with the company to develop the job contract and pay the rates involved.

The development of sites is often time consuming and difficult. Industries must be convinced of the economic advantages to such a program. In some cases, the sites are developed from workshop subcontracts. Contracts are also located through the reputation of the center in the general industrial market. In these instances, past successes in subcontract work have assisted the center in establishing industrial linkages on-site.

In addition to the industry-based contacts, the center has established a working relationship with the public sector. The rehabilitation center has provided janitorial and landscaping under federal and state contracts. Workers are paid at the established wage rate for a given job, which is set by the government. The individual client wage is dependent on the rate of productivity and the specific tasks performed on the job. Government contracts are made available by the Javits-Wagner-O'Day Legislation administered by the National Institute for Severely Handicapped (NISH).

This government initiative has many advantages. Federal contracts are financially sound because it is possible to keep a government contract indefinitely if the job is well done. The participating center can invest in equipment and can risk taking on new jobs because of the stability of these contracts. Long-term training opportunities are also provided by this type of contracting. The pay for federal jobs is usually higher than in the private sector as a result of established wage rate procedures. However, it is difficult to initiate a contract relationship with the federal government. Facilities often have to expend significant staff time and monies to become qualified to pursue the NISH contracts. This is of particular concern for many of the smaller rehabilitation centers. The final advantage of government contracts is that federal sites—often due to the size of the contract—have a ratio of disabled workers to the total number of persons employed that is much more favorable to an integrated mainstreamed program approach. Private industry sites tend to be smaller so that there is a higher ratio of disabled to nondisabled workers.

Site Development

There are many steps required in site development. For example, in a janitorial contract with the federal government, the site is visited, the job requested is priced—equipment needs, manpower needs, supplies, etc.—and the work area is zoned and broken down into required tasks. The number of client hours and financing is determined. Supervisors who know the job are hired, and appropriate clients who have the necessary mobility and gross motor tasks for the job are selected.

By breaking down jobs into tasks and assessing the necessary time required to perform them, a subjective evaluation of the skill level and the speed required of a worker can be determined. This breakdown allows the rehabilitation center to select the appropriate number of workers to complete the job. When a new site has been developed, clients have been selected and prepared by a case manager, and supportive services are in place, there is still an adjustment period until production reaches the appropriate level. Site development is a slow process and requires flexibility on the part of the center undertaking the activity.

Training

Training is an important part of the CREWS program. The first people to be trained are the supervisors, who are hired before a site opens and are trained by other supervisors who have participated in other sites. Supervisors are selected because of their work-related experience, and they then must be trained in human service skills. There are overall site supervisors and working supervisors who are in charge of specific jobs and zones. Working supervisors must also do the paperwork on their workers to see that they are paid according to their productivity. The ratio of workers to supervisors

varies from job site to job site and zone to zone, according to the geographics and the demands of the job. The average on an industrial site is 10 workers to 1 supervisor, whereas on a janitorial site the ratio is 6 workers to 1 supervisor.

Because of the type of jobs selected, a great deal of prior training for clients is not required. The increased motivation in a normalized setting helps individuals to learn the job with less training. The primary incentives for learning are the pressure of meeting the production deadlines and the opportunity for increased wages. Most of the training for the jobs is conducted on-site by the supervisor in a similar fashion to industrial training. A behavioral training approach is used that breaks jobs into tasks and segments. A major area of training at the center is teaching clients to use public transportation. Because in-depth training is not required by this program, workshop training is not needed before participants enter the CREWS program. Thus, clients may go directly to work in community settings in this program.

Workers in the CREWS Program

A full range of clients participate in the CREWS program. The coordinator of the program estimates that 70% of the clients are disabled due to retardation or learning problems. The remainder are emotionally disturbed or have substantial physical disabilities. The degree of disability varies from site to site, depending on the skill level required by the job. Fine motor skill jobs in industry sites require more capable workers, whereas janitorial sites may employ workers with more severe disabilities. Many of the clients have been previously institutionalized. Results this far show that the program is effective even for more severely disabled clients from an institutionalized setting. Most of the jobs require less than an 8-hour day so individuals can become accustomed to the world of work. There is some attention to activities of daily living skill training, with transportation training as a major focus. Individuals are taught to use public transportation to reach the site directly or to get to a central point from which they can be shuttled to the job. Clients are motivated to travel through the work incentive.

Supervision in the Design

The CREWS program requires ongoing supervision and thus can be fairly costly. However, the state mental health and vocational rehabilitation agencies pay for part of the cost for the supervisor, case management, support services, and training. Initial expenses diminish, as clients become more independent and more familiar with the tasks on the job and the work environment and need less supervision and training. Workers earn more, thus contributing more to taxes and decreasing their support payments. Some individuals move into competitive employment and become financially independent.

The rehabilitation center has encountered a problem in attaching suitable clients to meet the production demands when starting large contracts. Often, there is resistance from families and sheltered workshops who are familiar with more protective environments with less working demands. Concerns about loss of Supplemental Income Payments (SSI) and Medicaid, as was mentioned in Chapters 4 and 5, have been limiting factors at times in the development of this model.

Wage Payments to Workers

Earnings in this type of program range from 40% to 100% of the normal rate. Workers are paid according to their level of productivity and skill. In the private industrial sites, the workers function at 60% to 70% of the normal production level and often are able to move to competitive jobs. At these sites, however, wages are often lower than the federal contracts on an hourly basis, reflecting the lower overall rate per hour of the private sector.

At the federally sponsored janitorial sites, workers often function at 50% to 60% of normal production. The hours worked per day range from 5½ to 8 hours. Certain wage rates are determined by the wage determination rate as set in each federal contract. Earnings thus vary tremendously from $1.25 to $5.00 per hour. This rate, however, is considerably higher than what has been reported for those individuals in sheltered workshops (Whitehead, 1979).

Current Achievements: Future Directions

Since 1978 the number of clients in the sheltered workshop setting of the South Shore Rehabilitation Center has been reduced from 300 to 85. Over 200 individuals are presently placed in community settings. The CREWS program also offers work opportunities at different levels and is thus able to accommodate a wide range of disabled workers. Once seen as a stepping-stone out of the workshop, the program is now regarded as an initial placement with vocational evaluation and on-the-job training. The program offers long-term community placement, as well as movement to competitive employment. The nonhandicapped public is educated by contact with disabled workers at the work site.

The incentives to industry are of an economic nature: meeting market demands for varying production schedules and offsetting problems of high employee turnover. The success of the CREWS program is based on the expectation that the clients can perform adequately in a normalized community-based setting and on the ability of the rehabilitation center to perform job training. In more than 15 years of effort, which has been intensified since 1978, the program has grown to include a greater number of sites and clients who perform more complex tasks for more hours, thus increasing their degree of economic self-sufficiency. It has proven itself to be a successful supported employment program, a community option that allows clients to bypass or leave traditional workshop settings and enter competitive employment with specific support services.

SUMMARY

The concept of supported employment acknowledges that certain developmentally disabled adults require support over long periods of time, if not indefinitely. The basis of the support, both quantitatively and structurally, varies, depending on the degree of independence that the individual can achieve and the structure of the working environment in which the individual interacts.

The two projects reviewed present an expanded approach to the concept of supported employment. The TEC design looks not only at the work environment but at the external environment and how it may have an impact on the individual's performance on the job. It is an approach that maintains an individual in employment by responding to the residential, learning, and adjustment needs outside the workplace as well. The TEC Center assists employment retention by responding to problems outside the workplace as soon as they are identified and before they have an adverse effect on the job performance of the developmentally disabled worker.

The CREWS program supports the individual both in entering and remaining on the job. The CREWS design focuses on the skill training needs of the individual while responding to the production demands of the workplace. The use of group placement, on-site training, and continuous feedback ensures that the transition of the individual into the workplace is as smooth as possible. The CREWS design can provide indefinite support to the developmentally disabled worker while maximizing the productive capacity and degree of economic self-sufficiency realized in the workplace.

Although somewhat different in their approaches, these programs are able to provide ongoing support in such a way that the developmentally disabled adult can become more productive in a normalized employment environment. The use of the regular work environment to provide training and support while maximizing earnings is a key benefit of these supported employment designs.

REFERENCES

National Association for Retarded Citizens. (1973). *The right to choose*. Arlington, TX: National Association for Retarded Citizens, October 1973.

Rusch, F. (1979). Toward the validation of social/vocational survival skills. *Mental Retardation, 17,*143–145.

Rusch, F. R., & Schutz, R. P. (1979). Nonsheltered employment of the mentally retarded adult: Research to reality? *Journal of Contemporary Business,*

Wehman, P. (1981). *Competitive employment: New horizons for severely disabled individuals*. Baltimore, MD: Paul H. Brookes Publishing Co.

Whitehead, C. (1979). Sheltered workshops in the decade ahead: Work and wages or welfare. In G. T. Bellamy, G. O'Connor, and O. Karan (Eds.), *Vocational rehabilitation of severely handicapped persons.* Baltimore, MD: University Park Press.

∞ Chapter 12 ∞

Time-Limited Evaluation and Training

Claude W. Whitehead and Joseph Marrone

TRADITIONAL APPROACHES TO EVALUATION and training used by rehabilitation facilities and funded by state rehabilitation agencies have met with limited success in moving developmentally disabled adults into the competitive labor market. There seems to be a continuing trend by state rehabilitation agencies to refer most developmentally disabled individuals directly to sheltered workshops, rather than other diagnostic and training facilities. Also, developmentally disabled clients are much more likely to have their cases closed as "rehabilitated" when they are placed in sheltered workshops, rather than in competitive employment.

This chapter examines policies and practices, fiscal constraints, and other factors that influence the achievement of the optimal level of gainful employment by developmentally disabled individuals. It also describes major issues that must be addressed in order to improve existing service delivery systems and create alternative approaches that ensure a greater access to the competitive labor market. This steadily growing trend toward upgrading training and employment services for disabled individuals requires a careful reassessment of the existing systems, along with implementation of a broader scale of demonstrated alternative approaches.

DEFINITIONS

Before discussing the various issues and concerns involved in time-limited evaluation and training, it is important to define some of the key terms that are utilized in the vocational rehabilitation system. A clear and consistent definition of terms, such as vocational evaluation, work adjustment, training, and time-limited service, is necessary if a service system is to function as a unified system. Table 1 reviews the definitions of these terms and the current sources of the definition reported by the authors. Although there is not always concurrence in terminology, the authors feel that the definitions noted in Table 1 are the most commonly held in the vocational rehabilitation field.

The establishment of a time-limited service system has often imposed significant restrictions on the provision of services for developmentally disabled adults. Of major concern is the unrealistic restrictions that are placed on the duration of provided services if legitimate behavioral goals of the client are to be met. Because of the time constraints imposed by the vocational rehabilitation system, developmentally disabled adults are often viewed as ineligible for services or only eligible for services targeted exclusively toward assisting

Table 1. Definitions in vocational rehabilitation

Term	Definition	Source
Vocational evaluation	A comprehensive process that systematically utilizes work, real or simulated, as the focal point for assessment and vocational exploration, the purpose of which is to assist individuals in vocational development. Vocational evaluation incorporates medical, psychological, social, vocational, educational, cultural, and economic data in the attainment of goals of the evaluation process.	U.S. Department of Education, 1984a, June
Work adjustment	A vocational training process utilizing individual and group work or related activities to assist individuals in understanding the meaning, value, and demands of work to modify or develop attitudes, personal characteristics, and work behaviors and to develop functional capabilities as required in order to assist individuals toward their optimum level of vocational development.	U. S. Department of Health and Human Services, 1972
Training	Controlled, systematic manipulations of the environment, administered in such a way that their effects can be measured and rewarded.	Gold, 1973
Time-limited services	A program of services that is transitional in nature, with definable performance goals which, when achieved, will lead to the withdrawal of such services. Time-limited services do not connote a long or short period of time but a discrete service offering. This distinguishes such a service from those whose purpose is to maintain the status quo of client functioning.	Whitehead and Marrone, 1984

them in entering sheltered employment. Neither effort clearly allows the true potential of developmentally disabled adults to be realized.

RATIONALE FOR TIME-LIMITED EVALUATION AND TRAINING

Historically the types of services outlined in this section have been delivered through the federal/state vocational rehabilitation system. When reviewing evaluation and training services, it is thus impossible to ignore the importance of this tradition in the current state-of-the-practice. As can be seen throughout this entire chapter the provision of services to developmentally disabled individuals implies a mandate for change in the traditional vocational rehabilitation system. Adherence to the traditional model has placed major constraints on methods utilized by the vocational rehabilitation system to respond to the needs of this group of disabled individuals. The mandate for change calls for applying an existing structure to a newly targeted service group.

Basic Principles of Rehabilitation

There are some basic principles of rehabilitation that give people in the field their professional identity. These tenets are based on certain assumptions about human behavior and the change process. Although the concepts have not been presented in this format in the literature, each component has an importance that can—and often has been—validated by researchers and practitioners alike. These principles serve as a guiding force in moving rehabilitation into the sphere of responding to the needs of the developmentally disabled adult. The first principle reflects the importance of productive activity for an individual's physical and psychological well-being (Acton, 1981; Brenner, 1977). An associated principle reflects the need for people to consolidate their energy levels at certain plateaus as they undertake significant life changes (McCrory, Connolly, Hanson-Mayer, Sheridan-Landolfi, Barone, Blood, & Gilson, 1980). The importance of clients taking control and respon-

sibility for their own actions and the attendant consequences serve as another guiding principle in rehabilitation (Andersen, 1975; DeJong, 1979). Lastly, the need for support systems to enable an individual to effect major change successfully in his or her life is a primary principle if rehabilitation is to be effective (Ell, 1984; Smith & Sykes, 1981).

State/Federal Vocational Rehabilitation Service Delivery System

Some of the problems of time-limited evaluation and training are so pervasive because of the history and philosophy of the state/federal vocational rehabilitation initiative. Even though the mental health service delivery system has been more concerned than the vocational rehabilitation system with the needs of developmentally disabled adults, the fact remains that, historically, the mental health network has focused on such areas as housing, medical needs, and social/recreational opportunities, rather than on providing vocational evaluation and other employment-related services for this population. Since its inception in 1981, the state vocational rehabilitation program has consistently focused on employment and vocational training as the outcome for its service delivery system.

It was not until the passage of the Rehabilitation Act of 1973 that major modifications in the state/federal rehabilitation system were initiated. This legislation (PL 93–112) created civil rights protection for disabled workers through Title V. It also redirected the focus of the vocational rehabilitation program toward those persons who are most severely disabled. This latter provision was designed to ensure services to a larger number of developmentally disabled individuals, as well as other multiply disabled individuals. The most recent significant amendments were the Rehabilitation Comprehensive Services and Developmental Disabilities Amendments of 1978 (PL 95–602). This legislation opened the door for the provision of services to those individuals who were judged not feasible for achieving a vocational goal but who could benefit by functioning more independently in the community. The amendments further attempted to link the rehabilitation program with the developmental disabilities program activities.

Vocational Evaluation and Work Adjustment Services

Within the social and historical context of the rehabilitation legislation, time-limited vocational evaluation and work adjustment services became the primary vocational service offered to mentally retarded and other developmentally disabled individuals. Sheltered workshops and other vocational rehabilitation facilities were most likely to provide those services (U.S. Department of Labor, 1979). In the last decade, however, there has been increased emphasis on programming within the school system, due to the influence of the Education for All Handicapped Children Act (PL 94–142), and a trend toward provision of services in nontraditional settings (i.e., structured programs outside sheltered workshops).

The goal of vocational evaluation is to assess the individual's vocational development. A variety of techniques can be used to achieve this goal, such as psychological testing, job analysis, situational assessment, work sample evaluation, and job tryouts (Gannaway, Suik, & Becket, 1980). In the vocational rehabilitation phase of the rehabilitation process, one or more of these activities can be incorporated into the services that are rendered.

In a pure sense, vocational evaluation provides client information that serves as part of the data base for rehabilitation interventions involving changes both in client functioning and the environment in which that client will interact. However, because of the exigencies of public funding, limitations in evaluation technology, and the societal perception of the developmentally disabled population, assessment has often focused on the capacity of the client to change within narrow parameters.

Traditionally, work adjustment training has been the next service point along the rehabilitation services sequence after vocational evaluation services. The intent of providing work adjustment training is to give the client sufficient skills and abilities to meet the demands of the competitive workplace or the sheltered employment setting. If the individual cannot make the transition to an independent level of functioning, then it is felt that the highest plateau of employment potential has been reached. Thus, some form of supported or sheltered employment is sought. The current work of Bellamy and Wilcox (1981) and Wehman (1983), as well as the concepts of the Pathways Model (see Chapter 7), helps further the notion of a range of services, as well as a continuum of services. The intent is to look at vocational services as simultaneous options and choices, and as sequential activities.

Until fairly recently, vocational skill training for the developmentally disabled population has been largely ignored, in part due to societal stereotypes, employment discrimination, lack of appropriate educational opportunities, and lack of physical access to the training site. Too often the lack of interest in or apparent inability of a client to gain access to available skills training opportunities has been interpreted as a lack of vocational potential. Efforts to alter these perceptions have focused upon the development of such concepts as supported employment and increased attention to the transition from school to work (see Chapter 8).

Essential Components of Time-Limited Evaluation and Training Services

This section describes and analyzes the significance of several elements of effective rehabilitation programming in the areas of time-limited evaluation and training services.

Staff and Case Management　Perhaps the most crucial component of an effective evaluation and training model is competent, compassionate staff. Wehman (1976) suggests the need for rehabilitation counselors to be more behaviorally oriented than psychometric testing oriented in order to serve as the "behavioral engineers and change agents of the environment" (p. 235). Staff of evaluation and training programs must have a complete understanding and working knowledge of fundamentals and principles of behavioral management, a commitment to the data-based system of training programming, and an opportunity for practicum experience with a severely retarded population. These suggestions can be generalized to staff working with any severely disabled adult population.

Case management provided by staff skilled in the art of rehabilitation is a *sine qua non* of an effective program of evaluation and training. The need to identify goals, develop interventions, and measure progress is an essential part of time-limited services. Case management activities must also engage the client's natural supports, as well as the formal network of case service professionals in the rehabilitation process. This linkage mandates the need for staff to be able to communicate effectively with both the client and the family.

Sequence of Structured Assessments and Experience: Individual Diagnosis, Evaluation, Prescription, and Services In addressing the needs of the developmentally disabled adult, certain concepts need to be emphasized. One program element is the need to intervene not only with the individual but also with the total environment in which that individual is functioning (Bernstein & Karan, 1979). Concentrating solely on the client and the presenting deficits can only lead to frustration and failure on the part of both the provider and client, given the broad range of needs of many severely developmentally disabled adults. Implicit in this discussion is the focus on the client as an individual with specific skills, interests, and needs. As was noted earlier in Chapter 1 and in the model presented in Chapter 7, the needs of the individual are complex and require multiple points of intervention.

Appropriate Site and Environment Another program element that must be addressed relates to the framework in which problem identification and remediation take place. A viable program of evaluation and training services identifies those behavioral problems that can be remediated through training and/or environmental intervention—job site modification, employer education, accessible transportation—as well as those arising from limited cognitive capacities or severe physical disabilities.

Thus, the focus of the rehabilitation effort must be comprehensive in scope; it must assess the resources of the immediate environment, the evaluation data, the family support structure, and the training technologies that will assist the individual to adjust within the workplace. The rehabilitation program is not necessarily a sequential activity, but a series of simultaneous choices that should be available to the developmentally disabled adult. Additionally, these choices need to be offered at different points in time if the developmentally disabled adult is to achieve success in an employment setting. In certain instances specific plateaus or periods of inactivity may imply that the rehabilitation process is complete. However, past experiences have shown that such plateaus may reflect a momentary delay in the rehabilitation process, rather than a termination of that process.

Involvement of the Clients and their Support System One key element in the evaluation and training service that often is ignored is the need to engage effectively the client and family or other advocates in the rehabilitation process. This component is important for several reasons. First and foremost, client control and responsibility form one of the basic underpinnings of the entire philosophy of rehabilitation. Second, there is sufficient data in the literature that substantiate the effectiveness of client self-monitoring strategies (Rosine & Martin, 1983; Rudrud, Rice, Robertson, & Olsen, 1984). By definition, self-monitoring is a technique that calls for active involvement of the client in both the evaluation and training process.

The evaluation and training services that are provided to the client form only part of a complex system of interlocking relationships (e.g., client-family/friends, client-other caregivers). Although service providers sometimes view the client's family or friends as obstacles to be dealt with, rarely are they approached as allies who often have more involvement with or can exert more influence on the client than the program staff. Earlier data have shown that family expectations play a significant role in the achievements of the developmentally disabled adult in the rehabilitation process. Specifically, employment outcomes for developmentally disabled adults are influenced considerably by parental expectations. Thus, the positive and constructive involvement of the parents and friends is significant to the rehabilitation process and the achievement of a positive outcome.

Adequate Funding Determined by Client Need Although not strictly a program component, the issue of adequate funding is a reality that must be confronted. Most private service providers in the evaluation and training area receive public funding on a contractual or fee-for-service basis, primarily from state vocational rehabilitation agencies. Therefore, the extent to which these providers can continue to deliver services is dependent both on client need and the willingness and ability of a third party to finance the activities designed to meet that need. Many severely developmentally disabled adults can benefit from evaluation and training services, but they need a fairly extended period of time to achieve a positive outcome leading toward employment (Brolin, 1972; Gersten & Irvin, 1984). Although it is not realistic to assume that services can ever be totally controlled by client need without any concern for external financial constraints, inadequate funding, particularly of services for the developmentally disabled individual, will limit the effectiveness of the service and most likely compromise the outcomes achieved.

Major Issues in Time-Limited Evaluation and Training

In the 1980s, there has been a renewed national effort of planning and developing services for disabled individuals. Provider organizations, disabled consumers, and state rehabilitation agencies have been involved in the planning effort. Its major thrust has been toward employment. This outcome has been perceived as a logical sequence in the continuum of services designed to help disabled individuals live in the community.

This planning effort actually began in late 1978 in several states. Concurrently, the U.S. Department of Health and Human Services initiated a major policy study, "Training and Employment Services Policy Analysis" (U.S. Department of Health and Human Services, 1979), that evaluated services provided to disabled individuals in sheltered workshops. A national task force was convened as an advisory committee to this federal initiative.

A good deal of attention was given to services and needs of persons with developmental disabilities. This population was felt to represent a major client group in community-based sheltered workshops (U.S. Department of Labor, 1979). It was also believed that the population was the most underserved by the state rehabilitation agencies (Comptroller General, 1977; U.S. Department of Health and Human Services, 1980). Data provided by the state rehabilitation agencies indicated that mentally retarded persons represented only 12.6% of the clients rehabilitated in 1978, and nearly two-thirds of this group was classified as mildly or moderately mentally retarded. In addition, the 1978 report showed a higher-than-average rate of rejection for services for mentally retarded persons (U.S. Department of Health and Human Services, 1980). A study of mentally disabled individuals returning to the community by the General Accounting Office (Comptroller General, 1977) likewise indicated problems faced by these persons in gaining access to vocational rehabilitation services.

The findings of these various seminars, committees, and panels indicated the need for a wider variety of approaches to providing services to the developmentally disabled adult. Additionally there was a keen interest in expanding the capacity of the vocational rehabilitation system to respond to the employment and training needs of the developmentally disabled adult. Much of the effort has been reflected in expanding alternatives to sheltered employment. As can be seen by the discussions in several chapters in this book, sheltered employment should not be viewed as the sole resource for the developmentally disabled adult. It is essential that additional options, as noted in Chapter 7, be made available to enable the expansion of opportunities for developmentally disabled adults. Impediments to the expansion of opportunities for developmentally disabled adults within the vocational rehabilitation system and proposed solutions are reviewed in the following sections.

Entitlement versus Eligibility Although handicapped children and institutionalized persons have been granted entitlement to services through legislation, most disabled adults have no such entitlement. Those not part of the special entitlement class often are rejected for services because they are judged not feasible—that is, unable to benefit from the provision of vocational rehabilitation services, even though they are eligible by law for state rehabilitation services (U.S. Department of Health and Human Services, 1980).

Only a few states have enacted legislation giving a right to services to developmentally disabled adults. However, many states have a mandate to serve eligible clients of state mental retardation and developmental disabilities agencies. Because state rehabilitation agencies primarily serve mildly mentally retarded individuals, the need for entitlement to service for the more severely disabled individuals is critical.

Some states provide joint funding to several state agencies to ensure the movement of more severely disabled individuals from adult training and day activity programs to sheltered employment and ultimately into regular places of employment. Progress in this area is somewhat slow, however. Federal efforts by the Office of Special Education and Rehabilitative Services and the Administration on Developmental Disabilities have provided some leadership at the national level in encouraging agencies to be attentive to the needs of the more severely disabled in day activity programs.

Intensive versus Extended Training Services Traditionally, evaluation services purchased by state vocational rehabilitation agencies from rehabilitation facilities have been short-term in duration. Although extended evaluation has been available as an option through state vocational rehabilitation agencies for more than a decade, its use with severely disabled clients has been minimal. Training services for developmentally disabled indi-

viduals, on the other hand, have tended to be provided over a period of weeks or months in many states (U.S. Department of Health and Human Services, 1980). The premise behind this extension of training time, through the use of extended evaluation services, was that developmentally disabled adults responded more slowly in a training program and needed additional opportunities to learn required work skills, as well as to adjust socially to the working environment. The pacing of services according to the capacity of the individual client should be the most important determinant of the intensity and extent of services provided.

Bellamy, O'Connor, and Karan (1979), Karan (1978), and others have demonstrated that intensive training services can produce improved results in severely and profoundly retarded individuals previously considered unable to benefit from training. Traditional training programs provided in sheltered workshops are less expensive, even though also provided over an extended period of time, but the results achieved seem to be less significant in terms of increased productivity for the client (Bellamy, et al., 1979).

Some state rehabilitation agencies, including Michigan and New Jersey, have developed pilot projects involving intensive training services that pay a higher per diem fee for a shorter period of time. The results reflect limited success thus far. However, favorable results on intensified training services are reported in certain supported employment projects (see Chapters 9, 10, and 11).

Segregated versus Integrated Settings for Training

There is no consensus on whether it is more desirable to serve a client in an isolated, protected environment or to provide training on the job in a (competitive) industrial site. (An analogous issue is the movement toward mainstreaming in the school classroom that likewise continues to be challenged by some professionals.)

The most reasonable compromise seems to be a scheduling balance, in which instruction and training are initially provided in a structured, protected setting when such isolation seems necessary and then gradually phasing into an open competitive environment. Another approach would provide for intensive job coaching on-site with gradual reduction as the client progresses in the industrial setting. Obviously, in any design, the training should be success-oriented.

An absolute rule that advocates either a segregated or an integrated setting exclusively cannot reflect the changing needs of the developmentally disabled adult over time. When special guidance, support, and structured training are necessary, intensive supervision in a segregated environment would be more appropriate. When specific behaviors and social/interpersonal skills are to be acquired, movement into a natural setting may be more beneficial. Experiences have shown that the use of the normalized working environment in training developmentally disabled individuals can be very significant.

Although there is continuing debate on the merits of a segregated versus an integrated setting, the data show that many more developmentally disabled adults than had been anticipated can respond to a productive work setting (Wehman, 1983). The determination of the environment within which the work is performed depends to some extent on the needs of the industry, the skills of the individuals, and the ability of society to accommodate to such change.

Specific Skill Training versus Work Conditioning

Developmentally disabled adults, especially those who are mentally retarded, experience strong resistance in attempting to gain access to vocational skill training programs in public vocational or trade schools. Often, they are refused admission because of their perceived failure to meet the basic educational requirements of the school.

Sheltered workshops have experienced limited success in establishing ongoing skill training programs for developmentally disabled individuals mostly because of the lack of suitable referrals to the training programs by spon-

soring agencies. The U.S. Department of Labor (1977) study of sheltered workshops found very few vocational training programs for mentally retarded persons. Utilizing on-the-job training at commercial or industrial sites outside the workshop has been more successful.

This failure of sheltered workshops to provide relevant training has been reported often (Flexer, 1983; U.S. Department of Labor, 1979). Department of Labor studies found that more than one-half of the sheltered workshop clients had never used power tools or machinery. The rationale for not utilizing such equipment has been dispelled by programs in several states where severely retarded individuals have effectively used power-operated woodworking and metal processing equipment (Whitehead, 1981).

The type of skill training offered may relate more to the reluctance of workshop staff to expend the extra effort in developing training programs than to the inability of the workshop to secure the necessary capital to purchase equipment and hire skill trainers.

An offsetting factor in this issue is the effort by the workshop to respond to an increasing number of severely disabled individuals. Many of these individuals have little or no educational experience and are considered to have minimal potential for gainful employment, according to state vocational rehabilitation criteria. The unwillingness of the state rehabilitation agencies to support training for the severely mentally retarded and other developmentally disabled individuals is another barrier to eventual entry into specific skill training programs.

In the state validation studies conducted to field-test the findings of the Training and Employment Services Policy Analysis of the U.S. Department of Health and Human Services (U.S. Department of Health and Human Services, 1980), sheltered workshop directors consistently emphasized the need for work experience and wage earnings for severely disabled persons unable to benefit from vocational skill training. Their experience in implementing skill training programs in the workshop showed that the programs tended to exclude the majority of the severely disabled adults. They further suggested that prospective employers were more often concerned with hiring a worker with good production and attendance performance than a vocationally trained person. This belief was confirmed by employers who stated that, in most cases, workers could be trained in basic production skills on the job.

Use of Real Work versus Simulated Work (Job Samples)

The use of commercially developed job samples rather than real work in assessing skills and potentials has been surrounded by controversy for many years in the rehabilitation professional community. The thrust for improving and expanding rehabilitation services through the use of job samples evolved from the 1965 amendments to the Vocational Rehabilitation Act (PL 89-333). Unfortunately, most of the early job sample test systems were found to be not suitable for developmentally disabled clients, due to their focus on reading of both the instruments and the elements of the assessment package utilized. Subsequently more suitable systems were developed and marketed, but the utilization of commercially developed evaluation systems is still questioned by many in the field of rehabilitation.

Site visits to sheltered workshops in several states conducted as part of the TESPA studies (Whitehead, 1979a) revealed that facilities serving a predominately developmentally disabled client population tend to receive a lower-than-average level of rehabilitation services funding from the state rehabilitation agency. This limitation in funding seemed to result in a greater reliance on income from the work program and thus a focus on real rather than simulated work. The training and evaluation were more likely to involve situational assessment on the job, rather than isolated testing and training in a facility. However, advocates of the use of job samples note that the type of work performed by the workshops is overly simplified and lacks the diversity necessary to test effectively the client's skills and interests.

Further, the use of job-related samples enhances preparation of the client for eventual competitive job placement.

Gainful Employment versus Competitive Employment Goal Setting

This issue has been debated for many years both within and outside rehabilitation agencies. The mandate to provide services to severely disabled individuals, which was incorporated in the 1973 amendments of the Rehabilitation Act (PL 93-112), initially eased the competitive employment focus of state vocational rehabilitation agencies. However, subsequent federal funding restrictions may have triggered a return to the focus on clients with competitive employment potential.

The priority of the state agency is significant because it is a primary funding source for employment training services for developmentally disabled adults. It was earlier noted with alarm that only 12.6% of the rehabilitation closures were mentally retarded individuals (U.S. Department of Health, Education and Welfare, 1979). These data included persons considered as rehabilitated in sheltered workshops. The proportion of individuals placed in sheltered employment as opposed to competitive employment is not known.

A March 1984 memorandum to state rehabilitation agencies by the Commissioner of the Rehabilitation Services Administration (RSA) (U.S. Department of Education) advised that rehabilitation closures in work activities centers and sheltered workshops could be considered as valid rehabilitation, thus clarifying the federal definition of acceptable gainful employment (U.S. Department of Education, 1984). Response to this memorandum has been mixed. In some states, the VR agencies still do not provide training support if the client is not a competitive employment candidate. Other states have been allowing sheltered closures and may now tend to use this authority to place more clients in sheltered workshops, rather than exert the greater effort to place them in competitive employment. The position expressed by RSA has both positive and negative implications.

Amendments included in the 1973 Rehabilitation Act (PL 93-112) required state rehabilitation agencies to follow up clients placed in sheltered workshops. The purpose of the follow-up was to ensure that clients were not being abandoned by state vocational rehabilitation agencies. A 1979 U.S. General Accounting Office study showed that this requirement was not being followed (Comptroller General, 1980).

The debate on sheltered versus competitive employment also centers around the right of all disabled individuals to a job. A 1981 national conference on vocational and employment opportunities for individuals who are mentally retarded (President's Committee on Mental Retardation, 1983) adopted resolutions that affirmed that all handicapped individuals who want to work should have that opportunity. If the person cannot secure and hold a job without assistance in the competitive labor market, then sheltered employment and supported employment should be made available.

The U.S. Congress expressed concern about the appropriateness of sheltered employment and mandated two studies of sheltered workshops by the Department of Labor (U.S. Department of Labor, 1979) and a General Accounting Office investigation (Comptroller General, 1981). Although none of the studies or investigations found significant evidence of wrongful activities, there was concern expressed that only about 12% of the handicapped clients moved from the workshop into competitive employment jobs each year (U.S. Department of Labor, 1977). Recent follow-up data from a few states suggest that the level of "graduation" is not improving (Whitehead, 1984).

The 1976 U.S. Department of Labor interviews with 2600 clients in sheltered workshops produced the surprising finding that most clients are pleased with services being provided in workshops; mentally retarded clients had the highest level of satisfaction (U.S. Department of Labor, 1979). This finding raises new questions regarding who determines the suitability of the sheltered workshop as an appropriate placement and what influence should the cli-

ent's needs, interest, and preferences have on the determination of the employment environment. This finding has prompted increased controversy regarding efforts to move the client from the workshop to a competitive employment setting. Whitehead (1979b) suggests several reasons why a client may not graduate from the sheltered workshop, including lack of assistance in finding a job, lack of transportation to the job site, parent resistance to placement outside the security of the workshop, fear of loss of support services, and reluctance by the workshop staff to place a client outside it because of production demands within the workshop.

The Pathways Model (see Chapter 7) may present some strategies that could be brought to bear on this complex issue. Supported employment where staff support is provided for an indefinite period of time seems to be an alternative deserving further investigation and consideration.

Measuring Results and Evaluating Performance and Achievement

The standard measure of success in the provision of vocational rehabilitation services is the rehabilitation of the client—case closure—as gainfully employed. As noted earlier, the case closure for the developmentally disabled person is most likely in a sheltered workshop or work activity center, rather than in competitive employment. Further, the U.S. Department of Labor studies of the sheltered workshops indicated that less than 10% of the clients closed into gainful employment in sheltered workshops eventually moved out into competitive employment. Although developmentally disabled individuals represented only one-third of the total annual referrals to workshops by state departments of vocational rehabilitation, they constituted more than three-quarters of the population in the extended sheltered employment programs in one specific state (Whitehead, 1984).

In examining the appropriateness of evaluation and training services on an individual client basis, one should ask whether evaluation and training services were designed or planned toward a competitive employment goal or to a sheltered or subsidized employment goal. A continuing controversy among professionals, parents, and advocates addresses, without resolution, the issues of the individual's needs and interests, i.e., is that person happier and more secure in a sheltered workshop, or is the quality of life higher in the regular labor market employment setting (U.S. Department of Labor, 1979)? Recent demonstration projects involving competitive employment reflect significant success with mentally retarded individuals having similar functional levels and characteristics as those traditionally served in sheltered workshops in the extended employment program (Bellamy et al., 1979).

The standard measure of performance of clients rehabilitated in the state vocational rehabilitation program is the hourly or annual wage earnings of the client at closure. The anticipation of closure into competitive employment is a factor in the decision to accept a client for services. Such a practice by vocational rehabilitation counselors tends to discriminate against the developmentally disabled client for whom sheltered employment and subminimum wage earnings are the anticipated outcome. Until competitive employment-oriented programs are more extensively developed, a weighted closure system that recognizes the change in functional levels of the client should be used. Such a system could reflect economic returns realized when a client moves from a state institution in which the annual cost for services far exceeds $10,000—for residential and day program services—to employment in a community-based sheltered workshop and group home living in which costs total less than one-half of that amount. In this case, the public cost reduction should be given more importance than the hourly wage earnings of the client receiving evaluation and training services.

Unless there is a major policy or procedure change regarding the measure of performance utilized by state rehabilitation agencies, developmentally disabled individuals will continue to have limited access to vocational rehabilitation systems, especially time-limited

evaluation and training services. Unfortunately, in most states the rehabilitation agency is the only source of vocational evaluation and training (Whitehead & Rhodes, 1985).

SUMMARY AND RECOMMENDATIONS

The pathway to employment for many developmentally disabled adults involves travel through the vocational evaluation and training service system. Because the primary funding resource for such services is the state rehabilitation agency, eligibility for services is of crucial importance (rehabilitation services are not an entitlement). Developmentally disabled individuals have a higher-than-average rate of rejection from vocational rehabilitation services (Whitehead, 1981).

The tradition of time-limited evaluation and training services has been challenged because the services often fail to allow the severely disabled individual sufficient time to acquire needed personal and vocational skills. The appropriateness of sheltered workshops for training services and employment is also questioned. New technologies are emerging as alternatives to sheltered employment—supported employment, work-stations-in-industry, and on-the-job training in competitive employment sites. The controversy continues about the degree of importance given to the needs and interests of the developmentally disabled individual.

Federal laws designed to prohibit discrimination and ensure affirmative action in the employment of handicapped individuals have been relatively ineffective (Whitehead, 1979c). Private employers have acknowledged that forced hiring is neither effective nor efficient and have suggested an approach of marketing qualified handicapped individuals to potential employers.

Existing measures of performance by state rehabilitation agencies have been found to restrict access to services by severely disabled individuals when the expected outcome is employment in a sheltered workshop at wages below the statutory minimum. Efforts to implement a modified form of evaluating case closures have not been successful to date.

In light of the above discussions, the following specific suggestions seem appropriate. Access to training and employment services by developmentally disabled individuals must be improved. Existing barriers contained in training programs funded through the Rehabilitation Act, the Vocational Education Act, and the Education for All Handicapped Children Act must be removed. Action to revise entry criteria, eligibility, and outcome measures must be initiated at the federal and state levels.

The tendency to refer developmentally disabled individuals almost exclusively to sheltered workshops and to have state vocational rehabilitation agencies accept closure in sheltered employment without follow-up should be challenged. The routine stereotyping of developmentally disabled adults ignores their capabilities and results in programming generally restricted to a sheltered employment outcome, rather than competitive employment goals.

In addition, state rehabilitation agency policies and practices regarding cost reimbursement for evaluation and training services should also be revised. The policy of paying less than cost for rehabilitation services purchased in sheltered workshops restricts the capacity of the workshop to provide services of the quantity and quality needed by developmentally disabled individuals.

State rehabilitation agencies and state mental retardation/developmental disabilities agencies should develop cooperative service and funding arrangements to meet more effectively the needs of developmentally disabled adults. Although the state vocational rehabilitation agency has a federal mandate to provide training and employment services, the developmentally disabled client often needs transportation assistance and other support services on a continuing basis. Unfortunately, the vocational rehabilitation services system is designed as a time-limited program that assumes that job placement and limited follow-up end the need for further services (Whitehead & Rhodes, 1985).

Sheltered workshops should improve the quality and diversity of training and employment opportunities offered. They also should increase efforts to move the disabled individual from the workshop into competitive employment outside the workshop. Better jobs could produce benefits for the client and the workshop through increased income and wage earnings. Creating a bridge from the workshop to the regular labor market would enhance the status of the workshop as a rehabilitation facility and ensure a steadier flow of client referrals by the state vocational rehabilitation agency.

A national policy on employment of handicapped individuals, which has been advanced in the past, should be widely promoted in order to meet the growing needs and rights of all disabled adults who want to work on a job (Cox & Whitehead, 1980). To the maximum extent possible, handicapped individuals should have the opportunity to hold jobs in the competitive labor market. Yet, individuals who are limited in their ability to secure and maintain competitive employment should be able to obtain supported or sheltered employment when appropriate.

At least 36 states have laws prohibiting discrimination against handicapped individuals, but most of these are relatively ineffective in ensuring employment. An aggressive program of marketing the skills of qualified handicapped individuals would likely achieve better results. Without job opportunities appropriate to the capacities and potential of the developmentally disabled worker, the evaluation and training services provided cannot be justified, and the disabled individual will experience continued rejection and frustration.

The need to view the developmentally disabled adult as a worker is essential. The belief that all individuals should be given an opportunity to engage in employment will focus the attention of legislators, administrators, and industry on expansion of opportunities so that belief can be realized.

REFERENCES

Acton, N. (1981). Employment of disabled persons: Where are we going? *International Labor Review, 120*(1), 1–13.

Andersen, T. (1975). An alternative frame of reference for rehabilitation: The helping process vs the medical model. *Archives of Physical Medicine and Rehabilitation, 56,* 101–104.

Bellamy, G., O'Connor, G., & Karan, O. (Eds.). (1979). *Vocational rehabilitation of severely handicapped persons: Contemporary service strategies.* Baltimore, MD: University Park Press.

Bellamy, G. T., & Wilcox, B. (1981). Secondary education for severely handicapped students. Guidelines for quality services. In K. P. Lynch, W. E. Kiernan, & J. A. Stark (Eds.), *Prevocational and vocational education for special needs youth: A blueprint for the 1980s* (pp. 65–80). Baltimore, MD: Paul H. Brookes Publishing Company.

Bernstein, G., & Karan, O. (1979). Obstacles to vocational normalization for the developmentally disabled. *Rehabilitation Literature, 40*(3), 66–71.

Brenner, M. H. (1977). Personal stability and economic security. *Social Policy, 8,* 2–4.

Brolin, D. (1972). Value of rehabilitation services and correlates of vocational success with the mentally retarded. *American Journal of Mental Deficiency, 76,* 644–651.

Cox, J., & Whitehead, C. (1980). *Needed: A national policy on employment of handicapped individuals.* Address to American Association on Mental Deficiency, San Francisco, CA.

Comptroller General. (1977). Returning the mentally disabled to the community: Government needs to do more. Washington, D C : United States General Accounting Office.

Comptroller General. (1980). Better re-evaluations of handicapped persons in sheltered workshops could increase their opportunities for competitive employment. Washington, D C : United States General Accounting Office.

Comptroller General. (1981). Stronger Federal efforts needed for providing employment opportunities and enforcing labor standards in sheltered workshops. Washington, D C : United States General Accounting Office.

DeFazio, N., & Flexer, R. (1983). Organizational barriers to productivity, meaningful wages and normalized work opportunity for mentally retarded persons. *Mental Retardation,* 157–162.

DeJong, G. (1979). Independent living: From social movement to analytic paradigm. *Archives of Physical Medicine and Rehabilitation, 60,* 435–446.

Ell, K. (1984). Social networks, social support, and health status: A review. *Social Service Review, March,* 133–144.

Flexer, R. (1983). Habilitation services for developmentally disabled persons. *Journal of Applied Rehabilitation Counseling, 14*(3), 6–12.

Gannaway, T., Suik, J., & Becket, W. (1980). A predictive validity study of a job sample program with handicapped and disadvantaged individuals. *The Vocational Guidance Quarterly, 29*(1), 4–12.

Gersten, R., & Irvin, L. (1984). Vocational assessment for severely retarded adolescents and adults. The trainee performance sample. *Vocational Evaluation and Work Adjustment Bulletin, Summer,* 42–45.

Gold, M. (1973). Research in the vocational habilitation of the retarded: The present and the future. In N. Ellis (Ed.), *International review of research in mental retardation.* New York: Academic Press.

Karan, O. (Ed.). (1978). *Habilitation practices with the severely developmentally disabled adult.* Madison, WI: University of Wisconsin.

McCrory, D., Connolly, P., Hanson-Mayer, T., Sheridan-Landolfi, J., Barone, F., Blood, A., & Gilson, A. (1980). Rehabilitation crisis: Impact of growth. *Journal of Applied Rehabilitation Counseling, 2*(3), 136–139.

President's Committee on Mental Retardation. (1983). *The mentally retarded worker: An economic discovery. Report to the President.* Washington, DC: U.S. Department of Health and Human Services.

Rosine, L., & Martin, G. (1983). Self-management training to decrease undesirable behavior of mentally handicapped adults. *Rehabilitation Psychology, 28*(4), 195–205.

Rudrud, E., Rice, J., Robertson, J., & Olsen, N. (1984). The use of self-monitoring to increase and maintain production rates. *Vocational Evaluation and Work Adjustment Bulletin, Spring,* 14–17.

Smith, H., & Sykes, S. (1981). Parents' views on the development of social competencies in their mildly intellectually handicapped adolescents. *Australian Journal of Developmental Disabilities, 7*(1), 17–26.

U.S. Department of Education. (1984a, June). *Rehabilitation brief. Rehabilitation Services Administration.* Washington, DC: U.S. Government Printing Office.

U.S. Department of Education. (1984b). *Rehabilitation closure policies. Memorandum from the commissioner, #84-11.* Washington, DC: Rehabilitation Services Administration.

U.S. Department of Health and Human Services. (1972). *Annual report to the President and the Congress. Social and Rehabilitation Services Administration.* Washington, DC: U.S. Government Printing Office.

U.S. Department of Health and Human Services. (1979). Office of the Assistant Secretary for Planning and Evaluation. *Training and employment services policy analysis: A look at community based services for handicapped individuals. First year progress report.* Washington, DC.

U.S. Department of Health and Human Services. (1980). *Training and employment services policy analysis: Report on field testing seminars in six states.* Office of the Assistant Secretary for Planning and Evaluation. Washington, D C. 12–13 (unpublished).

U.S. Department of Labor. (1977). *Sheltered workshop study: Workshop survey. Vol. 1.* Washington, D C.

U.S. Department of Labor. (1979). *Sheltered workshop study: Study of handicapped clients in sheltered work-*

shops and recommendations of the secretary. Vol. 2. Washington, DC.

Wehman, P. (1976). Vocational training of the severely retarded: Expectations and potential. Rehabilitation Literature, 37(8), 233–236.

Wehman, P. (1983). Toward the employability of severely handicapped children and youth. Teaching Exceptional Children, Summer, 219–225.

Whitehead, C. (1979a). Sheltered workshops in the decade ahead: Work and wages, or welfare. In G. T. Bellamy, G. O'Connor, & O. C. Karan (Eds.), Vocational rehabilitation of severely handicapped persons—Contemporary service strategies. Baltimore, MD: University Park Press.

Whitehead, C. (1979b). The handicapped client comments on sheltered workshop services. Presentation to Annual Conference, National Association of Rehabilitation Facilities, Pittsburgh, PA.

Whitehead, C. (1979c). Sheltered workshops—Effective accommodation or exploitation. South Bend, IN: AMICUS.

Whitehead, C. (1981). Final report: Training and employment services for handicapped individuals. Washington, DC: U.S. Department of Health and Human Services.

Whitehead, C. (1984). Analysis of operations of vocational rehabilitation facilities in 1983. North Brunswick, NJ: New Jersey Association of Rehabilitation Facilities (monograph).

Whitehead, C., & Marrone, J. (1984). Time limited evaluation and training. Paper presented at the Conference on Pathways in Employment for Adults with Developmental Disabilities, Boston, MA.

Whitehead, C., & Rhodes, S. (1985). Guidelines for evaluating, reviewing, and enhancing employment-related services for people with developmental disabilities. Washington, DC: National Association of Developmental Disabilities Councils.

∞ Chapter 13 ∞

Contemporary Industrial, Managerial, and Production Innovations and Their Implications for Rehabilitation Practice

Kevin P. Lynch, Jeffrey A. Ditty,
Sheila Scott, and Vanessa C. Smith

THIS CHAPTER IS CONCERNED WITH CHANGES in the private sector in industrial management and production systems and the relationships of these changes to the broad issues of assessment, adjustment, training, and sheltered/competitive placement of developmentally disabled individuals. It is important to note that a chapter concerned with manufacturing and management changes in the private sector and their implications for rehabilitation would have been an anachronism only 5 years ago because of extensive reliance on federal, state, and local program conceptualization, funding, and evaluation. To survive in the rehabilitation profession during the late 1960s and throughout the 1970s, astute rehabilitation specialists needed contacts in their state capital and Washington, plus they had to be able to read and quickly respond to the *Federal Register.* Indeed, most popular graduate rehabilitation texts composed in the late 1960s and 1970s usually had (and still have) multiple chapters on state-federal rehabilitation system mechan-

ics and federal legislation (i.e., see Bitter, 1979). Although federal initiatives will continue to be important to rehabilitation programs, state priorities will probably be more significant in the future, and building relationships with industry to employ special treatment populations will become the most important focus of all.

The purpose of this chapter is to provide an understanding of the development of new technology and its impact on the employment of developmentally disabled individuals. This technology involves much more than machine-intensive use. It involves new developments in manufacturing and innovative management principles that have revolutionized the way goods are produced and services are delivered in this country. The authors' intent is to provide insight into the complex strategic planning and reorganization taking place in American industry. Attention is also given to proven production and management skills based on international research and development. In Chapter

7 the authors provided the *process*—through a model—for developing a successful pathway to employment. In this chapter, recommendations for the *content* of successful employment, particularly in the private sector, are made. These same content principles and techniques, however, also apply to agency-operated habilitation programs.

In this chapter, as in Chapter 22, future directions are discussed, and there are frequent references to Japanese management and manufacturing techniques. The many references should not be interpreted as evidence of the authors' new-found bias for matters Oriental. Rather, they are a function of the genuine innovations that have been derived from Japanese industry, many of which were taught to the Japanese by academic and industrial consultants retained under the postwar recovery provisions of the Supreme Commander of the Allied Powers treaty under the direct management of General MacArthur (Allen, 1958). What Denison (1976) and others have referred to as Japan's economic miracle is, in many instances, direct evidence of that nation's ability to be a worthy student. The influence of the Japanese system on the American production and management system will continue to be evident and thereby will have an impact on the private sector in its efforts to employ the developmentally disabled.

THE NEW INDUSTRIAL REVOLUTION

A number of industrially related works published within the past 5 years suggests that Western industry is in a process of change, as far-reaching in scope as was the Industrial Revolution. Works such as *Megatrends*, (Nessbitt, 1982), *Theory Z* (Ouchi, 1981), *In Search of Excellence* (Peters & Waterman, 1982), *The Art of Japanese Management* (Pascale & Althos, 1981), and others have forecast fundamental changes in what businesses produce and the means by which they accomplish their productive purpose.

Industrial productivity is the measure of the output of goods or services resulting from a given input, such as the number of fuel in-

jection kits assembled or rooms cleaned by a work team in a specific time period. Having led the world in output per worker for decades, this country has been shocked to learn that its national productivity is the lowest of all industrialized nations (10%) and that Japan's overall output, in particular, has increased by 90% (Cascio, 1978). The loss of traditional American dominance in foreign and domestic markets in such diverse areas as car manufacturing, electronics, and optics has reawakened interest in manufacturing processes and management strategies as vehicles to restore lost market share by improving employee qualitative and quantitative output (Pascale & Althos, 1981).

Manufacturing Changes

It is still commonplace for Western manufacturing industries to have large amounts of materials produced and stored in buffer inventory, a process referred to as job-lot manufacturing. With this process the manufacturer produces a medium-to-low volume of a variety of products and models. For example, in American automotive plants, employees produce hundreds and thousands of springs, steering wheels, seats, speedometers, door locks, spark plugs, and so forth, which are stored at the manufacturing site and also stored in buffer. This inventory guarantees the manufacturer that wide swings in consumer preferences can be met by instantly drawing on materials in inventory. The manufacturer must be able to respond rapidly to unpredictable and constantly changing product orders because a small change in end-product volume has ripple effects on work in process and raw material ordering. Western industry, especially in the United States, has learned to handle these data-processing tasks through computer-based manufacturing management, which is commonly known as materials requirement planning (MRP).

Interestingly, the Japanese also employed job-lot procedures in the past, but abandoned that approach for a mix of other approaches that they believe are superior. The industrial giants of Mitsubishi, Nissan, Nihon Radiator, Honda, IBM, or Lilly have not become megacorporations by catering to consumer whims, but have instead entrenched themselves in the market by producing a few products very well, often in market areas ignored by others. These companies believe that low cost and high quality lead to growth in market share, a belief that was first expounded by Henry Ford (Schonberger, 1982).

Additionally, as a company continues to gain a larger portion of the market share, this increase in volume requires longer production runs of the same product model. Such repetitive operations permit management to "fine tune" process and inventory variables even further, which then leads to a product that is so good that it becomes attractive to purchasers of all income levels, not just to those who must economize (e.g., witness the growth of Nikon 35mm cameras during the 1960s, which were priced, at that time, far below American and German products).

Again, as the company grows, marketing its high-quality Henry Ford-type basic black product, it then has sufficient capital to build plants to produce other models and products, which then gives it the force of a full line of models, all produced repetitively and sold in volume. The Western job-lot manufacturer is then left without even the competitive edge of diverse models.

Job-lot manufacturing processes, even when coupled with new and more sophisticated ("closed loop") MRP systems (MRP II), still have two inherent and serious deficiencies: storage costs and quality. As was noted earlier, job-lot manufacturing involves the comparatively slow production of a wide variety of items, which are then inventoried. These elements are available to respond to consumer preference, a process which is guided by statistical MRP systems. One of the most common examples of job-lot procedures in operation has been the selection of an American-manufactured automobile. A new General Motors, Ford, or Chrysler base-level product is available to the consumer at prices that are often competitive with the Japanese product. However, the base-level American product is little more than "transportation." The option list for

the base product is both extensive—for example, improved seats, more powerful engine, handling packages, interior options, multiple sound systems, wheel and tire combinations—and expensive. A base 1985 Pontiac 6000 may be sticker-priced at $8,200, whereas the same package, with a complete set of options, may be listed at close to $14,000. By contrast, there is one factory option for the Nissan 300ZX turbo: leather interior or cloth.

Being able to respond to multiple consumer preferences is not achieved without cost—in this case, storage. Japan, largely devoid of natural resources—a nation with slightly more than half the United States population situated on an island slightly larger in land mass than the State of California, with mountains constituting 80% of the terrain, and with less than 20% of the land available for farming—considers land, space, and efficiency as precious. The United States, rich in mineral and agricultural resources and with low population density, has never been greatly concerned with storage and related cost until recently.

In 1973, in response to American support for the Israelis in the short-lived Arab-Israeli conflict, the Organization of Petroleum Exporting Countries (OPEC) reduced oil production and, over a period of months and years, raised the per-barrel price of crude many times over, which had ripple effects through all the industrialized—and Third World—economies. Suddenly, storage costs multiplied, as did the cost of all forms of transportation. Buffer inventory suddenly became expensive.

Large inventory became expensive not only in terms of rent and maintenance of material, but also because rapid change in consumer preference made much of the inventory obsolescent. Suddenly, large and fuel-wasteful vehicles and the large optional wheels, springs, leather seats, luggage carriers, and "brightwork" were being overlooked for smaller and more fuel-efficient vehicles. Larger seats and chrome pieces suitable for placement on a Buick Estate Wagon cannot adapt to a Vega; thus the huge cost of reworking inventory had to be added to initial manufacture, transportation, and shipping expense.

Engineering the Workplace

Not only has large inventory become expensive, it has also led to the problems that were never foreseen in Economic Order Quantity (EOQ) calculations: production quality. This is not to suggest that Western industry has not been interested in work quality. Manufacturers have experimented with job simplification and functional effectiveness designs that speed task acquisition and ostensibly reduce production error (McCormick, 1979). However, in some work simplification settings, it is not uncommon for a worker to experience 800 or more unvarying repetitions of the same activity or movement in 1 hour, which may lead to reduced motivation and employee vigilance. During the 1950s, largely as a reaction against functional effectiveness, shops began to experiment with novel work designs, such as job enlargement, enrichment, and autonomous work conditions (Herzberg, 1968; Karlsen, 1972). Enlargement approaches attempted to give the work more meaning and less boredom by providing more responsibility to the worker. Enrichment procedures give employees even more responsibility for self-monitoring—for example, workers can work directly with other departments with regard to problems, etc.—functions that are usually the purview of middle management (Ford, 1973; Herzberg, 1968). Autonomous work group designs both enlarge and enrich work in that workers may decide among themselves how they are to address the work and what work assignments are to be meted out (Klein, 1976).

Most American manufacturing concerns usually employ job simplification or enlargement approaches, seldom use enrichment approaches, and rarely implement autonomous work group designs. Schonberger (1982) suggests that neither the more common simplification nor enlargement approaches—the other approaches being employed so seldom as to make their effectiveness academic—can overcome the difficulties inherent in job-lot production and large inventories. In brief, these difficulties are: 1) lack of employee re-sponsibility for quality and 2) slow feedback for good/poor quality.

In the typical job-lot manufacturing process, materials are processed by various departments. Some materials are immediately forwarded to the next operation, whereas others are stored in inventory to achieve economic order quantity, avoiding having to restart the line for multiple small orders. Processed materials from a department are checked by statistical process control down the line by a quality control department. The existence of a quality control department and the use of statistical process/quality control suggest two undesirable probabilities: First, the individual worker is not responsible immediately for the quality of his or her work, and second, the use of statistical process control, by definition, suggests that some level of error is both tolerated and acceptable.

Closely allied to defect tolerance is the second major problem associated with job-lot manufacturing. A worker whose machinery has migrated out of tolerance may be forwarding defective parts to another department or to inventory for long periods of time. Because statistical process control is by definition a sampling procedure, there is a probability that the locus of defects may not be identified for a long time, which can translate into potential slowdowns along the line or defective merchandise reaching the consumer with a low mean time between failure. In the automotive industry this factor can also translate into expensive product recalls and litigation for product liability.

Alternative Production Procedures

As an alternative to the work simplification and buffer inventory procedure, many companies are exploring the use of the Japanese JIT/TQC procedure. The just-in-time (JIT) concept seems to be at the core of Japanese production management and production improvement. The idea behind it is a simple one: Produce and deliver finished goods just-in-time to be sold, subassemblies just-in-time to be assembled into finished goods, fabricate parts just-in-time to go into subassemblies, and purchase materials just-in-time to be transformed into fabricated parts. Put another way, the Japanese industry produces small quantities "just-in-time"; Western industry produces massive quantities (buffer inventory) "just-in-case."

The JIT ideal is for all materials to be in active use as elements of work in process, never at rest collecting carrying charges. It is a hand-to-mouth model of operation with production and material movement. At the Kawasaki Motors subsidiary plant in Lincoln, Nebraska, this ideal serves as a target—a dominant objective for the entire plant to aim for year after year. Each move, everywhere in the plant, toward smaller production/delivery sizes achieves some of the promised JIT benefits.

The Total Quality Control (TQC) concept may stand alone or may operate in concert with JIT production. In the latter case, TQC greatly enhances the quality control aspects of the JIT model and is especially effective in reducing scrap, reducing rework labor hours, which in turn produces less material waste, and giving fast feedback to employees on defects.

In TQC all plant personnel are imbued with the view that quality is an end in itself. "Quality at the source" is the slogan that best epitomizes the TQC concept. What it means to the plant workers is that errors, if any, should be caught and corrected at the source (i.e., where the work is performed). This concept is in contrast to the widespread Western practice of inspection by statistical sampling *after* the item has been produced (e.g., defect detection as opposed to defect prevention). As was noted earlier, in the Western system the inspection is performed by individuals from a quality control department; in Japanese TQC, workers and foremen—not a quality control department—have primary responsibility for quality, and all other personnel are expected to contribute, often at the request of the workers and foreman. Engineers build automatic error-checking devices in addition to those supplied by equipment suppliers, personnel provide quality control training, management is quick to approve funding for any ideas that might enhance quality, and so forth.

High-Performance Organizations

Industry has increasingly come to realize that worksite and task design, in and of themselves, are not sufficient to produce high levels of output from workers, particularly those with additional deficits, such as the developmentally disabled. Largely as a result of this country's severe loss of market share in industries once regarded as untouchable by foreign competition—automotive, optics, electronics, musical instruments, etc.—American industry has begun to study Japanese management strategies in particular and high-performance corporations in general (Ouchi, 1981; Pascale & Althos, 1981).

High-performance industrial organizations, both Japanese and American, are reputed to care for the "whole employee" (Tsurumi, 1976). In practical terms, this concern is often expressed by the provision of medical care, recreational facilities, dormitories for unmarried personnel (exclusive to the Japanese), psychological counseling, family planning, and postretirement care (again, exclusive to the Japanese).

THE TOTAL WORKER IN THE EVOLVING INDUSTRY

Work fulfills a very important social function in the developmentally disabled individual's life, a role that used to be assumed by the extended family, the church, and the community (Ouchi, 1981). With the weakening of these institutions, largely a function of a highly mobile society, the workplace becomes increasingly important in meeting the individual's need for affiliation. To the extent that the employee's needs for affiliation are not met at the worksite, then it can be presumed that such individuals will not identify with the goals of the company. Many high-performance American firms are taking steps to reduce employee alienation, procedures that most successful Japanese companies have used for years. A number of these steps are outlined below.

Effects of Production and Management Changes on Rehabilitation Practice

Industry's new emphasis on product quality and reduction in buffer inventory will have a marked effect on traditional sources of revenue, particularly for sheltered facilities. As has been noted by the Greenleigh Associates, Inc. (1975) report, subcontract revenue is the largest source of income for sheltered facilities. It is derived from the facilities assembling or processing certain types of work that the parent industry does not wish to perform in-building. These subcontract products are then placed in the company's buffer inventory for use at assembly or processing time. As was noted, however, the emphasis on just-in-time (JIT) production procedures intentionally attempts to reduce buffer inventory; in turn, this suggests that facilities may have difficulty obtaining large subcontracts. Those subcontracts that are obtained must be produced rapidly, and more important, accurately. On the other hand, if facilities continue to receive only simplistic and low-paying contracts (see below) the changes that are occurring in more complicated manufacture will not affect them.

Closely allied to the just-in-time concept is the notion of total quality control, with workers and supervisors on-line carefully monitoring quality. As was noted earlier, the Greenleigh Associates, Inc. (1975) report determined subcontract revenue was the major source of revenue for facilities and that the subcontracts received by facilities involved very simple and low-paying work. Such tasks as envelope stuffing and simple sorting and assembling do not require high levels of quality assurance, and thus the facilities have little or no experience in maintaining product quality. This suggests that facilities expecting to derive revenue from subcontract activity will have to become literate in contemporary manufacturing thought. More important, they are going to have to prove to an industry that they are a "certified" vendor, capable of producing work precisely and rapidly.

Not all trainees/clients ought to or need to be employed in sheltered industry, and numerous authorities are calling for the competitive or on-site sheltered enclave employment of even the most severely handicapped adults. At face value, manufacturers' movement to JIT/TQC or similar processes would seem to bode ill for harder-to-train and more difficult-to-supervise clients in industrial settings. Individual workers will be responsible for higher degrees of work quality, will be required to communicate effectively with peers and managers on problem areas, and will be expected to be part of the industrial "family." On the other hand, implicit in high-performance manufacturing and management are higher levels of supervision and stronger and more personal relations between worker and manager. The habilitation literature of the past 15 years has demonstrated that even profoundly retarded workers are capable of complex task acquisition and will produce same at representative rates under conditions of higher supervision levels. High-performance organizations of the future may provide just the climate needed to maintain a worker with special needs (e.g., hiring a personality, not just a worker; provision of counseling; familiarity; family atmosphere).

In addition to affecting contract procurement, new manufacturing procedures and quality specifications are also going to affect long-standing rehabilitation practice, especially vocational adjustment procedures. Facilities have traditionally taught work skills by giving clients "real work." This practice, always considered questionable at best, will not be permitted when work production deadlines and quality standards are elevated. If a client is in work adjustment because he or she produces work slowly or sloppily, a facility would have to have compelling self-destructive urges to give important contract work to such an individual until his or her adjustment problems were addressed elsewhere. In the past, this practice was acceptable in that the subcontract work obtained by facilities was of such a low level and was so casual that almost any type of work was acceptable. If subcontract work continues to be simple with little regard for quality, facilities can persist in their current practice. However, those facilities that desire to increase their revenue and client employment opportunities will need to conduct adjustment services in new ways.

Perhaps most affected by the industrial changes discussed above are the variety of services referred to as vocational assessment. The authors of this book feel that contemporary vocational assessment has shed very little light on how trainers should "train" or how placement people should "place." Fundamentally, these assessment procedures require a solitary client/student to perform certain manipulative tasks or to follow written or oral instructions for which there are standards. A similar process is employed to determine a client's/student's vocational interest; the examinee generally specifies his or her interests, which are then compared to similar interests of others holding certain occupations. There are slight permutations and commutations to this formula, none of which are very helpful in the face of uninformed examinees whose test-retest reliability on such inventories approximates the random elevation of semiprecious metal (e.g., a coin toss).

New assessment procedures will have to be devised that provide the following, more realistic information on employees:

1. How fast does the client learn?
2. What training methods hasten task acquisition?
3. How long does the client remember acquired materials (e.g., how much retraining time?)
4. How fast does the client work under the following conditions:
   a) alone
   b) in groups
   c) under high supervision
   d) under moderate supervision
   e) under low supervision
   f) under no supervision
   g) with complex work
   h) with simplistic work
5. What is the client's work precision index?
6. Can the client recognize defects that are increasingly occurring?
7. Can the client correct defects?
8. How many times per hour can the client switch task on command?
9. Will the client switch tasks on perceived need?
10. What is the client's inoculation quotient against co-workers' inappropriate suggestions (e.g., let's go hide, etc.)?

SUMMARY

Industry is in a process of change that has been motivated by the loss of American dominance in fields that were considered unassailable merely 15 years ago. To be able to compete effectively in the international marketplace, management and production practices are being revamped along the lines of those employed by "high-performance" organizations, both foreign and domestic. In the past, when rehabilitation practice and funding were dominated by the federal government, awareness of industrial changes was irrelevant. We may now be experiencing the beginning of a long-term trend that emphasizes local and state initiative and employment of specialized populations through development of relationships with local businesses. Such changes require that the rehabilitation practitioner become familiar with contemporary business practice.

Generally, the authors suggest that contemporary business changes—management and manufacturing—are not going to be impediments to the sheltered enclave or competitive employment of special need workers. JIT/TQC procedures have many aspects of enrichment-enlargement job design attributes that may make work more intrinsically interesting for handicapped and nonhandicapped workers alike. Furthermore, although primarily designed for middle-level management and above, the management changes that are currently being implemented may create a work climate that is more accepting of special employees or industrial enclaves. As a result of these changes, rehabilitation facilities and state agencies that relied on funding from the federal government in the 1960s–1970s will have to undergo dramatic changes. As with antiquated industrial procedures, their ability to survive may depend on their flexibility in the face of certain and powerful changes.

REFERENCES

Allen, G. C. (1958). *Japan's economic recovery*. London: Oxford University Press.

Bitter, J. (1979). *Introduction to rehabilitation*. St. Louis, MO: C. V. Mosby Publishers.

Cascio, W. F. (1978). *Applied psychology in personnel management*. Reston, VA: Reston Publishing.

Denison, E. F. (1976). *How Japan's economy grew so fast*. Washington, DC: Brookings Institute.

Ford, R. N. (1973). Job enrichment lessons from AT & T. *Harvard Business Review, 51*(1), 96–101.

Greenleigh Associates, Inc. (1975). *The role of the sheltered workshops in the rehabilitation of the severely handicapped*, (3 volumes). Report to the Department of Health, Education, and Welfare, Rehabilitation Services Administration. New York.

Herzberg, F. (1968). One more time: How do you motivate employees? *Harvard Business Review, 46*, 53–62.

Karlsen, J. I. (1972). A monograph on the Norwegian Industrial democracy project. *Oslo Work Research Institute*, Document No. 15.

Klein, L. (1976). *New forms of work organization*. Cambridge, MA: Cambridge University Press.

McCormick, E. J. (1979). *Human factors in engineering and design*. New York: McGraw-Hill.

Nessbitt, J. (1982). *Megatrends*. New York: Warner Books.

Ouchi, W. G. (1981). *Theory Z*. New York: Avon Books.

Pascale, R. T., & Althos, A. G. (1981). *The art of Japanese management*. New York: Simon and Schuster.

Peters, T. J., & Waterman, R. J. (1982). *In search of excellence*. New York: Harper and Row.

Schonberger, R. J. (1982). *Japanese manufacturing techniques: 9 hidden lessons in simplicity*. New York: Free Press.

Tsurumi, Y. (1976). *The Japanese are coming*. Cambridge, MA: Ballinger Publishing.

∞ Chapter 14 ∞

Evaluation, Training, and Placement in Natural Work Environments

Stephen Shestakofsky,
Margaret M. Van Gelder, and William E. Kiernan

SINCE THE PASSAGE OF ITS INITIAL LEGIS-lative mandate, vocational rehabilitation has utilized time-limited training and support services as the primary means of moving disabled individuals from dependency to independence (Kiernan & Pyne, 1982). As the focus of vocational rehabilitation expanded to include services to mentally retarded individuals and later to the more severely disabled clients, the role of the sheltered workshop became more prominent in the service delivery system. Expansion of services to include extended evaluation was an attempt to respond to the longer-term training needs of the more severely disabled client. This feature, however, was frequently not utilized because the criteria for vocational rehabilitation systems continued to be job placement or case closures—classified as ''26'' status (Karan, 1978).

As the focus on services to the more severely disabled took hold, there was an increased awareness of the need to develop alternative training strategies and training environments. Movement away from the frequent, if not sole, use of a sheltered workshop environment was stimulated by the Department of Health and Human Services report on sheltered workshops and the recommendations from that study group (Whitehead, 1981) to modify the basic vocational rehabilitation model to provide more effective training and to realize more appropriate outcomes for the severely disabled client.

The Pathways Model presented in Chapter 7 reflects the movement toward a sequential service delivery system. This model looks to the development of a wide range of options and environments within which the developmentally disabled adult may enter the world of work. It presents a conceptual view of how both time-limited training and ongoing supported employment can be viewed as options. These options reflect the degree of independence at which the developmentally disabled individual can function in the work environment. The following section examines a statewide program focusing on time-limited training. A specific program design within that system is presented in more depth later.

MASSACHUSETTS SUPPORTED WORK PROGRAM

Background

In 1974 the federal government—primarily under the aegis of the Department of Labor—and the Ford Foundation undertook a 5-year research and demonstration effort of a supported work model to train severely disadvantaged individuals. Utilizing 15 states throughout the nation, the $80 million project sought to determine how this form of structured work experience of limited duration would affect four specific target groups: public assistance recipients of Aid to Families with Dependent Children (AFDC), ex-offenders, ex-drug addicts, and youths who had dropped out of school. The model emphasized the use of work crews, each with a supervisor and operating under conditions of graduated stress and performance requirements, employing close supervision and engendering peer support. The program was administered by the Manpower Demonstration Research Corporation (MDRC)—established for that purpose—and evaluated by Mathematica Policy Research. The Supported Work Model proved to be most effective with long-term female AFDC recipients, more marginally effective with addicts and ex-offenders, and ineffective with dropout youth (Riccio & Price, 1984).

One recommendation of the MDRC Study, however, was to assess the potential of supported work for such groups as mentally retarded and mentally restored individuals. In March 1979, Transitional Employment Enterprises (TEE) began implementation of its Work Opportunities for Retarded Citizens project (WORC), a model established during its participation in the national supported work demonstration. TEE's initial experience with its first 30 terminated clients was encouraging; 53% were placed in competitive employment, and of these, some 81% had retained their initial placement during the postplacement follow-up study. The TEE effort, which was initially funded by local Comprehensive Employment and Training Act (CETA) contracts and service revenues generated by the project's private sector partners, found its initial cost per placement to be approximately $18,000, with a net public sector cost of $15,000.

On the basis of this positive experience, the Massachusetts legislature appropriated $500,000 in July 1981 for programs of "Supported Work for the Retarded" during the state's 1982 fiscal year (July 1, 1981 to June 30, 1982). Although the appropriation had been requested by the Department of Mental Health, the legislature assigned the program to the Executive Office of Economic Affairs (EOEA)—the state unit responsible for economic development and manpower programs. The move was a statement of legislative intent to place the emphasis on private sector jobs, rather than therapeutic or day activity programs. On October 21, 1981 the EOEA assigned responsibility for program implementation to the Bay State Skills Corporation (BSSC), a newly formed entity. By January 1982 the corporation had hired a program director, established an advisory task force—including representatives from the Departments of Mental Health, Special Education, and Vocational Rehabilitation, as well as advocacy organizations and the private sector—issued a request for a proposal, and awarded contracts to eight agencies to provide services through the remainder of the fiscal year.

Program Elements

The BSSC understood its legislative mandate to be the replication of the TEE model with a focus on private sector jobs. Philosophically, the corporation was comfortable with this emphasis and set a 60% placement rate of all enrollees in full-time competitive employment as the primary goal for all service providers. Since the beginning of the project, service providers have been monitored to ensure compliance with their contract and to help assess the validity of the model, but clinical decisions have not been second-guessed by the funding agency. The contractors are held responsible and measured solely on the basis of their success in meeting employment, placement, and cost per unit goals.

The following program elements were considered essential to the development of a supported work model.

Eligibility All trainees have the diagnosis of mental retardation in order to be eligible to participate in the BSSC-funded program; however, this does not have to be the primary diagnosis. There is no minimum standard test score required to determine eligibility; rather, the BSSC accepts determinations by the State Rehabilitation Commission and the Department of Mental Health. Other enrollees are deemed eligible if the determination of disability can be documented to the BSSC by the service provider. The criteria utilized by both the state agencies and the BSSC are consistent with those of the American Association on Mental Deficiency (Grossman, 1983).

Definitions of the Work Environment The BSSC defines supported work as a training methodology to provide both job readiness and placement assistance to participants. Its primary goal is the transition of participants into permanent unsubsidized employment after a period of program employment, on the basis of individual readiness and specific skills gained through a work experience. The model emphasizes the following design features:

Work crews of four to eight trainees (all employees of the service provider) receiving at least minimum wage under the direction of a full-time supervisor/trainer provided by the BSSC-funded contractor

Intensive supervision at the worksite (gradually faded during the period of training), linked with a curriculum based on gradually increasing expectations of worksite performance and requirements

Comprehensive supported services to participants to facilitate their involvement in the training, as well as their transition to permanent unsubsidized employment

Private sector worksites that can provide "real work" for training purposes, financial compensation to the training agency for the work performed by the trainees, and placement opportunities for successful program completers after a 4- to 12-month training period

Additional Program Features Other features that were encouraged, but less emphasized, include the development of peer support at the worksite and the utilization of financial incentives, such as bonuses or step raises, linked to individual training performance. According to an evaluation of the statewide program's first 2 years—through June 30, 1983—the BSSC has taken a somewhat flexible approach to its model in the diversity of both the service providers' capabilities and private sector company needs. No contractor of the 17 funded adhered strictly to all aspects of the program design (Bailis, Jones, Schreiber, & Burnstein, 1984).

Premises of the Model

The premises underlying the Massachusetts Supported Work Model are simple: first, that there are substantial numbers of mentally retarded citizens capable of competitive employment who are currently unemployed or underemployed and receiving services or transfer payments subsidized by the taxpayers; second, that most of these individuals can be made job-ready through cost-effective, short-term, time-limited training; and finally, that private employers would hire those disabled individuals if they were made job-ready to the employers' specifications.

The private sector emphasis of the model is an essential element of its design. The BSSC sees the private sector as the growth sector of the economy; that is, preparing trainees for real world jobs therefore means preparing them for jobs in private industry. The program model seeks to provide a realistic training experience by having trainees do productive work in a real work setting, one where both disabled and nondisabled individuals are employed. The skills of the trainees are gradually increased so that they may be able to make a smooth transition into the status of employee without the need for major adjustments. At this stage of transition, a number of changes occur. The fading of the training supervisor is offset by the increased role of the company supervisor. The paycheck from the training agency is replaced by the paycheck from the company. The trainee has been trained in transportation skills and can get to work independently. Similarly, the trainee has received the minimum wage and now has experience in money management. In most training sites, the program participant has also learned the basic economic premise that good performance is financially rewarded through bonuses, raises, and/or promotions.

During training, usually a 4- to 12-month period, the supervisor/trainer provided by the training agency is seen as the key to program success for the individual. Responsive to both company and client needs, the trainer ensures that productivity levels are met while gradually shifting this responsibility to the trainee. Before the training period, the supervisor generally learns the job and develops a task analysis and training curriculum. During the training period, the trainer helps organize the work crew into a support group that meets regularly to reinforce positive behavior and to deal with group concerns. The trainer evaluates the trainee's performance and is the person most responsible for noting his or her needs and obtaining supportive and ancillary services when necessary.

BSSC Experience

The Massachusetts Supported Work Program entered its fourth year of state funding beginning July 1984 (see Table 1). It has grown from a $500,000 budget item serving 123 trainees through eight service providers to a $1,336,892 appropriation designed to serve about 325 persons through 23 service providers. Its contractors range from specialized training agencies, such as TEE, to traditional vocational rehabilitation providers that generally deliver sheltered employment services, and from educational agencies to university-affiliated programs, such as the Developmental Evaluation Clinic of Boston Children's Hospital. The BSSC project has demonstrated both the applicability and replicability of this model to a vast array of service providers.

The Supported Work Program has surpassed the desired results projected by earlier studies that were used to justify its initial appropriations (Bailis et al., 1984). In 3 full years of program operations, the overall placement rate has risen from 50.4% (1982) to 57.8% (1983) to 63.7% (October 1984) as the service providers, private sector employers, and referral agencies have become more familiar with the model. As of October, 1984, the placement rate of successful graduates has risen from 78.5% to 85% and finally to 95.5%. This

increase in the placement rate has occurred during a period of program expansion; new enrollments jumped from 123 in the initial year to 206 in 1983 to 246 in 1984, with over 300 new enrollments expected in 1985.

The actual cost of the program, originally projected to be between $12,350 and $15,000 per placement in the initial preprogram budget analysis, has proven to be much less than anticipated. In the first year of operation, the vendor cost was $7,520 per placement, due in part to high start-up costs and a short time available for placement. In the subsequent 2 full years of normal operation, the costs were reduced to $5,555 (1983) and $5,756 (1984) per placement. Evaluation of the program's first 2 years estimated that, for public assistance recipients placed, the public cost of the supported work program would be recouped by the taxpayer in less than 2 years of employment; for others, in about 7½ years (Bailis et al., 1984). These costs savings do not measure the value of the workshop slots being made available to new clients due to the movement of BSSC clients out of these slots.

The Cadmus Report in 1984 found that the population served by supported work was generally mildly mentally retarded adults with little employment experience. The participants' I.Q. scores ranged from 30 to 88, with a mean score of 67. The average number of weeks worked in full-time unsubsidized jobs during the year before enrollment was 1.8, with an average income of $571 in earnings. The postprogram statistics for those placed showed dramatic gains: a 10-fold increase in average earned income to $5,704 and a 20-fold increase in weeks worked in full-time competitive jobs to 39.3 weeks. The average placement wage of $3.76 per hour was seen as a significant achievement, considering the average per program wage of only $1.58 per hour for those employees who worked in the month before participation.

Source of Referrals

The majority of the employees were referred by the state Rehabilitation Commission (62%), with other significant sources being the De-

Table 1. Supported work for mentally retarded persons

OUTCOME DATA TO DATE
(October 31, 1984)

	FY 1982	FY 1983	FY 1984
Number enrolled	123	206	246
Carry-in from previous year	0	38	20
Total served	123	244	266
Total still in training	0	0	12
Total terminations	123 (38 in FY '83)	206 (19 in FY '84) (1 in FY '85)	234 (13 in FY '85)
Total completions	79 (23 in FY '83)	140 (16 in FY '84)	156 (8 in FY '85)
Completion rate	64.2%	68.0%	66.7%
Total placements	62 (21 in FY '83)	119 (12 in FY '84)	149 (6 in FY '85)
Placement rate of completers	78.5%	85.0%	95.5%
Placement rate of all enrollees terminated	50.4%	57.8%	63.7%
Actual vendor costs	$308,324	$711,001	$892,164
Cost per enrollee	3,627	3,174	3,717
Cost per completer	5,506	4,836	4,335
Cost per placement	7,520	5,555	5,756

Note: Costs are allocated to fiscal year in which trainee terminated.

partment of Mental Health (21%) and local educational programs (13%). It should be noted that, although the placement rate of trainees was found not to vary by I.Q. level, the program was found to be most successful for special education referrals, despite the lower I.Q. (60) score than the norm and the obvious lack of work experience (Bailis et al., 1984). This finding has encouraged an even greater emphasis on funding school-to-work supported work projects that would eliminate the need for special education students to enter an adult day activity or sheltered employment program.

Private Sector Perspective

The BSSC was established by state legislation in 1981 to help employers meet their personnel needs by expanding the capacity of Massachusetts training and education institutions. This objective is generally accomplished through the award of grants-in-aid to nonprofit or public institutions that obtain at least equivalent matching grants from private sector (for profit) industry partners. The BSSC's grants range from entry-level training to upgrading the skills of currently employed professionals to helping develop graduate-level programs in emerging technologies. The Corporation's purpose is to meet industry's unmet labor market requirements. Within that context, the BSSC views the host companies participating in the Supported Work program as its clients— of equal importance to it as the trainees themselves. If any program is to be deemed a success by the BSSC, it must meet real employer needs.

Because of the BSSC philosophy, the Corporation has required potential contractors to have verified "up front" commitments of industry participation before awarding any funding to a proposed program. As a result, industry involvement has largely reflected the abilities of service providers to market the value of the program to specific companies on the basis of economic need. In Massachusetts, trainees are generally most in demand in those entry-level service and manufacturing jobs where employee retention and reliability are chronic concerns to industry. Although gener-

ally "traditional" placement sites for mentally retarded individuals, these entry-level positions are now being filled in numbers previously thought impossible through the traditional placement process.

In the 1984–85 program year, the BSSC's 23 contractors worked with over 40 host companies as training sites, more than 90% of whom anticipated hiring the majority of successful program graduates trained at their site. Approximately 30% of all trainees were enrolled in hotel industry programs, another 25% in food services training at restaurants or institutional catering firms, and 10% in electronic assembly and quality control; the remaining 35% were involved in a wide array of other training activities, including apparel, bindery work, day care aide skills, laundry services, janitorial/maintenance/groundskeeping, plastics manufacture, sanding, shipping/packing/receiving, and silk screening.

Companies are urged to participate on the basis of their economic needs, not altruism. The Supported Work Model successfully provides companies with entry-level employees trained to company specifications. The company has 4 months to 1 year to observe each trainee's progress. Only after the trainee can meet objective criteria for employment is the company asked to extend an offer for employment (and the company can even then exercise its option to refuse). In most cases, the training site host company employs the trainee; in those cases where a participating company decides not to hire a job-ready trainee, the BSSC requires that the training agency find a suitable equivalent placement in private industry.

One might ask why do the companies participate? They participate because they need well-trained, reliable employees. They are willing to hire anyone who can do the job well, in a regular and responsible manner. The Supported Work Model provides them access to people who have already proven that they can meet company specifications. Second, the employer costs and risks during training are reduced in a number of ways. Due to the contractual relationship between the company and the training agency, the company pays only for the prearranged negotiated value of the work the trainees perform. Participating companies save costs in recruitment (advertising, interviewing, testing), liability for fringe benefits (health, workers' compensation, unemployment insurance), and overhead (payroll, personnel). Finally, companies can take advantage of other benefits available to anyone hiring handicapped mentally retarded workers, such as the federal Targeted Jobs Tax Credit and the On-the-Job Training support available through the Association for Retarded Citizens.

The design of BSSC is a model of supported work where outcomes benefit both industry and the mentally retarded individual. The model utilizes a real-work training environment to facilitate the training of the mentally retarded individual. The following section examines a specific project sponsored by this statewide initiative and run by the Developmental Evaluation Clinic at Boston Children's Hospital.

A Specific Model within the Supported Work Design

Since 1981 the Supported Work Project (SWP) at the Children's Hospital, Boston, has received funding from the BSSC. The SWP provides on-site job training, support services, job placement, and postemployment services to individuals diagnosed as mentally retarded. This project is designed to facilitate movement of trainees to unsubsidized competitive employment in food service occupations. It was established through a partnership between the Dietary Department and the Developmental Evaluation Clinic (DEC), a university-affiliated program, at the hospital. Through a contractual arrangement, the hospital agreed to transfer the equivalent of salary and fringe benefits for two full-time dishmachine operator positions, as well as the in-kind contribution of a supervisor's time, to the SWP. The DEC agreed to provide financial support for a percentage of professional staff effort in the project, with the remaining support coming from the BSSC. The Dietary Department received, in turn, a reliable work force to meet the daily operational needs of the dishroom and related

service area activities. A key element in this partnership is the liaison established with the private sector and a training agency, in this case the Dietary Department and the clinic.

Participants in the SWP received training in food service occupations for approximately 6 months and were then provided assistance in obtaining jobs in other similar employment settings in the greater Boston area. As in the case of other service providers for BSSC, participants do not always "roll over" into competitive jobs in the hospital. The SWP incorporates all the key components of the supported work training model as mandated by BSSC; however, there are several variations in its implementation. In addition to an emphasis on job training and placement in the private sector, the SWP focuses on providing the individual with increased opportunities to make decisions and assume responsibility for those decisions as a means of supporting movement toward greater independence and economic self-sufficiency.

The following sections review how the key components of the Support Work Training Model are incorporated into the SWP.

Real Work Environment All training as a dishmachine operator, dishroom attendant, and food server is done on-site in the main cafeteria of the hospital. This provides for a well-integrated work setting and extensive contact with other department employees. There are eight work positions, each having a specific training curriculum. Work hours reflect varying shifts and schedules from part-time to full-time hours. All trainees are employees of Children's Hospital and are granted the same rights and responsibilities of other employees. These rights include but are not limited to payment of minimum wage; new employee orientation through the Human Resources Department; and benefits of sick time, vacation time, 10 paid holidays, and health insurance. As with all employees in the hospital, participants in the program receive and wear a hospital identification badge.

Intensive Supervision On-site training and supervision are provided by a supervisor from the dietary department assigned full-time to the project. The supervisor is responsible for providing instruction, assigning job duties, and monitoring the performance of trainees. A curriculum utilizing a task analysis approach orients new trainees to the work area, teaches job functions, and monitors performance and maintenance of skills that are learned. Project staff serve as consultants to the supervisor and provide technical assistance and extra support to new trainees or those who are encountering specific performance difficulties on the job.

Graduated Increased Job Expectations Job functions are broken down into discrete tasks and progress from simple, very routine job duties to multiple, more complex duties emphasizing speed, judgment, and/or public contact. Initially, trainees perform the simpler, more structured tasks. With experience and increased proficiency, they gradually progress to more demanding, higher-level tasks. At the outset, trainees are given part-time shifts—usually 20 hours per week—during the more structured part of the day. Throughout the course of training, trainees may increase their hours up to full-time, with the possibility of working shifts that require greater independence and responsibility. Increases in hours may be granted when a trainee has met the initial requirements of the project, at an individual's request once he or she has met the necessary work performance expectations, and/or as an incentive to motivate individuals.

Financial Incentives All trainees earn the minimum wage at the outset of the training program. They have the opportunity to increase their earnings by receiving raises and/or through increases in the number of hours worked. Salary adjustments are awarded when trainees meet the general work performance requirements during the initial 8-week training period, which include regular attendance, punctuality, good grooming, cooperation, and general skill mastery. After this initial period, salary decisions are made on an individual basis, according to the degree of progress achieved by the trainee. This factor enables the SWP staff to emphasize development of work skills and behaviors while simultaneously being responsive to the variability of needs, capabilities, and rate of learning for each individual.

Special emphasis is placed on developing the concept of increased earnings as reinforcement for good work performance and demonstration of appropriate work behaviors, even for individuals who may not have well-developed money concepts. Trainees are encouraged to initiate requests for increased work hours and to become involved actively in developing goals that will lead to increased wages.

Peer Support Viewed as a critical component of the SWP, peer support is developed informally through weekly crew meetings led by the supervisor and a project staff person. Teamwork is emphasized. The work crew provides an important opportunity for trainees to learn how to develop co-worker relationships, as well as offering an opportunity for socialization. Crew meetings give trainees both positive and corrective feedback about their job performance; opportunities to talk about common work-related topics, such as safety concerns, how to request time off, scheduling and job position assignments for the coming week; and a chance to discuss work problems and concerns they may have experienced that week. Both peer camaraderie and competition develop, with important secondary gains being the establishment of social relationships that for many persons extend beyond the duration of their time in the project.

Counseling and Case Management Services These integral support services are designed to assist trainees in adjusting to the demands of the SWP and the new expectations placed on them as a worker. The focus of counseling is on such practical issues as transportation or contact with the local Social Security offices and on teaching individuals problem-solving and decision-making strategies in both work and nonwork-related areas. For individuals with personal or family problems that are having an impact on their job performance, counseling is a mechanism to share these concerns outside the workplace. When necessary, referrals for additional services in the community can be initiated.

Case management is ongoing and facilitates communication about an individual's progress, areas of need, and development of plans for the future with the referral agency and other service providers. Likewise, opportunities to work with families support the trainee's progress and movement toward competitive employment. Family support is critical to the success of the trainee. It is important to establish a network with community agencies, such as local vocational rehabilitation, advocacy, education, and mental health agencies, to build case management and personal supports for those trainees who will require ongoing services once they complete the SWP.

Job Placement and Follow-Up Services Planning toward job placement is an ongoing process while a trainee is in the SWP. Staff assess and develop with each trainee an individual profile of work skills, habits, behaviors, and temperament. An ecological approach is used in finding the best match of an individual's skills, strengths, needs, and interests with the structure and requirements of the workplace. Trainees are actively involved in the job planning and seeking process both to develop their skills in this area and to enhance their investment on the job once it is obtained. All trainees participate in a Job Seeking Skills Group that provides instruction in interviewing and completing applications. The group also helps the trainee identify those job situations that are most suitable. The placement specialist, together with the trainee, identifies job leads in other health care and university settings. Consideration is given to finding jobs that provide both wage and fringe benefits.

Follow-up is critical in assisting trainees to adjust to their new jobs and maintain themselves in employment. The provision of follow-up support is a very attractive feature to employers who want reassurance that they will be given assistance if problems arise. Initially, intensive follow-up services are provided, and they then decrease in frequency over a 6-month period of time. These services vary, depending on individual capabilities and needs. Specific follow-up services may include on-site visits to assist with problem-solving or job instruction, telephone contact with employers and trainee graduates, follow-up counseling appointments, and case management with other service providers and family members. In certain cases, individuals have been assisted in obtaining subsequent jobs.

Choice and Decision-Making within the Project Individual involvement and input into the decision-making processes are encouraged from the admissions process through placement. At the time of referral, clients and/or their families or service providers are invited in for an informal visit. Individuals are provided with concrete information about the project, as they visit the work area and meet with the work supervisor. This process gives the applicant and others a better understanding of the type of work performed. They are encouraged to think about their interest in food service work and their reason for attending the SWP. The application procedure is a dual decision process whereby each prospective candidate determines his or her preference for participation in the project and staff assess the appropriateness of each applicant. The procedure allows those not interested in the project to self-select out of the admissions process and terminate their application.

At the time of application, some of the primary factors that are assessed include the individual's expressed motivation to work, interest in food services as a vocational choice, physical capabilities and endurance, ability to use or learn to use public transportation, previous work experience, nature of the support system available to the individual, potential to acquire work skills and behaviors within a 6-month period, and a past history of significant behavioral and/or psychiatric difficulties. These factors have been found to be predictive of those who can successfully participate in the project; the literature has also described these factors as keys to developing a good fit of an applicant to such a program as the SWP.

An underlying premise of the project is that individuals need to be viewed within the context of their family environment and/or external support system. Therefore, an important component of the admissions process is the involvement of parents and family or other significant persons, such as community residence staff or case managers. Experience has shown that the support of the family and those persons who comprise the support system available to the individual is of critical importance to the individual's adjustment and successful transition into competitive employment. Some of the areas addressed with the family include the stability of the applicant's living situation, expectations or lack of expectations for him or her as a worker, the role of work within the family structure, willingness on the parts of all family members to facilitate more independent functioning in the individual, and the feeling of the family toward the economic incentives or disincentives of the project (specifically SSI and Medicaid benefits). Contact with families and others allows for sharing information, uncovering any misconceptions, and building an alliance that can be fostered throughout the SWP to facilitate the individual's movement toward greater independence. For the majority of individuals to maximize gains and maintain a higher level of functioning in employment, work that the person performs needs to be valued and supported in the family environment.

Trainee Characteristics and Outcome Observations From March 1982 through December 1984, 38 individuals participated in the SWP, of whom 58% were between the ages of 21 to 30 years. The ages of participants ranged from 19 to 55 years, and 76% were females. About two-thirds resided with their families. Over half received SSI benefits, with the balance (47%) dependent on their families for financial support. The average participant was diagnosed as functioning within the mild range of mental retardation, and 50% had another presenting disability of a physical and/or psychiatric nature. During the 6-month period before entering the SWP, 42% of the participants were unemployed and not actively involved in any program services, 39% were attending sheltered workshops or other vocational training programs, 16% were attending school, and 3% were attending a day treatment program (see Table 2). None of the applicants had been competitively employed during the previous 6-month period.

As of December 1984, 22 participants had successfully completed training, 8 were noncompleters (dropping out of training or not job-ready at the end of the training period), and 8 participants were still in training. Of the 22 participants who completed training, 20 were placed into unsubsidized competitive employment in hospitals, nursing homes, universities, and restaurants in the greater Boston area. This resulted in a placement rate of 91% for all trainees who completed the SWP, and 67% of all trainees who entered the project. Of those individuals who obtained jobs, the average hourly wage was $3.99 and the average number of hours worked per week was 29 (see Table 3).

Although the focus of the project is on job placement, it is also important to examine the group of noncompleters and their difficulty following through with training or acquiring the work skills and behaviors necessary to enter competitive employment. Some of the contributory factors that emerged included significant life changes that hindered performance on the job—for example, marriage, pregnancy—specific skill deficits, limited motivation compounded by poor external supports, and fear of loss of SSI benefits. Likewise, for the two trainees who completed training but did not enter employment, motivational problems and limited expectations to work held by significant persons in their living environment were the primary factors.

Employment Retention Although these numbers are small in size, thus far these placement results have been encouraging. However, it is too limiting to view job placement statistics only without examining job retention and some of the factors that seem to influence it. Employment retention figures for the SWP reflect a wide range of time intervals, as certain trainees obtained jobs over 2 years ago whereas

Table 2. Trainee characteristics

Age:			Means of support:	SSI/SSDI	50%
	- 20:	18%		Family	47%
	21 - 30:	58%		General relief	3%
	31 - 40:	13%			
	41 - 50:	8%	Referral source:	MRC	66%
	51 - 60:	3%		DMH	21%
Sex:	Female :	76%		School	5%
	Male :	24%		Family/self	3%
				Advocacy groups	5%
Living environment:			Major activity during		
Family:		68%	the previous 6 months:	Unemployed	42%
Community residence/staffed				Workshop/vocational	
apartment:		10%		training	39%
Independent/cooperative				School	16%
apartment:		16%		Day treatment	3%
Nursing home:		3%			
Foster care:		3%			
N = 38					

others entered unsubsidized jobs within the past few months. Of the trainees who were placed in jobs, 14 have maintained employment, yielding a retention rate of 70%. It is noteworthy that nine individuals (64%) are in the original jobs, whereas the other five (36%) have undergone at least one job change and obtained and maintained the new jobs. Some of the reasons for job changes were voluntary or due to parental pressures, whereas others were dictated by the employer because of layoffs or job performance problems.

Often service providers expect that the developmentally disabled individual will be placed in a competitive job and remain on that job indefinitely. Frequently, job change is viewed negatively. However it appears that in reality these assumptions are not valid and are not realistic even for the nondisabled working individual. It may be more useful to look at an individual's ability to maintain him- or herself in employment throughout the working years, rather than the ability to keep one job. This new concept does have service delivery implications, however, in terms of the availability of job follow-up and placement assistance to guide individuals in making job transitions. For many individuals, going through a job change can be a very important learning experience that can enhance their investment in the subsequent job obtained.

Of those individuals who were unable to maintain themselves in employment (n = 6),

the reasons included skill deficits, emotional instability in coping with the demands of the job, limited external support systems, and poor social skills that adversely influenced adjustment in the work setting. All of these individuals worked at their jobs for at least 4 months, and several individuals held their jobs for over 1 year. These findings raise some questions about job maintenance and retention and an individual's ability to cope with the demands of a job over a longer period of time. These results also have implications for the nature and duration of follow-up services for certain individuals if employment is to be maintained. A local vocational rehabilitation agency typically closes cases after a 60 day follow-up period once a job has been obtained. This would seem to be premature in some cases. There may be significant value in considering long-term case management or other services that would provide employment assistance when necessary.

Observations and Considerations for Supported Work

Certainly the supported work training model has proven its effectiveness in moving a large number of mentally retarded individuals from a status of public or family dependence to one of employment characterized by greater independence and some degree of economic self-sufficiency. Within this model, a variety of public and private sector partnerships can be

Table 3. Placement outcomes

22 participants completed training			Average hourly wage:	$3.90/hour
8 participants did not complete training			Average number of hours worked per week: 29 hours	29 hours
20 out of 22 completers placed in un-subsidized competitive employment	= 91%		Job retention:	
20 out of all 30 participants placed in unsubsidized competitive employment	= 67%		14 out of 20 participants placed are still in employment -9 participants are still in their initial job placements - 5 participants have experienced job changes	
N = 30				= 70%

developed, as well as different models of implementation. There are certain advantages to the model employed by the Children's Hospital's SWP in which the training site remains stable and trainees are ultimately placed in jobs in the greater Boston area. It allows for more consistency and control in the training situation and an opportunity to get to know trainees better before placing them in unsubsidized competitive employment. It also provides opportunities to work with families and other support systems to promote the individual's progress. However, this design has some limitations in terms of the types of trainees that can be served well, because for some individuals, generalization of acquired skills and adjustment to a work setting may be too difficult. In addition, training in the food service occupations may not be appropriate or of interest to a number of individuals who otherwise may benefit from this model of time-limited training. The advantages of using real work environments are significant. The emphasis on specific skill training and job placement is essential; however, it is also important to view individuals within the context of their external environment and the factors that can influence their vocational adjustment and success.

SUMMARY

The success of the Massachusetts Supported Work Program has proven that a wide variety of service providers can together train and place in unsubsidized competitive employment many developmentally disabled individuals who otherwise would have remained unemployed or in subsidized sheltered employment. The design features of this time-limited training model are not particularly unique. What is unusual, however, is the statewide, state-funded nature of the effort. This is not a small initiative or one by a single progressive service provider using federal funds to demonstrate innovative techniques. This is a large-scale effort that has enrolled over 735 trainees in almost 3 years, primarily conducted by over a score of traditional vocational rehabilitation and special education service providers, with over $3.7 million in tax dollars as part of the state's ongoing commitment of services to mentally retarded adults.

The success of the program is attributable to three specific factors. First, the program serves the needs of all major constituents concerned— from mentally retarded citizens seeking to maximize their economic opportunities, to private companies seeking to maximize their profit, to policymakers seeking to maximize the cost-effectiveness of their program dollars. Everyone shares the credit for the program's success: referral agencies seeking to close cases positively and move clients to the maximum utilization of their abilities, service providers seeking to demonstrate their abilities to deliver time-limited training, and advocates seeking to show the capabilities of their clients.

Second, the program does not try to be all things for all people, but rather limits itself to the Supported Work Model, a design not applicable to clients incapable of competitive employment or made capable only with continuing significant support. The model is based on transitional and diminishing supports, with no provision for postprogram services. Thus, supported work is not meant to be supported employment.

Third, the program does not ensure individual service providers of ongoing multiyear funding. Each year, all prospective supported work providers must competitively apply for funding and be objectively rated on their proposed program design and cost-effectiveness, as well as their past experience in meeting program performance standards. This competitive formula ensures that the funding of agencies that perform well can continue or expand, that the funding of those that do not

perform as well can be reduced in size or eliminated, and that new contractors can regularly bring new energy and new perspectives to the overall effort.

The Supported Work Program of the Bay State Skill Corporation reflects the move toward a provision of time-limited training services within the actual workplace. The project, a statewide funded initiative, has grown considerably over a 3-year period. The results continue to indicate that this design is both cost-effective and replicable. The outcomes realized show that training in the actual work setting is an effective strategy for preparing adults with developmental disabilities to enter the world of work.

REFERENCES

Bailis, L. N., Jones, R. T., Schreiber, J., & Burnstein, P. L. (1984). *Evaluation of the BSSC supported work program for mentally retarded persons*. Watertown, MA: The Cadmus Group, Inc.

Grossman, H. (1983). *Classification in mental retardation*. Washington, DC: American Association on Mental Deficiency.

Karan, O. (1978). *Habilitation practices with the severely developmentally disabled, Vol. 2*. Madison, WI: University of Wisconsin, Research and Training Center in Mental Retardation.

Kiernan, W. E., & Pyne, M. (1982). Hard to train: A history of vocational training for special needs youth. In K. P. Lynch, W. E. Kiernan, & J. A. Stark (Eds.), *Prevocational and vocational education for special needs youth: A blueprint for the 1980s* (pp. 3–13). Baltimore, MD: Paul H. Brookes Publishing Company.

Riccio, J. A., & Price, M. L. (1984). *A transitional employment strategy for the mentally retarded: The final STETS implementation report*. New York: Manpower Demonstration Research Corporation.

Whitehead, C. W. (1981). *Final report: Training and employment services for handicapped individuals in sheltered workshops*. Washington, DC: U.S. Government Printing Office.

∞ Chapter 15 ∞

Not Entering Employment
A System Dilemma

Jack A. Stark, William E. Kiernan, Tammi L. Goldsbury, and John J. McGee

THE CONTRIBUTORS TO THIS BOOK HAVE CON-tinuously maintained their belief that most developmentally disabled individuals who are physically able to work could and should be employed. The findings of the research conducted by many of the authors of this text have demonstrated that even severely disabled adults are capable of competitive employment if they are given proper training and have a supportive service system. While advocating the need to move from day activity centers and sheltered workshops to competitive employment and economic independence, these authors are fully aware that a segment of the developmentally disabled population—specifically, individuals with severe physical handicaps—may never be employed. Nevertheless, they are dedicated to minimizing the numerous barriers that prevent those who are capable of employment from attaining such goals.

Walter Reuther, then president of the United Auto Workers Union, expressed the premises underlying this viewpoint rather well.

The proper goals of manpower policy go far beyond assurance of a job for everyone willing and able to work. The job must provide a useful and rewarding outlet for the worker's highest capacities. The work environment must promote dignity and self-respect. The work must offer opportunity for development and advancement . . . . Manpower policy is, or at least should be, concerned with the nature of work and the elimination of its discontents; with the preparation of human beings for creative and constructive activities and for the enjoyment of leisure . . . . Most of all, however, manpower policy should aim at making obsolete such words and phrases as manpower and labor market, for our central concern must increasingly be with the worker as a human being rather than as an instrument of production. For example, the major purpose of education and training must not be simply to produce more effective human tools for the use of employers but, rather, more effective human beings for participation in, and for enjoyment of, all aspects of living. In the next two decades, substantial progress ought to be made in these new directions that are indicated by our evolving concepts of what is desirable and achievable. (Reuther, 1967)

Some fear that creating false hope is being raised among the adult developmentally disabled population and their parents as to what they can accomplish. Although overall unemployment rates for developmentally disabled adults are high, the authors feel that the hope of future employment is essential; without it, there is no reason to try or to be motivated (Buscaglia, 1973; Frankl, 1965). The poet Robert Browning stated it best: "Ah, but a man's reach should exceed his grasp / Or what's a Heaven for?" (Andrea del Sarto).

DESCRIPTIVE
POPULATION CHARACTERISTICS

The focus of this chapter is on the ways and means of helping that portion of the developmentally disabled population who will not enter the employment system for a variety of reasons. In Chapter 2, a developmentally disabled individual was defined as one who has substantial functional limitations in three or more of the seven major life activities: 1) self-care, 2) receptive and expressive language, 3) learning, 4) mobility, 5) self-direction, 6) capacity for independent living, and 7) economic sufficiency. The last issue, that of economic self-sufficiency, is explored in this chapter, with the recognition that the other life functions are essential to its achievement.

Survey data from Chapter 3 indicated that the majority of those individuals who are developmentally disabled and have or will have substantial functional limitations in economic self-sufficiency represent some 2 million non-institutionalized individuals or approximately 1.49% of the total disabled population.

In addition, since the landmark 1975 legislation—the Education for All Handicapped Children Act (Public Law 94-142)—unprecedented numbers of students with disabilities are graduating from public school systems. It is estimated that 250,000 to 300,000 students graduate from special education programs annually (Rehab Brief, April 1984). About 90% of these individuals are not moving into an employment status. (Figure 1 explains this process and the distinction of terms.) This very low rate of employment leads to what the authors consider to be the major problem for developmentally disabled citizens in America: *Special education students are "graduating" from school with no place to go, to live, and to work* (see Chapter 8).

THE UNEMPLOYED:
NOT ENTERING THE SYSTEM

It is easier to understand *who* the unemployed developmentally disabled are and *why* they find themselves in this situation if the barriers to the employment *process* are examined first. Figure 1 explains the interrelationships among work, employment, and jobs. For the members of the developmentally disabled population who will never be engaged in employment or supported employment, a comprehensive model must be developed to respond to their specific needs, thereby preventing or reversing their institutionalization. This model can then maximize our ability to move developmentally disabled individuals into employment status.

Several reasons for the lack of employment within the developmentally disabled population are described in the following sections.

Economic Disincentives

Economic disincentives and lack of long-term security in the current employment market present a major impediment to employment for many developmentally disabled individuals. They stay unemployed or underemployed because of their fear of losing essential benefits, such as health care, medication, monthly disability payments, food stamps, and rental subsidies. These systemic problems are directly related to federal policies. For example, of SSI recipients, more than 87% are not in the labor force, 9.6% work part of the time, and 2% are actively looking for work. The disincentives within the Social Security system that inhibit developmentally disabled individuals from entering employment are well documented by Noble, Conley, and Elder (see Chapters 4, 5, and 6).

Age Factors

There are a growing number of elderly developmentally disabled individuals who either are retired or who have been out of (or never entered) the employment area for so long that such a goal would be detrimental to their physical or emotional well-being. They have a right to enjoy a system of normalizing experiences involving social, recreational, and independent living activities. This group of developmentally disabled individuals therefore do not enter the employment system either by choice or lack of need.

Work: Work is an activity that consumes energy and effort typically reflecting a purposeful act directed at improving or maintaining one's level of independence.

Habilitation:

Habilitation is achieved when efforts to help the DD individual result in increased levels of independence — socially, vocationally, and residentially.

Employment: Employment is a subset of work and reflects an expenditure of effort toward remuneration or gain.

Jobs: Within employment, individuals have multiple jobs that reflect their employment history.

This figure demonstrates both the habilitation process and the distinction of terms. Habilitation is the generic term indicating a process toward developing meaningful work in a developmentally disabled person's life with a goal toward employment with specific jobs that overlap and change over time.

Figure 1.   Pathways to employment habilitation process.

Needs Factors

Other than those who do not work because of health factors, the largest group of developmentally disabled individuals who are not able to enter the employment system are those whose *needs* are not being met by the existing inadequate service delivery system. Stark, McGee, and Menolascino (1984) have identified seven reasons why the needs of developmentally disabled individuals are not met: 1) not enough staff; 2) too many clients to serve; 3) not enough money and equipment and poor facilities; 4) not enough time to accom-

plish all the demands of the job; 5) a focus on short-term results only; 6) lack of capacity to generalize skills; and 7) political intervention and barriers.

Even though these factors apply to *all* human services, they have a particular impact on the developmentally disabled population. Often, the unemployed developmentally disabled individual is not working due to a lack of resources, skills, and information. There is hope, however. The renewed emphasis on employment initiatives—which this book represents—has received the support of Congress, private industry, and state and community programs.

Although much remains to be done, the adoption of funding priorities by the Administration on Developmental Disabilities, state developmental disabilities councils, state departments of education, and public school systems in the early 1980s to support employment-related activities has served to stimulate greater employment opportunities for the developmentally disabled individual.

Many professionals in the field believe that more can and should be done with the available resources. To date, one major barrier to further accomplishments has been insufficient communication of technological advances and innovative program strategies among planners and operations staff at all levels. This barrier should be overcome soon with the establishment of a complete telecommunication network among national, state, and local programs serving the developmentally disabled individual (i.e., Administration on Developmental Disabilities, National Association of Developmental Disabilities Councils, state developmental disabilities councils, state mental retardation and vocational rehabilitation offices, and University Affiliated Facility programs). By facilitating rapid information exchange and stimulating new approaches to training and placement in various employment settings, this communications network can further our efforts of meeting the needs of the developmentally disabled individual who wants to enter the employment system.

HEALTH-RELATED
CONCERNS THAT HAVE
AN IMPACT ON EMPLOYMENT OPTIONS

That segment of the developmentally disabled population who are physically employable, but due to any number of barriers are prevented from working, has been the focus of this chapter. Certainly, we will continue our efforts to reduce economic disincentives so that more developmentally disabled individuals may move from the rolls of the unemployed to the employed. And we will continue to support the rights of developmentally disabled individuals to enjoy their retirement just as other Americans do. The remainder of this chapter focuses on those developmentally disabled individuals who are unemployed due to *health factors*; that is, those individuals with functional limitations in both the physical and cognitive domain who are frequently referred to as "medically fragile" and/or "severely/profoundly handicapped."

Although the segment of the developmentally disabled population that is unemployed due to health factors is rather small, it is perhaps the most controversial. The legal and emotional issues of "Baby Doe" and some politicians' complaints about the high costs spent on this small group are, in the authors' opinion, pivotal to the allocation of resources to the whole developmental disabilities movement. There seems to be a trend in which the decision makers of our society use an extreme example or exception to the rule as justification for decisions that have an impact on the total population. In this particular case, decision makers cite the severe/profoundly handicapped individuals with health problems as justification for their institutionalization, for opposing their movement into the community, and for cutting back resources for the entire developmentally disabled population. An example of this trend is the erosion of the legal strides that were made in the late 1970s and early 1980s with recent court decisions reversing the right to habilitation for severe/profoundly handicapped individuals.

Efforts in working with this segment of the population are two-fold. The first objective is to improve their level of functioning so they can become eligible for future employment if such an option is deemed appropriate. With the technological developments noted in Chapters 20 and 22, the authors are optimistic about the possibility of making great strides in this area. Remember that only a decade ago, many professionals in the field felt that tremendous progress had been made in placing moderately disabled individuals into competitive employment as they started to graduate from special education programs funded by PL 94-142 legislation.

Second, for those individuals who are not capable of advancing toward employment, our challenge, particularly in delivery of health care services, is to improve their level of functioning. Evaluation and training strategies addressed in the following section can be utilized to enhance the level of functioning of these developmentally disabled individuals (see also Chapter 18).

EVALUATION AND TRAINING

Developmentally disabled individuals have service needs in three major areas. The first major area is residential and physical care. Second, cognitive and social skill deficits need to be evaluated and addressed by comprehensive education and training programs. Third, developmentally disabled individuals need to live in environments that appropriately and constantly influence their behavior (Berkson & Romer, 1981).

New and innovative ways of training developmentally disabled persons who want to work but have difficulty because of the severity of their disability must be developed, and inadequate evaluation practices need to be examined (Gold, 1973; Karan, 1976). Few professionals are sufficiently trained to evaluate the vocational progress of developmentally disabled individuals. The vocational evaluation materials that are available have quite limited predictive validity at best. Often, evaluation facilities in school settings or assessment centers are not available to the developmentally disabled or more severely disabled student.

A major concern is that rehabilitation services follow clients placed in their vocational situations only for a short period of time. In fact, most developmentally disabled individuals do not receive vocational rehabilitation services at all because of eligibility restrictions. If an applicant to a state vocational rehabilitation agency cannot be placed into competitive employment within a reasonable period of time, they are deemed to be incligible for services. Rehabilitation services have traditionally placed more emphasis on short-term training than on extended evaluation; thus, many developmentally disabled individuals have not been able to enter the system.

Bernstein and Karan (1979) note that, because in the past developmentally disabled individuals have not been expected to become employed, efforts to encourage and assist them have been very limited. They point out the following obstacles that stand in the way of employment for handicapped individuals: 1) lack of work incentives, 2) caretaker overprotectiveness, 3) transportation problems, 4) lack of coordination, and 5) lack of accountability within the service system. The traditional vocational rehabilitation system has not been effective in providing guidance to developmentally disabled individuals to overcome these obstacles. However, during the past decade programs across the country have demonstrated that the new technology of applied behavior analysis approaches offers strategies that are useful for evaluating and training developmentally disabled individuals (Albin, Stark, & Keith, 1978; Lynch, 1978).

In most professions, evaluation processes are used to determine the direction, type, scope, quality, and duration of services. The authors suggest that the evaluation and training activities for a developmentally disabled individual incorporate information derived from task and functional analyses, as well as from a data-based system utilizing longitudinal data from criterion-referenced samples, rather than from normative groupings. Currently, research is being conducted on how environments change behavior (Karan & Schalock, 1983). Studies have found that it is best to provide skill training for severely impaired populations in natural settings that allow for stimulus control, skill maintenance, and skill generalization. (Horner, 1981; Rusch, Schutz, & Agran, 1982). Recent research by Schalock (1984) has shown the efficacy of teaching community and living skills in an environment similar to the one in which an individual will be living and working. Research by Stark et al. (1984), Rusch (1986), and Schalock (1984) demonstrate that staff and environmental factors may be critical components of the learning process for those with severe health and/or behavioral deficits. Both the settings in which evaluation and training take place and staff attitudes are crucial factors.

Comprehensive research and studies will also need to look at issues of acquisition, utilization, and maintenance of skills by developmentally disabled individuals (Rusch, 1986).

FUTURE STRATEGIES AND GOALS

If we are to provide opportunities for developmentally disabled individuals wanting to work, we need to implement programs based on the principles discussed in this chapter. Certainly, provision of health care is an essential first step. Teaching and training efforts to maximize the acquisition of skills that will lead to increased degrees of economic independence also need to be further developed.

Other areas to consider include the following:

1. Providing financial and programmatic incentives and support to enable families to care for their developmentally disabled family member(s) at home
2. Designing educational intervention through in-school experiences to maximize the acquisition of prevocational and vocational skills (see Chapter 8) and developing methods of facilitating the transition from education to work
3. Establishing safe, integrated, and attractive residential living facilities as an alternative to institutionalization (see Chapter 16)
4. Providing a health care continuum through primary, secondary, and tertiary health caregivers for the developmentally disabled population (see Chapter 18)
5. Allocating sufficient resources to serve the most severely disabled individual in such a fashion that the greatest degree of independence is achieved by that individual

For those developmentally disabled individuals not entering employment, we must look toward developing approaches, systems, and supports that minimize the barriers to achieving the highest degree of self-sufficiency possible—economically, socially, and emotionally. Only if we make use of all the resources of our knowledge, attitudes, creativity, and technology can we ensure that our hopes for the future for these developmentally disabled individuals will become reality.

REFERENCES

Albin, T. J., Stark, J. A., & Keith, K. W. (1978). *The vocational training and placement of developmentally disabled individuals.* Paper presented at the Timberline Conference on Vocational Habilitation of Severely Handicapped. Portland, OR, February 28–March 2.

Berkson, G., & Romer, D. (1981). A letter to a service provider. In H. C. Haywood & G. R. Newbrough (Eds.), *Living environments for developmentally disabled persons.* Baltimore, MD: University Park Press.

Bernstein, G. S., & Karan, O. C. (1979). Obstacles to vocational normalization for the developmentally disabled. *Rehabilitation Literature, 40*(3), 66–71.

Buscaglia, L. (1973). *The disabled and their parents: A counseling challenge.* Princeton, NJ: Charles B. Stack, Inc.

Frankl, V. (1965). *Psychotherapy and existentialism.* New York: Washington Square Press, Inc.

Gold, M. W. (1973). Research on the vocational habilitation of retarded: The present, the future. In N. Ellis (Ed.), *International review of research in mental retardation, (Vol. 6).* New York: Academic Press.

Horner, R. H. (1981). Stimulus control, transfer, and maintenance of upright walking posture in a severely mentally retarded adult. *American Journal of Mental Deficiency, 86*(1), 86–96.

Karan, O. C., (1976). Contemporary views on vocational evaluation practices with the mentally retarded. *Vocational Evaluation and Work Adjustment Bulletin, 9,* 7–13.

Karan, O. C., & Schalock, R. L. (1983). An ecological approach to assessing vocational and community living skills. In C. O'Connell-Mason (Ed.), *Vocational habilitation.* Columbus, OH: Charles E. Merrill Publishing Co.

Lynch, K. P. (1978). *A conceptual model for vocational education of the severely handicapped.* Paper presented at the Timberline Conference on Vocational Habilitation of Severely Handicapped. Portland, OR, February 28–March 2.

Rehab Brief. (1984). National Institute of Handicapped Research. Vol. III, No. 4.

Reuther, W. P. (1967). The human goals of manpower policy. In I. H. Siegel (Ed.), *Manpower tomorrow: Prospects and priorities.* New York, NY: Augustus M. Kelley.

Rusch, F. R. (Ed.). (1986). *Competitive employment issues and strategies.* Baltimore, MD: Paul H. Brookes Publishing Co.

Rusch, F. R., Schutz, R. P., & Agran, M. (1982). Validating entry level survival skills for service occupations: Implications for curriculum development. *Journal of the Association for the Severely Handicapped, 8,* 32–41.

Schalock, R. L. (1984). *Benefit-cost analysis and program evaluation.* Paper presented at 108th annual AAMD convention. Minneapolis, MN, May 29, 1984.

Stark, J. A., McGee, J., & Menolascino, F. (1984). *International handbook of community services for the mentally retarded.* Hillsdale, NJ: Lawrence Erlbaum.

∞ Section V ∞

OTHER ESSENTIAL HABILITATION COMPONENTS

No MATTER HOW COMPREHENSIVE AND SUCCESSFUL A MODEL AND ITS DESIGN ARE, IF THERE ARE no places for people to live, no mechanism for teaching social and interpersonal skills, and no people to care for their physical needs, the model will not succeed. This section examines the residential and learning and adjustment components of a total service system. A special focus is placed on health care needs because these are often viewed as major barriers to effective integration of the adult with developmental disabilities.

In Chapter 16, Bruininks and his colleagues—Lakin, Hill, and White—examine and document the trends in the delivery of residential services to adults with developmental disabilities. This chapter contains seldom-found data on the social objectives, philosophical principles, and growing knowledge base that have fostered the growth in residential services during the past decade. The authors provide a systematic guide to the delivery of residential services. The reader should find this chapter particularly helpful in identifying the barriers to residential services and responses to these barriers. The chapter concludes with recommendations for improving current practices to achieve a fuller social integration and effective residential service delivery for the developmentally disabled adult.

Educators and training staff will be particularly interested in Chapter 17, which focuses on the learning and adjustment needs of this population. Calkins, Walker, and Bacon-Prue present a model that reviews the behavioral, personal, and social adjustments that adults go through during the developmental process. These adjustments are essential components to successful integration of the developmentally disabled adult in the community. The authors present a systematic model to help accomplish these adjustments to learning that is based on eight major assumptions. Finally, they present a number of needs that should be addressed by research, services, and model development activities in the future.

The issue of medical care for the developmentally disabled adult has always been a major concern and has been receiving increased attention over the last few years. Chapter 18 presents a review of the medical needs of the population that is often missing in the literature. The authors—a geneticist, a psychiatrist, and medical psychologist—have diverse backgrounds and substantial experience in addressing these issues in their teaching, writings, clinical practices, and community consultations.

Buehler, Menolascino, and Stark first review the health care of developmentally disabled individuals, including their cognitive, physical, and/or emotional needs, through a historical analysis of views toward the developmentally disabled, particularly the mentally retarded. The medical needs of this population were sampled through data collected in a model health care program. Factors influencing the delivery of medical services and an evaluation of the new models of health care should be extremely useful to those personnel involved in this area of care. More important, however, is the issue of medical training. Recommended changes in the core medical curriculum and retraining through continuing education are presented, along with the role medical care personnel can play in ensuring the success of the developmentally disabled adult in the community.

∞ Chapter 16 ∞

Residential Options
and Future Implications

K. Charlie Lakin, Bradley K. Hill,
Robert H. Bruininks, and Carolyn C. White

IN RECENT YEARS THE RESIDENTIAL SERVICES system for developmentally disabled adults has changed rapidly under a policy and process termed deinstitutionalization. As the state institution populations have decreased from 196,000 in 1976 to 119,000 in 1982 (Lakin, 1979; Scheerenberger, 1983) the number of residential placements outside state institutions has grown from an estimated 22,000 to over 100,000 (Hill, Lakin, & Bruininks, 1984a; Lakin, Hill, Hauber, & Bruininks, 1982). These changes are the result of new social and fiscal policies, aggressive advocacy for the rights of developmentally disabled individuals to live in the community, a better understanding of improved habilitative environments, court cases challenging the adequacy of many specific institutional settings, and a new cadre of professionals educated in the need to increase, improve, and support community-based services.

This chapter discusses the social objectives, philosophical principles, and the growing knowledge base that have given direction to residential services for developmentally disabled individuals. Although the long-term care service system for developmentally disabled individuals in the United States falls far short of being based exclusively on the principles and

research described here, it is clearly evolving into greater congruence with them.

SOCIAL AND PHILOSOPHICAL CONCEPTS

No term has so reflected the changes taking place in long-term care for developmentally disabled individuals than has deinstitutionalization. The term is widely used to describe a variety of changes currently taking place, and because of its widespread use and perhaps its general acceptance, very few terms have suffered greater semantic abuse. The general concept of deinstitutionalization has been supported as a social goal by every branch of the federal government for over a decade. Currently, it is formally recognized as the central theme of residential services by virtually all consumer/advocate, professional, and policy groups in the United States. Therefore, from a practical standpoint, it is not surprising that many groups with varying interests in long-term care have attempted to include their particular vested goals under its rubric. As a result, the place of state institutions and other large facilities in the residential care system is constantly being defined and redefined as the interests of particular groups dictate.

Although there is no precise determination of what constitutes deinstitutionalization, the term is generally recognized as having three major aspects: 1) the movement of residents out of relatively large institutional facilities to smaller ones, 2) avoiding initial placements of individuals into relatively large institutional facilities in favor of placement in smaller ones, or 3) avoiding long-term care altogether.

A new social policy of *noninstitutionalization,* reflecting a commitment to systematic and irreversible efforts to close institutional settings as rapidly as possible—rather than gradual depopulation with continued capital investment—is increasingly being articulated and promoted by mainstream advocacy organizations, such as the Association for Retarded Citizens. The conceptualization of non-institutionalization derived from a sense that deinstitutionalization largely excluded severely and profoundly handicapped individuals who currently live in large institutional settings from the benefits of community-based care. Advocates of noninstitutionalization note that it has been well over a decade since the realities of large institutions have been fully documented and made public (Blatt, 1970, 1973; Goffman, 1961; Where Toys are Locked Away, 1965). Furthermore, long-term negative behavioral effects of institutional placements have been empirically established (Kiesler, 1982; Pilewski & Heal, 1980), and as for general treatment effectiveness, the single best predictor of future institutionalization is prior institutionalization (Kiesler, 1982; Rotegard & Bruininks, 1983).

Of increasing concern to many advocates is the tendency of institutions to move mildly and moderately handicapped individuals into communities but not to make such provisions for the more severely handicapped. This practice is seen as discriminatory and has long been a major factor in decisions about the appropriateness of placement in insititutional versus noninstitutional settings. State institutions have increasingly become residential care centers for the most severely retarded, a trend that has been noted for many years (Pense, 1946). Table 1 presents a breakdown of the extremes of impairment in resident population of state institutions from 1939 to 1982.

The high proportion of profoundly retarded clients in state institutions resulted from a much higher rate of discharge of the more mildly disabled residents and an implicit acceptance of the appropriateness of institutional placement for a large number of more severely retarded individuals. Although profoundly retarded individuals made up 15% of the state institution's population in 1939, they represented less than 4% of all discharges; mildly/borderline retarded individuals—40% of the state institution population—represented over 75% of all discharges (Bureau of the Census, 1941). Now 40 years later, comparative data from a 1978 national sample of 75 state institutions showed that profoundly retarded individuals made up 47% of all institution residents but only 19% of all discharges, whereas mildly/borderline retarded individuals made up 9% of state institution residents and 28% of discharges (Sigford, Bruininks, Lakin, Hill, &

Table 1. Resident population of state institutions by level of retardation

Year	Percent mildly or borderline retarded	Percent profoundly retarded
1939	40%	15%
1964	18%	27%
1982	6%	57%

Source: Bureau of the Census (1939), 1941; Scheerenberger (1964), 1965; Scheerenberger (1982), 1983.

Heal, 1982). At the same time, profoundly retarded individuals represented only 12% of the persons in long-term care outside state institutions (Hill et al., 1984a), a circumstance that is increasingly being viewed as unacceptable.

The provision of services to developmentally disabled individuals in the United States in the 1970s and 1980s has been immeasurably influenced by the concept of normalization. Normalization, however, has not been understood in exactly the same way by all who have used it. For example, some have implied—often in an attempt to deride the concept—that normalization is a demand for services to make disabled individuals "normal" or that service providers should essentially ignore the abnormalities of disabled individuals (Aanes & Haagenson, 1978; Schwartz, 1977; Throne, 1975; Wolfensberger, 1980). Most interpretations, however, derive from a human value, and increasingly from a societal value, that the treatment of developmentally disabled individuals should occur within a context that recognizes and acknowledges their personhood and natural membership in their native culture and community.

In general, the *normalization principle* means "making available to all mentally retarded people patterns of life and conditions of everyday living which are as close as possible to the regular circumstances and ways of life of society" (Nirje, 1976, p. 231). Normalization is not a specific service or habilitative practice; it sets a standard of value for a historically devalued group of people against which the human and professional qualities of services can be judged. The standard is simply whether the treatment of the individual reflects the acceptance of him or her as a valued member of society, providing the opportunity for those normal patterns and experiences of living that his or her disability reasonably allows.

Three significant movements have promoted a gradual reconstruction of long-term care services based on the normalization principle. First, there is a growing consensus that the fundamental meaning of normalization involves valuing the life, rights, and dignity of citizens with disabilities. Increasingly, the degradation of life, rights, or dignity in the name of treating a disability is seen as professional arrogance. Second, the development of skills that most greatly alleviate the effects of disability—that is, promote independence, self-care, and social participation—is best conducted in the environments in which these skills must ultimately be demonstrated. Increasingly, failure to reflect this concept, which is supported by research findings, is recognized as inadequate professional practice. Third, there is a growing questioning of arguments for continued institutionalization of developmentally disabled individuals that are based on political and economic interests (e.g., state legislatures wishing to recoup investments in institutional physical plants, opposition to deinstitutionalization expressed by state employees' unions seeking to retain state employment). Limiting participation of a particular group of citizens in a society because of the secondary interests of those who perceive benefits in maintaining their segregation is increasingly indefensible in light of current beliefs and knowledge.

Normalization is largely a philosophical and moral principle, its operationalization is most clearly evident in the concept of the *least restrictive alternative*. The concept can be defined as a semantic marker for a number of goals for residential services, including placement in the "most culturally normative environment feasible" or at the "level of maximum social integration." In a habilitative sense, the concept reflects the attempt to provide training under the optimal conditions for acquiring, maintaining, and generalizing the specific skills of daily living that are part of the expected behavioral repertoire of members of the culture.

PRINCIPLES FOR ORGANIZING RESIDENTIAL AND RELATED SERVICES

Today's service system for developmentally disabled individuals has been shaped by a number of interrelated principles. Changes in philosophy and practice have evolved into increasing consensus on the importance of achieving standards of appropriate services at all levels of the service delivery system. These trends in recent years support the following functions of community service programs, divided into direct and indirect service categories as identified in the Developmental Disabilities Act.

Direct Services

To provide basic maintenance (food, shelter, clothing) as necessary and a *range of residential options* that appropriately serves the varying needs of developmentally disabled individuals for different levels of care and different types of programs.

To provide *habilitation activities* that are focused on teaching developmentally disabled individuals the skills they need to increase their level of independence and degree of social integration and ability to fulfill valued social roles (e.g., work) and that promote the health, development, and psychological well-being of developmentally disabled individuals through appropriate, adequate, and timely intervention in response to their needs.

To provide *social, leisure, and recreation activities* that offer frequent and varied opportunities for productive and enjoyable uses of free time by developmentally disabled individuals in integrated settings.

To establish *resource allocation,* budgeting, service reimbursements, and income-maintenance policies and practices that are clear, well-publicized, and non-stigmatizing, that provide significant incentives for family and community living, and ensure continuity of noninstitutional alternatives.

To use individualized *assessment, planning, and placement* procedures that gather and utilize information to determine the nature and quantity of services needed.

To provide individual *case managers* or program coordinators to link developmentally disabled individuals with providers who will deliver appropriate services in the least restrictive, most normalized appropriate placement.

Indirect Services

To maintain *information and evaluation systems* that gather, aggregate, and utilize data on individual clients, programs, and systems to establish objectives for services and policies, assess the effectiveness of services and policies in meeting goals, and modify services and policies as indicated by evalution results.

To establish *personnel management* practices that recruit, train, utilize, and retain adequate numbers of skilled professionals and paraprofessionals to provide the services needed by developmentally disabled individuals.

To promote *social attitudes,* professional commitments, community experiences, and citizen expectations for public laws, regulations, and policies that increase the acceptance and integration of developmentally disabled individuals.

To develop and *share knowledge and experience* among service providers, academic and research institutions, government and private administrative agencies, advocacy/consumer organizations, and natural and surrogate family members about available services, effective practices, new technologies, special opportunities, and useful policies in local, state, and national spheres.

To promote the recognition of *human rights and dignity* for developmentally disabled individuals, including maximizing the opportunities for consumer involvement, personal choice, and self-advocacy.

CONTEMPORARY STATUS OF RESIDENTIAL SERVICES

Demographic data demonstrate significant trends in residential services, primarily in the decrease in the population of traditional state institutions and the corresponding increase in the development of a private residential services system. Figure 1 presents the relative change in three major segments of the residential care system since 1962. Licensed private mental retardation facilities (including specially licensed foster care homes) now have more developmentally disabled residents than public facilities (state or county operated). If one defines the residential care system more broadly to include nursing home placements, the private care sector of the residential service industry has been predominant for a number of years.

Unfortunately, the statistical focus on deinstitutionalization and the development of alternative care models have, at times, led to an overemphasis on the public/private dichotomy in service provision. Figure 2 presents the percentage of all persons in residential care (public or private) facilities of various sizes.

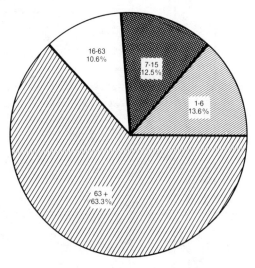

Figure 2. Percent of residents by size of facility (June 30, 1982). (From: K. C. Lakin, B. K. Hill, & R. H. Bruininks. [1986]. Basic facts and trends in residential services. In R. B. Kugel (Ed.), *Changing patterns in residential services for persons with mental retardation.* Washington, DC: President's Committee on Mental Retardation.)

On June 30, 1982, nearly two out of every three (63.3%) individuals in residential facilities for the mentally retarded/developmentally disabled resided in facilities serving 64 or more residents, whereas over one-half (55.9%) were in facilities with more than 100 residents. In 1984, the 50 states still spent 1.5 times as many dollars on institutional expenditures as they did on community residential services (Braddock, Howes, & Hemp, 1984).

Despite the fact that residential services have yet to reach their rapidly evolving ideals, significant change has been taking place. The following material briefly discusses the current status and recent changes in residential services for individuals with developmental disabilities, based on data gathered in national research conducted at the Center for Residential and Community Services, University of Minnesota, in 1977 and 1982. These data are summarized in Table 2.

Type and Size of Facility

Between 1977 and 1982, the total number of residential facilities for mentally retarded/developmentally disabled individuals increased from 11,025 to 15,633. The total num-

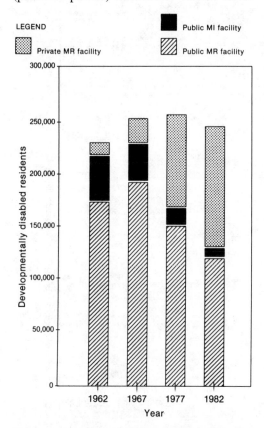

Figure 1. Number of persons with developmental disabilities in public and private facilities. (From: K. C. Lakin, B. K. Hill, & R. H. Bruininks. [1986]. Basic facts and trends in residential services. In R. B. Kugel (Ed.), *Changing patterns in residential services for persons with mental retardation.* Washington, DC: President's Committee on Mental Retardation.)

Table 2. Characteristics of residential facilities for mentally retarded people in the United States: June 30, 1977 and June 30, 1982

Characteristics	Specialized foster		Group residential 1-15		Group residential private 16+		Group residential public 16+		Semi-independent		Board and supervision		Personal care		Specialized nursing		Total	
	1977	1982	1977	1982	1977	1982	1977	1982	1977	1982	1977	1982	1977	1982	1977	1982	1977	1982
Facility characteristics																		
Number of facilities	5,332	6,587	3,225	6,414	850	886	362	369	236	306	210	185	561	583	249	303	11,025	15,633
Number of residents	15,435	18,252	24,331	43,588	43,336	46,068	167,212	134,943	2,356	3,155	2,955	2,559	9,185	7,956	21,103	24,521	285,913	281,042
M[a]	2.9	2.8	7.6	6.8	51.6	52.0	464.2	365.7	10.5	10.3	14.8	13.8	16.4	13.6	86.0	81.1	26.2	18.0
SD[b]	2.0	1.9	3.2	3.2	60.4	55.7	540.1	383.9	11.4	8.8	19.6	20.3	24.4	19.8	65.3	61.8	129.8	83.0
Number of MR residents	14,418	17,147	22,449	42,018	36,998	40,347	154,856	122,971	1,993	2,870	665	1,264	4,141	4,070	11,275	12,982	247,796	243,669
Operator																		
Private/proprietary	100.0%	100.0%	40.0%	27.1%	50.7%	50.2%	.0	.0	15.0%	13.4%	93.5%	94.6%	90.9%	90.4%	76.5%	70.6%	72.4%	62.2%
Nonprofit	.0	.0	48.2%	63.6%	49.3%	49.8%	.0	.0	75.8%	80.4%	5.5%	4.3%	4.5%	4.8%	18.0%	23.1%	20.2%	31.2%
Public	.0	.0	11.8%	9.2%	.0	.0	100.0%	100.0%	9.2%	6.2%	1.0%	1.1%	4.6%	4.8%	5.5%	6.3%	7.3%	6.6%
Average per diem per resident	$9.41	$16.15	$16.52	$38.31	$22.78	$45.15	$43.53	$85.84	$16.20	$27.40	$9.60	$15.97	$12.60	$17.05	$25.92	$49.81	$34.23	$61.89
Movement																		
New admissions	22.4%	19.0%	37.2%	25.7%	20.3%	15.7%	5.7%	5.9%	54.2%	31.9%	30.0%	12.7%	19.8%	14.7%	23.0%	14.4%	13.3%	12.8%
Readmissions	2.3%	.9%	2.6%	1.2%	1.3%	1.3%	1.9%	1.9%	1.1%	1.0%	3.0%	.9%	3.6%	2.3%	4.7%	2.0%	2.0%	1.6%
Releases	7.0%	7.9%	18.5%	13.4%	13.9%	12.0%	9.2%	11.4%	24.8%	18.5%	16.4%	13.0%	10.9%	8.5%	15.5%	8.0%	11.3%	11.5%
Deaths	.9%	.9%	.6%	.5%	.8%	.8%	1.5%	1.5%	.4%	.3%	.9%	.8%	1.1%	.8%	3.1%	2.3%	1.3%	1.2%
Estimated move due to close	8.7%	8.8%	6.2%	5.8%	2.4%	2.4%	.4%	.5%	9.5%	9.4%	7.4%	6.8%	6.7%	5.7%	2.5%	2.6%	2.0%	2.7%
Estimated net 12 month change	8.2%	2.3%	14.5%	7.3%	4.5%	1.7%	-3.5%	-5.6%	20.6%	4.9%	8.3%	-7.1%	4.6%	2.0%	6.6%	4.3%	.9%	-.8%
Opened within 4½ years	52.7%	46.7%	71.0%	60.0%	36.1%	19.7%	19.9%	8.8%	88.0%	62.5%	38.6%	21.4%	37.9%	27.4%	42.5%	23.4%	55.2%	48.6%
Resident characteristics																		
Age																		
<22	39.6%	37.4%	28.6%	19.8%	44.4%	32.0%	35.8%	22.0%	17.7%	7.7%	10.1%	5.9%	14.7%	10.2%	52.9%	38.2%	36.8%	24.8%
22-39	24.7%	32.0%	47.9%	53.3%	36.7%	41.8%	41.3%	50.2%	61.3%	65.4%	33.8%	38.3%	28.6%	31.6%	22.3%	33.6%	39.3%	47.0%
40-62	26.7%	23.1%	21.2%	23.8%	16.3%	22.1%	19.2%	22.9%	20.3%	25.5%	42.0%	40.5%	43.4%	41.1%	18.3%	21.8%	19.9%	23.3%
63+	9.1%	7.6%	2.2%	3.0%	2.6%	4.1%	3.7%	5.0%	.7%	1.5%	13.4%	15.3%	13.4%	17.1%	6.6%	6.4%	4.1%	4.8%
Level of retardation																		
Borderline/mild	28.0%	25.9%	34.4%	29.3%	29.6%	26.8%	9.3%	7.0%	66.1%	61.8%	49.5%	47.1%	30.6%	31.2%	12.6%	9.2%	16.9%	16.8%
Moderate	37.7%	37.7%	41.7%	37.9%	34.9%	29.9%	16.0%	12.9%	31.1%	32.5%	40.8%	33.6%	40.4%	39.8%	21.6%	16.2%	23.4%	22.8%
Severe	26.5%	26.0%	19.5%	23.2%	23.4%	24.0%	27.9%	24.3%	2.7%	5.3%	7.1%	17.6%	18.0%	20.6%	35.9%	26.2%	26.2%	24.0%
Profound	7.8%	10.4%	4.4%	9.5%	12.2%	19.3%	46.9%	55.8%	.1%	.3%	2.6%	2.7%	11.1%	8.4%	30.0%	48.5%	33.5%	36.4%
Nonambulatory	7.0%	9.3%	3.5%	5.3%	8.4%	14.4%	23.3%	25.5%	6.0%	3.7%	1.0%	1.7%	6.6%	5.4%	49.3%	43.3%	18.9%	19.5%
Cannot talk	18.6%	24.9%	11.2%	17.4%	19.7%	24.1%	43.5%	49.1%	3.3%	3.7%	6.5%	4.8%	13.0%	16.1%	48.5%	54.0%	34.7%	36.7%
Not toilet trained	8.8%	13.1%	4.2%	6.7%	11.6%	16.1%	34.1%	38.0%	.8%	.1%	1.0%	3.9%	6.8%	6.5%	45.2%	49.0%	26.1%	26.7%

From: B. K. Hill, K. C. Lakin, & R. H. Bruininks. (1984b). Trends in residential services for people who are mentally retarded: 1977–1982. *Journal of The Association for Persons with Severe Handicaps, 9,* 247.

[a] Mean.

[b] Standard deviation.

ber of mentally retarded residents in these facilities actually declined slightly from 247,800 to 243,700, and the average size of facilities decreased from 26.2 to 18.0 residents. During this same period the proportion of mentally retarded residents in facilities with 15 or fewer residents increased substantially from 16.3% to 26.1%. Most new facilities were specially licensed foster homes or small group residences. The number of specially licensed or contracted placements in boarding homes, personal care homes, and nursing facilities was relatively stable between 1977 and 1982 (17,081 and 18,316 respectively).

The number of staffed semi-independent living facilities increased from 236 to 306, but this model still served only 1.2% of all persons in residential care. Although there was some growth in the number of residents served by large private group residences, the population of large public facilities decreased by 20.6% over the 5-year period. No national data exist on the number of developmentally disabled individuals in generic foster, boarding, and nursing homes. However, movement statistics suggest that decreases in nursing home placements that were evident between 1977–1980 appear to have leveled off, perhaps because of the aging of the developmentally disabled population. It is also readily evident in discussions with state program agency personnel that there has been substantial growth in supported independent living. Again, no national data exist to indicate the extent of this growth.

Facility Operator and Reimbursement

Between 1977 and 1982, there was a moderate increase in the proportion of private nonprofit facilities—from 20.2% to 31.2% of all facilities—primarily because of a growth in the number of small nonprofit group residences. Most semi-independent living programs continued to be nonprofit, and most boarding homes, personal care homes, and specialized nursing facilities continued to be individual or family operated (proprietary).

The national average annual cost for residential care of a developmentally disabled individual in Fiscal Year 1982 was about $22,500—a substantial increase from about $12,500 in 1977. Foster homes, semi-independent living programs, boarding homes, and personal care homes had reimbursement rates that increased approximately 13% per year between 1977 and 1982, slightly above the 10% annual average rise in the Consumer Price Index over the same period. Reimbursements for group residences and nursing facilities increased much more rapidly over that period. A major contributing factor to those cost increases was the growth in the number of ICF/MR certified beds from 98,097 in 1977 to 138,738 in 1982. During that time period, ICF/MR costs nearly doubled from $41.96 to $79.53 per day. The rapid cost increases among Medicaid-reimbursed facilities may suggest that, when states pay half or less of the cost of care (the federal government pays 50% to 77% of states' ICF/MR costs, depending on their per capita income), they may be less concerned with how fast those costs are rising. Other factors such as resident characteristics and requirements necessary to meet Medicaid licensing standards, may also account in part for the major cost increases.

Resident Movement and Facility Opening

Data from surveys conducted in 1977 and 1982 present the total number of new admissions, readmissions, releases, and resident deaths during 1-year periods. Estimates of the net change in the number of residents served during each 1-year period generally correspond to the change in total number of residents in each type of facility between 1977 and 1982. The most rapid growth in facility beds was among small group facilities (15 or fewer residents) that added an estimated 3,255 new beds in 1977 and 2,773 new beds in 1982. Large public facilities (16 or more residents) accelerated their net outflow of residents with slightly increased rates of release and substantially increased numbers of "closed" beds. Large private facilities continued to grow in fiscal year 1982, but at a substantially decreased rate.

Information on year of opening, which accounts for both system growth and replacement of facilities that close or move, indicates a relatively large turnover among specialized foster homes, comparable to the national rate at which U.S. households move. Although the total number of residents in these facilities grew less than 20%, approximately half the foster home "beds" available on June 30, 1982 moved or were newly opened in that 5-year period. On the other hand, although the majority of small group residence beds were also newly created between 1977–1982, these beds tended to be in more stable facilities, therefore causing a near doubling of the number of small group residence beds. The highest percentage of new beds was in the semi-independent category, reflecting a significant growth in the number of residents served (34%).

Resident Characteristics

Comparison of the 1977 resident population to the 1982 populaton shows a slight decrease— approximately 4,000 or 1.6%—in the total number of developmentally disabled persons in residential care. This change is partly attributable to a decrease in the number of children being placed outside their natural family homes before adulthood (Lakin et al., 1982). During that 5-year period, the number of residents aged 21 or younger decreased by 30,000, from 36.8% to 24.8% of all residents. Some of this decrease is due to residents reaching the age of 22, contributing to an increase of 17,000 people in the 22–29-year-old age group. Some of it is also due to the national decrease of 3.5% in the total number of children. However, the decrease is a real one; fewer children entered residential facilities than in the past to replace those who are moving into older-age categories. The decrease in the proportion of residents under 22 in specialized foster care settings was less than that of any other model of care, although specialized foster homes continued to serve mostly adults.

The proportion of severely/profoundly retarded residents in residential care settings remained essentially the same between 1977 and 1982 (59.7% and 60.5% respectively). The near doubling of the number of small group homes—adding nearly 20,000 new beds— between 1977 and 1982 accommodated most of the 33,000 residents released or diverted from public institutions, increasing the proportion of severely/profoundly retarded residents in small group residences from 23.9% to 32.7%. The proportion of profoundly retarded residents in small group homes increased from 4.4% to 9.5%, but was still exceeded by the proportion in foster homes, large private, and large public institutions (10.4%, 19.3%, and 55.8% in 1982 respectively). Boarding homes and personal care homes tended to serve mildly handicapped older adults, whereas specialized nursing facilities—nursing homes with the mental retardation program licenses—served primarily severely handicapped children and young adults.

Information gathered on functional limitations of residents was largely congruent with the data on level of retardation. It was found that 19.5% of all residents were non-ambulatory, 36.7% could not talk, and 26.7% were not toilet-trained. Relative to other placement types, the most severely functionally impaired population was in specialized nursing homes.

Current populations of state-operated institutions—behaviorally difficult, multiply handicapped, medically needy, and profoundly retarded—are the individuals who must be targeted for services in community-based settings.

Behaviorally Difficult Behavior problems have long been considered a major obstacle to the successful community placement and adjustment of retarded individuals (Sternlicht & Deutsch, 1972; Windle, 1962). Next to severity of retardation, behavior problems may be the single most important factor in determining initial placement in state-operated institutions (Maney, Pace, & Morrison, 1964; Saenger, 1960; Spencer, 1974). In addition, a proportion of readmissions to state institutions—up to 55%—has been directly related to behavior problems (Keys, Boroskin, & Ross, 1973; Pagel & Whitling, 1978). Although overall the number of institutionalized retarded individuals has decreased at a fairly constant rate, smaller numbers of first admissions to state-operated facilities have been offset by larger numbers of readmissions. Therefore, some community residential facilities have been less able and/or less willing than state institutions to serve residents with certain behavior problems (Conroy, 1977; Lakin, 1979; Rotegard, Bruininks, & Krantz, 1984; Scheerenberger, 1979).

Data gathered by the Center for Community and Residential Services in a national probability sample of approximately 1,000 residents in state institutions and 1,000 residents in private (community) residential facilities on January 1, 1979 (±3 months) are presented in Table 3. These data showed substantially more

behavior problems among institutionalized residents than among residents residing in community facilities. However, more significantly, state institution residents engaged in aberrant behavior of a much more serious nature.

Although such data are sometimes used in the aggregate to argue for a continued need for state institutions as a placement for developmentally disabled individuals with behavior problems, it is important to note that in the 1979 study there is not a single category of

Table 3. Percent of residents reported to exhibit maladaptive behavior as reported by direct care staff

Category of behavior	Private facility residents (N = 964)	State institution residents (N = 997)	State institution new admissions (N = 286)	State institution readmissions (N = 244)
Injures self	11.1%	21.7%	22.0%	21.3%
Injures other people	16.3%	30.3%	42.0%	38.5%
Damages property	11.1%	17.6%	19.2%	23.4%
Unusual or disruptive behavior	28.8%	34.3%	37.8%	41.0%
Breaks rules; won't follow routine	19.1%	18.8%	32.4%	33.2%
Refuses to go to day program	7.2%	11.7%	20.9%	25.8%
Has spent one of last 30 days at home because of refusal to go	2.5%	5.7%	9.4%	13.8%
Has purposely run away	2.2%	3.6%	11.5%	13.5%
Has run away within the last six months	1.3%	2.5%	8.7%	8.2%
Has broken the law within the last year	1.5%	.5%	3.1%	7.4%
Court of law enforcement personnel involved	.7%	.1%	1.4%	4.1%
Total with one or more types of behavior	47.3%	59.7%	68.5%	68.4%

From: R. H. Bruininks, B. K. Hill, K. C. Lakin, & C. C. White. (1985). *Residential services for adults with developmental disabilities.* Logan: Utah State University, Developmental Center for Handicapped Persons.

aberrant or maladaptive behavior found among institution residents that was not also found among community facility residents. Therefore, there simply is no way to make a valid argument that the presence of maladaptive behavior prevents placement in community facilities. There does, however, seem to be a limited capacity and/or willingness of community residential placements to deal effectively with problem behaviors. These data suggest that there is a need to develop behavior management skills in persons who work in community settings, to identify community program models that are effectively dealing with problem behaviors, and to demonstrate the approaches and effects of the best community-based programs to professional trainees and the larger professional and lay public. The literature is rich with information on managing problem behaviors of developmentally disabled individuals.

Multiply Handicapped It is well documented that mental retardation is often accompanied by related disorders (Hardman & Drew, 1977). The two most commonly noted disorders are epilepsy and cerebral palsy. Pond (1979) reported rates of epilepsy from 3% to 6% among persons with mild/moderate retardation and about 33% among persons with severe/profound retardation. These figures compare with prevalence estimates of about .3% to .6% for the general population.

Cerebral palsy is also highly related to functional mental retardation. The proportion of the general population with cerebral palsy is only about .30% to .35% (EMC Institute, 1979; National Information Center for Handicapped Children and Youth, 1983). The proportion of persons who have cerebral palsy and are also mentally retarded is estimated to be 55% (United Cerebral Palsy, 1968). Additional disabilities, such as visual and hearing impairment and severe behavioral syndromes (autism, mental illness), are also significant to the provision of long-term care in community-based facilities.

In describing the nature of the mentally retarded target population in residential care with respect to multiple disorders, the 1979 national probability sample of approximately 1,000 institution and 1,000 community facility residents again is used. Summary data from this nationally representative study are presented in Table 4.

Mentally retarded individuals in public institutions have a significantly higher prevalence of epilepsy and physical handicaps than do the residents of community-based programs. However, other handicaps were not significantly more common among institutionalized residents. Forty-four percent of institutionalized residents had no secondary handicap whereas 60% of community facility residents did have a secondary handicap. These data point out the considerable overlap between institutional and community residence populations in terms of multiple handicapping conditions. Although statistical analyses did show a few statistically significant differences between the two groups, it is equally as important to note that the disorders that are more prevalent in institutions are nonetheless being treated in great numbers in community facilities.

Medical Needs Developmental disabilities are often accompanied by health problems (Nelson & Crocker, 1978; Smith, Decker, Herberg, & Rupke, 1969). Surveys on the health characteristics of developmentally disabled individuals in publicly operated institutions have indicated a prevalence of medical problems (Wright, Valente, & Tarjan, 1962) and mortality rates (deaths per thousand persons per year) that are far above those for the general population (Forssman & Akesson, 1970; Tarjan, Eyman, & Miller, 1969).

Although health problems have not been clearly identified as reasons for initial institutionalization (Maney et al., 1964; Saenger, 1960), they have often been cited as reasons for reinstitutionalization of released residents. Of 117 readmissions to one large state institution for retarded individuals, 25% were reported by social workers to be due to health problems and 10% to a combination of health problems and maladaptive behavior (Pagel & Whitling, 1978). Similarly, Keys et al. (1973) reported that, among 126 readmissons to a public institution, 28% returned for medical reasons and

Table 4. Handicaps in addition to mental retardation as reported by direct care staff

Handicap	Private facility residents (N = 964)	State institution residents (N = 997)	State institution new admissions (N = 286)	State institution readmissions (N = 244)
Epilepsy				
Recorded history	25.3%	12.8%	43.8%	41.4%
Medicated for epilepsy	20.8%	36.3%	32.2%	34.8%
Seizure observed within last year	12.9%	22.2%	19.3%	25.1%
Cerebral palsy	10.5%	11.0%	6.9%	12.2%
Physical handicap[a]	10.7%	14.5%	9.0%	7.3%
Vision				
Severely impaired[b]	3.4%	4.6%	5.0%	2.0%
Blind	2.6%	4.0%	4.6%	3.3%
Hearing				
Severely impaired[c]	1.7%	2.7%	2.5%	.8%
Deaf	1.3%	2.6%	2.8%	.8%
Behavior disorder[d]	1.6%	.7%	.7%	1.6%
Number of handicaps[e]				
None	59.5%	44.3%	55.9%	50.4%
One	31.2%	38.6%	32.9%	37.7%
Two	7.2%	14.5%	6.6%	9.8%
Three	1.7%	2.0%	3.1%	2.0%
Four	.3%	.6%	1.4%	.0%

[a]Includes spina bifida, contractures, missing extremities and paralysis; excludes residents with cerebral palsy.
[b]Cannot see a television size image from 8 feet away, but sees enough to walk around without usually bumping into things.
[c]Can hear only a few words said or loud noises.
[d]Autism, mental illness, alcoholism, or nonprescribed drug dependency.
[e]Of the six handicapping conditions in this table. Includes epilepsy if a seizure was observed during the last year or if resident had a recorded history of seizures and was currently receiving medication for epilepsy.
From: R. H. Bruininks, B. K. Hill, K. C. Lakin, & C. C. White. (1985). *Residential services for adults with developmental disabilities.* Logan: Utah State University, Developmental Center for Handicapped Persons.

6% because of uncontrolled seizures. In studying these data it is important to differentiate between the reasons why a previous placement was terminated and why the next placement was chosen. Health conditions are often cited as a factor in extrafamilial placements of developmentally disabled individuals and for changes in community placements. They are further cited as reasons for maintaining state

institutions as places where specialized medical/health services are readily available.

Table 5 presents data from the 1979 national probability sample of residents in state institutions and community facilities with respect to chronic health disorders. There seem to be many institutional residents with chronic health disorders for whom community health systems would have to be responsible if these

Table 5. Chronic health disorders of residents as reported by direct care staff

Health disorder category	Private facility residents (N = 964)	State institution residents (N = 997)	State institution new admissions (N = 286)	State institution readmissions (N = 244)
Infective or parasitic	.2%	.4%	.0%	.8%
Endocrine, nutritional or metabolic (e.g., diabetes, thyroid, hormone imbalances)	1.8%	3.5%	1.8%	2.0%
Blood and blood-forming organs (e.g., anemia)	.3%	1.0%	1.1%	.8%
Nervous system and sensory organs (e.g., cataracts, glaucoma, chronic ear infection, Parkinson's disease, muscular dystrophy)	.9%	.8%	1.1%	.4%
Circulatory system (e.g., heart problems, blood pressure)	7.2%	7.6%	3.5%	2.9%
Respiratory system (e.g., asthma, emphysema, chronic respiratory infection)	2.2%	2.7%	3.2%	2.5%
Digestive system[a] (e.g., ulcers, hernia, chronic constipation, colostomy)	2.5%	3.5%	2.1%	3.7%
Genitourinary system (e.g., kidney, urinary tract)	.6%	1.0%	1.1%	.8%
Skin and subcutaneous tissue	1.5%	1.1%	.7%	.4%
Neoplasms (malignant and nonmalignant)	.4%	.5%	1.4%	.8%
Teeth and gums	.1%	.7%	.0%	.0%
Other	2.5%	2.5%	6.0%	2.5%
Number of health disorders[b]				
None	82.5%	79.9%	83.3%	85.7%
One	14.9%	15.8%	12.1%	11.9%
Two	2.2%	3.2%	3.9%	1.6%
Three	.3%	.9%	.7%	.8%
Four	.0%	.1%	.0%	.0%

[a]Included with digestive systems disorders were problems that required tube feeding and chronic emesis that required medical care.
[b]Number of categories exhibited by each resident.
From: R. H. Bruininks, B. K. Hill, K. C. Lakin, & C. C. White. (1985). *Residential services for adults with developmental disabilities.* Logan: Utah State University, Developmental Center for Handicapped Persons.

individuals are to be placed in the community. However, in terms of health characteristics, community facilities residents seem to present essentially the same general health conditions as do their institutionalized peers.

The 1979 study by the Center for Residential and Community Services (Hill, Bruininks, & Lakin, 1983) documented the following: 1) The prevalence of significant health disorders (categorized according to the *International Classification of Diseases, 9th Revision,* 1980) is not substantially different among populations of institutional and community facilities, and 2) the prevalence of serious health disorders is quite low in both populations. These data suggest that the actual level of chronic health impairment among institutional populations is considerably overestimated in arguing for the maintenance of institutions with self-contained health care units (the quality of which have been challenged on more than one occasion).

Severely/Profoundly Retarded Adults Table 2 clearly showed the substantial variation among the proportions of severely/profoundly retarded residents in different types of facilities. If one looks only at the profoundly retarded portion of the residential population, the extent to which level of disability predicts placement is increased. In 1982, over 80% of public facility residents were severely/profoundly retarded compared to 33% of small community facility residents. Profoundly retarded persons made up 36.5% of the residential population nationwide but 56% of the public institution population. Although less than 10% of the residents of small community facilities (group homes, foster homes, small boarding homes, and personal care homes) were profoundly retarded, the proportion doubled from less than 5% between 1977 and 1982. Increasingly, opportunities are being made for profoundly retarded individuals in smaller community placements.

The most common residential placement for developmentally disabled individuals is, of course, the natural or adoptive family. Substantial evidence indicates that this is an increasingly popular placement. In 1967, public

and private residential facilities had 130.4 developmentally disabled individuals per 100,000 of the general population; in 1982, this rate had dropped to 106.3 per 100,000. Although some of the decrease may be accounted for by the use of alternate placement sites, such as nursing homes or independent living settings, there is little question that the average age at which handicapped children and young adults leave home has increased dramatically, resulting in fewer out-of-home placements (Hill et al., 1984a; Lakin et al., 1982).

Understanding the conditions that permit and encourage developmentally disabled children to remain at home has important cost and service implications. Placement at home can lead not only to reduced demand for expensive and slow-to-develop extrafamilial services but can also provide greater insight into important community-based supports. Services that form the basis of family support programs include the following:

1. Case management to oversee needed services
2. Day programs to ensure the continued opportunity to engage productively in developmentally beneficial activities
3. Training to help parents manage behavior and teach socially beneficial skills
4. Services to assist parents in care, training, and integration of their developmentally disabled children (e.g., transportation, recreation programs, counseling)
5. Respite care to allow parents some relief from the demanding tasks of caring for a developmentally disabled family member
6. Support groups to provide emotional and practical supports for parents

Summary

Overall, the 5 years of data on the residential services system indicate a highly dynamic service system. Residents in 1982 were older and slightly more impaired than those being served 5 years earlier. Public facilities, which continue to be depopulated at a fairly constant rate of 6,000 residents per year, are being replaced by smaller community programs that serve a greater number of severely/profoundly handicapped individuals. The number of residents in large private facilities did not decrease between 1977 and 1982, but the rate of growth slowed considerably, and the population shifted significantly in the direction of older more severely retarded and functionally impaired residents.

Changes in the Medicaid ICF/MR program between 1977 and 1982 generally paralleled those in the residential care system as a whole. The number of smaller ICF/MR certified facilities grew rapidly, mostly through the creation of new facilities. Of the 1,161 ICF/MR facilities with 15 or fewer residents in 1982, approximately 70% opened in 1978 or later. Although the total number of ICF/MR beds in larger facilities— 76 or more residents—increased substantially between 1977 and 1982 (101,709 to 122,456), almost all of this growth came through the certification of already existing facilities. Less than 10% of this growth in beds was created in larger facilities that opened after 1977.

In general, earlier trends in residential services for mentally retarded/developmentally disabled individuals in the United States were maintained between 1977 and 1982. Yet, during this period there was a significant decrease in the number of children and youth in the residential care system and an accompanying increase in the number of adults. This change, resulting from social policies creating and funding community-based education and support programs for children and their families, is one of which advocates should feel proud. However, it is accompanied by concern that community-based service systems may be less well prepared to deal with the developmental and/or vocational needs of the greater number of developmentally disabled adults in the system.

The increase in the number of severely/profoundly retarded individuals in family care and small group care demonstrates that severely and profoundly retarded individuals do not have to be placed in institutions. The data further suggest that there are numerous good (and, no doubt, some bad) examples of community-based care for severely handicapped individuals.

BARRIERS TO RESIDENTIAL SERVICES

A recent national survey of planners, providers, parents, advocates, and other professionals active in the field of services to individuals with developmental disabilities assessed barriers to residential services (Bruininks, Hill, Lakin, & White, 1984). Thirty-three respondents identified barriers to each of the 11 desirable functions of residential service systems presented earlier in this chapter. These barriers were categorized and organized under each specific function, although they frequently were related to more than one service area. Those barriers characterized as having national or statewide significance are described below with minimal editorial revision.

Direct Services
Function 1: Range of Residential Options A primary function of a residential service system for individuals with developmental disabilities is to provide both basic maintenance (food, shelter, clothing) as necessary and a range of residential options that appropriately serve their varying needs for different levels of care and different types of programs.

Barrier 1 There has been a failure to develop a continuum of cost-effective residential services in which placement can be based on individual needs, with a range of options for individuals needing different levels of residential care.

Barrier 2 There are definitional restrictions that limit residential and related support services to individuals with mental retardation, excluding some developmentally impaired individuals who are not retarded.

Barrier 3 There is a lack of accessibility within many existing residential sites for developmentally disabled individuals with physical disabilities.

Function 2: Habilitation Activities The residential service system must provide habilitation activities that are focused on teaching developmentally disabled individuals the skills they need to increase their level of independence, health, psychological well-being, and degree of social integration for fulfilling valued social roles (e.g., work).

Barrier 1 There is a severe shortage of appropriate training activities in community environments for work placement, including actual on-the-job training opportunities.

Barrier 2 There are too few appropriately trained staff to carry out needed habilitation activities.

Function 3: Social, Leisure, and Recreational Activities A community service system should provide social, leisure, and recreational activities that offer frequent and varied opportunities in integrated settings for productive and enjoyable uses of free time by developmentally disabled individuals.

Barrier 1 There is a shortage of recreational activities in integrated community settings, particularly in generic community recreation agencies.

Barrier 2 Community recreation staff are inadequately educated about the uses of environmental modifications and specific training techniques to foster social skills of developmentally disabled adults.

Function 4: Resource Allocation A community services system must establish resource allocation, budgeting, service reimbursements, and income-maintenance policies and practices that are clear, well-publicized, and nonstigmatizing, that provide significant incentives for family and community living, and that ensure continuity of noninstitutional alternatives.

Barrier 1 Budgeting, service reimbursement, and income maintenance policies generally provide greater amounts of funding that is more easily obtained for institutionally oriented programs, creating substantial relative disincentives for developing community-based services.

Barrier 2 Eligibility criteria in federal income maintenance and health care programs often create economic disincentives for developmentally disabled individuals to work and for employees to hire them.

Function 5: Assessment, Planning, and Placement Individualized assessment, planning, and placement procedures must gather and use information that can determine the nature and quantity of services needed by developmentally disabled individuals and evaluate the effects of those services once provided.

Barrier 1 There is often a mismatch between the needs of persons and the nature of their living environments because of inappropriate assessment and/or inadequate placement options.

Barrier 2 Personnel are poorly trained in client-oriented assessment, program planning, and intervention strategies that support placement in the least restrictive alternative.

Barrier 3 Existing practices for assessment, program planning, and intervention strategies often require too much time and are too removed from the ongoing programs of clients to be cost-effective or feasible to use.

Function 6: Appropriate Services The community service systems must provide the developmentally disabled individual with providers who will deliver appropriate services in the least restrictive, most normalized appropriate placement.

Barrier 1 There are inconsistent and often inadequate quantities of appropriate case management and related support services for the community residential programs of different states and communities.

Barrier 2 Many persons in case management roles have had insufficient training about or experience with the needs of developmentally disabled individuals in community settings.

Barrier 3 Provider agencies still do not adequately accept consumer-oriented case management systems in which clients and families are provided the opportunity for meaningful involvement in placement and program decisions.

Barrier 4 There remain inadequate clinical support services for individuals with multiple disabilities in community settings.

Barrier 5 Families of developmentally disabled individuals do not have adequate or consistent services that support family integrity and defray their care burden.

Indirect Services

Function 1: Information and Evaluation Systems Community service systems must maintain information and evaluation systems that gather, aggregate, and use data on individual clients, programs, and systems to establish objectives for services and policies, assess the effectiveness of services and policies in meeting goals, and modify services and policies as indicated by evaluation results.

Barrier 1 Data that are crucial for helping determine the types of residential care settings necessary to meet the needs of clients in specific areas are often unavailable or insufficient.

Barrier 2 Data for management information systems are often gathered through procedures whose reliability, validity, and relevance to user agencies have not been assessed or established.

Barrier 3 The technology for assessing client needs, long-range planning, and monitoring is currently not available or implemented in most states.

Function 2: Personnel Management Residential service systems must establish personnel management practices that recruit, train, utilize, and retain adequate numbers of skilled professionals and paraprofessionals to provide the services needed by developmentally disabled individuals.

Barrier 1 There is a lack of accessible and effective training programs for direct care staff for community-based programs.

Barrier 2 Few states or agencies have implemented programs to ensure the availability of qualified residential care staff and to combat the high rate of turnover in smaller community facilities.

Function 3: Social Attitudes The community services system must endeavor to promote social attitudes, professional commitment, community experiences, and citizen expectations in support of public laws, regulations, and policies that increase the acceptance and integration of developmentally disabled individuals.

Barrier 1 There are relatively few systematic and ongoing programs that attempt to build positive citizen attitudes toward individuals with developmental disablties and toward community-based programs for this population.

Barrier 2 The general citizenry still does not have opportunities to know persons with disabilities in a positive, natural way.

Barrier 3 There is still a belief, held by the public and many policy-makers and professionals, that some individuals are too disabled to live in community settings.

Function 4: Share Knowledge and Experience The community services system must develop and share knowledge and experience among service providers, academic and research institutions, government and private administrative agencies, advocacy/consumer organizations, and natural and surrogate family members about available services, effective practices, new technologies, special opportunities, and useful policies in local, state, and national spheres.

Barrier 1 There are serious delays and dissemination problems in increasing the use of existing technology for information exchange and training across agencies.

Barrier 2 There is a lack of readily available technical assistance to help programs address individual client problems.

Barrier 3 There is a shortage of funds and opportunities for training to upgrade the skills of program personnel and parents.

Function 5: Human Rights and Dignity The residential service system must promote the recognition of human rights and dignity for developmentally disabled individuals, including maximizing the opportunities for consumer involvement, personal choice, and self-advocacy.

Barrier 1 There is insufficient consumer involvement in policymaking and operation of community services.

Barrier 2 Developmentally disabled individuals and key people in their lives are given insufficient training in determining their own needs and identifying effective strategies for obtaining appropriate opportunities and assistance.

RECOMMENDATIONS

This section presents recommendations for improving current practices that are based largely on the findings of a special project reported by Bruininks et al. (1984). The recommendations were offered by project respondents to overcome the major barriers to fuller social integration and effective services that were presented above. They are stated here in succinct form under four headings: *training, service, information services* (including applied research, demonstration, and dissemination), and *policy development*.

Training

1. Training within community programs is needed to provide direct service staff in community programs with the skills necessary to deal with increasingly difficult populations found in and projected for community settings (e.g., severely and profoundly handicapped, medically impaired, behaviorally disordered clients).
2. Efforts are needed to identify model programs that are effectively serving individuals with severe problem behaviors. It is recommended that experimental demonstration sites be organized through federal and state funding to provide effective training programs for direct service personnel who work in community settings.
3. Many direct service personnel report that one of the reasons for leaving their jobs is to accept positions that offer greater professional development opportunities. It is recommended that career ladder options for attracting and maintaining professional and paraprofessional employees in community residential and other service programs be developed through the creation of consortia of individual facilities and small agencies and through state agency involvement in creating professional community care providers.
4. The services system for developmentally disabled adults, in most instances, is a generic system serving a variety of at-risk

clients. If the needs of developmentally disabled clients are to be met, case management providers must identify the needs, obtain access to the resources, and evaluate the services provided to such clients. It is recommended that social work programs, paraprofessional casework training programs, and other case management training programs be designed and provided to address the often-cited deficiencies in obtaining access to, organizing, and managing services for developmentally disabled adults.

Service

1. In most residential programs, insufficient attention is given to developing employment and community independence skills. It is recommended that training and development projects offered in community residential programs be expanded to address these needs more effectively and to demonstrate successful practices through special federal and state initiatives.
2. Research and descriptive data reviewed in this chapter indicate that most residential service programs provide training, employment, and day care activities in segregated activities. Because work and daily living activities are required for community integration, it is recommended that residential programs be encouraged and aided, both technically and financially, in developing a more effective range of working and living opportunities that are integrated into community settings, including service programs for individuals who live in supervised and semi-independent residential placements.
3. Research and descriptive data clearly indicate that case management services are insufficient in quantity and quality of staffing to serve adequately the needs of developmentally disabled clients, particularly those living in community residential settings. It is recommended that model case management services be de-

veloped and evaluated to address the needs of developmentally disabled individuals and their families with support through federal, state, and local agencies.

4. This chapter, consistent with other research projects, points out that many families would be better able to maintain developmentally disabled members in their home if there were at least minimally adequate in-home services, information and referral services, crisis intervention services, respite care options, and assistance in modification of physical environments to accommodate their family members. Because of cost savings, the realization of a social ideal, and the generally positive outcomes when developmentally disabled individuals are maintained in natural and surrogate families, it is recommended that efforts be undertaken to improve in-home support services, local case management, crisis intervention and respite care options, and to provide assistance in modifying the physical environments for families through actions of state and local agencies.

5. Communities are encountering considerable difficulty in providing effective services to low-income incidence handicapped populations. Improved technical assistance and consultation to parents and service providers are needed to achieve further deinstitutionalization and provide appropriate services to this group of people. It is recommended that states support the development of special case coordinators and consultation teams through collaboration of institutions of higher education and other agencies to improve community services for low-incidence populations.

6. The expansion and improvement of services over the last decade have been clearly influenced by advocacy efforts and self-advocacy of handicapped individuals. It is recommended that colleges and universities, as well as other agencies, develop programs in collaboration with advocacy groups to train professionals,

parents, and other interested parties in the skills of promoting the self-advocacy of developmentally disabled individuals. Such programs should increase the sensitivity of service personnel to ethical implications of practice, and the need for strategies to enhance community integration and acceptance of developmentally disabled individuals.

Information Services

1. Although successful community-based residential programs for developmentally disabled individuals—especially those with severe/profound levels of mental retardation, serious behavioral problems, and various physical and medical disabilities—exist in almost every state, insufficient effort has been given to describing such programs and disseminating information about them to encourage replication of effective programs or successful components of such programs. It is recommended that support be provided to enable service agencies to identify specific program models that are successful and encourage replication of either the total program or outstanding components as a means of improving available services. This strategy is particularly needed to improve adult services.

2. Many residential service programs have developed in an independent manner and are isolated from the main flow of information and state-of-the-art practices. A critical need exists to identify such information and disseminate it effectively to various treatment programs. It is recommended that clearinghouse functions be assigned to universities in each state to identify successful practices and research findings and make this information available to individual residential treatment programs.

3. Research points out that very few programs use adequate client-based assessment. Without such assessment instruments, planning and evaluation of services

are difficult, if not impossible. It is recommended that additional attention be given to promoting the adoption of individual assessment techniques that have been carefully validated for their technical aspects, as well as their relevance to the purposes to which they are applied.

4. Environmental analysis and the use of prosthetic procedures to adapt environments to the physical learning and emotional needs of developmentally disabled individuals are essential activities improving their community integration and adjustment. It is recommended that institutions of higher education initiate research studies on the instruments and techniques of environmental analysis and the use of prosthetic procedures for adapting environments to facilitate the physical, learning, and emotional needs of developmentally disabled clients.

5. Research literature points to the benefits and feasibility of improving the evaluation of outcomes of services for developmentally disabled adults. Very few practitioners are trained in the techniques and methodology to conduct such research. It is recommended that university training programs initiate coursework at a preservice or inservice level to prepare professionals to expand evaluations on the efficacy of services for developmentally disabled children and adults.

6. There is a lack of services to help parents evaluate the potential value and actual effects of services in their family decision making and in their lifelong planning for their handicapped children. It is recommended that training be undertaken to prepare case managers and other personnel to assist in this capacity and that materials be designed to assist parents in their lifelong planning and evaluation of services for family decision making.

Policy Development

1. Profoundly retarded individuals and individuals with behavioral difficulties, multiple handicaps, and medical needs are disproportionately represented in large publicly operated institutions and in large privately operated ICF/MR facilities at relatively high public cost. It is recommended that options for moving such individuals to less restrictive community service settings be pursued through continued focus on depopulating existing public institutions and larger private facilities, with a concomitant focus on developing adequately staffed community-based programs for "difficult-to-place" individuals.

2. Many communities throughout the United States have insufficient program options to prevent or reduce institutionalization. Program options that urgently need expansion include family subsidy and support programs including respite care, foster family care options, small group homes, and semi-independent and independent living programs. It is recommended that the full range of residential services be expanded through reimbursement strategies that facilitate—or at the minimum do not create disincentives for—placement of developmentally disabled adults in the least restrictive living environment.

3. Many community residential sites are not accessible to individuals with physical handicaps. It is recommended that capital improvement funds be made available to assist with the costs of physically adapting residential service sites and community settings, including homes of families with developmentally disabled members.

4. Current funding mechanisms focus on support to the agency program, rather than to the handicapped individual. It is recommended that various experimental funding alternatives be established and evaluated that allow case managers to negotiate directly with providers for services on the basis of an individual's need, including the use of vouchers, contracts for specific services, or other means of linking the funds for service to the identified need for specific types and levels of services.

5. A variety of disincentives operate against the integration and the employment of developmentally disabled adults in community settings (e.g., as noted in Chapters 4, 5, and 6, pursuit of gainful employment may cause loss of medical benefits and income support). It is recommended that eligibility criteria for work, income support, habilitation, and other programs be studied carefully to assess how they operate as incentives or disincentives for institutionalization, productive employment, and community integration.

6. High staff turnover is a major obstacle in managing and operating community residential services. It is recommended that states devise more effective staff development systems for personnel by providing career ladder options, uniform job descriptions, and salary structures equivalent to other human service programs. Such mechanisms should allow for movement between institutions and community-based service systems without serious loss of benefits and wages, provided prospective employees possess attitudes consistent with the goals of community integration and are sufficiently trained to assume their new roles and responsibilities.

7. A variety of laws and regulations inhibit the integration of developmentally disabled adults in community settings, including regulations that govern residential housing, transportation, zoning, and location of programs for developmentally disabled individuals. It is recommended that states undertake studies of existing laws and regulations to determine their effects on integrating and encouraging movement into and/or retention in community settings.

8. Current fiscal accounting procedures make it difficult, and sometimes impossible, to transfer resources from institutional settings into community residential programs. It is recommended that federal and state governments develop more effective means of permitting the transfer of resources from institution to community services.

9. The service system for developmentally disabled adults is characterized by an unclear designation of state and federal agency responsibilities. For example, the mental retardation agencies and educational agencies of some states have similar or overlapping responsibilities with the young adult populations; in other states, no agency has explicit programmatic responsibility for nonretarded individuals with developmental disabilities. Such ambiguous designations of responsibility often produce significant gaps in the services to needful individuals. It is recommended that clear-cut lead agency status be designated for community service programs, that sufficient control be established to direct necessary resources to areas of need, and that agencies be required to achieve clear agreements to increase the continuity, coordination, and effectiveness of service programs.

10. Almost all accreditation, certification, and licensing standards are based on process or effort, rather than evidence of effectiveness. It is recommended that funds be provided to support research projects to assess the potential for using process *and* outcome criteria in accreditation and certification practices.

11. Capital funds for developing new community facilities are extremely limited. It is recommended that federal and state governments implement tax incentives to generate the private capital needed for expanding small-scale living arrangements and adult day programs.

SUMMARY

During the past two decades, residential services have evolved along four main directions: from large to small facilities, from public to private operation, from isolated to integrated locations, and from self-containment to utilization of community resources and services. Although deinstitutionalization has been remarkably successful as a national effort, it remains far from an ultimate goal of enabling all persons in need of residential services opportunities to live in ways that approximate as closely as is feasible the situations of their nondisabled peers. Future efforts in the deinstitutionalization process must involve on going development of a continuum of programs in community settings where all levels of care are available. At present, virtually all states utilize public and private institutions to serve severely/profoundly handicapped persons. Future evolution of these systems will demand that the technical expertise presently concentrated in colleges and universities and in state institutions for mentally retarded individuals be diffused through training, research, and demonstration of creative personnel practices to the community-based service sector. Increased reliance on the program models that are presently meeting the primary challenges facing the future of residential services will also be required.

The development of a community-based continuum of care for developmentally disabled individuals is ultimately based on recognition of: 1) the uniqueness of each individual handicapped person, so that a full range of options (from total support to independent living) is provided in the community to meet individual needs; 2) the developmental potential of handicapped individuals, so that provisions exist for the training of residents, and mechanisms are established for moving clients to less restrictive, more independent placements as developmental accomplishments warrant; and 3) the dignity of handicapped individuals, to ensure that they live as similarly to other community members as the nature and severity of their impairment maximally allow. To achieve such goals requires that the realities of service provision closely match the ideals set forth for achieving fuller development and integration of developmentally disabled citizens.

Observers of deinstitutionalization now realize that there is no point at which this process is destined to be halted. Although the depopulation of institutions will not be precipitous, it will be continuous, and its success will be largely determined by the availability in the community of persons with sufficient skills and commitment and the improvement of policies and regulations to support more fully the community living and integration of developmentally disabled citizens.

REFERENCES

Aanes, D., & Haagenson, L. (1978). Normalization: Attention to conceptual disaster. *Mental Retardation, 16*(1), 55–56.

Blatt, B. (1970). *Exodus from pandemonium: Human abuse and reformation of public policy*. Boston, MA: Allyn and Bacon.

Blatt, B. (1973). *Souls in extremis*. Boston, MA: Allyn and Bacon.

Braddock, D., Howes, R., & Hemp, R. (1984). *A summary of mental retardation and developmental disabilities expenditures in the United States: FY 1977–1984*. (Preliminary data; Public policy monograph series #3). Chicago: University of Illinois, Institute for the Study of Developmental Disabilities.

Bruininks, R. H., Hill, B. K., Lakin, K. C., & White, C. C. (1984). *Residential services for developmentally disabled citizens*. Minneapolis, MN: University of Minnesota, Department of Educational Psychology.

Bruininks, R. H., Hill, B. K., Lakin, K. C., & White, C. C. (1985). *Residential services for adults with developmental disabilities*. Logan: Utah State University, Developmental Center for Handicapped Persons.

Bureau of the Census. (1941). *Mental defectives and epileptics in institutions, 1939*. Washington: DC: U.S. Government Printing Office.

Conroy, J. W. (1977). Trends in deinstitutionalization of mentally retarded. *Mental Retardation, 15*(4), 44–46.

EMC Institute. (1979). *Defining the developmentally disabled population*. Philadelphia: EMC Institute.

Forssman, H., & Akesson, H. O. (1970). Mortality of the mentally deficient: A study of 12,903 institutionalized subjects. *Journal of Mental Deficiency Research, 14*, 276–294.

Goffman, E. (1961). *Asylums: Essays on the social situation of mental patients and other inmates*. Garden City, NJ: Doubleday.

Hardman, M. L., & Drew, C. J. (1977). The physically handicapped retarded individual: A review. *Mental Retardation, 15*(5), 43–47.

Hill, B. K., Bruininks, R. H., & Lakin, K. C. (1983). Physical and mental characteristics of mentally retarded people in residential facilities. *Health and Social Work, 8*(2), 85–95.

Hill, B. K., Lakin, K. C., & Bruininks, R. H. (1984a).

Trends in residential services for mentally retarded people. 1977–1982 (Brief No. 23). Minneapolis, MN: University of Minnesota, Department of Educational Psychology.

Hill, B. K., Lakin, K. C., & Bruininks, R. H. (1984b). Trends in residential services for people who are mentally retarded: 1977–1982. *Journal of the Association for Persons with Severe Handicaps, 9,* 247.

Keys, V., Boroskin, A., & Ross, R. T. (1973). The revolving door in an M.R. hospital: A study of returns from leave. *Mental Retardation, 11*(1), 55–56.

Kiesler, C. A. (1982). Mental hospitals and alternatives. *American Psychologist, 37*(4), 349–360.

Lakin, K. C. (1979). *Demographic studies of residential facilities for mentally retarded people: A historical review of methodologies and findings.* Minneapolis, MN: University of Minnesota, Department of Educational Psychology.

Lakin, K. C., Hill, B. K., & Bruininks, R. H. (1986). Basic facts and trends in residential services. In R. B. Kugel (Ed.), *Changing patterns in residential services for persons with mental retardation.* Washington, DC: President's Committee on Mental Retardation.

Lakin, K. C. Hill, B. K., Hauber, F. A., & Bruininks, R. H. (1982). Changes in age at first admission to residential care of mentally retarded people. *Mental Retardation, 20,* 216–219.

Maney, A., Pace, R., & Morrison, D. (1964). A factor analysis study of the need for institutionalization: Problems and populations for program development. *American Journal of Mental Deficiency, 69,* 372–384.

National Information Center for Handicapped Children and Youth (NICHCY). (1983). *Autism fact sheet.* Washington, DC: NICHCY.

National Institute of Mental Health. (1956). *Patients in mental hospitals, 1955.* Washington, DC: US Government Printing Office.

Nelson, R. P., & Crocker, A. C. (1978). The medical care of mentally retarded persons in public residential facilities. *New England Journal of Medicine, 299,* 1039–1044.

Nirje, B. (1976). The normalization principle. In R. B. Kugel & A. Shearer (Eds.), *Changing patterns in residential services for the mentally retarded* (rev. ed.). Washington, DC: US Government Printing Office.

Pagel, S. E., & Whitling, C. A. (1978). Readmission to a state hospital for mentally retarded persons: Reasons for community placement failure. *Mental Retardation, 16*(2), 164–166.

Pense, N. W. (1946). Trends in institutional care for the mental defective. *American Journal of Mental Deficiency, 50,* 453–457.

Pilewski, M. E., & Heal, L. W. (1980). Empirical support for deinstitutionalization. In A. R. Novak & L. W. Heal (Eds.), *Integration of developmentally disabled individuals in the community.* Baltimore, MD: Paul H. Brookes Publishing Company.

Pond, D. (1979). Epilepsy and mental retardation. In M. Craft (Ed.), *Tredgold's mental retardation* (12th ed.). London: Bailliere Tindall.

Rotegard, L. L., & Bruininks, R. H. (1983). *Mentally retarded people in state-operated residential facilities: Years ending June 30, 1981 and 1982.* Minneapolis,

MN: University of Minnesota, Department of Educational Psychology.

Rotegard, L. L., Bruininks, R. H., & Krantz, C. G. (1984). State operated residential facilities for people with mental retardation: July 1, 1978–June 30, 1982. *Mental Retardation, 22,* 69–74.

Saenger, G. (1960). *Factors influencing the institutionalization of mentally retarded individuals in New York City.* Albany, NY: New York State Interdepartmental Health Resources Board.

Scheerenberger, R. C. (1965). A current census of state institutions for the mentally retarded. *Mental Retardation, 3*(1), 4–6.

Scheerenberger, R. C. (1979). *Public residential services for the mentally retarded: 1979.* Madison, WI: National Association of Public Residential Facilities for the Mentally Retarded.

Scheerenberger, R. C. (1983). *Public residential services for the mentally retarded: 1982.* Madison, WI: National Association of Superintendents of Public Residential Facilities for the Mentally Retarded.

Schwartz, C. (1977). Normalization and idealism. *Mental Retardation, 15*(6), 38–39.

Sigford, B. B., Bruininks, R. H., Lakin, K. C., Hill, B. K., & Heal, L. W. (1982). Resident release patterns in a national sample of public residential facilities. *American Journal on Mental Deficiency, 87*(2), 130–140.

Smith, D. C., Decker, H. A., Herberg, E. N., & Rupke, L. K. (1969). Medical needs of children in institutions for the mentally retarded. *American Journal of Public Health, 59,* 1376–1384.

Spencer, D. A. (1974). Redevelopment of a hospital for the mentally handicapped. *Nursing Times, 70*(3), 1172–1173.

Sternlicht, M., & Deutsch, M. R. (1972). *Personality development and social behavior in the mentally retarded.* Lexington, MA: D. C. Heath.

Tarjan, G., Eyman, R. K., & Miller, C. F. (1969). Natural history of mental retardation in a state hospital revisited: Releases and deaths in two admissions groups, ten years apart. *American Journal of Disabled Children, 177,* 609–620.

Throne, J. M. (1975). Normalization through the normalization principle: Right ends, wrong means. *Mental Retardation, 13*(5), 23–25.

United Cerebral Palsy Association (UCP). (1968). *Annual report of 1968.* New York: Author.

Where toys are locked away. (1965). Senator R. F. Kennedy's indictment of New York State's institutions for mentally retarded children. *Christian Century,* September 29, pp. 1179–1180.

Windle, C. (1962). Prognosis of mental subnormals. *American Journal of Mental Deficiency, 66*(5). (Monograph Supplement).

Wolfensberger, W. (1980). The definition of normalization: Update, problems, disagreements, and misunderstandings. In R. J. Flynn & K. E. Nitsch (Eds.), *Normalization, social integration, and community services.* Baltimore, MD: University Park Press.

Wright, S. W., Valente, M., & Tarjan, G. (1962). Medical problems on a ward of a hospital for the mentally retarded. *American Journal of Disabled Children, 104,* 142–148.

Chapter 17

Learning and Adjustment
Future Implications

Carl F. Calkins, Hill M. Walker, Ansley Bacon-Prue,
Beth Gibson, James Intagliata, and Marty Martinson

THIS CHAPTER PRESENTS AN OVERVIEW OF THE learning and adjustment process as it applies to developmentally disabled adults. In an effort to develop a more complete view of learning and adjustment for the reader, the authors have organized this chapter into several sections: a statement of need, a description of types of adjustment, a conceptual model for learning and adjustment, a brief discussion of the assumptions underlying the learning and adjustment model, and a delineation of directions for future efforts in learning and adjustment that will affect pathways to employment for developmentally disabled adults.

STATEMENT OF NEED

"What does it mean to be an adult? What are the root issues of adult life—the essential problems and satisfactions, the sources of disappointment, grief, and fulfillment?" When Daniel J. Levinson (1978) raised these questions in his book, *The Seasons of a Man's Life*, he was advocating the need to study adult development. The subsequent popularity of such books as Gail Sheehy's *Passages* and *Pathfinders* suggests that these questions are of great importance to many adults who are trying

to understand better the meaning and quality of their lives. Although these authors were not specifically describing growth processes for the developmentally disabled adult, their work is clearly relevant to these individuals because it identifies and analyzes the challenges and needs that *all* persons face in their adult years.

The concern for the quality of life of developmentally disabled individuals is evident in a variety of current philosophical approaches to service delivery, such as normalization, the developmental model, or the least restrictive alternative. Similarly, the significant shifts that have occurred in residential placement programs through deinstitutionalization reflect a concern for the quality of care and attention to the rehabilitation needs of developmentally disabled individuals (Bruininks, Hill, Lakin, & White, 1984).

Deinstitutionalization and community program development efforts have produced significant changes in the needs and priorities for services to adult developmentally disabled individuals. As Willer and Intagliata (1984) note:

> In response to the idea that mentally retarded persons can live more normally and function more fully than we had grown accustomed to expect, the community-based service network

A detailed description of the learning and adjustment process, a more complete description of the supporting literature, and a data base for learning and adjustment can be found in Calkins, C. F., Walker, H. M., Bacon-Prue, A., Gibson, B. A., Martinson, M., and Offner, R. (1984). *The learning and adjustment process*. Kansas City, MO: University of Missouri.

has not only expanded to provide more varied residential settings but has also given considerably greater attention to the importance of providing needed educational and habilitative training programs. (p. 181)

Habilitation services include such programs as self-care and community living skill training, leisure/recreation programs, physical and mental health care, educational services, vocational services, transportation services, and case management services. It is the access to and utilization of these programs and services that enables developmentally disabled adults to take advantage of the opportunities afforded by community living. Such services allow these individuals to meet the challenges and demands of community living.

The quality of life for developmentally disabled individuals and their ability to remain in and cope effectively with less restrictive community settings are determined to a large extent by their behavioral adjustment status and levels of personal-social competence (Bjaanes, Butler, & Kelly, 1981; Butler & Bjaanes, 1983; Edgerton, 1983). The ability to have access to work settings, to use community resources, to live independently, and to develop social support networks are all highly dependent on the basic adjustment process and its outcomes. For example, it has been determined that more jobs are lost among developmentally disabled populations because of social behavior problems and deficits than because of lack of job skills (Bellamy, O'Connor, & Karan, 1979; Foss & Peterson, 1981; O'Connor, 1983). A developmentally disabled individual's ability to establish meaningful patterns of social affiliation and support networks is mediated by his or her repertoire of social behavior skills and competencies, as well as the number and type of opportunities and support for the development of enduring social contacts (Intagliata, Willer, & Wicks, 1981; Landesman-Dwyer, Berkson, & Romer, 1979; O'Connor, 1983; Romer & Heller, 1983; Singh & Winton, 1983).

Although we have made great strides in developing a community-based system of care for developmentally disabled individuals, the extent to which important needed services are available, adequate, and offered in an equitable fashion to clients and their families varies considerably within most states and across the country (Willer & Intagliata, 1984). The authors reviewed a representative sample of 11 developmental disabilities state plans for evidence of services that directly support the learning and adjustment processes of mentally retarded adults. This review clearly indicated that nonvocational social development services, which most directly contribute to the learning and adjustment process, did not rank among the most common high priorities of the state plans reviewed. Rather, child development and alternative living (residential) services were identified as high priority needs twice as often as case management and nonvocational services. If these adults are to be assisted in acquiring skills and competencies that facilitate their successful community functioning, more attention will need to be given to the nonvocational support services that facilitate the learning and adjustment process.

These findings also raise some interesting questions in relation to the Developmental Disabilities Act of 1984. This act is intended to ensure that all developmentally disabled individuals receive comprehensive, coordinated, and appropriate services that meet their individual needs and result in their achievement of the ultimate goals of *increased productivity, community integration, and independence*. Because many of the learning and adjustment needs of adult clients are not being assigned high priority in state service plans, it seems unlikely that adult clients are currently being provided all the important support services they need to attain the goals identified for them in the Developmental Disabilities Act of 1984. In order for relevant services to be developed to support such goal attainment, policymakers, service planners, and care providers will need a clear understanding of adult development.

In response to this need, the Administration on Developmental Disabilities supported a study designed to produce a national profile of services, program practices, and program models that directly support the learning and adjustment process of developmentally disabled adults. University Affiliated Facilities, which are in an excellent position to plan, develop, and implement exemplary services that support the learning and adjustment process for adult developmentally disabled individuals, were assigned primary responsibility for conducting this study. It had four major objectives:

1. To define the learning and adjustment process
2. To review the existing knowledge base in the community adjustment of adult developmentally disabled individuals
3. To develop a conceptual framework for the learning and adjustment process
4. To survey the learning and adjustment practices of developmental disabilities program models nationally

The study findings are described in the larger report (Calkins et al., 1984) referred to above.

TYPES OF ADJUSTMENT

The concept of adult development and its relation to the learning and adjustment process is complex. The services that are required to support learning and adjustment are multifaceted and cannot be categorized into a simple framework. They are, for example, considerably more varied and diverse than are residential or vocational programs and services. Learning and adjustment encompasses the complex processes in which developmentally disabled adults participate in order to enhance the quality of their lives. Thus, we may define an enhanced quality of life as the end-product of the learning and adjustment process.

The learning and adjustment of the developmentally disabled client population has not been well defined in the professional literature, perhaps because there is no widespread consensus on what constitutes adjustment or effective performance (Edgerton & Bercovici, 1976). For some professionals, adjustment is primarily social-behavioral in nature, whereas others would add a component that includes skills in such domains as self-help, community living, and vocational competence. In general, however, a review of the relevant literature

suggests that three interrelated but distinct areas of adjustment can be identified: behavioral, personal, and social. Each is briefly discussed and illustrated below.

Behavioral adjustment refers to the extent to which the individual conforms to the social norms and behavioral expectations governing acceptable forms of conduct that are consensually validated by our society. Successful behavior adjustment is reflected in behavior that includes following established rules, initiating appropriately, complying with requests or commands, sharing, cooperating, making assistance needs known in an appropriate manner, and so forth. Poor behavioral adjustment is reflected by such behaviors as stealing, having tantrums, engaging in stereotypical forms of behavior, aggression, antisocial or hostile forms of behavior, defiance, or public masturbation. One can be perceived as being outside the normal or expected range of behavioral adjustment in two ways: 1) by enaging in expected forms of appropriate behavior at unacceptably low rates or frequencies and/or by enaging in maladaptive forms of behavior (rule violations, noncompliance) at unacceptably high rates, or 2) by engaging in social norm violations that have a high degree of salience for care providers or the general public (e.g., intense aggression or antisocial behavior, public masturbation, consuming feces, and so forth).

Personal adjustment refers to the individual's ability and opportunity to manage his or her life effectively and with a maximum degree of independence. Two general classes or sets of skills underlie personal adjustment: daily living skills (Cuvo & Davis, 1982) and community living skills (Close, Irvin, Taylor, & Agosta, 1982). Daily living skills can be grouped into domestic (cooking, cleaning), self-help/self-care (grooming), leisure (time management), and work-related (punctuality, productivity, following task sequences) categories. Illustrative community living skill areas, including fiscal accountability, community mobility, social interaction, communication, and skills for interacting with community services, have been identified by Close et al. (1982).

Social adjustment refers to the ability to initiate and maintain positive social relationships, friendships, and enduring patterns of affiliation with social agents in the environment (e.g., peers, co-workers, parents, guardians, supervisors). Developmentally disabled adults, as do their nonhandicapped peers, manifest their socal adjustment in the context of two types of relationships that are important in their daily lives: relationships with peers and co-workers and relationships with guardians, supervisors, parents, and teachers (Walker, McConnell, & Clarke, 1985).

Because the focus of each type of relationship is somewhat different, the skills and competencies required to maintain each effectively are different. For example, in peer relationships, social skills, such as *sharing*, initiating communication, continuing interactions over time, and *complimenting*, assume great importance and directly affect the quality of the relationship and the degree of adjustment. In contrast, skills that are important in relationships with adults—parents, teachers, supervisors, care providers, or guardians—often serve the convenience needs of the dominant individual and include following directions, listening, attending, cooperating, following specified rules of conduct, and being socially responsive. Both types of relationships are very important to the mental health, general well-being, and life satisfaction of developmentally disabled individuals (Berkson & Romer, 1980; Landesman-Dwyer, 1981; O'Connor, 1983; Romer & Heller, 1983; Willer & Intagliata, 1981).

All these types of adjustment—behavioral, personal, and social—seem to be very important to the overall quality of life of developmentally disabled individuals in community settings. Each form of adjustment serves a slightly different purpose. For example, behavioral adjustment seems to be the primary determinant of whether a developmentally disabled client is able to remain in the community and to have continued access to its normalizing benefits and greater freedoms. Personal adjustment determines to a very significant degree the quality of life and level of independence in the community. Social adjustment provides for the development of social support networks and patterns of affiliation that are increasingly being perceived as crucially important to mental health, life satisfaction, coping skills, the ability to handle stress, and a host of other indices of adaptive functioning (O'Connor, 1983; Romer & Heller, 1983; Willer & Intagliata, 1984).

CONCEPTUAL MODEL

Client competence within social, behavioral, and personal adjustment domains has been recognized as a major component in the successful adjustment of developmentally disabled individuals to community settings (Gollay, Freedman, Wyngaarden, & Kurtz, 1978; Landesman-Dwyer, 1981; Romer & Heller, 1983). Traditionally, the *failure* of developmentally disabled individuals to adjust successfully to community settings has been attributed to person-specific, rather than setting-specific, variables. Person-specific variables are usually examined in order to identify the sources or causes of such failure. This represents a skill-based approach to the problem(s) of adjustment failure among developmentally disabled populations and does not adequately take into account the powerful role that setting variables can play in accounting for such failure (e.g., performance pressures and demands, behavioral requirements, tolerance levels of key social agents—supervisors, teachers, care providers—environmental arrangements, critically important skills, response opportunities, degree of supportiveness, setting complexity, and so forth).

The conceptual model of the learning and adjustment process presented here adopts the social ecological approach to community adjustment as described by Romer and Heller (1983). Although individual attributes, such as client motivation and skill level(s) in adjustment-related domains, are important factors in the adjustment process, the skill/ competency-based approach as described above neither has sufficient breadth nor inclusiveness to explain adequately the common adjustment problems of developmentally disabled adults in community settings. The social ecological approach, with its dual emphasis on: (1) measuring and programming of person-specific *and* setting-specific factors and (2) facilitating the match or fit between persons and environments, seems to be far more appropriate. Conceptually, this approach makes it possible to take into account individual characteristics, setting or environmental characteristics, and the complex interactions that occur between these two sets of variables in the generic adjustment process.

The social ecological approach argues that successful adjustment to the enviroment depends less on individual characteristics per se and more on the match between the person and environmental attributes (Romer & Heller, 1983). A number of recent investigations suggest that setting variables are better predictors of developmentally disabled individuals' adjustment and behavioral status than are individual characteristics (see Intagliata & Willer, 1982; Landesman-Dwyer, 1981). Although the concept of person-environment fit has been in evidence for some time (see Jahoda, 1961), such investigators as Sundberg, Snowden, and Reynolds (1978) and Berkson and Romer (1980) have advocated strongly for a new commitment to this concept given the powerful influence of environmental setting on developmentally disabled persons' behavior and their ability to adjust to community settings (Kerans, Begab, & Edgerton, 1983).

In pragmatic terms, the emphasis of the social ecological approach on facilitating an optimal person-environment requires that the following tasks in the adjustment process be performed systematically:

1. Identifying critically important skills and behavioral requirements associated with different settings and performance domains in which the developmentally disabled individual is expected to function
2. Assessing the developmentally disabled client's ability to fulfill these skills/requirements
3. Teaching and remediating such deficits

4. Providing a carefully designed transition program to support the integration process and the movement from one placement setting to another
5. Altering the target environment, to the maximum extent possible, to support and be responsive to the developmentally disabled client's needs and skills/behavioral status
6. Providing continuing support, monitoring, and technical assistance both to the developmentally disabled client and social agents in the receiving environment(s)
7. Focusing on teaching functional independence in socially valid skill domains to the developmentally disabled client over the long run

A systematic and comprehensive approach that would include all these tasks would, in the authors' view, incorporate the minimum elements necessary to ensure satisfactory adjustment levels of developmentally disabled individuals in community settings.

Figure 1 provides a graphic illustration of this conceptual model for the learning and adjustment process. The model is sequential in nature and consists of three general classes of variables: person-setting, intervention, and outcome variables. Person-setting variables refer to client needs and setting-specific barriers that influence adjustment status. Intervention variables are defined as client- and environmental-focused intervention procedures that can be applied to remediate client deficits and/or provide for more supportive environments. Outcome variables contained in the model refer to the results or products of client and environment-based intervention procedures applied within the context of the social ecological approach. These outcomes include: 1) an improved person-environment fit or match, 2) enhanced behavioral, social, and/or personal adjustment, and 3) improved quality of life.

The model assumes that adjustment failure can result from client-specific characteristics, such as skill deficits and motivational problems, setting-specific characteristics, such as

Person/setting variables accounting for adjustment failure

Person-specific needs

1. Skill deficits
2. Motivational problems
3. Behavioral excesses/norm violations
4. Absence of social process competencies

Setting-specific barriers

1. Inadequate support services
2. Barriers to service delivery
3. Low performance expectations
4. Unreasonable behavioral demands and low tolerance levels of specific settings (residential, vocational) and care providers
5. Societal attitudes toward devalued populations
6. Limited choice options available to DD persons

Intervention variables

Person-specific intervention(s)

1. Skills development procedures
2. Instruction and behavior management of crucial behavioral competencies
3. Training in behavioral self-control and self-management strategies
4. Instruction in problem solving approaches and strategies

Setting-specific intervention(s)

1. Implementation of ecological support/intervention procedures
2. Design of supportive environments
3. Provision of response opportunities
4. Provision of advocates/benefactors
5. Systematic education of the general public

Intervention outcomes

Improved person-environment fit or match

Enhanced, behavioral, social, and personal adjustment

Improved quality of life

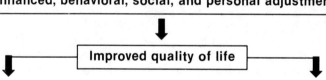

1. Enhanced decision-making ability
2. Positive self-ratings of life satisfaction
3. Higher levels of competence
4. Breadth and variety in daily activities
5. Greater independence
6. Absence of stress

7. Adaptability and autonomy in work-related responding
8. Behavioral self-control
9. Access to community resources, settings, and services
10. Improved ability to manage one's daily life
11. Greater community understanding and acceptance
12. Broader patterns of affiliation and social support networks

Figure 1. A conceptual model governing the learning and adjustment process.

inadequate or inaccessible support services, or some combination of the two. In the great majority of cases, it is likely that some interaction of these two sets of factors accounts for the adjustment failure.

Similarly, it is assumed that client-focused intervention procedures would be used to address directly and teach/remediate client-specific problems that impair the adjustment process, whereas environmental intervention procedures would be applied to create maximally supportive environments and to remediate barriers to the delivery of exemplary client services. It is expected that intervention with both clients and environments would be necessary to address adequately the adjustment impairments of most developmentally disabled adults in community settings.

Systematic and detailed attention to both clients and environments makes it possible to assess and provide for an improved person-environment fit or match for the majority of developmentally disabled clients. An improved fit or match may lead to enhanced adjustment levels in behavioral, social, and personal domains as prior research has demonstrated (Moos & Insel, 1974). These improved adjustment levels are likely to be reflected over time in an improved quality of life.

As yet, controlled and scientific studies have not conclusively demonstrated that the outcomes listed in Figure 1 under *improved quality of life* are an inevitable result of achieving an improved or maximized person-environment fit. However, empirical evidence reviewed in Section II of *The Learning and Adjustment Process* (Calkins, Walker, Bacon-Prue, Gibson, Martinson, & Offner, 1984) strongly suggests that the technological capacity to achieve these goals exists and has been demonstrated and replicated in a number of settings. It seems equally certain that model programs of the type described in Figure 1 have not been systematically developed across relevant adjustment domains or widely implemented within existing service systems. Reviews of existing service systems for developmentally disabled clients by Flexer (1983) and McCord (1982) suggest that our technological innovations in serving the developmentally disabled population have far outstripped our capacity to deliver those services effectively.

The major thrust of the conceptual model presented in Figure 1 is the critical importance of a balanced approach to client-specific and setting-specific variables in accommodating the adjustment needs and problems of developmentally disabled clients in community settings. A social ecological approach that maintains a dual emphasis on the interactive nature of client and setting variables in both accounting for and facilitating adjustment holds great promise for developing an effective solution to the widespread community adjustment problems observed among developmentally disabled clients in recent years.

ASSUMPTIONS UNDERLYING THE LEARNING AND ADJUSTMENT PROCESS

The conceptual model described above is based on nine assumptions, which reflect the collective biases and values of the authors. They also help define the nature of learning and adjustment services that should be applied to the developmentally disabled population and specify some of the conditions under which such services should be delivered.

Assumption One: Learning and adjustment is a dynamic process that can lead to desirable life outcomes for developmentally disabled clients as defined by an improved quality of life and enhanced life chances.

Assumption Two: The learning and adjustment process is client-referenced and requires that the service delivery process be truly adapted to the unique needs of developmentally disabled individuals, rather than generated primarily by the organizational and professional needs of the developmental disabilities service system.

Assumption Three: The learning and adjustment process should systematically prepare developmentally disabled adults to function effectively in less restrictive settings and to use generic, rather than specialized, services whenever possible.

Assumption Four: The developmental disabilities service system should assume responsibility for teaching individuals to be more independent in their personal decision making. This will enhance the growth of developmentally disabled individuals in personal, social, and behavioral domains and enable them to lead more normal life-styles.

Assumption Five: The learning and adjustment process should be actively used to develop social support networks for developmentally disabled adults and to provide for friendship-making opportunities in vocational, residential, and other community settings.

Assumption Six: The learning and adjustment process is life-span inclusive and represents a process that occurs over the entire life-span of a developmentally disabled individual.

Assumption Seven: Services and activities conducted in support of the learning and adjustment process should be interdisciplinary in nature and carefully coordinated within and across disciplines.

Assumption Eight: To the maximum extent possible, the learning and adjustment process should be used to develop competence and functional independence within vocational, residential, and other community settings.

Assumption Nine: The learning and adjustment process is holistic in nature and takes place within larger societal contexts. Therefore, the public and community need to be educated about the general characteristics of clients with developmental disabilities and the basic philosophies of community integration that are consistent with the civil rights of persons with developmental disabilities. The goal of these activities should be to better prepare society to assimilate persons with developmental disabilities.

In contrast to the above assumptions, the great majority of habilitation efforts designed for developmentally disabled populations continue to focus on the development of skills of the individual, rather than on the design of new environments or the restructuring of existing ones to support the special needs of developmentally disabled clients. Well-developed instructional and habilitative techniques, such as task analysis, use of various prompting procedures, peer tutoring, and monitoring, represent the skill-based or competency approach to remediating the adjustment problems of developmentally disabled clients. Although these techniques are powerful and of proven cost-effectiveness, they are often not applied in an ecologically valid manner within natural settings, (i.e., skills are not taught in a manner that matches the specific behavioral/performance requirements that exist in different settings). Further, many of the adjustment problems of developmentally disabled clients are due less to specific skill deficits than to the lack of opportunity to participate in less restrictive settings and to have access to community services because of either naturally occurring or service-system-generated barriers.

In this conceptual model, the application of skill-based training procedures is clearly inappropriate. Instead, ecological intervention strategies are called for that would create the necessary response opportunities and environmental support that ameliorate the barriers preventing access and client participation. This sort of ecological analysis and intervention holds great promise for improving the generalized adjustment status of developmentally disabled adults in community settings.

FUTURE DIRECTIONS

The professional literature and empirical knowledge base relating to the learning and adjustment of the developmentally disabled population suggest a number of areas of need to which future research, services, and model development activities ought to be directed.

1. *There must be continued theoretical and empirical work focused on describing and delineating the learning and adjustment process.* As already noted, the learning

and adjustment process among adult developmentally disabled populations is extremely complex and not well understood. Additional ecologically focused and direct observation studies of the type conducted by Landesman-Dwyer, Stein, and Sackett (1978) and Berkson and Romer (1980) are urgently needed to develop a more complete picture of the processes and constraints impinging on the adjustment of developmentally disabled adults in community settings.

2. *There must be continued attention to conceptualizing and systematically describing environments.* The precise and reliable assessment of environmental variables that relate to adjustment status is a central feature of the conceptual model of the learning and adjustment process presented above. Some progress has been made in this area during recent years (see Intagliata, 1983; and Kerans et al., 1983). However, there needs to be a great deal of additional research and development before it will be possible to construct meaningful profiles of social environments and placement settings on such dimensions as: 1) the number of skill development response opportunities provided daily, 2) the nature and type of available friendship-making and affiliation opportunities, 3) the degree to which existing social contingencies support adaptive versus maladaptive client behavior, 4) the behavioral demands, expectations, and tolerance levels of care providers and supervisors, and 5) the services and resources available in the setting to respond to or match client needs. Such comprehensive assessments play an important role in the development of habilitation settings for developmentally disabled clients.

3. *Interventions that focus on constructively adapting and modifying environments must be developed and refined.* At present, a true technology of ecologically valid, environmental intervention procedures is not available for enhancing the adjustment status of developmentally disabled adults in natural settings. In part, this may be due to the following factors: 1) a traditional focus on remediation of person-specific skill deficits in responding to the adjustment problems of developmentally disabled clients, 2) the absence of environmental assessment measures and procedures that make it possible to diagnose the habilitative capacity or level of natural environments, and 3) a lack of awareness of the extent to which developmentally disabled client adjustment status is mediated by setting-specific variables (see Kerans et al., 1983). A well-developed technology of this type would generate a broad array of ecological intervention options and, in combination with the skill-based client/competency approach, would provide a powerful foundation for facilitating the adjustment of developmentally disabled individuals in community settings.

4. *The critically important behavioral, personal, and social skills that underlie adjustment in vocational, residential, and other community settings must be identified.* Effective adjustment in vocational, residential, and other community settings depends in large part on individuals attaining important benchmarks in behavioral, personal, and social skill domains. To date, however, relatively little has been done to identify systematically such benchmarks or develop training programs designed to assist individuals to meet them. Foss and Peterson (1981) are a notable exception, having systematically identified social skills that are essential to job tenure. It is essential to identify skill clusters that are empirically related to success not only in vocational programs but also in residential and other community settings as well. Although there is likely to be overlap in such clusters or groupings across settings, the limited data on this topic suggest that setting-specific skills exist and are critically important to adjustment in such settings (McConnell, 1982; Strain, 1983).

5. *The most effective technologies, standardized training curricula, and program models must be more widely disseminated and implemented.* In the past decade, some very powerful standardized training programs have been developed, validated, and replicated that could have a dramatic impact on developmentally disabled client competence in vocational, residential, and other community settings, as well as on adjustment in personal, social, and behavioral domains (see Paine, Bellamy, & Wilcox, 1984). These programs are designed for use in community settings, are highly cost-effective, and represent the best that our current technology has to offer in the habilitation process. If implemented with reasonable degrees of fidelity, they will produce treatment gains for developmentally disabled populations with high levels of social validity.

6. *A wide variety of systematic transition programs to support the movement of developmentally disabled individuals from setting to setting must be designed and implemented.* Social policy and federal mandates relating to transition services for the developmentally disabled populations are currently focused on the movement from school to the world of work (OSERS Policy Statement on Transition, 1984). However, systematic transition services and programs should have a broad-based design in order to support the learning and adjustment process during the various transitions any adult may encounter throughout the life-span (job changes, residential environment changes, retirement, etc.). These programs and services should be designed with attention to relevant variables that support the learning and adjustment process.

SUMMARY

This chapter described the need for services that support the learning and adjustment process. A conceptual model for the learning and adjustment process was presented and the assumptions of this model discussed. Implications for habilitation programming and future directions for research and program development were also presented.

The importance of learning and adjustment in enabling developmentally disabled adults to reach employment and community integration goals and to function effectively in the world at large is acknowledged widely in the literature. Services and programs that support the learning and adjustment process need to be developed. University Affiliated Programs could serve a major facilitative role by utilizing their considerable expertise and resources to support state planning and program development in this area. With primary responsibility for leadership training, manpower development, the demonstration of exemplary services, information dissemination, and research, University Affiliated Facilities can help plan and develop those services that will support the learning and adjustment process for developmentally disabled adults.

REFERENCES

Bellamy, G. T., O'Connor, G., & Karan, O. (1979). *Vocational rehabilitation of severely handicapped persons.* Baltimore, MD: University Park Press.

Berkson, G., & Romer, D. (1980). Social ecology of supervised communal facilities for mentally disabled adults. I. Introduction. *American Journal of Mental Deficiency, 85,* 219–228.

Bjaancs, A., Butler, E., & Kelly, B. (1981). Placement type and client functional levels as factors in provision of services aimed at increasing adjustment. In R. H. Bruininks (Ed.), *Deinstitutionalization and community adjustment of mentally retarded people* (pp. 337–350).

Washington, DC: American Association on Mental Deficiency.

Bruininks, R. H., Hill, B. K., Lakin, K. C., & White, C. (1984). *Residential services for developmentally disabled citizens.* Minneapolis, MN: Residential Services Working Group.

Butler, E., & Bjaanes, A. (1983). Deinstitutionalization, environmental normalization, and client normalization. In K. Kernan, M. Begab, & R. Edgerton (Eds.), *Environments and behavior* (pp. 73–87). Baltimore, MD: University Park Press.

Calkins, C. F., Walker, H. M., Bacon-Prue, A., Gibson,

B. A., Martinson, M., & Offner, R. (1984). *The learning and adjustment process*. Kansas City, MO: University of Missouri.

Close, D., Irvin, L., Taylor, V., & Agosta, J. (1982). Community living skills instruction for mildly retarded persons. In P. Strain (Ed.), *Social development of exceptional children* (pp. 127–128). Rockville, MD: Aspen Publications.

Cuvo, A., & Davids, P. (1982). Home living for developmentally disabled persons: Instructional design and evaluation. In P. Strain (Ed.), *Social development of exceptional children*. Rockville, MD: Aspen Publications.

Edgerton, R. (1983). Failure in community adaptation: The relativity of assessment. In K. Kerans, M. Begab, & R. Edgerton (eds.), *Environments and behavior*. Baltimore, MD: University Park Press.

Edgerton, R. & Bercovici, S. (1976). The cloak of competence: Years later. *American Journal of Mental Deficiency, 80*, 485–497.

Flexer, R. (1983). Habilitation services for developmentally disabled persons. *Journal of Applied Rehabilitation Counseling, 14*(3), 6–12.

Foss, G., & Peterson, S. (1981). Social-interpersonal skills relevant to job tenure for mentally retarded adults. *Mental Retardation, 19*(3), 103–106.

Gollay, E., Freedman, R., Wyngaarden, M., & Kurtz, N. (1978). *Coming back: The community experiences of deinstitutionalized mentally retarded people*. Cambridge, MA: ABT Books.

Intagliata, J. (1983, May). *Enhancing the fit between mentally retarded persons and their environments*. Paper presented at the meeting of the American Association on Mental Deficiency, Dallas, TX.

Intagliata, J., & Willer, B. (1982). Reinstitutionalization among mentally retarded persons successfully placed into family care and group homes. *American Journal of Mental Deficiency, 87*(1), 34–39.

Intagliata, J., Willer, B., & Wicks, N. (1981). Factors related to the quality of adjustment in family care homes. In R. Bruininks, C. E. Meyers, B. Sigford, & K. C. Lakin (Eds.), *Deinstitutionalization and community adjustment of mentally retarded people* (pp.217–230). Washington, DC: American Journal of Mental Deficiency.

Jahoda, M. (1961). A social psychological approach to the study of culture. *Human Relations, 14*, 23–30.

Kernan, K., Begab, M., & Edgerton, R. (1983). *Environments and behavior*. Baltimore, MD: University Park Press.

Landesman-Dwyer, S. (1981). Living in the community. *American Journal of Mental Deficiency, 86*(3), 223–234.

Landesman-Dwyer, S., Berkson, G., & Romer, D. (1979). Affiliation and friendship of mentally retarded residents in group homes. *American Journal of Mental Deficiency, 83*, 571–580.

Landesman-Dwyer, S., Stein, J., & Sackett, G. (1978). A behavioral and ecological study of group homes. In G. P. Sackett (Ed.), *Observing behavior (Vol. 1). Theory and applications in mental retardation*. Baltimore, MD: University Park Press.

Levinson, D. J. (1978). *The seasons of a man's life*. New York: Ballantine Books.

McConnell, S. (1982). An observational study of the social behavior of handicapped and nonhandicpped elementary pupils. Eugene, OR: University of Oregon (unpublished dissertation).

McCord, W. (1982). From theory to reality: Obstacles to the implementation of the normalization principle in human services. *Mental Retardation, 20*(6), 247–253.

Moos, R., & Insel, P. (1974). *Issues in social ecology*. Palo Alto, CA: National Press Books.

O'Connor, G. (1983). Social support of mentally retarded persons. AAMD Presidential address. *Mental Retardation, 21*(5), 187–196.

OSERS Transition Policy Statement. (1984). Washington, DC: Office of Special Education and Rehabilitative Services, U.S. Department of Education.

Paine, S., Bellamy, G. T., & Wilcox, B. (1984). *Human services that work*. Baltimore, MD: Paul H. Brookes Publishing Co.

Romer, D., & Heller, T. (1983). Social adaptation of mentally retarded adults in community settings: A social-ecological approach. *Applied Research in Mental Retardation, 4*(4), 303–314.

Sheehy, G. (1976). *Passages: Predictable crises of adult life*. New York: Bantam Books.

Sheehy, G. (1981). *Pathfinders*. New York: Bantam Books.

Singh, N., & Winton, A. (1983). Social skills training with institutionalized severely and profoundly mentally retarded persons. *Applied Research in Mental Retardation, 4*, 383–398.

Strain, P. (1983). Identification of social skill curriculum targets for severely handicapped children in mainstream preschools. *Applied Research in Mental Retardation, 4*(4), 369–382.

Sundberg, N., Snowden, L., & Reynolds, W. (1978). Toward assessment of personal competence and incompetence in life situations. *Annual Review of Psychology, 29*, 179–221.

Walker, H. M., McConnell, S., & Clarke, J. Y. (1985). Social skills training in school settings: A model for the social integration of handicapped children into less restrictive settings. In R. McMahon & R. Peters (Eds.), *Childhood disorders: Behavioral-developmental approaches* (pp. 140–168). New York: Brunner/Mazel.

Willer, B., & Intagliata, J. (1981). Socio-environmental factors as predictors of adjustment of deinstitutionalized mentally retarded adults. *American Journal of Mental Deficiency, 86*(3), 252–259.

Willer, B., & Intagliata, J. (1984) *Promises and realities for mentally retarded citizens*. Austin, TX: Pro-Ed Publishers.

∞ Chapter 18 ∞

Medical Care of Individuals with Developmental Disabilities
Future Implications

Bruce A. Buehler, Frank J. Menolascino, and Jack A. Stark

MEDICAL CARE, ALONG WITH RESIDENTIAL services (Chapter 16) and learning/personal adjustment aspects (Chapter 17), is an essential component in developing a successful pathway to employment for the developmentally disabled adult (Schalock, 1983). Due to the lack of a comprehensive health care delivery system, medical care is critically important for developmentally disabled individuals, particularly in rural settings (Stark, McGee, & Menolascino, 1984). The importance of health services can perhaps best be illustrated in the case of an individual with epilepsy. Community service personnel can develop excellent vocational, residential, and counseling services only to see their efforts diminished when uncontrolled seizures suddenly appear without adequate and immediate medical support.

By definition, developmental disability includes either cognitive, physical, or emotional—all of which have health care involvement—limitations and quite frequently a combination of all three. Although the health status of a developmentally disabled adult can affect each of the seven major life activities, it probably has a greater impact on self-care, mobility, and capacity for independent living. The incidence data on the number of developmentally disabled individuals vary based on the age grouping, location (whether institutionalized individuals are included), categorical or functional definition, and research criteria (Boggs & Henry, 1979; Bruininks, 1983; Gollay, 1981). For purposes of this chapter, in devising a health care delivery system, the authors use the incidence figure of 1.6% of the total population.

Throughout this book, the focus has been on the removal of barriers to employment for the developmentally disabled adult. This chapter on medical care was included here because there is perhaps no other component that can remove the developmentally disabled adult more quickly from the employment pathway than major health-related deficits. The objective of this chapter then is to present the health care needs of the developmentally disabled adult, a model delivery system, and recommendations for training medical personnel in order to better meet the complex needs of this population.

HEALTH CARE OF ADULTS WITH DEVELOPMENTAL DISABILITIES: HISTORICAL PERSPECTIVES

The historical development of health care services for the developmentally disabled adult has shaped the current delivery system and provides a background against which to understand and plan future directions.

The ancient world—300–500 B.C.—was dominated by superstition. Demon worship and a harsh physical environment played important roles in health care. Most primitive societies permitted the killing of sickly or defective infants, and the weak and infirm survivors of these rituals were later eliminated by the natural rigors of the environment (Hewett & Forness, 1977). The Greek and Roman Period that followed—500–400 B.C.—introduced scientific understanding, medical treatment, and human respect for the sick and disabled. In particular, Hippocrates and Aristotle introduced the concept of natural causes of disease, rather than the superstitious causes espoused by religious practices (Coleman, 1972).

Unfortunately, the basic approaches to health care have been cyclical in nature. The Middle Ages—400–1500 A.D.—and the 16th and 17th centuries were characterized by deep religious beliefs that resulted in cruel persecutions of those who looked, acted, or thought differently. Institutions and hospitals were established as shelters for the socially unfit, sick, and poor (Sheps, 1971). Some of the stigmata of the "charitable institution" are still evident in attitudes toward public nonprofit hospitals today.

The 18th, 19th, and early 20th centuries were shaped by the Industrial Revolution, which in turn provided a supportive atmosphere for technological advancements. Natural causes of disease and disability were systematically studied. Knowledge gains from the large numbers of military examinations and

treatment of veterans during World Wars I and II resulted in significant improvements in health care delivery and reinforced the humanity of the Greco-Roman Period (Scheerenberger, 1983).

The rapid technical advancements of the 20th century have been accompanied by changes in the social structure of health care delivery. Urban areas grew as a result of the rapid industralization required to meet the armament needs of World War II. By 1945, with the influx of returning veterans, some with chronic and/or permanent disabilities, health care needs began to change. Many underserved rural and urban centers in the country experienced a shortage of medical facilities and services. In 1946 the Hill-Burton Act was passed in an attempt to remedy these shortcomings, as federal funds were made available to subsidize construction of hospitals in underserved areas, with primary attention to rural communities. This effort was not entirely successful because a large number of hospitals were not adequately staffed with physicians and frequently were capable of providing only limited services. Despite these problems, this trend of building inpatient facilities has been difficult to redirect, and much of the thinking on improving medical care in the 1960s was tied to the idea of constructing new facilities.

The financing of medical care changed in the 1960s with the advent of the federal Medicare and Medicaid programs. Individuals who became disabled and persons 65 years of age and older were often unprepared to assume the financial burdens placed on them by their health care needs, particularly after they lost employee benefits as a result of termination or retirement from the labor force. In response to these concerns, Medicare and Medicaid programs were established by Congress in 1965.

During these years of increasing government support for health care needs, there was a major increase in the number and kinds of private insurance policies. By the mid-1980s, approximately 89% of the civilian, noninstitutionalized population was covered by some form of health insurance plan, either through public or private programs. Although the extent of this protection speaks positively for the availability of health care services for the American people, the stipulations of most of these insurance policies have created reimbursement incentives for hospitalization, thus contributing to inflated cost factors.

CURRENT MEDICAL NEEDS

As developmentally disabled children grow into adulthood, they present a range of medical needs to health care professionals that are often difficult to assess and treat for a number of reasons: the person's inability to express him- or herself, the severity of the person's cognitive deficits, and the associated behavioral problems, and the professional's lack of familiarity with treatment techniques for developmentally disabled persons. There is no systematic national data-based system available to indicate the exact nature or number of medical needs in developmentally disabled adults. Chapter 16 contains perhaps the best data available on the health care needs, which were obtained by sampling both institutional and community-based programs.

To increase the available data, the authors analyzed a limited sample of developmentally disabled adults seen in a Midwestern medical and psychiatric center over a 4-year period. The sample consisted of 610 adults who had been referred by family members, physicians, service agencies, or themselves. The levels of mental retardation of this sample were as follows: mild–25.3%; moderate–55.7%; and severe/profound–19.0%. It is likely that many mildly retarded persons seek out their own medical care. It is further likely that the more severely retarded adults were referred to the special services of this medical center due both to the severity of their mental retardation and the allied diagnostic complexity that their clinical status imparts.

The specific major medical needs noted in this sample of 610 adults were as follows:

Seizure control, 52%
  Grand mal, 36%
  Psychomotor, 8%
  Petit mal, 8%
Psychiatric disorders, 35%
  Organic affective disorders, 12%
  Severe adjustment disorders, 12%
  Schizophrenia, 11%
Auditory disorders, 15%
  Chronic otitis media and secondary deafness, 11%
  Congenital deafness, 4%
Visual disorders, 13%
  Esotrophia, 4%
  Severe acuity problems, 9%
Other medical disorders, 22%
  Persistent acne and/or severe dermatitis, 5%
  Hypothyroidism, 3%
  Diabetes mellitus, 4%
  Major dental disorders/prostheses, 4%
  Uncorrected congenital defects, especially orthopedic defects, 4%
  Severe recurring upper respiratory infections, 2%[1]

Clearly, the developmentally disabled adult displays the entire range of medical needs as shown in the non-developmentally disabled population. Seizures and their control are the highest frequency medical challenge among this population, according to this limited sample. A further major medical need, and a frequent underlying reason for medical referral noted in this sample, is psychiatric disorders. It should be noted that recent studies report mentally retarded persons to be twice as vulnerable to mental illness as the general population and thus require appropriate psychiatric diagnosis and specific treatment intervention (Menolascino & Stark, 1984; Szymanski & Tanguay, 1980).

Despite the limited nature of the sample and its potential biases, the experience of major medical centers confirms that this sample reflects a general and consistent pattern of health care throughout the United States and is prob-

---

[1]This compares with the SIE data. Of the total developmentally disabled population, 35% are mentally retarded, 10% are seriously disturbed, 77% are sensory impaired, and the remaining 38% are physically impaired (see Chapter 3).

ably representative of community-based adults with developmental disabilities. These data do not address institutionalized individuals; however, Chapter 16 contains perhaps the best data available on this subject derived from its authors' impressive data-based system on residential care. Their data and that of other authors (Keys, Boroskin, & Ross, 1973; Pagel & Whitling, 1978) indicate that health care problems, although not usually the reason for initial institutionalization, were the major reason given for admitting approximately one-third of those who were reinstitutionalized. However, as Lakin, Hill, Hauber, and Bruininks (1982) point out, the chronic health impairments among institutional and community residents are essentially the same. It has also been the authors' experience that the argument of health care needs tends to be overused as a reason for institutionalization.

FACTORS INFLUENCING
THE DELIVERY OF MEDICAL SERVICES

The American health care delivery system has and will continue to undergo massive changes in the 1980s and 1990s. This process will have a dramatic impact on developmentally disabled individuals, particularly the medically fragile. Factors that influence population changes (fertility, morbidity, morality, migration, and inflation—see also Chapter 23) have a direct causal relationship with health habits, beliefs, attitudes, and practices of patients and subsequently influence health care delivery systems (Black, 1974).

Demographic Data

The following summary of 20th-century demographic trends within the United States points to several population changes that will be a major influence on the general health status of the nation.

1. In 1900 life expectancy at birth was 47.3 years. By the mid-1980s life expectancy increased to 75 years. Most of this increase was realized between 1900 and 1950 when medical advances were made in immunization against infections and parasitic diseases.
2. The rate of population growth slowed substantially between the 1950s and mid-1980s, with a decrease in annual births from 4½ to 3 million.
3. If the population continues to grow at the current rate, it will double in size by the year 2060.
4. The death rate declined during the first half of the century, rose slightly in the 1950s and 1960s, and resumed a downward trend in the 1970s and 1980s. However, as the number of elderly persons increases over the next 25 years, the death rate is expected to rise again.
5. By the year 2000 the number of people over the age of 65 is projected to increase from 10.7% to 12.2% of the total population. A logical deduction from this trend is that medical staff and facilities will be subject to increased demands as the elderly generally are in greater need of health care services.
6. The health care challenge of today is different from that of 20 or even 10 years ago. Cancer, heart disease, stroke, accidents, and suicide have replaced communicable diseases as the leading killers; that is, 90% of deaths are attributable to these causes, demonstrating the stressful effects of modern-day living.

Economic Data

The major driving force behind changes in the American health care delivery system will be economic factors. Data on Nationwide total and per capita expenditures demonstrate that health care costs have been rising 2½ times faster than the cost of living during the last 10 years. The federal government now spends 12 cents of every taxpayer dollar on health care, with 9 cents going to the hospital industry alone. The cost of the average hospital stay was less than $350 in 1965; by 1985 it was over $3,000 per stay. The average American works 1½ months each year to pay health care costs. During the last 10 years medical schools have increased enrollment by 3½% each year, and it has been estimated that for each new doctor that begins practice the nation's medical bill will increase $250,000 a year due to additional services generated. Thirteen billion dollars were spent on health care in 1950, $26 billion in 1960, $78 billion in 1970, $234 billion in 1984, and $700 billion is predicted for 1990. In 1950, 4.5% of the gross national product was spent on health care; today that figure is over 11%, and in 10 years it is predicted that it will be approximately 20%.

The major impact on developmentally disabled individuals is the limitations placed on Medicare funding through recent national efforts to freeze fees and place caps on payment for various diagnostic groupings. These groupings, referred to as DRGs (Diagnostic Related Groupings), essentially limit or establish standard fees on what a physician and hospital can charge to Medicare patients. This legislative change will force hospitals and physicians to streamline their treatments. Economic factors are already having an impact, as various politicians question the expenditure of great sums of money on the educational and medical care for severely disabled individuals.

Surveys of large companies indicate that average medical claims costs per employee amounted to $1500 a year in the mid-1980s. General Motors spends more on employee health benefits each year than it does on steel for its entire production line. The Chrysler Corporation reports that its health care benefits add $600 to the cost of every car. In short, in response to escalating costs it should be anticipated that there will be significant reductions in the delivery of medical care over the next decade that will affect developmentally disabled individuals.

NEW MODELS FOR HEALTH CARE

The problems of the past, along with their attempted solutions, have brought some new and very complex difficulties to modern medical care. Health care delivery has evolved from the institutional model, in which hospitals were either final solutions for the terminally ill or the sole alternative for those unable to function within the social mainstream. Although this model has been greatly improved over time, and, in fact, provides physical medicine with an ideal treatment setting, this approach does not always fulfill all patient needs (Tharp & Wetzel, 1969). Current political, economic, and social conditions demand a new health care system for rehabilitation and general medicine that emphasizes prevention, patient screening, appropriate treatment referrals, and a healthy life-style. A new concept of overall health encompasses biological, physiological, psychological, and philosophical aspects of disease and teaches individuals how to gain control over their lives in order to remain healthy (Rama, 1978).

Two new major models of health care delivery that emerged in the 1970s and early 1980s are expanding even more rapidly than predicted and will have a dramatic impact on the way medicine is delivered to the developmentally disabled population in the next decade. These two models are the health maintenance organization and preferred provider organization.

The health maintenance organization (HMO) is a prepaid medical plan in which participants pay set monthly fees in advance. They are then entitled to use services provided by physicians and other health care professionals participating in the HMO. The major advantages are that unexpected illness is already paid for through the monthly premiums and physicians have an incentive to keep individuals out of the hospital and hold health costs down. The disadvantages are that: 1) participants can use the services as often as they want and may tend to abuse the system, 2) physicians may lack the incentive for providing comprehensive quality care due to the costs involved, and 3) participants are not able to seek out the physician of their choice, but can only go to those physicians and health care professionals who are part of this HMO program. Despite these potential problems, HMOs continue to show small but steady gains. In 1969 there were 26 HMOs in the United States, with an enrollment of 3 million;

by the mid-1980s there were 300 HMOs, with an enrollment of over 13 million.

The preferred provider organization (PPO) is an agreement among health care providers, the insurance company, individuals, and the employer. Under the PPO concept, the employer pays the premium directly to the health care providers, who in turn can lower their fees because of a large volume of patients. Insurance companies benefit by lowered costs and an increased ability to maintain some control over the health care delivery system. However, PPOs have the same potential abuses as do HMOs. PPOs have grown from 3 million participants in 1970 to over 14 million by the mid-1980s.

These new models will have a major impact on developmentally disabled individuals, particularly those who are medically fragile. These models, however, may indeed be more normalizing than the traditional health care delivery system because they emphasize outpatient care and health maintenance prevention. Unfortunately, the care of the handicapped adult may be too costly for these programs, and developmentally disabled adults may be excluded from them.

MEDICAL TRAINING

Many professionals, service providers, and consumers have long voiced concern about the lack of training and exposure of physicians to developmentally disabled individuals, as indicated by national surveys of physicians (Task Force in Pediatric Education, 1978; Wolraich, 1982) and medical school training programs (Guralnick, Richardson, & Heiser, 1982) (see Chapter 19). There are very few lectures and even fewer specific courses offered in medical school on handicapping conditions. Residency programs provide opportunities for physicians to have some exposure to this population, but this exposure is generally loosely organized, not a part of the required curriculum, and often requires a good deal of initiative to obtain. The growing demand for continuing education in developmental disabilities among physicians,

particularly pediatricians, psychiatrists, family practitioners, and internists, is encouraging.

It is possible to make some general statements about the skills physicians must possess in order to deal with adults with developmental disabilities. Training in modern concepts and practice in the control of seizures with a focus on the appropriate use of seizure medications are essential. Physicians need specific training in the diagnostic approach to treatment of mental illness in retarded individuals and an understanding of the multiple therapy approaches to behavioral components in adults with developmental disabilities. Surprisingly, the necessity for in-depth training in motor disorders may not be as great as previously anticipated. It also appears that physicians will need better training in treatment of common dermatologic problems and a further understanding of the contribution of preventive hygiene measures to chronic skin disorders. Finally, the physician must be aware of and fully understand the necessity of having visual and auditory testing available.

Medical Specialties Serving
Adults with Developmental Disabilities

When dealing with a population of individuals from birth to age 18, it is relatively easy to identify the specialists most involved in medical care: pediatricians and family practitioners have been incorporated in the majority of medical training programs throughout the United States. Unfortunately, medical specialization has not identified a specific practitioner who is trained to deal with the 18- to 64-year old individual with developmental disabilites. A recent review of medical personnel at established University Affiliated Programs, developmental centers, and institutional settings indicates that pediatricians currently comprise the majority of their medical staff positions. Therefore, it would appear that pediatricians are presently delivering much of the medical care to adult individuals with developmental disabilities in these programs. Data from the American Medical Association indicate that community physicians dealing with nondisabled individuals from 18 to 64 years of age are primarily family practitioners and physicians trained in internal medicine. No data are available indicating which physicians specifically work with adults with developmental disabilities in community settings.

The above data suggest that pediatricians, family practitioners, and internal medicine specialists are the major resource for the delivery of medical services to adults with developmental disabilities. However, at the present time, most pediatricians in community practices do not see individuals over the age of 21. It may be possible to convince pediatricians that developmental disabilities may negate this age limitation, or it may be more prudent to concentrate training efforts on family practitioners and internal medicine physicians in the delivery of services to adults with developmental disabilities.

Medical Curriculum

If one assumes that pediatricians, family practitioners, and internal medicine physicians are the primary resources for delivery of medical services to adults with developmental disabilities, then the next logical step is to incorporate a training program that reflects the needed training and clinical experience for these physicians into existing medical school and postgraduate training curricula. In an attempt to obtain the current medical school curriculum information regarding adult developmental disabilities by questionnaire, the response rate was very poor. In order to obtain limited data, phone calls were then made to randomly selected colleges of medicine throughout the United States; 10 of these colleges volunteered information regarding their present medical school curriculum. None of the colleges of medicine contacted had a specific curriculum requirement in pediatrics, family practice, or internal medicine for training in adult developmental disability medical services. Two of the medical schools indicated that *elective* postgraduate rotations in developmental disabilities were available and had been utilized by residents in all three specialties

in the past. A review of the training programs listed by University Affiliated Programs does not indicate a significant number of training programs with a specific curriculum in this area. Four of the curriculum officers polled by phone indicated a willingness to consider programs in the adult developmental disabilities, but suggested that their present curricula were so demanding that it may not be possible to *require* this area of study. All four of these individuals indicated an interest in this area of medicine, but they suggested that training limitations and board certification requirements may severely limit the addition of this curriculum component.

An extensive review of existing medical literature verifies the limited attention paid to adults with developmental disabilities. There are a number of references on behavioral management of adults with developmental disabilities, but there are virtually none on other specific medical problems in the adult developmentally disabled population. Recently there have appeared a number of review articles suggesting the need for increasing services to adults with developmental disabilities and discussing potential delivery models, but the medical component is not a major issue in these publications (Menolascino & Stark, 1984).

A review of birth statistics available from the Communicable Disease Center in Atlanta, Georgia, indicates that at least 3% of the newborn population have identifiable birth defects. This figure, which has remained constant for the past decade, includes any major birth defect, such as cleft lip and palate, heart disease, or developmental disability. Individuals with birth defects have a marked decrease in infant mortality and an increased life span. These data suggest that the percentage of adults with developmental disabilities as defined by onset of disability prior to age 22 will increase due to better medical care, improved perinatal survival rates, and the increasing overall longevity of individuals in the United States.

Based on the data presented in this chapter, the number of appropriately trained physicians appears to be woefully inadequate to meet the overall and highly specialized needs for sophisticated medical services of the ever-increasing population of adults with developmental disabilities now and in the foreseeable future.

Recommended Changes

It is suggested that all local-state-federal agencies involved in the daily care and management of adults with developmental disabilities engage in a major advocacy effort to focus attention on educating and acquainting the medical licensing boards of pediatrics, family practice, and internal medicine with the key medical problems so frequently noted in the adult developmental disabilities. It is also suggested that these agencies work with the Association of American Medical Colleges to develop curriculum components that address the specific problems of adults with developmental disabilities, thereby increasing medical students' awareness of this growing population of individuals with specific medical needs. It is suggested that federal and state agencies fund demonstration projects for medical colleges to develop these curriculum activities and to test the short- and long-term effects of this training

on the specialties of pediatrics, family practice, and internal medicine. These demonstration programs will help determine which medical subspecialties are most interested in the provision of services to this population and will act accordingly to require board certification for those subspecialties in the future.

While prospective data collection systems and new training programs are being developed, it is suggested that continuing education training programs be established for primary care physicians in the community. The purpose of such programs will be to familiarize these physicians with: 1) the diagnosis and treatment of behavioral components in adults with developmental disabilities, 2) modern approaches to seizure control, 3) dermatologic problems, and 4) motoric difficulties that so often unduly complicate the lives of adult citizens with developmental disabilities. The absence of a large cadre of physicians who are willing and capable of treating the many medical complications noted in adults with developmental disabilities may limit the ability to maintain adults in community-based programs.

REFERENCES

Black, L. S. (Ed.). (1974). *Population change: Strategy for physicians*. Proceedings of the International Conference of the Physician & Population Change. Stockholm, Sweden, September 4–6. World Foundation for Medical Education, Bethesda, MD.

Boggs, E., & Henry, D. (1979). *A numerical and functional description of the developmental disabilities population*. Washington, DC: Administration on Developmental Disabilities.

Bruininks, R. H. (1983). *Client oriented service indicators for evaluating the targeting of resources to reduce dependency and provide appropriate care*. Washington, DC: Administration on Developmental Disabilities. (Submitted to Bureau of Social Science Research).

Coleman, J. C. (1972). *Abnormal psychology and modern life, 4th Ed*. Glenview, IL: Scott Foresman.

Gollay, E. (1981). *Summary report on the implications of modifying the definition of a developmental disability*. Washington, DC: Department of Health, Education, and Welfare.

Guralnick, M. J., Richardson, H. B., & Heiser, K. E. (1982). A curriculum in handicapping conditions for pediatric residents. *Exceptional Children, 48*, 338–346.

Hewett, F., & Forness, S. (1977). *Education of exceptional learners, 2nd Ed*. Boston, MA: Allyn & Bacon.

Keys, V., Boroskin, A., & Ross, R. T. (1973). The

revolving door in an M.R. hospital: A study of returns from leave. *Mental Retardation, 11*(1), 55–56.

Lakin, K. C., Hill, B. K., Hauber, F. A., & Bruininks, R. H. (1982). Changes in age at first admission to residential care of mentally retarded people. *Mental Retardation, 20*, 216–219.

Menolascino, F., & Stark, J. (1984). *The handbook of mental illness in the mentally retarded*. New York: Plenum Press.

Pagel, S. E., & Whitling, C. A. (1978). Readmission to a state hospital for mentally retarded persons: Reasons for community placement failure. *Mental Retardation, 16*(2), 164–166.

Rama, S. (1978). *A practical guide to holistic health*. Honesdale, PA: The Himalayan International Institute.

Schalock, R. (1983). *Services for developmentally disabled adults*. Baltimore, MD: University Park Press.

Scheerenberger, R. (1983). *A history of mental retardation*. Baltimore, MD: Paul H. Brookes Publishing Co.

Sheps, C. G. (1971). Trends in hospital care. *Inquiry, 8,* 1.

Stark, J., McGee, J., & Menolascino, F. (1984). The delivery of services in rural settings. In: *International handbook of community services*. Hillsdale, NJ: Lawrence Erlbaum Associates, Publishers.

Szymanski, L., & Tanguay, P. (1980). *Emotional dis-*

orders of mentally retarded persons: Assessment, treatment and consultation. Baltimore, MD: University Park Press.

Task Force in Pediatric Education. (1978). *The future of pediatric education.* Evanston, IL: American Academy of Pediatrics.

Tharp, R., & Wetzel, R. (1969) *Behavioral modification in the natural environment.* New York: Academic Press.

Wolraich, M. L. (1982). Communication between physicians and parents of handicapped children. *Exceptional Children, 48,* 324–329.

∞ Section VI ∞

IMPLICATIONS
FOR THE FUTURE

IN SECTION VI, TRAINING, RESEARCH AND EVALUATION OF SERVICES ARE ADDRESSED WITH A VIEW toward the future. In Chapter 19, Karan and Knight present a comprehensive review of the training demands and issues in preparing individuals to work with developmentally disabled adults. The authors emphasize the education of allied health professionals and the need to involve parents and paraprofessionals in the training process. They also discuss the role that University-Affiliated Facilities (UAFs) can play in training professionals and paraprofessionals who will be providing services to adults with developmental disabilities. A specific model for training community developmental disabilities associates is detailed by the authors. This chapter will serve as a model analysis of training needs of both professionals and paraprofessionals who provide services to adults with developmental disabilities.

As essential as proper training is the need for improved research strategies and activities that examine employment opportunities for adults with developmental disabilities. Stark, Schalock, and Berland review past research activities and analyze current research publications. They note the need to expand research activities, both qualitatively and quantitatively. Finally, the chapter addresses the major problems of research utilization. Often, for the practitioner in the field, the gap between completion of research activities and the dissemination of results leads to long delays in utilization of research findings. The authors recommend how this gap can be reduced and how research findings may be more effectively integrated into day-to-day service delivery.

Schalock and Hill present a series of models and options for evaluating the effectiveness of employment services in Chapter 21. The authors provide both a content and a process to help the reader conceptualize and implement a systematic monitoring and evalution strategy. The chapter is divided into three parts: systems design, a three-phased approach to monitoring, and evaluation of outcomes in formative, summative, and benefit-cost designs. Program evaluation is a mechanism for identifying those activities and approaches to employment training that are successful for adults with developmental disabilities.

∞ Chapter 19 ∞

Training Demands of the Future

Orv C. Karan and Catherine Berger Knight

DESPITE THE FACT THAT MANY DIFFERENT persons provide many kinds of service within many settings to many different developmentally disabled persons (Beauregard & Indik, 1979) the shortage of qualified personnel capable of serving adults is a critical and growing national concern (Benson, 1979; Bilvosky & Matson, 1977; Fifield & Smith, 1985). How best to respond to this shortage is a complicated issue because there are no statutory mandates nor has a single agency been designated to provide services to this age group (Middendorf, Fifield, & Smith, 1985). Yet, adult service providers are expected to respond to changing conditions that are being radically influenced by recent ideologies, technologies, priorities, and opportunities.

Today's developmentally disabled young adults, for example, having been exposed to educational opportunities that were simply unavailable a decade ago, are a qualitatively different group than the generation who preceded them. Generally speaking, this new breed of young adults has more skills, more normalized life experiences, and more potential at all levels of disability (Brown, 1984). Both they and their parents rightfully expect the same opportunities for further education and/or jobs that are available to their nondisabled peers (Valera, 1982). Unfortunately, of the estimated 90,000 handicapped students leaving the school system each year (Moran, 1984), 80% will either be unemployed or underemployed and living below the poverty level within 1 year after graduation (McInerney & Karan, 1981).

As these recent graduates push the adult system from one end, residents of large public institutions, who are slowly being returned to the community, are pushing it from another end. Many of these adults grew up before the passage of PL 94-142 and therefore missed training opportunities that today are all but taken for granted. The majority of the over 100,000 developmentally disabled persons now living in public institutions (Janicki, Mayeda, & Epple, 1983; Lakin, Krantz, Bruininks, Clumpner, & Hill, 1982) are severely or profoundly handicapped adults (Best-Sigford, Bruininks, Lakin, Hill, & Heal, 1982), with over 60% at all mental retardation levels exhibiting frequent maladaptive behaviors (Bell, 1976; Vittelo, Atthowe, & Cadwell, 1983). Given the impetus of the waiver authority of the Budget Reconciliation Act of 1981 (PL 97-35), many—and it is hoped all—of these individuals may someday become community residents. However, community service providers have not had much success nor experience serving these adults as reported recidivism rates of 50% and higher indicate (Sutter, Mayeda, Call, Yanagi, & Yee, 1980). For the community placements of such individuals to succeed, continuous staff and parent training is essential (Novak & Heal, 1980).

Further complicating matters is that this additional demand for better services is being made on a system that is already notorious for its fragmentation, duplication, and limited options. Thus, in trying to anticipate future personnel training needs for such a volatile system, we are reminded of some of Murphy's Laws, such as the Parouzzi Principle that states, "given a bad start, trouble will increase at an exponential rate," and his fourth and fifth corollaries that warn that "whenever you set out to do something, something else must be done first," and "every solution breeds new problems" (Bloch, 1984).

Paying full heed to these wise words and making no claims to be accurate crystal ball readers, the authors offer a vision of future training needs. Fortunately, to assist in this task, some tentative projections can be made based on the training literature (e.g., Neufeldt, 1978, 1980) and trends in employment statistics.

A STARTING POINT

In recent years, segregated service models have been increasingly replaced by integrated initiatives in education, employment, housing, and leisure activities (Office of the Inspector General, 1984). This change has resulted in a shortage of qualified staff, particularly in community residential settings (Bruininks, Kudla, Wieck, & Hauber, 1980), as well as the unavailability of essential support services, such as educational, vocational, recreational, and medical services (Bruininks et al., 1980; Novak & Heal, 1980; O'Connor, 1976). To accommodate greater community integration, certain professionals are, and will be, taking on increasing importance.

According to the Federal Bureau of Labor Statistics (1980), faster than average growth in the 1980s is projected for several health professions. The primary reason for this growth is the increasing need for professionals to work in community programs. It is anticipated that these needs will be most prevalent in rural areas and in some inner-city locations. The professions include nursing, physical therapy, occupational therapy, speech pathology, audiol-

ogy, social work, and psychology. However, preparing better trained individuals will require the removal of such existing barriers as the lack of well-trained faculty, the lack of faculty interest, the lack of trainee time, the lack of trainee interest, and the lack of well-defined curricula (Guralnick, Richardson, & Heiser, 1982; Jadkins & Harrison, 1979).

EDUCATING THE PROFESSIONAL: A CASE IN POINT

Although many of the professionals already identified will play critical roles in ensuring the provision of necessary support services, the chronicity and/or complexity of some of the health conditions of developmentally disabled persons and the high prevalence of their psychopathology (Matson, 1984) suggest that physicians will retain highly critical responsibilities for their care and treatment in the future. Whether they will be prepared to respond adequately to these responsibilities is another question. The following case study presents the complex and unusual problems that developmentally disabled persons present to their community physicians.

David was born with seral rubella syndrome, and in addition to his profound retardation, he was also congenitally deaf and blind. Further, David had only a rudimentary communication system, understanding a few simple signs and expressing even less. He was institutionalized shortly after birth and remained in one institution or another until the age of 21 when he was selected to participate in a deinstitutionalization project (Karan, 1981).

In an attempt to minimize the stress of transferring from the institution to the community, a two-step process of transition was used. First, David began attending a community work activity center while continuing to reside in the institution. Within a year he adjusted to the routines of the activity center and started the second stage of the transition process. During this stage he moved into a group home while still continuing to attend the work activity center. Once he was discharged from the institution, all his ancillary service needs, such as occupational and speech therapy, were to be obtained from community service providers. In addition, the group home staff identified a physician who was willing to accept

David and the other group home residents as his patients.

Although his progress was slow, the staffs at both the work activity center and the group home felt that David was adjusting to the change. After about 3 months he seemed to have settled into his new routines and was expanding his base of experiences through various supervised community excursions. Then, for no apparent reason, David began displaying unusual behaviors and symptoms. He seemed more lethargic than usual, had diarrhea and blood in his stool, was throwing up frequently, and was spending significant portions of his day sleeping. Concerned about these changes, the group home staff took David to the physician's office. On examination, David's physician concluded that he probably had a case of the flu, advised bed rest, and prescribed some medication to control the diarrhea and vomiting.

David died in his sleep a few days later, and an autopsy showed that he had a hairline skull fracture and a subdural hematoma.

David's limited communication skills and cataracts, which interferred with a good test of his pupil reflexes, obviously hindered his physician's ability to make an accurate diagnosis. Whether anyone could have detected David's problem more accurately remains a moot question, and David's death can only be attributed to accidental causes. But had David's physician received training to familiarize himself better with severely handicapped persons, perhaps he might have been more likely to consider other diagnostic options.

National reviews of medical school training programs and practices reveal serious gaps and omissions. For example, Guralnick et al. (1982) surveyed all the accredited pediatric residency programs to determine the extent of resident training in the area of handicap. They found that, although many responding programs—the initial response rate was 55%—offered at least some training, the programs were loosely organized and apparently made only minimal efforts to include systematic experiences with individuals having a range of handicapping conditions. An absence of formalized curricula or even educational objectives was frequently noted. In addition, a follow-up of those programs that did not respond to the survey indicated that 45% did not have any organized program in the area of handicap. In a similar review, Willer, Ross, and Intagliata (1980) found that even among

medical school programs offering either course work or clinical practica in the field of mental retardation, almost half had only minimal coverage and offered inadequate clinical experiences.

Surveys of physicians show they are concerned about their lack of adequate specialized training (Cooke, 1966; Task Force in Pediatric Education, 1978; Wolraich, 1982), their need for continuing education to prepare them not only to work with handicapped persons but also to interact with nonphysician professionals, and their limited knowledge of such basic resources as local parent organizations (Wolraich, 1982).

If present trends continue, it appears as if physicians will neither be prepared adequately to meet the future needs of developmentally disabled adults nor to participate successfully in cooperative interdisciplinary interactions with other caregivers (Bennett, 1982; Garrard, 1982; Guralnick, 1982; Haggerty, 1974; Powers & Healy, 1982; Richmond, 1975). That this is a legitimate concern is evidenced by the authors' recent Medline search of the National Library of Medicine's Retrieval System; out of all the medical journals in the system from 1980 to 1984, *only seven* citations on educating allied health professionals in mental retardation were identified.

THE NEED FOR A NEW TYPE OF PROFESSIONAL

It has been suggested (Magrab & Elder, 1979) that the challenge of the 1970s was one of providing equal services to handicapped persons that were traditionally available to nonhandicapped persons, whereas the challenge of the 1980s is to develop a coordinated collaborative human service delivery system that enables the handicapped person to receive services in an expeditious and coordinated manner. The essential element of coordinated, effective systems is a well-trained staff. Yet, although there are many professionals calling for program excellence, there are few mandates that exist for staff excellence (Ziarnik & Bernstein, 1980).

Given the chaotic state of affairs within the adult service delivery system and the fact that most states lack sufficient plans and information to identify the specific occupations and skills desired for either their generic or specific programs (Scheerenberger, 1981), systems for personnel preparation must respond reactively to rapidly changing service needs and demands.

Despite the chaos within the delivery system itself, it is clear that a new type of trained person is needed—one who is able to transcend traditional discipline boundaries in his or her efforts to assist developmentally disabled adults in full community integration. Personnel preparation programs, however, are only just beginning to reflect a movement from specific disciplinary staff training to an increased emphasis on functional skills training (Carlin et al., 1981).

Our systems of higher education must be more responsive to future training needs. Unfortunately, institutions of higher education have generally failed to provide the training necessary to develop and improve community systems. Further, there has been a lack of synchronization between universities, community colleges, and service agencies in the development of joint planning to meet training needs (Gartner, 1979; Stedman, 1977). Thus, although the complex organizational environment within which developmentally disabled adults seek and receive services dictates complex training needs for professionals, preservice training programs are generally discipline-specific. The traditional unidimensional approach to training neither provides mutual understanding of the role of each professional nor emphasizes the need for integration and coordination among professionals (Richardson, West, & Fifield, 1985).

Preparing personnel either to work with adults or to assist students in bridging their transitions into adulthood also requires an expansion of many preservice training programs now geared primarily to the needs of developmentally disabled children (Boyan & Kaplan, 1980). Today's secondary-level special educators, for example, must be trained to assume a particularly critical role in facilitating their students' vocational preparation and transitions from school to work. To ensure that there is a functional basis to their preservice training, as well as that of other professionals, interdisciplinary training models need to incorporate employers and business persons into the curriculum planning processes. Further, working relationships between the academic and business communities must be strengthened. Along these lines, Colby (1984) recommends that preservice professional training include at least one practicum in a business setting.

These training needs imply a new role for the University Affiliated Facilities (UAFs) in preparing professionals to assist developmentally disabled adults (Fifield & Smith, 1985). However, a recently completed telephone survey (Berger, 1984) conducted with the training coordinators of all the UAFs revealed that almost half of those responding limit their current involvement with developmentally disabled adults to occasional evaluations or special projects. Although these findings are consistent with what has been the major thrust of services and funding to UAFs, it is an unfortunate commentary on our collective roles as planners, educators, and policymakers that to our mutual surprise we have only just discovered that developmentally disabled children grow up. And as they grow and become more integrated into their local communities, the range and complexities of the training issues that must be addressed also increase, as shown by the following case study.

> Betty is a 28-year-old mildly mentally retarded woman who has a history of emotional problems related to her unpredictable moods. She often misinterprets what people say to her and frequently reacts in ways that appear to be out of context to the casual observer. Those who know her well simply accept her behavior as one of Betty's quirks. For those who do not know her, however, she can appear "confused," "strange," or "wierd." Betty's psychiatrist, whom she has known for years and sees regularly, periodically prescribes psychotropic medication. Betty hates taking the medication because it makes her "spacey," and she will usually avoid it unless someone monitors her closely.

Betty's parents live in town, but she rarely sees them, except on occasions when she needs money. Then she will stop at her mother's office and get a few dollars.

Before moving into her supervised apartment, which she shares with three other persons, Betty lived in a foster home. Her foster mother has remained a friend, and occasionally the two will still do activities together. All her apartment mates also have emotional difficulties, and frequently there is considerable tension in the house; one person's moods will affect another's mood, leading to chain reactions of bickering, yelling, and fighting. A residential supervisor, who lives in another apartment downstairs, tries to resolve these problems if they get out of hand by imposing various restrictions on the residents. This intervention, however, has backfired, causing even more problems because those residents who are grounded or restricted are likely to maintain their anger throughout their restricted period, thus contributing to a continuing volatile environment.

Betty's case manager readily acknowledges that her living conditions are unsatisfactory, but he has been unsuccessful in helping her locate more suitable alternatives. Also, because there is a large waiting list for community housing, Betty's situation is not given a high priority. Thus, her chances of finding more appropriate housing in the immediate future look dim. Betty has had three different case managers in the last 3 years, and she resents her current one because she feels he puts too many restrictions on her.

Betty is well known to many of the city merchants, bar owners, bus drivers, and police officers. In her free time, and particularly on weekends, she likes to go downtown to meet new people. Although she usually has fun dancing, shopping, drinking, or just "hanging out," she sometimes gets into heated arguments with others over matters that she later admits to not quite understanding. The police have been called on occasion, and although they have threatened her with fines and/or nights in jail for disturbing the peace, this punishment has yet to happen. Instead, an officer usually drives her home. On such occasions, the residential supervisor either grounds Betty or imposes some restriction on her for having caused trouble.

Betty has a part-time job working in one of the buildings on the university campus as a janitor's helper. The building houses faculty, staff, and students in a number of disciplines, such as social work, psychology, and special education. As a result, there is never a lack of sympathetic ears and kindly suggestions for Betty, who is usually in the middle of one crisis or another. Un-

fortunately, Betty has considerable difficulty sorting out the various helpful messages she receives. Complicating matters even further is that Betty seeks advice from lots of people, even total strangers she meets on the bus, and has difficulty discriminating the value of one person's advice from another's.

Betty is usually agitated when she reports to work, upset about one matter or another related to the ongoing events in her life. Yet, her work has probably been the most stable part of her life. After years of sporadic employment in sheltered workshops, lasting no more than a few months in any setting, Betty has remained on her present job for almost 3 years. Despite the fact that she was declared unemployable by the division of vocational rehabilitation, she can do good work and likes her job. She has also been accepted by the other members of the janitorial crew and often joins several members for coffee breaks or lunch. This is not to say that she does not have difficulties. In the last 2 months, for example, she has had a series of problems and has been considerably more unpredictable, both in her attendance and in the quality of her work. The primary difficulty involves another janitor. She claims that he continuously pressures her to have sex with him both on the job and after work at his home and that he also touches her when she does not want to be touched.

Because Betty confides in so many people, her allegations came to the attention of the building director. He appointed a sexual harassment officer to meet separately with both Betty and the other janitor to discuss her allegations. In addition, the security and protection unit on the campus sent an officer to speak to both of them. No specific action was taken, although the sexual harassment officer will remain involved to check with Betty periodically to see if a problem still exists.

The janitor denied Betty's allegations and is now so angry that he will not even speak to her anymore. This reaction has been very unsettling to her, and she has been threatening to harm herself. Further, she is having more difficulties than usual at home, and her work performance has also suffered. There have been several complaints about her work from various units within the building, and unless she makes some significant improvements soon her job may be terminated.

Meanwhile, Betty's mother has initiated efforts to have her sterilized, a plan with which Betty agrees. The doctor's attorney has advised him not to proceed until Betty's competence in this matter has been determined. A private psychologist has agreed to see Betty to try to determine her competence in making this decision. At the same time, representatives of the state's protection and advocacy agency have taken steps to ensure that Betty's rights in this matter are protected.

THE NEED FOR A NEW APPROACH: THE RECIPROCITY OF INFLUENCE

Betty is not atypical, and there are many Bettys trying to make their way in society. As her case study indicates, working in the community is more than simply doing a set of specific tasks. As noted in Chapter 7, clearly one's vocational life cannot be separated from all the other events, activities, and experiences in which

one is involved on a 24-hour basis (Bellamy, Rhodes, Wilcox, Albin, Mank, Boles, Horner, Collins, & Turner, 1984).

Figure 1 is a conceptual model that represents the reciprocal relationships among individuals and the multiplicity of persons, places, and things with which they interact (Karan & Berger, 1986).

Considerable evidence suggests that social interpersonal difficulties are the major reason why mentally retarded people fail vocationally (Crawford, Aiello, & Thompson, 1979; Edgerton & Bercovici, 1976; Foss & Bostwick, 1981; Greenspan & Shoultz, 1981; Niziol & DeBlassie, 1972; Richardson, 1978; Rosen, Clark, & Kivitz, 1977; Rusch, 1979; Sowers,

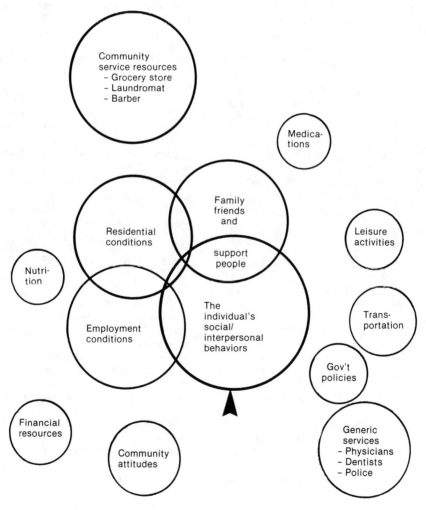

Figure 1.   An individual's ecological system.

Thompson, & Connis, 1979; Wehman, 1981). For this reason, the individual's social interpersonal behaviors have been purposely balanced on a rather precarious base in Figure 1 to convey how fragile these behaviors sometimes are and how easily they can be shifted as a function of changing environmental conditions. It is almost amazing that so many developmentally disabled persons function as well as they do, considering the mass of conflicting information they process regularly as a result of their involvement with so many different individuals (Karan & Schalock, 1983).

Within this framework, every part of an individual's ecological system is related to its fellow parts, and changes in one part may cause changes in other parts, which could then affect the total system (Jeger & Slotnick, 1982). Thus, in the area of transportation, for example, if one had difficulty getting to and from work, one's job could be in jeopardy. An individual's residential placement might then be jeopardized because in many cases the individual must be employed or participating in daily vocational services as a condition for living in that placement. When considering the variety of possible permutations in the model that could occur as a result of changing conditions, it becomes evident that various levels of support across settings (Gardner, Karan, & Cole, 1984) are needed to keep developmentally disabled adults employed.

Implications for Training

The reciprocity of influences among service providers, people on the street, parents, and developmentally disabled persons has important implications for training. Beyond any specific skills unique to a given profession, occupation, or role, all training must sensitize individuals to the importance not only of their own social-interpersonal relationships with developmentally disabled persons but also to the influence of others as well (Humm-Delgado, 1979; Tjosvold & Tjosvold, 1981, 1983). It is not enough for people to know only the specific skills and knowledge base of their own profession or role. Parents, professionals,

paraprofessionals, and generic service providers must learn to increase their understanding of and sensitivity to the possible effects and influences of their own interactions and the interactions of others on developmentally disabled individuals.

As further indicated in Figure 1, employment, residence, and family, friends, and support people have been conceptualized as the primary influences within a given individual's ecological system. Each of these in turn has its own unique set of ecological variables. Figure 2, for example, depicts a community residence—in this case, a group home—as both a workplace for the staff and as a home for its residents. Among other duties, staff are responsible for contributing to a healthy psychosocial environment for the residents (i.e., by providing support, training, security, and comfort). Yet, at the same time, the staff have their own employment and personal needs related to their job satisfaction, which is influenced by salary, growth opportunities, working conditions, and supervisory support. As conceptualized in Figure 2, the greater the overlap between the two circles, the greater the degree of compatibility between the staff and resident needs (Karan & Berger, 1986).

Figure 2 also reveals another important concern that has significant implications for training. Basic learning theory principles tell us that behavior is not maintained unless it is reinforced. Therefore, unless supportive managerial practices with well-defined expectancies and the right incentives (pay, fringe benefits, respect) are available to support individuals trained to work with developmentally disabled persons, there may be insufficient reason for them to sustain these skills or provide their services (Bernstein & Rudrud, 1980; Bernstein & Ziarnik, 1982; Byrd, Sawyer, & Locke, 1983; Lattimore, Stephens, Favell, & Risley, 1984). For instance, Gotowka, Johnson, and Gotowka (1982) found that when dentists experienced financial disincentives for providing dental services to mentally retarded adults, they simply provided fewer services.

Among community residential providers, attrition rates exceed 70% per year (George &

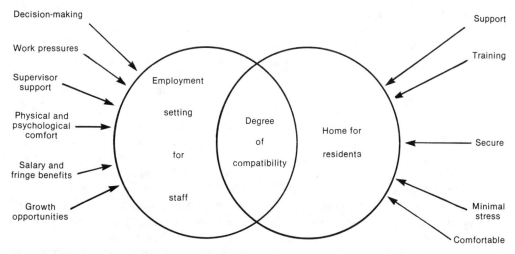

Decision-making

Work pressures

Supervisor
support

Physical and
psychological
comfort

Salary and
fringe benefits

Growth
opportunities

Support

Training

Secure

Minimal
stress

Comfortable

Employment

setting

for

staff

Degree

of

compatibility

Home for

residents

Figure 2.   The group home as both a workplace and a residence.

Baumeister, 1981; Skarnulis, 1976). This is a national problem (O'Connor, 1976), and in a 1980 nationwide survey (Bruininks et al., 1980), the preparation of direct service staff was listed as the major concern of over 2,000 program administrators. Without question, the need for well-trained personnel who can respond appropriately to the complicated and persistent problems of severely handicapped citizens is a serious concern; however, of equal, if not greater, importance is the need to find ways to support these individuals—financially and in other ways—and to sustain them in the continuing provision of their services. Continuous staff turnover not only precludes the development of meaningful relationships but also mitigates the implementation of well-formulated habilitation programs over time.

The Role of Parents

In recent years, an increasing number of professionals have recognized that parents and paraprofessionals are invaluable sources of information, as well as the primary instructors in most activities of daily living. Parents, of course, are their child's first teachers, and they are involved in not only the instruction of different skills and activities but also have a substantial impact on the values and attitudes that their children have toward work. Once a

child reaches adulthood, his or her parents play a

> major and ever-critical role in facilitating the advantageous aspects of competitive employment. By helping to overcome transportation problems, working out SSI limitations and providing strong moral support to their son or daughter in the job placement, parents can make a competitive placement successful or completely block it. (Wehman, 1981, p. 7)

The importance of the parents' role has many training implications. Parents need to be prepared early for their child's movement toward independence and to learn to balance their own protective needs with the child's need for independence and its associated risks (Bernstein & Karan, 1979). Further, as their child grows into adulthood, it is important to recognize that parental concerns are different from those of parents of young children and that each new transition, such as the one from school to work, may stimulate new stress for the family (Arnold, 1985). Such issues have not been adequately considered in the planning of many parent training programs (Guralnick et al., 1982).

Parents may play a variety of roles in promoting their adult son's or daughter's successful integration into the community. Therefore, at the very least, they must be trained and treated as equal members of the interdisciplinary team (Arnold, 1985). Because developmentally disabled adults are usually served by a variety of agencies, the team process is particularly important (Schalock, 1983), and parents can contribute to this process as advocates and/or case managers (Arnold, 1985).

A variety of approaches are available for training parents (Intagliata & Doyle, 1984), including information services, emotional support groups, therapy, and specific technical skills training (i.e., behavior management). Such training has been offered through university credit courses, workshops and minicourses, and networks and groups (Arnold, 1985).

Developers of parent training programs must be responsive to the limitations placed on parents' schedules. Programs must also be relevant, timely, and often creative. As an example, one parent obtained independent funding from a local bank to provide a minicourse on legal and financial considerations for parents whose interests paralleled her own (Arnold, 1985).

Program developers must also be aware of obstacles to parent training. A primary obstacle is the traditional professional view that roles of authority and expertise should be assigned solely to the professional team. Given that the two most significant predictors of successful community placement are parental acceptance of and involvement in community-based programs (Schalock, Harper, & Genung, 1981), the absurdity of this outdated viewpoint is apparent. All training programs need to incorporate a greater emphasis on the parents' role, and both service providers and parents must learn how to work more effectively with each other (Arnold, 1985).

The Role of the Paraprofessional

Since the paraprofessional movement first began in the 1960s (Schalock, 1983), the term "paraprofessional" has come to mean many things. It generally refers to any individual involved in direct care who lacks a baccalaureate degree and who serves in a position for which a professional person has ultimate responsibility (Gartner, 1979). Representing

> an extremely heterogeneous group in terms of characteristics, background, and job-related . . . activities . . . paraprofessionals include full-time, salaried staff with training ranging from a grade school to a college education and such part-time unpaid volunteers as homemakers, students, parents and the elderly. (Durlak, 1982, pp. 446–447)

Their importance to the field of developmental disabilities is evident, given that more than 80% of the personnel who come into daily contact with the developmentally disabled adult in service programs are paraprofessionals (National Institute on Mental Retardation, 1972; Schalock, 1983).

Paraprofessionals have played increasingly important roles in the delivery of human services and can be expected to play new roles that will involve them more in programmatic decision making and interdisciplinary problem-solving processes (Durlak, 1982; Jeger & Slotnick, 1982). With the increasing demand for more intensive programs to serve more severely handicapped persons with more complex needs at a time of reduced revenues, paraprofessionals will continue to be an important and critical person-power resource in the future (Fiorelli, 1982; Menolascino, 1980).

Given that paraprofessionals represent the overwhelming majority of individuals with whom mentally retarded citizens have daily contact, the need for improved training and incentives to retain such individuals in the field is critical. However, it has been estimated that anywhere from 70%–90% (Bilvosky & Matson, 1977; Schalock, 1983) of all those now providing direct care services never had any formal training for their jobs. Instead, the majority of employees in community-based programs are entry-level personnel with no prior experience and little, if any, appropriate education (Pfriem, 1979).

In response to this growing need, staff training programs addressing a variety of topics have been developed (Schalock, 1983) by government agencies, and by institutions of higher education in cooperation with service delivery agencies. For the most part, inservice models have been designed to promote career mobility within a civil service system (Gartner, 1979; Pickett & Humm, 1981).

The importance of career development ladders must be underscored (Pfriem, 1980; Roeher, 1981) because "in the absence of planned coordinated approaches to training and career development and mobility, the goal of developing a trained cadre of community-based direct service workers will be almost impossible to implement and may in fact jeopardize the movement toward communitization" (Gartner, 1979, pp. 19–20). Most paraprofessionals are not involved in any career advancement program that would enable them to move into jobs with increased responsibilities and higher salaries. At the same time, current salaries for direct service jobs are inadequate, thereby reducing the motivation for enrolling in and completing rigorous training programs (Kregel, 1985).

Attention must also be paid to the issues of high staff turnover and low morale, the lack of credentialing and certification programs, and logistical problems in delivering effective staff development training (Kregel, 1985). Staff development must address both the generic and highly specialized skills required by direct service personnel (Kregel, 1985) and must begin to utilize systematic, research-oriented approaches to determine the content required in these programs (Bernstein & Ziarnik, 1982; Ziarnik, Rudrud, & Bernstein, 1981). Because of scheduling and time constraints, creativity and flexibility must be used in planning training programs (Mittler, 1981), which themselves should promote professionalism (Bernstein & Rudrud, 1980; Fiorelli, 1982; Fiorelli, Margolis, Heverly, Rothchild, & Keating, 1982). Methods could include the establishment of Associate of Arts degree programs, minicourses and institutes, technical assistance and consultation, and computer-assisted activities (Kregel, 1985; Middendorf, Fifield, & Smith, 1985).

Paraprofessional training is extremely critical to the successful implementation of the supported employment concept described elsewhere in this book because those who assist developmentally disabled adults in employment settings do not need advanced degrees. Increasingly, however, what they do need is experience with private industry and the accompanying skills—business management, peer model, line-level worker—for working effectively in a variety of employment sites. They also need orientation and sensitization to developmental disabilities (Neufeldt, 1978). Thus, contemporary approaches to non-sheltered employment depend on trained personnel who can balance a practical business sense with a humanistic approach.

Neufeldt (1978) recommends two complementary training models for achieving this balance: 1) a preservice model with considerable flexibility in entry-exit-reentry requirements and credits for practial experience, and 2) a continuing education model of supplementary, short-term training. Coordination between the training and service systems is essential in either model. The following section describes a paraprofessional training model in Wisconsin that addresses both business and humanistic concerns.

The Wisconsin Technical College Model In response to the need for qualified paraprofessionals in Wisconsin, a 2-year associate degree program was developed. This program, entitled the "Community Developmental Disabilities Associate (CDDA)," is offered within Wisconsin's Technical College system. The following guiding principles provided direction for the program.

1. The program should be located within a generic educational system.
2. The curriculum should reflect functional skills and be responsive to current and new skill demands.
3. The program should be closely monitored and regularly evaluated to determine if it is meeting its objectives.
4. The program should be flexible enough to respond to varying training needs of its students.

There are 16 district technical colleges throughout Wisconsin's Technical College System, and each district is responsive to the employment needs of its area. The single most important criterion in planning any training program is whether there will be jobs available for the graduates. New programs that cannot meet this criterion are not implemented and existing programs that do not continue to meet it are eventually phased out. Within the state technical college system, districts provide different training based on their regional employment needs. All proposed new programs must pass reviews at both the state and district levels before they are approved. However, once approved at the state level a program may then be implemented in any other district college as well. The Community Developmental Disabilities Associate program has been operating within the Madison Area Technical College since 1983, having just entered its fourth year of implementation. Two other district colleges have expressed an interest in establishing this program in their regions.

Establishing the CDDA program within the Wisconsin Technical College system required almost 2 years, partly because of the normally lengthy review process and partly because of fiscal concerns of the Madison Area Technical College, which limited all new program initiatives. Despite this delay, the program's benefits outweighed the inconveniences. First, it has been established within a generic educational system, which gives it both community visibility and respectability as a legitimate vocational training program. This status is particularly important to student recruitment efforts at the high school level. Second, as a fully sanctioned training program, its budget comes from local and state property tax revenues that support the entire college. So, unlike grant-funded demonstration projects that usually disappear at the end of the grant period if they are not absorbed within an existing system, this program has a permanent place within the Wisconsin Technical College system as long as students enroll and its graduates obtain jobs.

The actual planning and implementation of the program itself can serve as a model of cooperative, system-wide, integrated efforts among a variety of adult service agencies, advocates, consumers, parents, and educators. Representatives of the university, the State Association for Retarded Citizens, and New Concepts Foundation for the Handicapped, Inc.—the largest provider of community residential services in Wisconsin—initiated the planning efforts. They were subsequently joined by representatives of the Wisconsin Council on Developmental Disabilities, the State Bureau of Community Services, the Department of Public Instruction, and the American Federation of State, County, and Municipal Employees (AFSCME Council 24), several directors of vocational and residential programs in the Madison area, the County Unified Services Board, United Cerebral Palsy of Wisconsin, parents, advocates, and consumers. This group evolved into the program's advisory committee.

The following six objectives were established for the program:

1. Establish a basic, yet comprehensive, quality statewide training program that will provide training, skills, and competencies needed by employees who work in community programs with people who have developmental disabilities.

2. Meet and upgrade standards for personnel working in community programs for developmentally disabled persons.

3. Assist current and future employers by providing personnel who can deliver quality community support services.

4. Increase job satisfaction and reduce job turnover among personnel.

5. Increase the number of persons with developmental disabilities being appropriately served in the community.

6. Aim for student growth in their: 1) perceptions of themselves as individuals, 2) development of good communication skills, 3) development of an understanding of human behavior, 4) development of an appreciation for the skills, abilities, and

needs of individuals with developmental disabilities, and 5) development of a working knowledge of the community service system.

A curriculum subcommittee of the advisory group was formed to review training materials from throughout the country, to modify these where appropriate, and to develop new curricula as needed. A vital component of these activities was the ongoing input and review by residential and vocational service providers to ensure that the curriculum was functionally synchronized with local job demands. Their input provided the major direction for the curriculum.

The curriculum consists of 66 semester hours of coursework. There are approximately 39 hours in the major field of developmental disabilities. In addition there are five credits of field placement during the second year, in which students are actively engaged in applying the skills learned from their classes under supervision available at the site and through instructor visits and meetings.

Now that the program is operational, the advisory committee reviews program activities and identifies new training needs on an ongoing basis. Two of the new options being considered include a course in middle management and an adult education practicum in which students will serve as teachers/tutors for developmentally disabled adults who enroll in adult education classes at the college. Considerable flexibility will be built into this program so that student teachers will provide individualized instruction either on-site at the technical college or at the person's home, job, or any other location relevant to the individual's specific needs.

Monitoring a training program to identify its strengths and its weaknesses is often limited, if even done at all, to ascertaining whether the trainees were satisfied or whether they learned the new material as determined by pretest-posttest differences. Usually missing are data on which to evaluate the program's impact (i.e., Did it make a difference in the service system?, Are employers pleased with the performance of the trainees?).

Long-term monitoring and evaluation is a vital component of the CDDA program. Not only will this monitoring provide the fine tuning needed to make it a high-quality program but it will also provide a means to determine whether the program is meeting its objectives. A 5-year evaluation plan, in which both graduates and their current and future employers are followed on an annual basis, is now in place. Specifically, the evaluation will provide answers to the following questions:

1. Where, in which contexts, and under what conditions are CDDA graduates working, and how do these change over time?
2. To what extent are the skills taught in the program relevant to the positions the graduates obtain in the developmental disabilities field?
3. What are the turnover and absenteeism rates for CDDA graduates?
4. Do employers view the CDDA degree as an asset and how do the graduates compare to non-CDDA trained personnel?
5. What are the areas of job satisfaction and dissatisfaction for graduates?
6. What relationships exist among the work environment, job satisfaction, turnover, and absenteeism?
7. How do graduates' expectations about their future work change as a function of the programs, and how do they change when graduates are actually working in the field?

Sufficient flexibility is built into the program to allow it to meet the needs of a variety of different trainee constituencies. For example, individuals with prior experience in the field may have some of their practicum course requirements waived. In addition, because each course is competency-based, students who are able to demonstrate their knowledge through pretesting can "test out" of a course.

Many of the students now enrolled in the program are already employed and are not as interested in obtaining the degree as they are in taking a specific course(s), such as behavior management. Some of the parents who have enrolled have also been primarily interested in acquiring specific information through a course or two, rather than the full degree. Of course, the program is also interested in attracting new students to the field too. Through program advertising, high school career days, and word-of-mouth, this year's class is made up of many young people who have entered the field because they have a relative or friend who is handicapped or simply because they are interested in the area.

In Wisconsin, as well as in other states, the waiver provisions of the Budget Reconciliation Act of 1981 (PL 95-35) have renewed interest and activity in deinstitutionalization. Retraining of institutional staff who are preparing for jobs in the community service system is another important consideration. This group represents a constituency whose numbers, although relatively small at this time, are expected to grow in the future.

Although the first class has yet to graduate from the CDDA program, a range of job possibilities and opportunities await them within the existing community services structure. And, of course, new possibilities, such as those within nonsheltered supported employment— serving as job coaches, transitional assistants, or ongoing support persons—are gaining in popularity and represent an important new area in which these graduates could make significant contributions.

At this point, the most critical issue that the advisory committee is attempting to address is to reduce the pay differentials between state employees who work for the public institutions and community service providers who work for private agencies. It is obviously imperative, not only for the long-term success of the CDDA program but also for the whole community services movement in general, to ensure that people who have the skills and training to provide quality services are able to receive compensation, benefits, and career ladder opportunities (Schalock, 1983) that are better than would normally be available to people without these additional skills and training.

SUMMARY

In this chapter an array of training concerns and issues pertinent to preparing personnel who are qualified to serve developmentally disabled adults have been reviewed. This has not been an easy undertaking, given the rapidly changing adult services system and the diverse clientele it is expected to serve. Nevertheless, the authors have attempted to integrate their own visions of future training needs with projections based on the available literature. Although there was a brief review of some of the health-related professions that are projected to increase in the future, it was the authors' position that over and above any specific skills there is a general knowledge base that must underlie all training programs. Important components of this base are developing one's sensitivity to the importance of one's interactions with developmentally disabled adults and recognizing how influential these and others' interactions are across time and settings.

Many individuals, including professionals (generic and specialized), parents, paraprofessionals, community service providers, and the person on the street, play important direct and indirect roles in facilitating the integration of developmentally disabled adults into normal community settings. In the school system alone, we will need vocational rehabilitation counselors to work with teachers, and special education and vocational education teachers who not only assist in job development, placement, and supervision but also serve as liaisons between special education and vocational education programs. In the community we need job developers who market developmentally disabled adults to employers and paraprofessionals who serve as on-the-job coaches and support personnel.

Parents and/or significant others—as well as handicapped consumers themselves in some cases—are usually in the best position to advocate for individual needs. However, because of their lack of information about adult services and resources and their limited knowledge about what can be accomplished and how to best have access to services, they are often in reactive rather than proactive positions as they try to work effectively with the service delivery system. Through effective training, parents and/or significant others can become the "glue" that reduces system fragmentation and makes interagency collaboration work for their handicapped family member.

We need to continue expanding our efforts to utilize the generic service system better. Improved training of mental health service providers (Reiss & Trenn, 1984; Szymanski & Grossman, 1984) whose biases currently limit these services (Alford & Locke, 1984) certainly ranks as a high priority, given that the prevalence of psychopathology among mentally retarded persons is four to five times that of the normal population (Matson, 1984).

Bus drivers (Queen City Metro, 1981), police officers, firefighters, barbers, and taxicab drivers all need to become more familiar with the special characteristics and needs of developmentally disabled individuals while simultaneously becoming desensitized to their own fears, biases, and stereotypes that inter-

fere with serving them as part of their daily clientele.

As the primary training arm of the Administration on Developmental Disabilities, UAFs are the most logical choice for playing a critical leadership role in reorienting training to serve the needs of adults with developmental disabilities and the individuals who have an impact on their lives.

Finally, we must not lose sight of our continuing need to find better ways through training to improve the social competency of developmentally disabled persons. Presenting only a minimal discussion on their training needs has been by design because it is the authors' contention that the social-interpersonal difficulties of developmentally disabled persons are often an indication of a broader system problem (Karan & Berger, 1986). Yet, as participating members in any human interaction, the better the social competencies of developmentally disabled adults, the greater the likelihood of their sustaining rather than repelling important social relationships.

REFERENCES

Alford, J. D., & Locke, B. J. (1984). Clinical responses to psychopathology of mentally retarded persons. *American Journal of Mental Deficiency, 89*, 195–197.

Arnold, M. (1985). Parent training and advocacy. In M. G. Fifield & B. C. Smith (Eds.), *Personnel training for serving adults with developmental disabilities* (pp. 99–116). Logan: Utah State University Developmental Center for Handicapped Persons.

Beauregard, R., & Indik, B. (1979). *A human service labor market: Developmental disabilities.* New Brunswick, NJ: Center for Urban Policy Research.

Bell, N. J. (1976). IQ as a factor in community lifestyle of previously institutionalized retardates. *Mental Retardation, 14*(3), 29–33.

Bellamy, G. T., Rhodes, L. E., Wilcox, B., Albin, J., Mank, D. M., Boles, S. M., Horner, R. H., Collins, M., & Turner, J. (1984). Quality and equality in employment services for adults with severe disabilities. Unpublished manuscript. Eugene, OR: University of Oregon.

Bennett, F. C. (1982). The pediatrician and the interdisciplinary process. *Exceptional Children, 48*, 306–314.

Benson, A. (1979). *University Affiliated Facilities: A*

primary resource in improving services for developmentally disabled persons. Washington, DC: American Association of University Affiliated Programs.

Benson, F. A., Hitzing, W., & Kozlowski, R. (Eds.). (1981). *Linking service and training systems in the 1980s.* Columbus, OH: Nisonger Center, The Ohio State University.

Berger, C. L. (1984). Survey of UAF training coordinators on training activities with developmentally disabled adults. Madison, WI: Rehabilitation Research and Training Center in Mental Retardation, University of Wisconsin.

Bernstein, G. S., & Karan, O. C. (1979). Obstacles to vocational normalization for the developmentally disabled. *Rehabilitation Literature, 40*(3), 66–71.

Bernstein, G. S., & Rudrud, E. R. (1980, May). The case for professionalization skill maintenance for direct care staff. Paper presented at the American Association on Mental Deficiency. San Francisco, CA.

Bernstein, G. S., & Ziarnik, J. P. (1982). Proactive identification of staff development needs: A model and methodology. *The Journal of The Association for The Severely Handicapped, 7*(3), 97–104.

Best-Sigford, B., Bruininks, R. H., Lakin, K. C., Hill,

B. K., & Heal, L. W. (1982). Resident release patterns in a national sample of public residential facilities. *American Journal of Mental Deficiency, 87,* 130–140.

Bilvosky, D., & Matson, J. (1977). *Community colleges and the developmentally disabled.* Washington, DC: American Association of Community and Junior Colleges.

Bloch, A. (1984). *Murphy's Law 1984.* Los Angeles, CA: Price/Stern/Sloan Publishers, Inc.

Boyan, C., & Kaplan, P. (1980). Preparing teachers to work with exceptional adults. *Exceptional Children, 46,* 557–559.

Brown, L. (1984). Keynote address. State Vocational Planning Conference. September 22, 1984. Madison, WI.

Bruininks, R. H., Kudla, M. J., Wieck, C. A., & Hauber, F. A. (1980). Management problems in community residential facilities. *Mental Retardation, 18* 125–130.

Byrd, G. R., Sawyer, B. P., & Locke, B. J. (1983). Improving direct care via minimal changes in conventional resources: An empirical analysis. *Mental Retardation, 21,* 164–168.

Carlin, E., Nelson, A. S., Richardson, M., Sills, C. J., & West, M. A. (1981). *Human resources assessment project.* Seattle, WA: Child Development and Mental Retardation Center, University of Washington.

Colby, A. (1984, October). *Pathways to employment for the developmentally disabled adult conference.* Boston, MA.

Cooke, R. E. (1966). Residency training—A summary of the findings of the PREP Committee. *Pediatrics, 38,* 720–725.

Crawford, J. L., Aiello, J. R., & Thompson,D.(1979). Deinstitutionalization and community placement: Clinical and environmental factors. *Mental Retardation, 17,* 59–63.

Durlak, J. A. (1982). Training programs for paraprofessionals: Guidelines and issues. In A. M. Jeger & R. S. Slotnick (Eds.), *Community mental health and behavioral-ecology* (pp. 445–457). New York: Plenum Press.

Edgerton, R. B., & Bercovici, S. M. (1976). The cloak of competence: Years later. *American Journal of Mental Deficiency, 80,* 485–497.

Federal Bureau of Labor Statistics. (1980). Reported in *Occupational Outlook Handbook: 1982–83.* Washington, DC: U.S. Government Printing Office (Stock Number O 29-001-02651-0).

Fifield, M. G., & Smith, B. C. (Eds.). (1985). *Personnel training for serving adults with developmental disabilities.* Logan: Utah State University Developmental Center for Handicapped Persons.

Fiorelli, J. S. (1982). Community residential services during the 1980's: Challenges and future trends. *The Journal of the Association for the Severely Handicapped, 7*(4), 14–18.

Fiorelli, J. S., Margolis, H., Heverly, M. A., Rothchild, E., & Keating, D. J. (1982). Training resident advisors to provide community residential services: A university-based program. *The Journal of the Association for the Severely Handicapped, 7*(1), 13–19.

Foss, G., & Bostwick, F. (1981). Problems of mentally retarded adults: A study of rehabilitation service consumers and providers. *Rehabilitation Counseling Bulletin, 25*(2), 66–73.

Gardner, W. I, Karan, O. C., & Cole, C. L. (1984). Assessment of setting event influencing functional capacities of mentally retarded adults with behavior difficulties. In A. S. Halpern & M. J. Fuhrer (Eds.), *Functional assessment in rehabilitation* (pp. 171–185). Baltimore, MD: Paul H. Brookes Publishing Company.

Garrard, S. D. (1982). Health services for mentally retarded people in community residences: Problems and questions. *American Journal of Public Health, 72,* 1226–1228.

Gartner, A. (1979). *Career ladders and a training model for the (re)training of direct service workers in community-based programs for the developmentally disabled.* New York: New Careers Training Laboratory, Center for Advanced Study in Education, City University of New York.

George, M. J., & Baumeister, A. A. (1981). Employee withdrawal and job satisfaction in community residential facilities for mentally retarded persons. *American Journal of Mental Deficiency, 85,* 639–647.

Gotowka, T. D., Johnson, E. S., & Gotowka, C. J. (1982). Costs of providing dental services to adult mentally retarded: A preliminary report. *American Journal of Public Health, 72,* 1246–1250.

Greenspan, S., & Shoultz, B. (1981). Why mentally retarded adults lose their jobs: Social competence as a factor in work adjustment. *Applied Research in Mental Retardation, 2,* 23–28.

Guralnick, M. J. (1982). Pediatrics, special education, and handicapped children: New relationships. *Exceptional Children, 48,* 294–295.

Guralnick, M. J., Richardson, H. B., & Heiser, K. E. (1982). A curriculum in handicapping conditions for pediatric residents. *Exceptional Children, 48,* 338–346.

Haggerty, R. J. (1974). The changing role of the pediatrician in child health care. *American Journal of Disabled Children, 127,* 545–549.

Humm-Delgado, D. (1979). Brief reports: Opinions of community residence staff about their work responsibilities. *Mental Retardation, 17,* 250–251.

Intagliata, J., & Doyle, N. (1984). Enhancing social support for parents of developmentally disabled children: Training in interpersonal problem solving skills. *Mental Retardation, 22,* 4–11.

Jadkins, B. L., & Harrison, A. (1979, August). Education of nurses in mental retardation: National survey of NLN accredited baccalaureate nursing programs in the United States.

Janicki, M. P., Mayeda, T., & Epple, W. (1983). Availability of group homes for persons with mental retardation in the United States. *Mental Retardation, 21,* 45–51.

Jeger, A. M., & Slotnick, R. S. (1982). *Community mental health and behavioral ecology.* New York: Plenum Press.

Karan, O. C. (1981). Project deinstitutionalization: Using extended evaluation to enable institutionalized severely developmentally disabled persons to demonstrate their vocational rehabilitation potential. *International Journal of Rehabilitative Research, 4*(1), 69–71.

Karan, O. C., & Berger, C. L. (1986). Developing support networks for individuals who fail to achieve competitive employment. In F. R. Rusch (Ed.), *Competitive employment issues and strategies.* Baltimore: Paul H. Brookes Publishing Co.

Karan, O. C., & Schalock, R. L. (1983). Who has the problem? An ecological perspective on habilitation programming for behaviorally involved persons. In O. C. Karan & W. I. Gardner (Eds.), *Habilitation practices with the developmentally disabled who present behavioral and emotional disorders* (pp. 77–91). Madison, WI: Research and Training Center in Mental Retardation.

Kregel, J. (1985). Training direct-care providers. In M. G. Fifield & B. C. Smith (Eds.), *Personnel training for serving adults with developmental disabilities* (pp. 84–98). Logan: Utah State University Developmental Center for Handicapped Persons.

Lakin, K. C., Krantz, G. C., Bruininks, R. H., Clumpner, J. L., & Hill, B. K. (1982). One hundred years of data on populations of public residential facilities for mentally retarded people. *American Journal of Mental Deficiency, 87,* 1–8.

Lattimore, J., Stephens, T. E., Favell, J. E., & Risley, T. R. (1984). Increasing direct care staff compliance to individualized physical therapy body positioning prescriptions: Prescriptive checklists. *Mental Retardation, 22,* 79–84.

Magrab, P. R., & Elder, J. O. (1979). *Planning for services to handicapped persons: Community, education, health.* Baltimore, MD: Paul H. Brookes Publishing Company.

Matson, J. (1984). Psychotherapy with persons who are mentally retarded. *Mental Retardation, 22,* 170–175.

McInerney, M., & Karan, O. C. (1981). Federal legislation and the integration of special education and vocational rehabilitation. *Mental Retardation, 19,* 21–24.

Menolascino, F. J. (1980). Preparing paraprofessionals to serve the severely-profoundly retarded in the '80's. In *Symposium on issues in training paraprofessionals and professional persons to work with severely and profoundly handicapped children and adults* (pp. 7-16). Omaha, NE: Meyer Children's Rehabilitation Institute, The University of Nebraska Medical Center.

Middendorf, K. L., Fifield, M., & Smith, B. (1985). Personnel training needs assessment. In M. G. Fifield, & B. C. Smith (Eds.), *Personnel training for serving adults with developmental disabilities* (pp. 42–66). Logan: Utah State University Developmental Center for Handicapped Persons.

Mittler, P. (1981). Strategies for manpower development in the 1980's. *Journal of Practical Approaches to Developmental Handicap, 4*(3), 23–27.

Moran, W. (1984). *Program inspection on the transition of developmentally disabled young adults from school to adult services.* Paper presented at the Administration on Developmental Disabilities Regional Forum West, Denver, CO.

National Institute on Mental Retardation. (1972). *National manpower model.* Toronto, Canada: National Institute on Mental Retardation.

Neufeldt, A. (1978). Training of personnel for mental retardation programmes. In *Vocational rehabilitation of the mentally retarded* (pp. 59–68). Geneva, Switzerland: International Labour Office.

Neufeldt, A. (1980). Future training issues. In *Symposium on issues in training paraprofessionals and professional persons to work with severely and profoundly handicapped children and adults* (pp. 36–37). Omaha, NE: Meyer Children's Rehabilitation Institute, The University of Nebraska Medical Center.

Niziol, O. M., & DeBlassie, R. R. (1972). Work adjustment and the educable mentally retarded adolescent. *Journal of Employment and Counseling, 9,* 158–166.

Novak, A. R., & Heal, L. W. (1980). *Integration of developmentally disabled individuals into the community.* Baltimore, MD: Paul H. Brookes Publishing Company.

O'Connor, G. (1976). *Home is a good place: A national perspective on community residential facilities for developmentally disabled persons* (Monograph 2). Washington DC: American Association on Mental Deficiency.

Office of the Inspector General. (1984). *A program inspection on transition of developmentally disabled adults from school to adult services.* Washington, DC: U.S. Government Printing Office.

Pfriem, D. C. (1979). *Inservice training: A follow-up survey.* Unpublished report. Minneapolis, MN: REM, Inc.

Pfriem, D. C. (1980). *Tinkers-to-evers but no chance: Staff training as a cooperative effort.* Unpublished report. Minneapolis, MN: REM, Inc.

Pickett, A. L., & Humm, A. (1981). *Paraprofessional bibliography: Training materials, resources, and programs for paraprofessionals working in educational programs for persons with handicapping conditions.* New York: New Careers Training Laboratory, Center for Advanced Study in Education, City University of New York.

Powers, J. T., & Healy, A. (1982). Inservice training for physicians serving handicapped children. *Exceptional Children, 48,* 332–336.

Queen City Metro. (1981). *An instructor's manual, disability awareness, for bus operators.* Adapted from the George Washington University Medical Center Rehabilitation Research and Training Center Number 9 Transportation Project. Cincinnati, OH: Queen City Metro/SORTA.

Reiss, S., & Trenn, E. (1984). Consumer demand for outpatient mental health services for people with mental retardation. *Mental Retardation, 22,* 112–116.

Richardson, S. A. (1978). Careers of mentally retarded young persons: Services, jobs, and interpersonal relations. *American Journal of Mental Deficiency, 82,* 349-358.

Richardson, M., West, P., & Fifield, M. (1985). Preservice and professional training. In M. G. Fifield & B. C. Smith (Eds.), *Personnel training for serving adults with developmental disabilities* (pp. 67–83). Logan: Utah State University Developmental Center for Handicapped Persons.

Richmond, J. B. (1975). An idea whose time has arrived. *Pediatric Clinics of North America, 22,* 517–523.

Roeher, G. A. (1981). Service systems and human resources issues: A cost benefit approach to personnel utilization. In F. A. Benson, W. Hitzing, & R. Kozlowski (Eds.), *Linking service and training systems in the 1980's* (pp. 8–27). Columbus, OH: Nisonger Center, The Ohio State University.

Rosen, M., Clark, G. R., & Kivitz, M. S. (1977). *Habilitation of the handicapped: New dimensions in programs for developmentally disabled.* Baltimore, MD: University Park Press.

Rusch, F. (1979). Toward the validation of social/vocational survival skills. *Mental Retardation, 17,* 143–145.

Rusch, F. R., & Mithaug, D. E. (1980). *Vocational training for mentally retarded adults*. Champaign, IL: Research Press.

Schalock, R. L. (1983). *Services for developmentally disabled adults*. Baltimore, MD: University Park Press.

Schalock, R. L., Harper, R. S., & Genung, T. (1981). Community integration of mentally retarded adults: Community placement and program success. *American Journal of Mental Deficiency, 85*, 478–488.

Scheerenberger, R. (1981). Human service person power for developmentally disabled persons. In T. Muzzio & J. Koshel (Eds.), *Alternate community living arrangements and non-vocational social services for developmentally disabled people*. Washington, DC: The Urban Institute.

Skarnulis, S. (1976). Least restrictive alternatives in residential services. *American Association for the Education of Severely Profoundly Handicapped Review, 1*, 1–20.

Sowers, J., Thompson, L., & Connis, R. (1979). The food service vocational training program: A model for training and placement of the mentally retarded. In G. T. Bellamy, G. O'Connor, & O. Karan (Eds.), *Vocational rehabilitation of severely handicapped persons: Contemporary service strategies* (pp. 151–205). Baltimore: University Park Press.

Stedman, D. (1977). Special concerns summary and issues on service delivery. In *Awareness papers*. Washington, DC: White House Conference on Handicapped Individuals.

Sutter, P., Mayeda, T., Call, T., Yanagi, G., & Yee, S. (1980). Comparison of successful and unsuccessful community placed mentally retarded persons. *American Journal of Mental Deficiency, 85*, 262–267.

Szymanski, L., & Grossman, H. (1984). Guest editorial: Dual implications of "dual diagnosis." *Mental Retardation, 22*, 155–156.

Task Force in Pediatric Education. (1978). *The future of pediatric education*. Evanston, IL: American Academy of Pediatrics.

Tjosvold, D., & Tjosvold, M. M. (1981). *Working with mentally handicapped persons in their residences*. New York: The Free Press.

Tjosvold, D., & Tjosvold, M. M. (1983). Social psychological analysis of residences for mentally retarded persons. *American Journal of Mental Deficiency, 88*, 28–40.

Valera, R. (1982). Self advocacy and changing attitudes. In *A public awareness viewpoint*. Washington, DC: American Coalition for Citizens with Disabilities.

Vittelo, S. J., Atthowe, J. M., & Cadwell, J. (1983). Determinance of community placement of institutionalized mentally retarded persons. *American Journal of Mental Deficiency, 87*, 539–545.

Wehman, P. (1981). *Competitive employment: New horizons for severely disabled individuals*. Baltimore, MD: Paul H. Brookes Publishing Company.

Willer, B., Ross, M., & Intagliata, J. (1980). Medical school education in mental retardation. *Journal of Medical Education, 55*, 589–594.

Wolraich, M. L. (1982). Communication between physicians and parents of handicapped children. *Exceptional Children, 48*, 324–329.

Ziarnik, J. P., & Bernstein, G. S. (1980, September). Evaluation of a program designed to teach behavioral skills to direct care staff. (Manuscript submitted for publication.)

Ziarnik, J. P., Rudrud, E. H., & Bernstein, G. S. (1981). Data vs. reflections: A reply to Moxley and Ebert. *Mental Retardation, 19*, 251–252.

∞ Chapter 20 ∞

Research Demands of the Future

Jack A. Stark, Robert L. Schalock, and Betty Jo Berland

THE PURPOSE OF THIS CHAPTER IS TO PROVIDE A comprehensive review of past, present, and future research strategies on employment of the developmentally disabled adult. The intent of the authors is to present a basic overview of the nature and types of research on this topic, where the research is being conducted, by whom, and a past-present-future analysis of research foci. In addition, the utilization of this research, as well as recommendations for future directions as they relate to the Pathways model presented in this volume, are shared with the reader.

THE NATURE OF RESEARCH

Research is defined as the systematic application of empirical methods for specifying which interventions cause change in clients. Although the parameters of research can include interventions applied to individuals, groups, programs, models, or locations, the major purpose of research as proposed in this chapter is to predict which habilitation approaches will produce the greatest independence and productivity. There are an enormous number of variables to control for and evaluate when we seek answers to such questions as "which specific techniques work best?, which model programs are most effective?, who are the best teachers or trainers?, and under what environmental conditions can learning and behavioral change best take place?" These variables, which include health factors, medication, living environments, and staff turnover, make it difficult to conduct quality research.

In his classic chapter on vocational preparation and placement of developmentally disabled individuals, Wolfensberger (1967) was highly critical of research in the vocational area. He noted that the quality of research was low because there was poor design and control, lack of cross-validation, lack of confirmation across studies, emphasis on variables associated with deficiencies within the individual rather than the conditions under which training takes place, and weak testing instruments used in making predictions. Although Wolfensberger's analysis of research efforts in the area of employment of developmentally disabled adults was made almost 20 years ago, much of the same criticism could be leveled against research undertaken today. The extensive costs and time involved in conducting research are not the major barriers, it is the lack of researchers.

THE RESEARCHERS

Who are the researchers? Where are they located? And what do they need in order to advance heuristically the knowledge of strategies that will enable the developmentally disabled adult to reach greater levels of economic self-sufficiency? These are difficult questions to answer because there are very few formal academic or scientific societies of researchers in this field. In fact, there are very few full-time researchers on employment of the developmentally disabled adult. Additionally, those individuals who are doing research are most likely doing so on a short-term basis, contingent on soft money. A recent review of the major journals published and presentations made each year in this specialty found approximately 50 authors who contribute to research in a variety of ways. However, the nucleus of individuals in this field include many of the contributors to this book. There are probably another 100 individuals who occasionally contribute to research in this area, depending on the goals and directions of the programs that they help to coordinate or administer. In addition, a survey of the major associations— American Association on Mental Deficiency, The Association for Persons with Severe Handicaps, Council on Exceptional Children, American Psychological Association, and the National Rehabilitation Association—revealed that individuals who work in the vocational habilitation process make up approximately 5%–10% of each professional organization's membership. Of this smaller group, 10% usually engage in research at one time or another. These researchers are located in academic institutions, medical centers, community-based programs, University Affiliated Facilities, research and training centers, and research-demonstration projects.

One of the major trends in research in the area of developmental disabilities has been the involvement of disciplines other than psychology. Along with individuals who have advanced training in vocational rehabilitation, psychologists and special educators continue to dominate employment and training-related research in developmental disabilities. However, psychiatrists, social workers, pediatricians, and occupational therapists have also become interested in this area, as seen by the number of journals outside the mainstream areas of developmental disabilities that are publishing articles about vocational habilitation (e.g., *American Journal of Psychiatry*, *Journal of Occupational Therapy*, and *Pediatrics*).

Until recently, the major journals in developmental disabilities rarely contained articles on employment or rehabilitation issues. However, in the last few years the following major journals have usually carried one article in each of its issues on this topic; this represents about a 5% share of the research published in the major journals listed below:

American Journal of Mental Deficiency
Mental Retardation
Journal of The Association for Persons with Severe Handicaps
Analysis and Intervention in Developmental Disabilities
Research in Mental Retardation
Journal of Exceptional Children

Despite an increase in journal coverage, the major problem still remains the lack of researchers, particularly the development of new researchers coming into the field. An excellent review of this problem is provided by Berkson (1984) who analyzed over 4,000 contributions to two major journals during the past 20 years. He found almost all the researchers in the field of developmental disabilities have doctorates, that these researchers are aging (mean age of 54), and there is a lack of interest on the part of new researchers in the field. Most younger— ages 25–40 years—researchers who contribute to journals have, on the average, a career of somewhat less than 4 years. Further, there is a direct correlation between federal funding and research productivity. His major contention is that the lack of training and decreasing federal funding for traineeships at the doctoral level have resulted in a decline in the number of researchers and the quality of the research conducted. To enable research in this area to continue to expand and grow in view of the changing conditions and needs of the population, new strategies and new approaches will need to be developed (Berkson, 1984).

TYPES OF RESEARCH

Generally, research is broken down into two categories: basic and applied research. Although the authors feel quite strongly that we need to continue to conduct basic research in both the biomedical and behavioral tracks, only a review of applied research is provided here.

There has been a major shift in the last 10 years in research with the developmentally disabled to a greater emphasis on applied research. Applied research in this field is conducted in three major areas: biomedical, behavioral, and psychosocial or "needs" research.

Biomedical Research

In the following areas in the biomedical field, research is beginning to show that we can either prevent disability or improve significantly the level of functioning of developmentally disabled individuals and thus have an impact on their ability to attain economic self-sufficiency (Menolascino, Neman, & Stark, 1983).

Gene Therapy Through gene splicing techniques, the chromosomal abnormalities in Down syndrome, Fragile X syndrome, and other genetic disorders can now be identified; the ability to alter the abnormalities looks particularly encouraging.

Inborn Errors of Metabolism The ability to provide early screening and detection of potentially damaging conditions, such as phenylketonuria (PKU),is but one example of available techniques of identifying and correcting inborn errors of metabolism early enough to prevent a significant developmental disorder.

Infectious Diseases Major research findings have been reported in recent years in this field. The National Institute of Health's research into infectious diseases that produce diminished cognitive functioning has developed intervention strategies at the prenatal, perinatal, and postnatal levels through new vaccines and antibiotic medications.

Developmental Neurobiology Our ability to understand the development of the brain, its maturation, and causes of abnormalities in the fetus has been advanced in the last decade, particularly through the development of expanded computerized diagnostic procedures.

Brain Impairment The ability of the brain to regenerate and repair itself—neuronal plasticity—and the technique of cellular

"transplantation" have gone beyond the basic research stage of animal investigation and are now being utilized with such disorders as Parkinson's disease. Soon, they may be applicable to the treatment of developmentally disabled individuals.

Learning and Memory Enhancers The development and discovery of neuropeptides that increase visual memory, as well as an understanding of the biochemical basis of learning, should enable us to duplicate those biochemical neurotransmitters that can enhance and improve learning and retention.

Nutritional Approaches Serious research investigations in the field of nutrition have revealed an ability to improve intellectual functioning through orthomolecular supplementation, particularly with the mildly disabled population.

Immunology Our ability to identify certain immune system deficiencies has led an initial understanding of causative factors of brain impairments in individuals with autism and other severe neurological impairments.

Neuropharmacological Approaches The burgeoning of new medications has led to better control of such disorders as schizophrenia, epilepsy, and neuromuscular diseases.

Behavior Research

New research findings in the behavioral area tend to be less spectacular than those in biomedical research. Nonetheless, they have just as powerful an impact, particularly on moderately and mildly disabled individuals. These findings in behavioral research are grouped in three major areas.

Cognitive Aspects Development of such techniques as task analysis, systematic reinforcement, contingency management, and shaping procedures has enabled developmentally disabled individuals to acquire sophisticated skills, particularly in the vocational field.

Language Development From laboratory and animal research to the more sophisticated symbolic and complex psycholinguistic theories, we are witnessing a rapid improvement in enhanced language development, which after all is basic to both the way we assess intellectual functioning and teach in our educational system.

Behavioral Disorders Particularly with the population that is the focus of this book—the more moderately and severely disabled individual—and with the movement to de-institutionalization, behavioral disorders have received a great deal of attention in the last decade. In the past, mainly because of environmental demands and the lack of treatment programs, developmentally disabled individuals often learned inappropriate behavioral repertoires. Behavioral research has now provided us with some 200 techniques that have proven useful in teaching sophisticated skills to individuals who have severe behavioral disorders. The development of alternative ways of behaving is thus enabling the developmentally disabled individual to be much more successful in his/her employment endeavors.

A survey of a number of contributors to this book indicated that some very specific areas of behavior research need additional attention. As this population moves toward economic independence, the issues of generalization, maintenance, and acquisition of skills take on great importance. In addition, emphasis should be placed on the utilization of technology with more severely handicapped individuals and the investigation of the ecological/environmental factors that facilitate successful community-based programs and employment. The authors urge the development of good longitudinal studies that provide quality program evaluation and cost-benefit analysis. Finally, a national data-base system with standardized measures should be developed to determine criteria that can be used to evaluate whether treatment approaches and programs have been successful with specific populations.

Support Systems Research

In conjunction with biomedical and behavioral areas, there are a number of research areas that can be identified as ancillary or "needs research" and are critical to successful habilitation of developmentally disabled individuals. These include residential services, family support services, interagency coordination, respite care, recreation, counseling, and transportation. If not addressed successfully, these need areas can inhibit progress and provide tremendous barriers to success even to the best programs, models, and staff.

THE DEVELOPMENT OF REHABILITATION RESEARCH

In this section, the development of research and associated legislation is analyzed, and their interactive impact on services and care of the developmentally disabled individual is examined. The history of the rehabilitation movement in this country has been described in great detail by Obermann (1965) and Cull and Hardy (1972). From an earlier period of public apathy toward the developmentally disabled individual, attitudes have now changed to recognize the economic necessity and social obligation to help the developmentally disabled person move toward independence and economic self-sufficiency. The application of rehabilitation goals to this population is a relatively recent phenomenon, first appearing in the mid-19th century. This philosophy of rehabilitation, particularly regarding the mentally retarded, has been described (White & Wolfensberger, 1969) as a shift from the *desire* to "make the deviant undeviant" (1850–1880), to a *concern* to "shelter the deviant from society" (1870–1890), to *alarm* over "protection of society from the deviant" (1880–1980). The first institutions in this country for disabled individuals were designed for youth and usually had a vocational emphasis. Indeed, in 1885 the superintendent of the Utica, New York State Lunatic Asylum wrote at some length about the conditions and needs of mentally retarded individuals in that state:

> We are of the opinion that much may be done for their improvement and comfort, that many instead of being a burden and expense of the community may be so improved as to engage in useful employment and to support themselves; and also to participate in the enjoyments of society. (Obermann, 1965, p. 81)

The healers of the mid-19th century gave way to the moral teachers of the early 20th century. Some individuals lived to see the pendulum swing back again and to regret their earlier words. The habilitation ideas of Itard and Seguin seemed all but forgotten in the early 20th century, as the emphasis on preparing developmentally disabled adults for return to society was replaced by the focus on eliminating these groups of human beings from society to avoid "contaminating" the general population. For instance, in 1913, Fernald generalized about the moral sensibilities of the mildly retarded and thought them all to be potential criminals. This eugenic movement peaked in the 1920s and then abated.

During the period between the late 1920s and 1950s there was an emphasis both on rehabilitation and on segregation in institutions. In general, the climate became more positive, as there was a reaffirmation of the original habilitation and education principle that disabled individuals could be trained to live within the community setting. Yet, large institutions continued to be the primary mode of treatment for many developmentally disabled individuals, particularly mentally retarded and autistic persons. In most instances, conditions within these caretaker-oriented institutions were directly antithetical to the idea of habilitation.

Passage of Public Law 236 by the 66th Congress in June 1920 was a landmark in the history of rehabilitation in this country. The Civilian Vocational Rehabilitation Act provided for the vocational rehabilitation of individuals disabled in any legitimate occupation and for their return to civil employment. During the period between 1920 and 1943, vocational rehabilitation was a federal system serving *only* physically disabled individuals. The Vocational Rehabilitation Amendments in 1943 expanded the concept of vocational rehabilitation to include *any* services necessary to enable a disabled individual to engage in work. For the first time, mentally retarded citizens, as well as those who were physically disabled, were accepted as rehabilitation clients.

However, little progress in serving developmentally disabled individuals was made until 1954, when rehabilitation services, training, and research were expanded through the National Office of Vocational Rehabilitation. *Rehabilitation research with developmentally disabled began at this time through federal allocations and the awarding of the first research grants.* During the 1950s and 1960s, research efforts focused primarily on behavior modification, which led to new training approaches in the United States. Two avenues of research began to formalize the principles of behavior modification as a clinical approach. One avenue explored the application of learning principles based on Pavlov's conditioning model; the other examined the application of learning principles based on Skinner's analysis of the behavior of organisms (Skinner, 1938).

Kasdin (1978) points out that present-day behavior modification techniques are a cumulative development of earlier research, which resulted in two major approaches: applied behavior analysis and behavior therapy. *Applied behavior analysis* adheres to Skinner's operant psychology, and much of the research developed to date has been formulated on Skinnerism structural theories and paradigms (Skinner, 1953). It is based on such empirical concepts as single subject and multiple baseline research designs. Its initial focus was on research of mentally retarded individuals and behaviorally disordered children in schools and in community and institutional settings. It was through the pioneering efforts of Sidney Bijou, more than any other researcher, that Skinnerian principles were applied to the education and training of developmentally disabled individuals (Bijou, 1966).

Behavioral research during the 1950s and 1960s focused on four areas: diagnosis and assessment, training procedures and techniques, monitoring the progress of training, and maintenance and generalization of acquired learning (Bijou, 1981a). Research on the diagnosis and assessment of developmentally disabled individuals resulted in a wide range of assessment tools, including behavioral interviews, self-reports, behavioral checklists, inventories, rating scales, criterion-referenced tests, and most important, a reliance on direct observation. These training procedures and techniques tended to focus on the role of response consequences in shaping behavior and in developing skills and on the identification of critical antecedent stimuli that maintain behavior. Early research—for example, by Ferster and Skinner, 1957—explored the issue of reinforcers and the impact of different schedules of reinforcement on behavior. A later research thrust—monitoring progress in training—helped establish procedures for data collection, determining the reliability of observations, coding stimuli responses, and determining the effects of systematically altering training techniques and program contents. Particular emphasis was placed on developing a systematic process of ascertaining reliability measures through observation (Birkimer & Brown, 1979). Research on the maintenance and generalization of acquired skills and knowledge explored how stimuli and response flexibility is affected by altering training methods, such as rotating trainers or teachers assigned to individual clients, or by varying the stimuli, response contingencies, materials, and settings. Researchers also investigated the specific conditions that maintain and generalize learned behavior after training has been completed (Stokes & Baer, 1977).

In sum, the early rehabilitation research conducted by Bijou and his colleagues during the 1950s and 1960s applied the learning principles of Skinner, Wolpe, and Eysenck to the population of developmentally disabled individuals with minimal disabling conditions or mild levels of cognitive functioning. This pioneering work was further developed in the 1960s by Zeaman & House (1963) and Crosson (1969) who began to apply learning principles to more moderately and severely retarded individuals, particularly as they related to programming in sheltered workshop environments. In an experimental setting they demonstrated that even severely handicapped individuals were capable of productive behavior in a sheltered workshop.

Their efforts were further advanced by Gold (1973, 1975a, 1976), who demonstrated that

moderately and severely handicapped individuals were capable of performing complex tasks in controlled and sheltered settings. However, it was more his style of presentation and the visual materials and workshops that he presented around the country than his research efforts that led to the reawakening of the national impetus to change our philosophy and attitude toward severely handicapped individuals (Gold, 1975b).

At about the same time, in the early 1970s, many of the contributors to this book began to establish programs, write research grants, and develop replication studies demonstrating that behavioral principles could be applied to entire systems and community-based programs (Bellamy, O'Connor, & Karan, 1979; Lynch, Kiernan, & Stark, 1982; Rusch & Mithaug, 1980; Schalock, 1983).

In addition, in the late 1960s and throughout the 1970s, new legislation greatly expanded eligibility criteria for services and the types of services provided, giving further impetus to the already growing area of rehabilitation research. The 1965 amendments to the Vocational Rehabilitation Act not only expanded research and demonstration projects that developed new methods and techniques for serving developmentally disabled individuals but also created Research and Training Centers. The 1968 amendments emphasized vocational evaluation and work adjustment services, and the Rehabilitation Act of 1973 included a strong mandate to state-federal vocational rehabilitation programs to serve the more *severely* disabled and to involve clients actively in the planning and delivery of vocational rehabilitation services.

The Rehabilitation Act of 1973 marked a major redefinition of rehabilitation efforts in this country. The sole eligibility requirement was no longer the ability to perform "substantial gainful activity," as comprehensive services for independent living, particularly those designed for the severely disabled adult, were also included. The purpose of this new eligibility criterion was to provide alternative living systems to help the individual engage in employment or to support his or her ability to function independently of family or institution. For the first time, funding was provided for such ancillary services as transportation and attendant care, recreational activities, health maintenance, services for children of pre-school age, and appropriate attendant services to decrease the developmental needs of severely handicapped individuals. These 1973 amendments were further strengthened by the 1978 amendments, which included Sections 503 and 504. Although these amendments created a great deal of controversy, they strengthened the emphasis on reducing prejudice and assisting developmentally disabled individuals, particularly in the area of employment. They established a legal mandate by which each employer must make a reasonable effort to hire a disabled individual who has equal talents and skills as a nondisabled applicant. In short, every major piece of national rehabilitation legislation since 1943 has contained references to developmentally disabled individuals—although they have not always been labeled in that way—as a target population for vocational rehabilitation services and has funded concomitant research studies to determine how to best deliver services to that population.

It is anticipated that, as a result of this book and the new emphasis on adult services, research efforts into the 1990s will be expanded. The arms of these efforts will be to measure the effectiveness and efficiency of various employment models—competitive and supported employment—to replicate them, and to exporting them to other state and local communities. These efforts will attempt to establish causal linkages between intervention-training approaches and such dependent or outcome variables as long-term adjustment and economic self-sufficiency. Research projects will also identify those factors that improve the quality of life among developmentally disabled individuals so that service delivery efforts can be structured accordingly. The next section outlines a habilitation formula that can serve as the basis of research and evaluation efforts.

Habilitation Formula
of the Pathways Model

In researching and evaluating the Pathways Model, the following habilitation formula can serve as a helpful guide: Habilitation Formula $(H) = f (L + O + SI + R \times EI5)$.

In this formula, H represents habilitation, which indicates the degree of success in helping developmentally disabled individuals achieve a level of economic independence that they so choose. The letter f signifies that habilitation is a function of five major variables. The first variable, *living (L)*, indicates the quality of one's living or environmental conditions. As has been pointed out in many different chapters, the developmentally disabled individuals' living conditions contribute to the degree of employment success realized by them. The second major variable represents *occupational (O)* status. Occupation is used here to specify those critical aspects surrounding the employment process that determine employment success. A third major determinant of the degree of habilitation success is *social integration (SI)*. This factor reflects the level of integration of the developmentally disabled individual into those social environments and situations that help promote success. Social integration of the individual in the community embodies the principles of normalization, in which appropriate modeling and support systems, such as friends, relatives, and meaningful individuals in their lives, are available to the individual. The fourth major variable in habilitation success is *recreation (R)*. This is a generic term encompassing all those activities or situations that help promote effective utilization of leisure time and provide some meaning and enjoyment for the individual. The last major variable of habilitation is *environmental intensity (EI)*. Obviously, it varies from program to program, but it includes the following common elements essential in achieving success: staff, equipment, finances, facilities, and attitude. It is quite obvious that without the staff, equipment, finances, program facilities, and positive attitude of the staff helping implement all the above components, success cannot be achieved. Often, the lack of some of these elements of environmental intensity is responsible for the failure of a well-designed program, rather than the design and implementation process itself.

This particular concept can best be described by an explanation of the following more specific formula: Occupational Formula (0) = f (P + Opp + S − D × DI).

The first of the five variables that determine occupational success is *preparation (P)*. This is the appropriate amount of evaluation and training that an individual receives before entering employment. The second variable, *opportunity (Opp)*, indicates the options or simply the opportunity that an individual has available. Obviously, many individuals in different parts of the country succeed where others may fail, simply because of the geographic or environmentally specific opportunities available to them. The third variable, *support system (S)*, reflects those critical persons in a developmentally disabled individual's life who provide ongoing emotional support and reinforcement. These individuals may include friends, parents, siblings, or agency personnel. This suport system is similar to that which is available to nondisabled persons. The fourth variable is the negative impact of *disincentives (D)*. As was noted in Chapters 4, 5, and 6, there are a number of disincentives or barriers that keep a person from even entering or becoming successfully employed (e.g., the loss of health care benefits). The fifth major variable represents the multiplication of all these previous variables by a factor reflecting *degree of intensity (DI)*. This concept reflects the level of effort and the degree of sophistication manifested in the preparation, opportunity presented, and the support systems available, minus the disincentives.

RESEARCH UTILIZATION

One of the major criticisms frequently leveled against research is that research findings are not applicable to practice. Consumers complain that the journal articles are too abstract and are read by only 20% of the subscribers,

who are also researchers. Because of this communication gap, less than 10% of the research findings for a given field are ever implemented.

Research utilization is a process by which research results are produced in response to client needs and communicated to policymakers for their use. In short, it is a continuous and ongoing effort. As with any process, it is useful to use "stop action" at discrete points in time to delineate its stages. Figure 1 presents the six important steps and three subsystems in the research utilization process.

Essential elements in the research utilization process include three social systems: 1) the research system that creates and develops research results, 2) the linking system that performs the functions of translating client needs to researchers and disseminating innovations to clients, and 3) the client system that recognizes the needs of research, encourages its initiation, and later adopts innovations that may result.

Research utilization is a reciprocal flow of client needs to researchers. It is important to note that utilization attempts are more likely to succeed when they begin with the user's needs

---

RESEARCH SYSTEM
(Research component)
Function: Create and develop innovations

LINKING SYSTEM — DISSEMINATION
(Training component)
Function: Translate client needs to researchers, and diffuse innovations to clients

CLIENT SYSTEM
(Service component)
Function: Recognize needs for research, and adopt innovations

---

Figure 1. Research utilization in rehabilitation. The communication process in this model involves the constant identification of client's needs, relayed to the linkers for clarification, and then on to the developers to refine. This process continues back and forth in a heuristic fashion leading to further advancement of research findings.

and include a capability to receive and process messages. In the past, research utilization has frequently failed because of its emphasis on messages of research orientation, rather than client use. Investigations into the utilization of research findings demonstrate that research centers frequently fail in their end result because of four common errors: The process does not start with the users' needs, users are bombarded by an information overload, linkages are not provided in the process or not accorded the appropriate attention because it is assumed that if the information is good it will sell itself to the users, and little attention is paid to user feedback about the adequacy of the research utilization activity so that utilization agencies rapidly become outdated and inappropriate, rather than self-renewing.

Finally, a major task of our country's research centers will be to provide a workable and meaningful system for the communication of research results to those who utilized the data for the benefit of the clients (i.e., an intersystemic process versus an intrasystem communication among researchers). As Figure 2 demonstrates, this process involves a constant reciprocal communication process among the developers, users, and clients.

FUTURE DIRECTIONS
OF RESEARCH STRATEGIES

The purpose of this last section of the chapter is to sensitize the reader to the complexity of programmatic research and evaluation. Two premises underlie this discussion of the future direction of research strategies. First, the direction of research in the next decade will be toward more applied and policy-oriented research. Second, the demand for program accountability will increase, along with measurability and reportability requirements.

To be accountable is to be responsible and clear. Yet, questions are often raised regarding "accountable to whom" and "accountable for what." Our experience tells us that we are accountable to a heterogeneous constituency composed of consumers, taxpayers, politicians, staff, and other professionals. Each of us has his or her own accountability perspective and acceptance criteria. In the area of employment services for developmentally disabled adults, we are accountable to this population for their gaining economic benefits and an improved quality of work life and for determining the effectiveness and efficiency of the employment model proposed throughout this book. How this accountability might be realized is described in the following discussion that outlines four proactive research strategies for the next decade.

Research Strategies in the Next Decade

This section briefly discusses four research strategies that individuals in this field may want to use in evaluating the Pathways to Employment Model, given the two premises discussed above. The type of research one

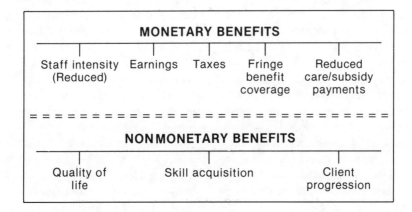

Figure 2. Monetary and nonmonetary benefits.

attempts is dependent on the questions asked, the complexity of available data, and the sophistication of the research efforts. The four research strategies are experimental, formative, summative, and outcome-cost.

Experimental Research   Some research efforts will continue to focus on evaluating hypotheses, determining cause-effect relationships, and conducting experimental-control studies. This research strategy will require random assignment to groups, the ability to control internal and external variance, and informed consent. Experimental research will most likely explore policy considerations concerning such issues as the following:

Programmatic/Intervention Effects   Studies involving random assignment to experimental/control or Program 1/Program 2 conditions will be conducted to determine the effectiveness of such model components as short-term training or supported employment.

Impact Studies   Different employment programs and strategies will be evaluated to determine their impact on outcome measures and quality of community and worklife.

Controlled Multivariate Analysis   Multivariate analysis as an experimental research design will be used to determine the relationship(s) between client and environmental characteristics, including training, employment, and support systems, and selected outcome measures.

Formative Research   Formative research will focus on providing feedback to program managers about their program's effectiveness and efficiency. These data can be used to formulate management hypotheses that can be answered through experimental research. Examples include client-referenced progress variables, such as skill acquisition, wages, quality of life, and movement into environments characterized as more independent, productive, and community integrated; utilization patterns; unit of service costs; quality assurance measures; staff turnover rates; consumer satisfaction surveys; and employer satisfaction surveys. This level of research requires standardized process and outcome measures, a computerized management information system, and management's ongoing commitment to formative research and program evaluation.

Summative Research   The focus of summative research will likely be on planning, budgetary, and systems-level management issues. The purpose of this research strategy is to compare *comparable* programs on standardized outcome measures to determine which of a number of approaches to supported employment or short-term training (as examples) is the most effective and efficient. It is important to realize, however, that summative research can be conducted only on programs with similar goals, objectives, client characteristics, program components, and outcome measures. This research strategy is more sophisticated and demanding because it requires comparable data from similar programs, but it should yield valuable information to policymakers and funding sources regarding the most efficient and productive way to provide pathways to employment for developmentally disabled adults.

Outcome-Cost Research   This research strategy explores strategies and procedures to provide managers and policymakers with some indication of the benefits accruing from a specific program vis-a-vis its cost (see also Chapter 21). The results of outcome-cost research can be used not only to make comparisons among programs but also to answer a critical accountability question among some constituents: "What are we getting for our money?"

As is discussed more fully in Chapter 21, the following important points need to be kept in mind regarding outcome-cost research:

Multiple Perspectives on Outcomes   The majority of current perspectives focus on a social benefit-cost model that calculates both economic and noneconomic aspects into the benefits, as opposed to merely how much the person pays back to society—the "payback model."

Multiple Perspectives on Cost   There is currently no agreed-on formula for cost determination. Hence, some models include opportunity costs, time-related costs, and systems-level (rules and regulations) fixed costs.

Multiple Outcomes   Not all programs have

the same goals and objectives. Therefore, it is necessary to conceptualize a benefits spectrum that focuses on both monetary and non-monetary benefits that might result from employment services for developmentally disabled individuals. The two major components of this spectrum are presented in Figure 3.

The reason for approaching cost-outcome research from a multiple outcome perspective is to minimize the tendency to view cost-outcome as a simple ratio of outcome to cost. Rather, it is essential to realize that benefits and outcomes are multivariate and that the total outcome mosaic must be analyzed before making definitive statements.

These four types of research are presented in Table 1. The four research strategies are not ranked according to level of sophistication, but should be determined by the questions asked,

the available data sets, the research capabilities of the program or system, and the sophistication of the management information system. Any of the four evaluation strategies results in information that should be useful to program managers and policy-level personnel in reaching the objective of developing employment services for developmentally disabled individuals.

In short, we are currently involved in a social experiment, the hypothesis of which is that we can make a difference in the lives and employment status of persons with developmental disabilities. This experiment not only can be conducted, but it must be conducted. Some of the strategies will require experimental research, some formative and summative research activities, and some outcome-cost studies based on a multiple outcome design.

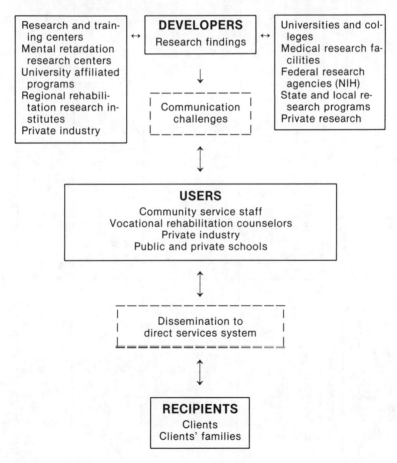

Figure 3. Dissemination chart.

Table 1. Research strategies for the next decade: focus, data requirements, and products

Research strategy	Focus	Data requirements	Products
Experimental	Evaluating hypotheses Determining cause-effect rela- tions Conducting experimental-con- trol studies	Random assignment to groups Control internal-external vari- ance Informed consent — Reliable/valid measures	Programmatic/intervention effects Impact studies Controlled multi-variance analysis
Formative	Management hypotheses Outcome-referenced data re- flecting a program's effective- ness and efficiency	Standardized process and out- come measures Computerized management in- formation system Commitment to formative re- search	Client-referenced outcomes Staff utilization patterns Unit of service costs Quality assurance measures Consumer satisfaction surveys
Summative	Planning Budgetary Systems-level management is- sues	Programs with similar goals, objectives, client characteris- tics, program components, and outcome measures	Comparisons of different pro- grams' effectiveness and efficiency
Outcome-cost	Program benefits	Multiple outcomes Costing-out methodology and capability	Program comparisons Benefit/cost statements

SUMMARY

The authors have attempted to provide the reader with both practical and stimulating information on research strategies relevant to employment issues of developmentally disabled adults. Topics presented were the basic nature of research, the various types of research on this particular topic, who the researchers are, where they are conducting their research, some of the major problems faced by reseachers, the history of rehabilitation research, the habilation formula, and a blueprint for the future direction of research strategies.

It is apparent that, during the next decade, research required by programs that serve adults with developmental disabilities will focus on program effectiveness, efficiency, and outcome measures. Research will take on a much more important status in the development and guidance of policies and legislative mandates. In the future, research activities and findings will have an international perspective, with a reciprocal exhange of research knowledge on the developmentally disabled adult.

In general, scientific achievements grow and develop at an exponential rate, doubling every 10 to 15 years. This phenomenon is reflected in this field at least on a quantitative basis, as one-half of the total accumulated research knowledge on employment issues of the developmentally disabled is the result of research done primarily in the last decade. The authors predict that the growth of scientific research in this field will continue at perhaps an even more accelerated rate. It is hoped that this book will contribute toward that goal.

REFERENCES

Bellamy, G. T., O'Connor, G., & Karan, O. C. (1979). *Vocational rehabilitation of severely handicapped persons: Contemporary service strategies.* Baltimore, MD: University Park Press.

Berkson, G. (1984). *The next generation: The relation between funding and productivity in mental retardation research.* Paper presented at the American Academy on Mental Retardation and the American Association on Mental Deficiency. Minneapolis, MN: May 28, 1984.

Bijou, S. W. (1966). Application of experimental analysis of behavior principles in teaching academic tool subjects to retarded children. In N. B. Haring & R. J. Whelan (Eds.), *The learning environment: Relationship to behavior modification and implications for special education.* Lawrence, KS: Kansas Studies and Education, Unversity of Kansas, School of Education.

Bijou, S. W. (1981a). *Behavioral techniques as the focus of training the developmentally disabled person.* Paper presented at the International Year of the Disabled Person. Commemorative International Symposium on Developmental Disabilities, September 1981. Tokyo, Japan.

Bijou, S. W. (1981b). Behavioral teaching of young handicapped children: Problems of application and implementation. In S. W. Bijou & R. Ruiz (Eds.), *Behavior modification: Contributions to education.* Hillsdale, NJ: Lawrence Erlbaum Associates.

Birkimer, J. C., & Brown, J. H. (1979). Back to basics: Percentage agreement measures are adequate but there are easier ways. *Journal of Applied Behavioral Analysis, 12,* 523–533.

Crosson, J. (1969). Technique of programming sheltered workshop environments for training severely retarded workers. *American Journal of Mental Deficiency, 73,* 814–818.

Cull, J. G., & Hardy, R. E. (1972). *Vocational rehabilitation profession and process.* Springfield, IL: Charles C Thomas.

Eysenck, H. J. (1957). *The dynamics of anxiety and hysteria: An experimental application of modern learning theory to psychiatry.* London: Routledge & Kegan.

Fernald, W. E. (1913). The burden of feeblemindedness. *Journal of Psycho-Asthenics, 17,* 90–91.

Ferster, C. B., & Skinner, B. F. (1957). *Schedules of reinforcement.* New York: Appleton-Century-Crofts.

Gold, M. W. (1973). Research in the vocational habilitation of the retarded: The present, the future. In N. Ellis (Ed.), *International review of research in mental retardation,* Vol. 6. New York: Academic Press, Inc.

Gold, M. W. (1975a). *Remarks from Gold—related research needs in the education of the severely handicapped.* Conference on Research Needs Related to the Education of Severely Handicapped. Princeton, NJ: Education Testing Service and Bureau of Education for the Handicapped.

Gold, M. W. (1975b). *Try another way.* Film Production of Indianapolis, Indiana. (Film)

Gold, M. W. (1976). Task analysis of a complex assembly test by the retarded blind. *Exceptional Child, 43*(20), 78–84.

Kasdin, A. E. (1978). *History of behavioral application: Experimental foundation of contemporary research.* Baltimore, MD: University Park Press.

Lynch, K. P., Kiernan, W. E., & Stark, J. A. (1982). *Prevocational and vocational education for special needs youth: A blueprint for the 1980s.* Baltimore, MD: Paul H. Brookes Publishing Company.

Menolascino, F. J., Neman, R., & Stark, J. (1983). *Curative aspects of mental retardation: Biomedical and behavioral advances.* Baltimore, MD: Paul H. Brookes Publishing Company.

Obermann, C. E. (1965). *A history of vocational rehabilitation in America*. Minneapolis: T. S. Dennison.

Pavlov, I. P. (1927). *Conditioning reflexes: An investigation of the physiological activity of the cerebral cortex*. G. V. Anarp (Ed. & trans). London: Oxford University Press.

Rusch, F. R., & Mithaug, D. E. (1980). *Vocational training for mentally retarded adults: A behavior analytic approach*. Champaign, IL: Research Press.

Schalock, R. L. (1983). *Services for developmentally disabled adults: Development and implementation and evaluation*. Baltimore, MD: University Park Press.

Skinner, B. F. (1938). *Behavioral organisms*. Englewood Cliffs, NJ: Prentice-Hall.

Skinner, B. F. (1953). *Science and human behavior*. New York: Macmillan.

Stokes, T. F., & Baer, D. M. (1977). An implicit technology and generalization. *Journal of Applied Behavioral Analysis, 10*, 349–367.

White, W. D., & Wolfensberger, W. (1969). The evolution of dehumanization in our institutions. *Mental Retardation, 7*, 5–9.

Wolfensberger, W. (1967). Vocational preparation and occupation. In A. Baumeister (Ed.), *Mental retardation*. Chicago: Adeline Publishing.

Wolpe, J. (1958). *Psychotherapy by reciprocal inhibition*. Stanford, CA: Stanford University Press.

Zeaman, D., & House, B. (1963). The role of attention in retardate discrimination learning. In N. Ellis (Ed.), *Handbook of mental deficiency*. New York: McGraw-Hill.

∞ Chapter 21 ∞

Evaluating Employment Services

Robert L. Schalock and Mark L. Hill

IF PROGRAM MANAGERS WERE ASKED WHETHER they were trained to do the tasks they are currently doing the majority would most likely answer "no." They would add that they were not trained in program monitoring and evaluation, that the terms were not in their lexicon 5 years ago, and that program monitoring and evaluation are still not their favorite activity. If one adds the lack of comprehensive data systems and the confusion over operationalizing and quantifying factors that some consider to be "nonquantifiable," it is no wonder why program personnel become frustrated when asked to provide outcome data of their program's effectiveness, efficiency, and benefit (Boschen, 1984). This chapter does not completely eliminate that frustration. It is hoped, however, that it will cause readers to think, conceptualize, and implement systematic monitoring and evaluation activities regarding their employment services for developmentally disabled adults. It might even change their attitude about those activities.

The authors' approach to monitoring and evaluating employment services for developmentally disabled adults is based on two premises. First, if the end product of employment is a degree of economic self-sufficiency, then the focus of monitoring and evaluation should be on the outcomes from employment services. In focusing on these outcomes, the authors utilize a systems model that allows one to monitor and evaluate employment services

based on quantifiable input, process, and output variables. The second premise is that the suggested approach to monitoring and evaluation complements the Pathways Design Model presented in Chapter 7. Because program monitoring and evaluation are essential to that model's success, an attempt has been made to integrate relevant input, process, and outcome variables from other chapters in this book. The result should be two complementary models: one reflecting the desired person-referenced habilitation process and the other outlining the procedures used to evaluate the effectiveness, efficiency, and benefit of that process.

The chapter is divided into three parts. The first section outlines an approach to *systems design* that focuses on three levels of a system (employee, service delivery consortia, and developmentally disabled system) and three components for each level (input, process, and outcome). A systems approach in monitoring and evaluation activities recognizes that a developmentally disabled adult's decision process and options are affected significantly by service delivery and systems-wide variables. In the same way, the outcomes from employment services should have an impact on all three levels of the system. In the second part, a three-phase approach to *monitoring the system* is proposed that includes selecting critical performance indicators, implementing a management information system, and conducting a systems review. The last part focuses on *evaluating the outcomes* through formative, summative, and benefit-cost designs.

A number of figures and tables are used throughout the chapter to facilitate its readibility. By design, the model presented is global, so that it can be generalized across the vast number and diversity of employment training-placement programs. Where appropriate, references are included that describe specific techniques or additional monitoring and evaluation models.

PART 1: SYSTEMS DESIGN

Systems Levels

Bronfenbrenner (1977) has sensitized us to the major social contexts or systems that affect a person's progression through the life cycle. Extrapolating from that notion, the authors propose that the goals and outcomes from employment services for disabled adults can be conceptualized at the level of the employee, the service delivery network, and the larger developmentally disabled system. The diagram in Figure 1 shows goals and desired outcomes for each of the three social contexts or systems that affect adults with developmental disabilities. The purpose of this is to illustrate that monitoring and evaluation activities must be based on clearly articulated goals and desired outcomes. Without these roots, activities will frequently flounder for lack of direction, purpose, and relevance. When one operationalizes and quantifies these components, outcome-oriented service delivery, monitoring and evaluation can be accomplished. This process is discussed in the next section.

System Components

Employment services for developmentally disabled adults need more than eloquently stated goals and outcomes. The plethora of pamphlets, video-slide presentations, and grant applications attest to our ability to promise outcomes; however, what is sorely lacking today are integrated employment services that fulfill these promises by implementing and

evaluating the critical input and process variables associated with each desired outcome as depicted in Figure 1. The input, process, and outcome variables, and the variables related to employment services for adults with developmental disabilities, are listed in Table 1.

Employee Employment services for adults with developmental disabilities are currently affected by a number of concepts, including: 1) that environments have significant effects on behavior (Landesman-Dwyer, 1981); 2) that assessment and training activities should have both ecological and social validity (Brooks & Baumeister, 1977; Hawkins, 1979; Kazdin & Matson, 1981; Rusch, Schutz, & Agran, 1982); 3) that functional and relevant behavioral skill training should occur in the natural environment, where stimulus control, skill maintenance, and skill generalization are maximized (Freagan & Rotatori, 1982; Horner, 1981); 4) that both persons and their environments can be assessed and that job training should focus on critical mismatched client skills/work environment requirements (Schalock & Koehler, 1984; Wehman, Hill, & Hill, 1984); and 5) that the quality of persons' work and community lives should be commensurate with their movement into environments that are more productive and independent. These five concepts coalesce at the employee component pathway summarized in Chapter 7. The inputs are essential in that there must be employment training-placement options, person-environment congruence analysis (see Chapter 18), and individual transition plans (see Chapter 8). Once in place, then training will occur in the natural environment, focus on job/client compatibility requirements, and be phased down when appropriate (Wehman et al., 1984). The resulting outcomes will be those listed in Table 1 and defined more fully in Part 3 of this chapter.

Service Delivery Network/Consortia A consortium is a voluntary alliance of public and private agencies within the same geographical area that is organized for a specific purpose (Baum, Flanigan, Hoke, Parker, Rydman, & Schalock, 1982). This concept is used throughout the chapter to emphasize the need for and benefits from such an alliance (Schalock,

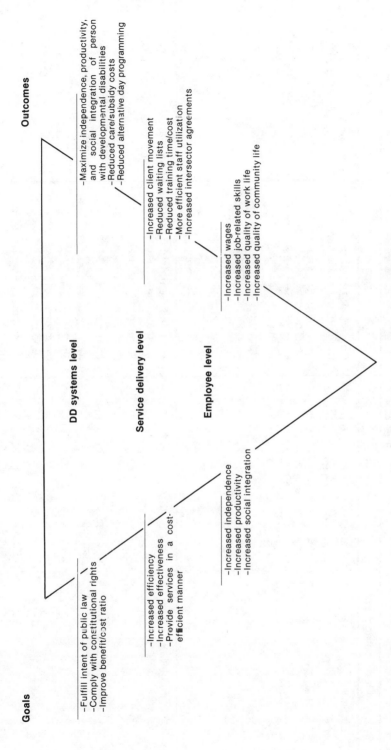

Goals

- Fulfill intent of public law
- Comply with constitutional rights
- Improve benefit/cost ratio

- Increased efficiency
- Increased effectiveness
- Provide services in a cost-efficient manner

- Increased independence
- Increased productivity
- Increased social integration

DD systems level

Service delivery level

Employee level

Outcomes

- Maximize independence, productivity, and social integration of person with developmental disabilities
- Reduced care/subsidy costs
- Reduced alternative day programming

- Increased client movement
- Reduced waiting lists
- Reduced training time/cost
- More efficient staff utilization
- Increased intersector agreements

- Increased wages
- Increased job-related skills
- Increased quality of work life
- Increased quality of community life

Figure 1. Goals and directed outcomes from employment services for individuals with developmental disabilities.

287

Table 1. Critical systems level component pathways and variables related to employment services for adults with developmental disabilities

Systems level component	Input	Process	Outcome

Employee	−Employment/training options
	
	−Person-environmental assessment and goodness to fit/congruence analysis
	
	−Development of individual transition plan
		−Community integrated job training and placement
		
		−Training based on relevant required compatible factors from person-environment analysis
		
		−Community integrated employment services including:
		  −skill acquisition training
		  −generalization training
		  −supervision
		  −case management support
			−Increased wages
			
			−Increased person to job compatibility
			
			−Increased quality of work life
			
			−Increased quality of community life

Service delivery network/consortia	−Intersector agreements →
	
	−Systems-level case man-→ agement
	
	−Employment services → available
		−Establish employment/training/placement options
		
		−Training in natural environment
		
		−Training options
		
		−Appropriate training techniques
		
		−Movement or withdrawal of support
		
		−Employment services provided
			−Increased client movement
			−Reduced waiting list
			−Reduced training time/cost
			−More efficient staff utilization
			−Intersector agreements reflecting shared:
			  −money −facilities
			  −manpower −experience

DD System	HHS employment initiative	-Job-site employment services	-Maximize independence, productivity, and community integration of person with developmental disabilities
Sections 1619 (a) and (b) of Social Security Demonstration program		-Adequate funding	-Reduced alternative programming costs
Public Laws 97-300, 98-199 and 98-221)[a]		-Public/private intersector initiatives	-Reduced care/subsidies to DD persons
		-Technical assistance	

[a]Public Law 97-300, Jcb Training Partnership Act of 1982; 98-199, Education of Handicapped Act of 1983; 98-221, Helen Keller National Center Act of 1984.

1984). The benefits to the developmentally disabled adult include increased training-placement options provided by the interface of public and private entities; training in the natural environment; systems-level case management; and more efficient staff utilization due to the gradual fading of skill acquisition, production, and generalization training to follow-along and case management support. The essential components of intersector agreements can be found in Schalock (1983).

Developmentally Disabled System There have recently been a number of initiatives focusing on the transition of adolescents and adults into the mainstream of social and economic life, rather than into day activity centers or sheltered workshops. If federal, state, and local initiatives continue, and if the previously discussed consortia and employee critical pathways are realized, then Jean Elder's (1984) goal should be achieved to "reduce the prevalence of lifetime dependency which presently is the fate of the great majority of people with developmental disabilities (p. 53).

PART 2: SYSTEMS MONITORING

Selecting Critical Performance Indicators

An essential ingredient in program monitoring and evaluation is to specify objective, measurable, and relevant performance indicators (Rockart, 1979). These indicators reflect a program's effectiveness and can be used, as discussed in Part 3, to determine its efficiency and benefit. A number of critical performance indicators appropriate to the monitoring of employment services for adults with developmental disabilities are summarized in Table 2. References are also included for those readers desiring additional information and/or specific techniques.

The critical performance indicators (CPI) outlined in Table 2 reflect a multiple-outcome approach to monitoring and evaluation. No one program will necessarily focus on all the CPIs, because particular CPIs are related to specific program goals. For example, assume that a consortium's major goals are to improve a

person's economic condition, the consortium's staff utilization patterns, and the development of additional training-placement options. In that case, the CPIs that should be monitored and evaluated would include: 1) at the employee level, fiscal and skill acquisition and 2) at the consortium level, staff functions, unit of service costs, and the number of optional training-placement environments. The purpose of Table 2 is to demonstrate the variety of variables that can be both monitored and evaluated. Before this monitoring and evaluation can occur, however, a management information system must be designed and implemented. The requirements of such a system are outlined in the next section.

Implementing a Management Information System

The major purpose of a management information system (MIS) is to provide data for monitoring a program's or system's CPIs and evaluating the effectiveness and efficiency of the services provided. Data needs vary across organizations, in part because of the relationship among programmatic goals, services provided, and desired outcomes. This notion is illustrated in Figure 2. In general, the authors have found that service delivery programs have three principal MIS needs, which are related to: 1) client characteristics and client tracking/movement, 2) services performed and service costs, and 3) quantifying client and programmatic outcomes. Detailed descriptions of the mechanics and computerization of these data needs can be found in Attkisson and Broskowski (1978), Carter and Newman (1976), Ramanathan (1982), Rossi (1979), Schalock (1983), Suchman (1972), and Sutherland (1977).

Table 3 lists a number of input and outcome MIS data sets that are necessary to monitor and evaluate employment services for the developmentally disabled adult. The data sets relate to the CPIs summarized in Table 2 and the desired outcomes listed in Table 1. They include *only* the employee and consortia/systems level components because the development and implementation of valid state

Table 2. Critical performance indicators used to monitor and evaluate employment services

Systems level component	Critical performance indicators	Examples	References
Employee	-Fiscal	-Wages, taxes paid, subsidies received	Schalock (1986)
	-Quality of work environment	-Quality variables including:	Wehman, Hill, and Hill (1984)
		–decreased intrusive training/supervision	
		–accessibility of company to persons with developmental disabilities	Hill and Shafer (1984)
		–integrated work, lunch, and break areas	
		–marketable skills learned	
		–same work schedules as regular employees	
		–absence of negative stereotypes	
		–variety of jobs	
		–percent of work force and percent of average wage	
		–increased accessibility to promotions	
	-Quality of community life	-Quality variables including:	Brown, Diller, Gordon, Fordyce, and Jacobs (1984)
		–mobility	
		–appearance/physical condition	
		–activity level	
		–independence and community involvement	
		–social/recreational environment	Keith and Schalock (1984)
		–individual decision-making	
		–living arrangements	

(continued)

Table 2. (Continued)

Systems level component	Critical performance indicators	Examples	References
	–Job-related skill acquisition and maintenance	–Skill indicators –Skill acquisition index –Job/person compatibility index –Skill maintenance index	Brown, Diller, Gordon, Fordyce, and Jacobs (1984) Schalock and Harper (1982, 1983) Wehman, Hill, and Hill (1984) Schalock, Gadwood, and Perry (1984)
	–Habilitation techniques employed	–Current skill acquisition and maintenance training techniques –Intervention time required –Prosthetics procurement and use –Environmental modification	Schalock (1983); Weisgerber, Dahl, and Appleby (1980)
Service delivery Network/consortia	–Common service delivery staff functions	–Staff functions including: –skill training –generalization training –case management support –supervision –transportation –on-site advocacy	Schalock (1985)
	–Fiscal	–Units of service cost –Training/placement costs	Thornton (1984) Schalock (1983) Hill and Wehman (1983)
	–Individual transition plans (ITP)	–ITP components including: –person/environmental assessment –transitional objectives –training activities –evaluation strategies –intersector and parental participation –multi-environmental training –integration of living and work learning experiences	Brown, Diller, Gordon, Fordyce, and Jacobs (1984) Schalock and Jensen (in press)

-Intersector agreements	-Agreement components including:
	  -goals and objectives
	  -specific programs and services offered
	  -specific roles, actions, and responsibilities
	  -evaluation strategies
		Lacour (1982)
		Magrab and Elder (1979)
		Schalock (1983, 1986)
		Hill (1984)

-Optional training-placement environments	-Competitive employment -Competitive employment with support -Supported enclaves in industry	Revell, Wehman, and Arnold (1984) Wehman, (1981); Bellamy, Rhodes, and Albin (Chapter 9, this volume)
	-Specialized industrial training -Work training stations in industry -Projects with industry	Bellamy, Horner, and Inman (1979) Paine, Bellamy, and Wilcox (1984) Rusch, Schutz, and Agran (1982) Schalock, (1986) Brickey, Browning, and Cambell (1982) Schalock and Harper (1983)
-Client/employee movement	-Client movement index -Training/placement time -Employees in regular full time/part time employment -Ratio of wages/promotions	Whitehead and Marrone (Chapter 12, this volume) Hill and Wehman (1983)
DD System Service provision Fiscal parameters	-Waiting lists -Number of work activity centers/sheltered workshops -Transfer payments -Support costs -Subsidy payments	Conley, Noble, and Elder (Chapters 4, 5, and 6, this volume)

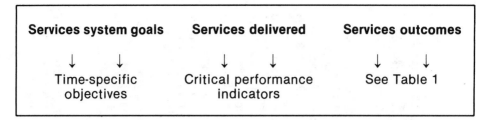

Figure 2.   Relationship among programmatic goals, services provided, and desired outcomes.

and federal MIS systems are beyond the scope of this chapter. References are again provided for those wishing additional details or specific procedures. The MIS data sets listed in Table 3 are not exhaustive, but do represent those sets that the authors consider to be most relevant to monitoring and evaluating employment services. Only when these or comparable data sets are in place can the monitoring process described in the next section occur.

Conducting a Systems Review

The systems approach to service delivery has been advocated throughout this chapter as the most efficient and effective way to conceptualize, monitor, and evaluate services. It assumes that each discrete element of the service delivery system affects each of the other parts; therefore, the monitoring of a system should employ a responsibility center approach that specifies for each critical systems level component the major responsibilities in regard to the input, process, and outcome variables. The proposed systems review process is an internal, self-correcting, monitoring-evaluation process that focuses on the status of a program's critical input, process, and outcome variables. It is not the same as the accreditation process that focuses primarily on input and process (Schalock & Harper, 1982). Systems review is made easier if one also remembers that monitoring is most feasible when it is an integral part of the organization's activities and most effective when it is a continuous process of feedback and planned change. Specific procedures for conducting a systems review can be found in Baum et al. (1982), Bellamy and Wilcox (1983), Schalock (1983), and Schalock

and Harper (1983). The proposed systems review process involves the following six steps:

1. Select the Critical Performance Indicators (CPI) to monitor. Examples are presented in Table 2.
2. Link the selected CPIs to data sets within the Management Information System (MIS). Exemplary MIS data sets are presented in Table 3.
3. Define when and how data will be gathered and the party, entity, or critical pathway from which it will be obtained. These potential sources are listed in Table 1.
4. Establish judgment criteria for acceptance or rejection of evidence in relation to each CPI. Options include "yes/no," "good/ satisfactory/unacceptable," median split absolute scores, or other mutually established judgment criteria.
5. Conduct on-site the activities specified in steps 3 and 4. These activities usually require at least 1 day per program component.
6. Interpret the data and specify the action or correction strategy if needed. Suggestions frequently relate to needed staff competencies, programmatic/data system changes, or training/placement organizational changes, which then become management objectives that are reviewed during the subsequent (usually 6 months) systems review.

PART 3: EVALUATING THE OUTCOMES

All the prerequisites for evaluating program outcomes have been discussed thus far in this chapter. Table 1 outlined the critical input,

Table 3. Management information data sets

Data sets/component level	References
Input/employee level	
1) **Client demographics**	Schalock (1983)
Age; skill acquisition/maintenance production; IQ; wages; taxes paid; hours worked; progression/movement record	
2) **Training/placement environmental profiles**	Schalock and Koehler (1984)
Skills/behaviors required Goodness-of-fit measure Job/client compatibility index	Schalock and Jensen (in press) Wehman, Hill, and Hill (1984)
3) **Quality of life data**	
Quality of work environment variables[a]	Brown, Diller, Gordon, Fordyce, and Jacobs (1984) Wehman, Hill, and Hill (1984)
Quality of community life variables[a]	Keith and Schalock (1984)
Input/consortia level	
1) **Staff functions**[a]	
Referenced to employee Expressed in time/position values	Carter and Newman (1976) Ramanthan (1982)
2) **Individual transition plans**	
Goals/objectives Evaluation criteria	Wehman, Kregel, Barcus, and Schalock (Chapter 8, this volume)
3) **Fiscal**	
Units of service cost[b]	Bellamy, Sheehan, Horner, and Boles (1980)
Transfer payments Subsidy costs	Hill and Wehman (1983) Long, Mallar, and Thornton (1981)
Outcomes/employee level	
Wages per hours worked Number of hours worked/week Taxes paid Job duration Subsidy/transfer costs	Hill and Wehman (1983)
	Brown, Diller, Gordon, Fordyce, and Jacobs (1984)
Skill acquisition and maintenance indices Quality of work and community living indices	Schalock and Harper (1983)
Outcomes/consortia level	
Client movement indices Training time to placement Training/placement cost Unit of service costs	Hill (1984) Schalock (1983) Thornton (1984)

[a]See Table 2.
[b]Allocated to employee and resource center.

process, and outcome variables around which a service delivery network should organize its employment services for developmentaly disabled adults. Table 2 summarized the CPIs that reflect a program's service delivery and can be used to monitor—and now evaluate—a system's effectiveness and efficiency. Table 3 listed those management information data sets that permit quantitative analysis for both formative (internal) and summative (external, comparative) program evaluation activities.

An extensive analysis of the various approaches to program evaluation, design, and techniques is beyond the scope of this chapter. Excellent detailed reviews can be found in Attkisson, Hargreaves, Horowitz, and Sorenson (1978); Hagedorn, Beck, Neubert, and Werlin (1979); Haveman (1976); Long, Mallar, and Thornton (1981); Ramanathan (1982); Rossi, Freeman, and Wright (1975); Rothenberg (1975); Sorensen and Grove (1977, 1978); and Warner and Luce (1982). The purpose of this discussion is to sensitize the reader to four critical factors in outcome evaluation of employment services for the developmentally disabled adult. These are: 1) different program evaluation foci, 2) the distinction between formative and summative evaluation and how it relates to benefit-cost analysis, 3) a proposed "benefits spectrum" that distinguishes between monetary and nonmonetary outcomes, and 4) a proposed procedure for determining the benefits and costs resulting from employment services for developmentally disabled adults.

Program Evaluation Foci

A number of different program evaluation approaches are listed in Table 4 and discussed more fully in each reference cited there. The procedure proposed later in this section incorporates the efficiency and outcome measure focus presented in Table 4, as opposed to an effort on process orientation.

Formative versus Summative Evaluation

Formative evaluation is usually conducted during program or project operation to provide immediate feedback on how well the program is doing in relation to its stated goals, processes, and outcomes. It results in summary statements regarding the status of previously discussed CPIs and/or desired outcomes. Formative evaluation refers to single-program evaluation and requires the MIS outlined in Table 3. Its results are not comparable among programs.

In contrast, summative evaluation is usually conducted after a process has been completed or between programs that have similar input and process variables, such as those listed in Table 1. It incorporates the concept of benefit-cost analysis.

Benefit-cost analysis (BCA) refers to formal analytical techniques for comparing the negative and positive consequences of alternative uses of resources, including money, manpower, facilities, and experiences. BCA requires an analyst or an evaluator to identify, measure, and compare all the measurable significant costs and desirable consequences of alternative programs that are addressing the same problem, such as employment services for developmentally disabled adults. *Its principal objective is to structure and analyze information to assist policymakers.* To quote Warner and Luce (1982):

> It is these individuals, not analysts, who will decide which, if any, of the competing programs will be proposed or implemented. BCA [is] not [a] formula for making decisions. This reflects the subjective, often political, nature of the policies at issue and the conceptual and practical limitations of BCA. If their program is to produce "correct" policy decisions, [BCA] will be found wanting. (p. 47)

Proposed Benefits Spectrum

It is because of both the conceptual and practical limitations of BCA discussed above and the need to provide quantifiable outcome measures for programs for either severely or profoundly handicapped individuals or geriatric disabled persons that the authors propose the benefits spectrum illustrated in Figure 3. The essential premise underlying this spectrum is that a valid distinction can be made between nonmonetized and monetized benefits.

Nonmonetized benefits link monetary input

Table 4. Historical approaches to program evaluation

Effort:

Amount and distribution of resources into program (Suchman, 1967)

Staff utilization patterns (Schalock & Jensen, in press)

Process:

Extent to which program was implemented as designed and services the target population (Posavac & Carey, 1980)

Information about the underlying process by which effort is translated into outcomes (Suchman, 1972)

Review of critical performance pathways and indicators (Schalock, 1983)

Efficiency:

The extent to which the program achieves its success at a reasonable cost (Posavac & Carey, 1980)

Comparison of resource inputs to specified process or outcome variables (Sorensen & Grove, 1977; 1978)

Explanation about how effort is organized to get greatest performance and adequacy (Suchman, 1972)

Outcome:

Assessment of outcomes achieved by the program (Posavac & Carey, 1980)

Assessment of social or economic benefit (Long, Mallar, & Thornton, 1981; Sorensen & Grove, 1977)

Assessment of benefits and effectiveness related to program costs (Carter & Newman, 1976; Warner & Luce, 1982)

to nonmonetary outcome measures. The advantage is that client benefits do not have to be monetized (translated into dollars), only the costs (Rossi et al., 1975). The authors propose that this approach to program evaluation be referred to as "outcome-cost analysis" and that it focus on those person-referenced outcomes that are difficult, if not impossible, to monetize. Examples include quality of work/community living indices, skill acquisition and maintenance indices, and the movement of persons into environments that are more independent, productive, and socially integrated. Similar programs should be comparable on these outcome-cost measures.

In contrast, benefit-cost analysis would focus on those outcome measures that can be monetized. Examples include client-level outcomes, such as earnings and taxes. At the network or consortia level, examples might include training-placement costs, unit of service costs, and direct-indirect cost ratios. At the developmentally disabled system level, model or program comparisons can be made.

Proposed Benefit-Cost Procedure

Decisions need to be made concerning the ultimate value of programs. The questions to be answered are "do the costs justify the outcomes?" and "is this program design the most

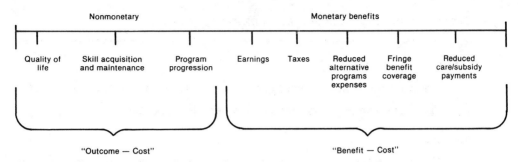

Figure 3.   Components of a benefit spectrum.

efficient way to meet the stated outcome needs?'' The following proposed techniques begin to answer these questions.

The proposed approach can be utilized in two ways. The first, which is less complex, compares a program to the alternative of no program. The second compares a number of programs that are attempting to meet the same goals. This more complex approach should only be utilized when the performance indicators or outcomes of the compared programs are the same. The goal is to identify processes that work and to refine processes so that they work better.

Figure 3 identified some programmatic outcomes for the developmentally disabled population, including wages earned, taxes paid, reduced alternative program expense, and reduced government care/subsidy payments. Each of these factors can be measured whether a program is in place or not, and one can compare the effects of differing program designs on these outcomes. Furthermore, as we begin to objectify and quantify the less tangible nonmonetary outcomes by establishing measurement of their CPIs, we are well on our way to effective monitoring and evaluation.

In applying the proposed benefit-cost procedure, the authors present a model described by Thornton (1984) and utilized by Wehman et al. (1984). The focus is on group data and is from three perspectives: the participant, the taxpayer, and society as a whole.

Thornton (1984) describes five major steps in developing a benefit-cost accounting framework:

1. *Define the program and the standard against which it will be compared.* In this example, the framework is designed to compare a program's effects with the alternative of no program.

2. *Specify the analytical perspectives to be adopted.* The authors look at the outcome effects from the viewpoint of the participant, the taxpayer, and society as a whole.

3. *List the specific benefits and costs.* Tables 5 and 6 outline the factors to be considered.

4. *Establish the prices used to value the various outcomes.* Critical performance indicators (CPI) must be identified for each benefit and cost outcome. Selection must be relevant; that is, there must be flexibility in determining each CPI to reflect differences in individual program and community ecologies. Factual data are used whenever possible. Yet, best estimates can also yield accurate results and are used in some cases. (For example, factual data would be based on the actual budget of an alternative program, whereas a best estimate would be based on a national average of similar programs).

5. *Determine the appropriate techniques for assessing effects that occur at different times.* A detailed analysis of time-related problems associated with valuing monetary effects is presented by Thornton (1984). The major time-related issues include the effects of inflation, discounting, and extrapolation (Ramanathan, 1982).

Table 5. Accounting framework. Monetary benefit-cost of an employment program for the participant, the taxpayer, and for society.

	Benefits	
Society	Participants	Taxpayer
Increased earnings + Fringe benefits + Taxes collected + Decreased cost of alternative support program + Decreased government care/subsidy payments	Increased earnings + Fringe benefits ——— ——— ———	——— Taxes collected + Decreased cost of alternative support program + Decreased government care/subsidy payments
SUBTOTAL +	+	+
	Costs	
Cost of program	———	Cost of program
SUBTOTAL –	0	–
=	Net outcome	
Net monetary societal value	Net monetary participant/ client value	Net monetary taxpayer value

With this framework in mind, Table 5 is presented as the accounting format for operationalizing the BCA. Table 6 is the accounting framework for the nonmonetized factors in the benefit/cost spectrum. In Table 6, the taxpayer is not differentiated from society because separating the taxpayer is for monetary evaluative purposes only.

SUMMARY

There is little doubt that creating viable employment services for developmentally disabled adults will improve significantly their quality of life. Research on these services will also provide the data to test an important social experiment that hypothesizes that this group of

Table 6. Accounting framework. Nonmonetary outcome-cost of an employment program for the participant and for society

Benefits	
Society	**Participant**
Improved quality of life	Improved quality of life
+	+
Increased productivity	Increased skills
+	+
Decreased dependence	Increased independence
+	+
Increased heterogenous representation	Increased mobility
+	+
Decreased segregation	Increased integration
+	+
Improved resource management	Increased programming resources available
− Costs	
− Cost of program	− − − − − − − − − − − − − −
= Net outcome	
− Societal net outcome value	Net participant outcome value

people can become more independent, productive, and socially integrated. An additional hypothesis is that these benefits can be gained with positive monetary consequences. This chapter has suggested that policy decisions concerning each of these goals should be based on tangible systems designs, monitoring, and evaluation. Goals that can and must be measured are: 1) more independence, reflected in community living alternatives, reduced staff assistance and supervision, normalized activity patterns, and reduced care/subsidy payments;

2) increased productivity as measured in competitive wages, hours employed per week, and job duration; and 3) social acceptability as seen in supervisory/co-worker evaluations, appearance changes, person-environment compatability analysis, and parent/guardian surveys.

If something good happens to people because of human service programs, then the task before us is to create the employment and support services that demonstrate that independence, productivity, and social integration are not elusive concepts, but have value for developmentally disabled adults. Goethe expressed this concept well when he is purported to have said, "If you treat an individual as he is he will stay as he is, but if you treat him as if he were what he ought to be and could be, he will become what he ought to be and could be."

REFERENCES

Attkisson, C. C., & Broskowski, A. (1978). Evaluation and the emerging human service concept. In C. C. Attkisson, W. A. Hargreaves, M. J. Horowitz, & J. E. Sorensen (Eds.), *Evaluation of human services programs* (pp. 1–25). New York: Academic Press.

Attkisson, C. C., Hargreaves, W. A., Horowitz, M. J., & Sorensen, L. E. (Eds.). (1978). *Evaluation of human services programs.* New York: Academic Press.

Baum, B. H., Flanigan, P. J., Hoke, G., Parker, R., Rydman, R. J., & Schalock, R. L. (1982). *A sourcebook for developing consortia and community living alternatives systems.* Springfiled, IL: Governor's Planning Council on Developmental Disabilities.

Bellamy, G. T., Horner, R., & Inman, D. (1979) *Vocational training of severely retarded adults.* Baltimore: University Park Press.

Bellamy, G. T., Sheehan, M. R., Horner, R. H., & Boles, S. M. (1980). Community programs for severely handicapped adults: An analysis. *Journal of The Association for the Severely Handicapped, 5*(4), 307–324.

Bellamy, G. T., & Wilcox, B. (1983). *STP model implementation review packet.* Eugene, OR: Specialized Training Program, University of Oregon.

Boschen, K. A. (1984). Issues in evaluating vocational rehabilitation programs. *Rehabilitation Psychology, 29* (1), 37–48.

Brickey, M., Browning, L., & Campbell, K. (1982). Vocational histories of sheltered workshop employees placed in projects with industry and competitive jobs. *Mental Retardation, 20*(2), 52–57.

Bronfenbrenner, U. (1977). Toward an experimental ecology of human development. *American Psychologist, July,* 513–531.

Brooks, P., & Baumeister, A. (1977). A plea for consideration of ecological validity in the experimental psychology of mental retardation. *American Journal of Mental Deficiency, 81,* 407–416.

Brown, M., Diller, L., Gordon, W. A., Fordyce, W. E., & Jacobs, D. F. (1984). Rehabilitation indicators and program evaluation. *Rehabilitation Psychology, 29*(1), 21–35.

Carter, D. E., & Newman, F. L. (1976). *A client-oriented system of mental health service delivery and program management. A workbook and guide.* Rockville, MD: National Institute of Mental Health.

Elder, J. K. (1984). Priorities of the Administration on Development Disabilities for FY 84. *Mental Retardation, 22* (2), 53–54.

Freagan, S., & Rotatori, A. F. (1982). Comparing natural and artificial environments in training self-care skills to group home residents. *Journal of the Association for the Severely Handicapped, 8,* 73–86.

Hagedorn, H. G., Beck, K. J., Neubert, S. F., & Werlin, S. H. (1979). *A working manual of simple program evaluation techniques for community mental health centers.* Rockville, MD: National Institute of Mental Health.

Haveman, R. H. (1976). *The economics of the public sector.* New York: John Wiley & Sons, Inc.

Hawkins, R. P. (1979). The functions of assessment: Implications for selection and development of devices for assessing repertoires in clinical, educational, and other settings. *Journal of Applied Behavior Analysis, 12* (4), 501–516.

Hill, M. (1984). *A rationale and plan for funding a transitional support work approach to competitive employment through the vocational rehabilitation system.* Richmond: Rehabilitation Research and Training Center, Virginia Commonwealth University.

Hill, J., & Scafer, M. (1984). *Research protocol of quality of life factors in competitive employment for severely disabled individuals.* Richmond: Rehabilitation Research and Training Center, Virginia Commonwealth University.

Hill, M., & Wehman, P. (1983). Cost-benefit analysis of placing moderately and severely handicapped persons into competitive work. *Journal of The Association for the Severely Handicapped, 10,* 25–40.

Horner, R. H. (1981). Stimulus control, transfer, and maintenance of upright walking posture in a severely mentally retarded adult. *American Journal of Mental Deficiency, 86*(1), 86–96.

Kazdin, A. E., & Matson, J. L. (1981). Social validation in mental retardation. *Applied Research in Mental Retardation, 2,* 39–54.

Keith, K., & Schalock, R. L. (1984). *Quality of life questionnaire and index.* Lincoln, NE: Governor's Planning Council on Developmental Disabilities.

Lacour, J. A. (1982). Interagency agreement: A rational response to an irrational system. *Exceptional Children, 49*(3).

Landesman-Dwyer, S. (1981). Living in the community. *American Journal of Mental Deficiency, 86* (3), 223–234.

Long, D. A., Mallar, C. D., & Thornton, C. V. D. (1981). Evaluating the benefits and costs of the Job Corps. *Journal of Policy Analysis and Management, 1*(1), 55–76.

Magrab, P. R., & Elder, J. O. (1979). *Planning for services to handicapped persons: Community, education, health.* Baltimore: Paul H. Brookes Publishing Co.

Paine, S., Bellamy, G. T., & Wilcox, B. (1984). *Human services that work: From innovation to standard practice.* Baltimore: Paul H. Brookes Publishing Co.

Posavac, E. J., & Carey, R. G. (1980). *Program evaluation: Methods and case studies.* Englewood Cliffs, NJ: Prentice Hall.

Ramanathan, K. V. (1982). *Management control in non-profit organizations: Text and cases.* New York: John Wiley & Sons, 1982.

Revell, G., Wehman, P., & Arnold, S. (1984). Supported work model of employment for mentally retarded persons: Implications for rehabilitative services. *Journal of Rehabilitation.*

Rockart, J. F. (1979). Chief executives define their own data needs. *Harvard Business Review, 79*(3), 81–93.

Rossi, P. (1979). *Evaluation: A systematic approach.* Beverly Hills, CA: Sage Publications.

Rossi, P. H., Freeman, H. E., & Wright, S. R. (1975). *Evaluation: A systematic approach.* Beverly Hills, CA: Sage Publications.

Rothenberg, J. (1975). Cost-benefit analysis: A methodological exposition. In M. Guttentag & E. L. Struening (Eds.), *Handbook of evaluation research (Vol. II).* Beverly Hills, CA: Sage Publications.

Rusch, F. R., Schutz, R. P., & Agran, M. (1982). Validating entry-level survival skills for service occupations: Implications for curriculum development. *Journal of The Association for the Severely Handicapped, 8,* 32–41.

Schalock, R. L. (1983). *Service for the developmentally disabled adult: Development, implementation and evaluation.* Baltimore, MD: University Park Press.

Schalock, R. L. (1984). Comprehensive community services: A plea for interagency collaboration. In R. Bruininks & C. K. Lakin (Eds.), *Living and learning in the least restrictive environment* (pp. 37–63). Baltimore, MD: Paul H. Brookes.

Schalock, R. L. (1986). Service delivery coordination. In F. R. Rusch (Ed.), *Competitive employment issues and strategies.* Baltimore: Paul H. Brookes Publishing Co.

Schalock, R. L., Gadwood, L. S., & Perry, P. G. (1984). Effects of different training environments on the acquisition of community living skills. *Applied Research in Mental Retardation, 5,* 425–438.

Schalock, R. L., & Harper, R. S. (1982). Skill acquisition and client movement indices: Implementing cost-effective analysis in rehabilitation programs. *Evaluation and Program Planning, 5,* 223–231.

Schalock, R. L., & Harper, R. S. (1983). Untying some Gordian knots in program evaluation. *Journal of Rehabilitation Administration, 7,* 12–20.

Schalock, R. L., & Jensen, H. (in press). Training in the natural environment: Critical issues related to training techniques, manpower utilization and program evaluation. *Journal of The Association of the Severely Handicapped.*

Schalock, R. L., & Koehler, B. (1984). *Ecobehavioral analysis and augmentative habilitation techniques.* Hastings, NE: Mid-Nebraska Mental Retardation Services.

Sorensen, J. E., & Grove, H. D. (1977). Cost-outcome and cost-effectiveness analysis: Emerging nonprofit performance evaluation techniques. *The Accounting Review, 52*(3), 658–675.

Sorensen, J. E., & Grove, H. D. (1978). Using cost-outcome and cost-effectiveness analyses for improved program management and accountability. In C. C. Attkisson, W. A. Hargreaves, M. J. Horowitz, & J. E. Sorensen (Eds.), *Evaluation of human services programs* (pp. 371–410). New York: Academic Press.

Suchman, E. A. (1967). *Evaluative research: Principles and practice in public service and social action programs.* New York: Russell Sage Foundation.

Suchman, E. A. (1972). Action for what? A critique of evaluative research. In C. H. Weiss (Ed.), *Evaluating action programs: Readings in social action and education* (pp. 240–256). Boston: Allyn and Bacon, Inc.

Sutherland, J. W. (1977). *Managing social service systems.* New York: Petrocelli Books.

Thornton, C. (1984). Benefit-cost analysis of social programs. In R. H. Bruininks & C. K. Lakin (Eds.), *Living and learning in the least restrictive environment.* Baltimore: Paul H. Brookes Publishing Co.

Warner, K. E., & Luce, B. R. (1982). *Cost-benefit and cost effectiveness analysis in health care.* Ann Arbor, MI: Health Administration Press, 1982.

Wehman, P. (1981). *Competitive employment: New horizons for the severely disabled.* Baltimore: Paul H. Brookes Publishing Co.

Wehman, P., Hill, J., & Hill, M. (1984). *Employment opportunities for handicapped youth and adults: Enhancing transition.* Richmond, VA: Rehabilitation Research and Training Center.

Weisgerber, R. A., Dahl, P. R., & Appleby, J. A. (1980). *Training the handicapped for productive employment.* Rockville, MD: Aspen Systems Corp.

∞ Section VII ∞

MANDATES FOR THE FUTURE

THIS FINAL SECTION PRESENTS AN ANALYSIS OF THE MAJOR FORCES—POLITICAL, ECONOMIC, occupational, legislative, living and health care conditions—that will have an impact on the establishment and delivery of employment services for adults with developmental disabilities. It is the authors' contention that to plan for services today without anticipating the changes that affect tomorrow's services will result in a system that is unresponsive to our dynamic society. Ten major forces must be considered if a meaningful relationship between employment and industry is to be achieved for the developmentally disabled adult.

∞ Chapter 22 ∞

Current and Future Directions in the Employment of Adults with Developmental Disabilities

William E. Kiernan and Jack A. Stark

HOW MANY TIMES HAVE WE WORKED EX-tremely hard at establishing services, training students, conducting research projects, or advocating on behalf of the developmentally disabled individual only to find that within a few years our approaches and strategies are no longer effective or useful? How many times have we said to ourselves, "I only wish I knew then what I know now"? The authors and editors of this text would be remiss if they did not attempt to address these very concerns. For developmentally disabled adults, their family members, and those who work with them, this chapter presents an analysis of the major factors that will have an impact on the adult with developmental disabilities over the next two decades. If human service workers are to cope successfully with the rapid changes that are predicted, they will need to go beyond their individual areas of expertise and become more knowledgeable about those major evolutionary factors that will define the kinds of services that developmentally disabled adults will need. Workers will need a broad-based knowledge of the political, economic, occupational, legislative, living and health care conditions that they will encounter if they want to avoid saying, "If I only knew then what I know now."

An analysis of the social conditions of the 1960s reveals that a major concern of the time was *civil rights*. Since then, a body of laws has been directed at giving most minorities access to the mainstream of society. In the 1970s, there was an emphasis on *human rights*—a concern for the basic rights of every person—both on a national and international scale. Now in the 1980s, we are witnessing an emphasis on *societal rights*. Concern with the needs of society as a whole, sometimes minimizing the needs of individuals and minority groups, is the benchmark of the 1980s. It appears that the 1990s will be an era marked by an emphasis on *individual rights*. With an improvement in social and economic conditions on an international scale, a return to a focus on the needs of the individual may be at hand. Members of minorities, among them developmentally disabled individuals, will organize into more effective and aggressive grassroots coalitions that will attempt to hasten improvements in living standards and employment opportunities for themselves.

Some of the macroevolutions—a borrowed biological term connoting large changes of a species evolving over time—that will have dramatic implications for the developmentally disabled adult population are discussed in the rest of this chapter. Suggestions of ways in which professionals can maximize their effectiveness are also presented.

MACROEVOLUTION: SHAPING OF THE FUTURE

Macroevolution 1: World Economy

Global economic development tends to proceed on a 50-year boom/bust cycle, with 25–30 years of growth followed by 20 years of slowdown and then a group recovery, leading to another spurt in the economy. Since the beginning of the Industrial Revolution in Britain some 200 years ago the economy has followed a wave-like pattern with four separate stages. During Stage 1, there is a vigorous boom that is usually triggered by technological breakthroughs and large-scale investments in industrial innovations. This period tends to last about 20 years. The second stage, often referred to as a recession, is a time when business is still fairly good but growth is slow. Profits tend to shrink, and stiffer competition leads to increased tension and debts. Inflation and surplus production capacity also result. Stage 3 is a depression. This downturn usually lasts 10 to 15 years and is characterized by unemployment, widespread bankruptcies, and a reduction in private investment. The fourth stage is a time of recovery when expenditures are reduced to increase efficiency and chronic unemployment leads to reduced labor costs. These conditions bring about improved profits and renewal of investment.

As demonstrated by Figure 1, the economy seems to be currently in a recovery phase. It is anticipated that, after approximately 10 years, the economy will enter a fifth stage characterized by improved economic development spurred on by new technological advances. However, many economists are concerned about the possibility of renewed inflation and huge government deficits. Technological advancement will be slowed by obsolete equipment, inflated pay scales, and the inability of Third World nations to retire their indebt-

edness. It appears now that the economic problems of the next 10 years will lead to a pattern of growth for the following 30 years. Efforts during this 10-year period to reduce the federal deficit will cause programs for developmentally disabled individuals to be scrutinized more closely, particularly at the state and local level. During this time an understanding of economic policies and the use of systemic advocacy skills will be essential in the effort to secure funding for services for developmentally disabled individuals. Community-based programs may need to be especially creative in administrative and fiscal operations during this period.

Macroevolution 2: Occupational Outlook

The current restructuring of the economy is characterized by a shift from manufacturing to information processing and telecommunications industries. Our nation's dominance in the production of goods and services is being challenged by foreign competition, particularly in high technology fields. Overseas producers now make one of every four cars sold in America, one-fifth of the personal computers, two of every three pairs of shoes, and almost all of our more complex electronic gadgetry. Occupational changes will continue to have an important impact on the U.S. labor market. For example, in the last 25 years employment has increased by 40 million, with approximately 105 million people being employed in 1984. Less than two million of these new jobs were in manufacturing, whereas 3.3 million of these jobs dealt with computers and high technology. Nearly three-fourths of all people employed today work in service fields. The latest Department of Labor's *Occupational Outlook Handbook* indicates that there will be 125 million jobs in the United States by 1995 (U.S. Department of Labor, 1984). Almost 75% of the new jobs will be in service industries, such as transportation, communications, utilities, finance, insurance, real estate, and government. Figure 2 lists occupations demonstrating better-than-average, average, and below-average prospects for growth.

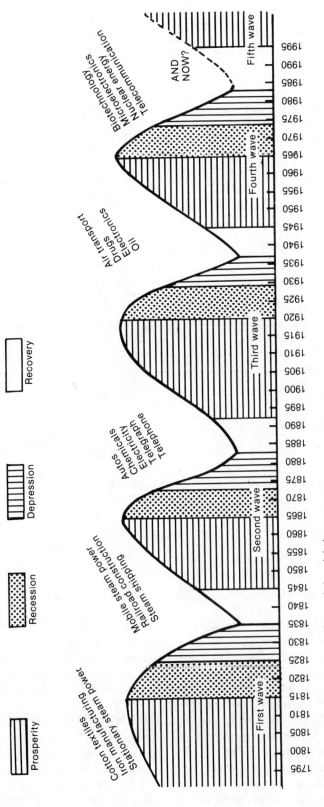

Figure 1. Over 2 centuries: pulsing of the global economy.

Better-than-average prospects

	Jobs in 1995	Change from 1982
Auto mechanics	1,168,000	38%
Cashiers	2,314,000	47%
Clinical-lab technicians	292,000	40%
Computer programmers	471,000	77%
Computer-service technicians	108,000	97%
Cooks, chefs	1,613,000	33%
Guards	937,000	47%
Nursing aides, orderlies	1,641,000	35%
Receptionists	861,000	45%
Waiters, waitresses	2,227,000	34%

Average prospects

	Jobs in 1995	Change from 1982
Assemblers	1,645,000	25%
Auto-body repairers	196,000	26%
Bank tellers	693,000	29%
Computer operators	737,000	27%
Custodians	3,607,000	28%
Machinists	298,000	26%
Secretaries	3,160,000	29%
Teachers' aides	593,000	28%
Telephone repairers	171,000	28%
Tool-and-die makers	187,000	21%

Below-average prospects

	Jobs in 1995	Change from 1982
Bus drivers	551,000	17%
Library technicians	32,000	10%
Photographers	102,000	18%
Postal clerks	252,000	−18%
Reservationists, ticket agents	110,100	2%
Shipping clerks	431,000	18%
Shoe repairers	18,400	15%
Stenographers	250,000	− 7%
Typists	1,145,000	16%

Figure 2.   Job outlook.

One challenge facing those trying to maximize employment for developmentally disabled adults will be finding job oportunities in the service and high technology fields. The majority of jobs—particularly for the developmentally disabled adult—will be in the service industry. If unemployment rates remain low the picture is quite promising. It is also predicted that there will be stricter enforcement of immigration quotas, which will limit the size of the pool of potential service workers. However, developmentally disabled workers will be competing with the less expensive labor force available to foreign producers. Nevertheless, employment of developmentally disabled adults in service-related fields should be encouraged.

Macroevolution 3: Changing Society

An increasingly older population is reshaping the social, economic, and political landscape of America. For the first time in history, there are more Americans over the age of 65 than there are teenagers. By 1990 the number of older citizens is expected to surpass 31 million, whereas the teenage population will shrink to 23 million. Demographic data from the Census Bureau show that lower birth rates, combined with greater life expectancy, are leading to the "aging of America."

Because the vast number of individuals born between 1946 and 1964—the baby boom generation—are now moving toward middle age, there will be a growing concern about planning for the future and less emphasis on short-term goals, a major trend noted in Nesbitt's book, *Megatrends* (1982).

The aging of our society will have important societal and political implications. There will be greater emphases on relationships and commitments. Politically, we can expect to see a more conservative environment. Unlike the 1960s and 1970s when general economic prosperity was accompanied by relative generosity in funding programs for the developmentally disabled population, the 1980s and 1990s will be characterized by a shrinkage in the pool of resources available to provide programs and services. Some analysts predict conflict between the elderly population and younger people. The older generation will be placing higher priority on spending for Social Security and health care, whereas younger persons will favor expenditures for educational programs. The concerns of older Americans are reflected in the "New Federalism" being espoused by the Reagan administration. Conservative members of Congress may be reluctant to provide for the needs of developmentally disabled individuals. Restrictive interpretation of both existing and future legislation by conservative members of the Supreme Court could further reduce the economic and civil rights of disabled individuals. Developmentally disabled individuals and others working with them will have to begin to speak for themselves through legislative activism and the formation of grass-roots coalitions.

Macroevolution 4: Population Distribution Shift

Population migration and work force shifts will lead to a concentration of the population, including those with developmental disabilities, in western and southern states. During the 1970s the population of these two regions increased over 22%. The northeast section of the country is experiencing very little population growth, and the population of major urban cities, such as New York and Chicago, is actually decreasing. Partly because of lower pay scales, tax incentives, government regulations, and favorable climates, two out of every three jobs created in the last 10 years are located in the west or south. Figure 3 illustrates the growth in population predicted between the

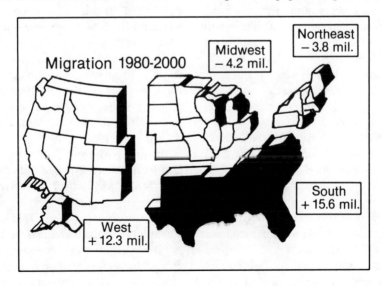

Figure 3.   Basic data: U.S. Department Labor.

years 1980 and 2000. In only the 5 years between 1985 and 1990, the population of the Sunbelt states is expected to increase by 20%.

Because of their reduced mobility, developmentally disabled individuals are less likely than others to move to a part of the country where job opportunities are being created or are expanding. Those handicapped individuals who do move with their families to economically thriving areas may find that community-based services are not expanding as rapidly as the population. In addition, economies dependent on one industry, such as oil or electronics, are subject to boom and bust cycles. Certainly, planners and directors of programs for the developmentally disabled should be aware of the economic, social, and political implications of the new patterns of population distribution.

Macroevolution 5:
Electronic Technology Revolution

Computer and video technology will help determine the shape of educational, occupational, and living environments in the future. The impact of computer technology will be felt most dramatically in the workplace. Computers are designing products, operating robots, manufacturing materials, and controlling the flow of materials and production lines. The most significant increase in the use of computers will occur in the service sector. Banks, insurance companies, and utilities will lead the rest of the economy in their utilization of computer technology.

Futurists also predict the widespread use of telecommuting and telecommunication devices. Video technology may reshape the educational system. Figure 4 depicts the major characteristics of this new information-based society.

Computers and telecommunications will provide developmentally disabled adults with the first tools to extend their cognitive capability. Computer-aided instruction, videotapes, and home video terminals may lead to the following outcomes: 1) allowing students to learn at an individualized pace, thereby reducing the stigma of slower-than-normal progress, 2) enabling parents and developmentally disabled individuals to work in their

home or wherever it is convenient, 3) providing learning aids tailored specifically to the developmentally disabled population, 4) teaching more individualized techniques and methodologies, and 5) helping developmentally disabled individuals acquire new information. New technology may assist the developmentally disabled adult in learning how to use public transportation or how to perform job tasks. For example, the disabled adult could wear a memory belt that can be plugged into information stations to provide and repeat audiovisual task instructions. Or he or she could have a miniaturized communication device that would contact a centralized station when assistance was needed in explaining a task or when physical difficulties are experienced. The potential use of computers for both service and training is significant.

Macroevolution 6:
Changing Family Structure

High divorce rates, smaller family size, and the large proportion—60%—of women in the work force will dramatically alter the nature of families in which developmentally disabled individuals live. In 1950 only a few women held jobs outside the home. Today more than two-thirds of the women between 25 and 44 are employed. Fifty-seven percent of working women hired have children, an increase from 31% noted 20 years ago. Women now outnumber men 52% to 48% in undergraduate enrollment. Fewer women are getting married, and those who do are waiting later in life to do so. In 1970 only 10.5% of women aged 25–29 had never been married. By 1995 this figure is projected to rise to 26%. Because women are having fewer children, the birth rate has fallen by half since 1960.

Divorces have more than doubled. It is now estimated that at least one-third of all children will spend a part of their formative years in a single-parent household, and more than half will have working mothers. This is a dramatic alteration from the traditional nuclear family, in which a full-time housewife/mother took care of the children. Data indicate that only 15%–20% of all households conform to this traditional pattern. Although single-parent

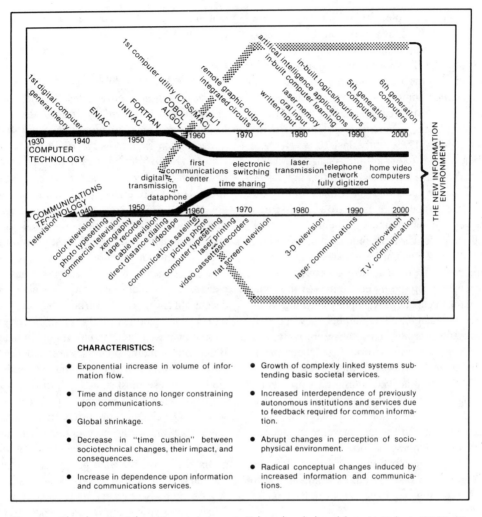

Figure 4.   The changing information environment. (Adapted and altered from McHale, J. [1971]. The changing information environment: A selective topography.)

women now head one in seven households, they head half of all families living in poverty. In 1960 one in ten families was headed by a single-parent woman, and roughly 40% of these families lived below the poverty line.

Changing family structure will have an impact on developmentally disabled individuals growing up in their natural families in the community. Working mothers will have less time to spend with their sons or daughters. Two-parent families will have more income with which to maintain a household and perhaps purchase supportive devices, but a single working woman will experience the effects of inflation and the rising costs of caring for a

developmentally disabled child without the benefit of added financial resources. There will be a growing need to provide more in-home care while parents are working. However, if telecommunication devices are available, developmentally disabled individuals may be able to provide care and secure employment for themselves.

Macroevolution 7: Changing Patterns in the Work and Living Conditions Leading to Improved Social and Economic Status for the Minorities

This country's racial composition is being altered by immigration and differential birth rates. For example, 30 million blacks now constitute 13% of the population. U.S. citizens with Spanish surnames now number about 16 million. The Hispanic population increased by 51% during the 1970s, and it is expected that they will outnumber blacks within another decade. Asian Americans are the fastest growing segment of the American population. Having increased by 128% in the last 10 years, there are now close to four million Asian Americans. Sociologists report that minorities are losing some of the economic gains made during the 1960s and that there is a growing disparity between the economic well-being of the rich and the poor. Until the predicted upturn in the 1990s, developmentally disabled individuals will continue to feel disproportionately the effects of a struggling economy. At the same time the occupational composition of the work force is changing. The number of workers is increasing, earning capacity is improving, and fewer people now work with their hands whereas more work with their intellect.

With newly arrived immigrants now competing for many of the unskilled labor jobs, the increasing intellectual complexity of many occupations, and the loss of some production jobs to developing countries with low wage scales, the occupational prospects for developmentally disabled adults would appear to be bleak. However there *are* some reasons for optimism.

First, with the upgrading of our educational system, workers now holding unskilled or semiskilled jobs may aspire to better paying ones. The jobs they vacate may become available to currently unemployed or underemployed developmentally disabled individuals. Additionally, service jobs, which can be performed by handicapped workers who have proper training and supervision, will constitute an ever-increasing portion of the labor force. Hotels, restaurants, office buildings, home care, and agriculture are potential worksites for developmentally disabled individuals. Not all the skilled jobs can, in all practicality, be exported. Costs, possible embargoes, and the possibility of cheaper production because of technological breakthroughs should all encourage manufacturers to maintain facilities in the United States.

Macroevolution 8:
Changing Governmental Roles

Decentralization of governmental control and the transfer of decision making to state and local agencies or governing bodies will result in a situation similar to the 1960s where advocacy groups played a critical role in the development of control and services. Before 1980, many futurists predicted that the government would continue to grow in size, scope, and number of services provided. They also predicted a relative decrease in military spending and an increase in social program budgets. Instead, military spending has increased in absolute terms; there has also been decentralization of governmental decision making and control, with the return of many of these functions to state and local governments. Block grant funding processes are evidence of the recent return of decision-making responsibility to those most directly concerned with the day-to-day management of programs and services. As evidence of current trends, social scientists point to the proliferation of *private* day care centers for preschoolers, despite minimal support for such programs as Headstart and public school full-day kindergartens. A growing body of research supports the cost-effectiveness of these programs. These trends will probably continue throughout the 1980s.

Certainly for the remainder of this decade, involvement by parents, developmentally disabled adults, and advocacy groups will be necessary in order to ensure the continuation of state and local funding. We seem to be returning to an era of grassroot movement and coalitions similar to that witnessed in the 1960s. It seems plausible that, as the economy continues to expand, we will witness less of a backlash-type reaction to federal control. We will probably begin to see a gradual return to such programs as subsidies for low-income families, child day care center programs, funding for in-home educational instruction programs, adult education, and most importantly, subsidies for low-cost housing and a national health insurance plan (Plog & Santamour, 1980.) In the 1990s, it is predicted that the government will once again exercise control over programs for developmentally disabled individuals.

Macroevolution 9: Education Growth

Improvements in our educational system, particularly in higher and continuing education, will lead to a higher educational index. This improvement will not be commensurate with the change in occupational demands. Improved educational opportunities for minority and special education students have led to an increase in the proportion of the American population that has graduated from high school. Between 1960 and 1980 the number of persons earning bachelors degrees from college more than doubled. Yet, the Bureau of Labor Statistics has found that the largest number of new jobs are of the type that requires little education. In the next 10 years, 20 occupations will account for 35% of the new jobs created. Only two of these categories—

elementary educators and accounting—will require a college degree. Figure 5 shows those areas of the job market that will experience the greatest growth before 1995. For example, there will be a greater need for service maintenance workers than for computer specialists. Forecasts by labor (AFL-CIO) indicate that by 1990 there will be a half-million college graduates without employable skills within the labor market. There will be an increased demand for continuing education that might be provided by telecommunications.

The areas of employment that will experience the greatest growth in the future will be those jobs that require fewer educational skills, in which a relatively large number of disabled individuals have been placed over the last 30 years. Many disabled individuals, particularly mentally retarded adults, have been placed in jobs as building custodians, nurses aides, waiters, waitresses, and kitchen helpers. Most service jobs, with the exception of teachers, truck drivers, accountants, and registered nurses, appear to be accessible to develop-

---

What Jobs Will Be Expanding the Most

Growth in Jobs
1982-95

Building custodians 779,000
Cashiers 744,000
Secretaries 719,000
Office clerks 696,000
Salesclerks 685,000
Registered nurses 642,000
Waiters, waitresses 562,000
Teachers (elementary) 511,000
Truckdrivers 425,000
Nursing aides, orderlies 423,000
Accountants, auditors 344,000
Auto mechanics 324,000
Blue-collar supervisors 319,000
Kitchen helpers 305,000
Guards, doorkeepers 300,000

Figure 5.   Basic data: U.S. Department of Labor.

mentally disabled adults when good training and supervision are available. There is thus a need to emphasize vocational training and preparation, rather than the acquisition of academic skills.

Macroevolution 10:
Biomedical and Behavioral Technology

This new technology will do a great deal to improve the quality of life while decreasing the number of individuals with developmental disabilities. We are entering an era of unprecedented breakthroughs in both the biomedical and behavioral sciences. We seem to be moving close to controlling many of the diseases that have afflicted children for centuries. For example, in 1983 approximately 3200 children contracted mumps, a decrease from 150,000 in 1968. In 1962 there were almost a half-million cases of measles; in 1983 there were only 1500 cases. Polio, which was the major medical problem in the 1950s, has been virtually eliminated. The infant mortality rate, which now stands at 11.2 per 1,000 live births, is only half of the rate in 1960. Average life expectancy has increased from 69 years to 75 years. Many of these advances have been made possible by the development of computer-assisted devices, such as computed tomography scanners, radioisotopes, ultrasound, and fiberoptic nuclear magnetic resonance machines, as well as our improved ability to conduct sophisticated laboratory analyses.

Behavioral programming has also benefited developmentally disabled individuals. Educational and training techniques that use behavioral analysis strategies to teach social and work skills have improved the functional abilities of many developmentally disabled individuals, particularly those with mild and moderate levels of disability.

Scientific knowledge is doubling every 5 to 10 years, particularly in the biomedical and behavioral fields. This unprecedented growth rate makes it difficult to imagine the accomplishments that await us in the future. Listed below are a number of biomedical and behavioral breakthroughs that could benefit developmentally disabled individuals.

1. Development of immunizations for viral infections, such as meningitis and encephalitis, can reduce the incidence of brain damage.

2. With intrauterine surgery on fetuses with suspected defects, such as hydrocephaly, it may be possible to remove the developing child from the mother's womb and return it after prenatal surgery.

3. One of the most exciting developments in biomedicine is gene therapy, the ability to manipulate or replace defective genes in order to cure or reverse such genetic disorders as Down syndrome, Fragile X syndrome, and other genetic abnormalities that lead to neurological deficits (Gerald, 1983).

4. The discovery of the biological basis of memory and learning by Lynch and his associates at the University of California, Irvine, may lead to the development of better memory mechanisms for those developmentally disabled individuals with cognitive deficits (Lynch, 1983).

5. The ability to fuse spinal cords and promote nerve regeneration may improve the quality of life for individuals with physical disabilities and loss of motor functioning (Ommaya, 1983).

6. The development of neuropeptides is a possible means of improving the memory of individuals with mental deficiencies. Research has already been conducted that demonstrates improved memory functioning in mentally retarded individuals who have been given low doses of the peptide M.S.H. (Kastin, Sandman, Miller, & Schally, 1982).

7. Nutritional research utilizing megavitamin therapy is receiving renewed attention. Its results hold promise for improving the cognitive function of disabled individuals.

8. Those individuals with organ deficiencies may benefit from laser surgery and the use of artificial organs and implants to improve overall physical and mental ability.

9. Research is also pointing toward the pos-

sibility within the next 20 years of implanting a biochip in which memory can be stored and called on.

10. Twenty-five years of vigorous research have led to significant increases in the level of sophistication in methods of teaching and improving the levels of learning and functioning in developmentally disabled individuals.

Our major challenge then in the future will be to ensure that these medical and behavioral breakthroughs and new technologies will be available to developmentally disabled individuals. We will need to emphasize the cost-effectiveness of programs for the developmentally disabled because questions of economy and ethics will be central to decisions about who will benefit from the use of expensive technology.

SUMMARY

In addition to the factors mentioned above, there are probably many other major forces operating in our society over the next one to two decades that will have an impact on our developmentally disabled citizens. The previous review selected the most important changes.

Economic and societal changes will have a direct and long-lasting impact on the provision of services to the developmentally disabled adult. The return to the acknowledgement of individual rights, through focusing on the person, does represent a challenge to the human service professional. We must teach the developmentally disabled adult to be assertive if he or she is to be successful.

Changes in employment and the marketplace mandate changes in the training at the high-school level as well as the postsecondary level if the developmentally disabled individual is to be prepared to enter the world of work. The continuation of fiscal disincentives to employment for the developmentally disabled adult in Social Security, and specifically, Supplemental Security Income, and Medicaid is being seriously questioned. The role of government is shifting from acting as the eternal parent to becoming a supportive partner. The move to a more mutually supportive relationship between the developmentally disabled adult and publicly sponsored projects is essential if economic self-sufficiency is to be a realistic goal for all individuals in our society.

It should be noted that the forces or factors discussed above reflect trends—and only trends. A trend is only an indicator; we are the ones who set the actual course. It is up to us to ensure that employment opportunities are available for the developmentally disabled adult and that the goal of economic self-sufficiency is a real possibility.

REFERENCES

Gerald, P. S. (1983). Chromosomal derangement and treatment prospects. In F. J. Menolascino, R. Neman, & J. A. Stark (Eds.), *Curative aspects of mental retardation: Biomedical and behavioral advances* (pp. 27–35). Baltimore: Paul H. Brookes Publishing Co.

Kastin, A. J., Sandman, C. A., Miller, L. H., & Schally, A. V. (1982). Some questions related to MSH. *Mayo Clinic Proceedings, 57,* 632.

Lynch, G. (1983). The cell biology of neuronal plasticity: Implications for mental retardation. In F. J. Menolascino, R. Neman, & J. A. Stark (Eds.), *Curative aspects of mental retardation: Biomedical and behavioral advances* (pp. 99–109). Baltimore: Paul H. Brookes Publishing Co.

McHale, J. (1971). *The changing environment: A selective topography.* Boulder, CO: Westview Press.

Nesbitt, J. (1982). *Megatrends: Ten new directions transforming our lives.* New York: Warner Books, Inc.

Ommaya, A. K. (1983). Current uses of peripheral and central nervous system transplants and their future potential for reversing mental retardation. In F. J. Menolascino, R. Neman, & J. A. Stark (Eds.), *Curative aspects of mental retardation: Biomedical and behavioral advances* (pp. 111–118). Baltimore: Paul H. Brookes Publishing Co.

Plog, S. C., & Santamour, M. B. (1980). *The year 2000 in mental retardation.* New York: Plenum Publishing.

United States Department of Labor. (1984). *Occupational outlook handbook.* Washington, DC: U. S. Government Printing Office.

Index